PowerPoint For Litigators

How to Create Demonstrative Exhibits and Illustrative Aids for Trial, Mediation, Arbitration, and Appeal

PowerPoint For Litigators

How to Create Demonstrative Exhibits and Illustrative Aids for Trial, Mediation, Arbitration, and Appeal

Deanne C. Siemer
Frank D. Rothschild
Edward R. Stein
Samuel H. Solomon

Reproduction Permission
National Institute for Trial Advocacy
Notre Dame Law School
Notre Dame, IN 46556
(800) 225-6482 FAX (219) 282-1263
E-mail: nita1@nd.edu Web site: www.nita.org

Siemer, Deanne C., Frank D. Rothschild, Edward R. Stein, Samuel H. Solomon, *PowerPoint for Litigators* (NITA 2000).

ISBN 1-55681-674-X
Second printing, 6/00

Library of Congress Cataloging-in-Publication Data
PowerPoint for litigators: how to create deomonstrative exhibits and illustrative aids for trial, mediation, and arbitration / Deanne C. Siemer ... [et al.].

p. cm.

Includes index.

ISBN 1-55681-674-X

1. Trial practice--United States--Graphic methods. 2. Microsoft PowerPoint (Computer file) I. Siemer, Deanne C. II. National Institute for Trial Advocacy (U.S.)

KF8915.Z9 P69 1999

006.6'869—dc21 99-051508

SUMMARY OF CONTENTS

SUMMARY OF CONTENTS

TABLE OF CONTENTS

REFERENCE GUIDES

GLOSSARY

A glossary, located at the back of the book, will help with any specialized PowerPoint terms. See page 405.

NITA "HOW-TO" FINDER LIST

A finder list, located at the back of the book, provides an alphabetical index of each of the methods used in creating the PowerPoint slides described in the book and the exercise where each is explained. See page 415.

ICONS

How to use this book. This icon marks paragraphs that describe how to navigate through the exercises and chapters in this book.

Important tip. This icon marks paragraphs that provide helpful shortcuts or warnings that will save you time.

Persuasive quality. This icon marks paragraphs that offer strategies for making your presentations more persuasive to judges and juries.

Go to Appendix. This icon marks places where you should refer to the appendix for the particular case file (criminal, tort, contract) with which you are working to see illustrations.

PowerPoint 97. This icon marks exercises or steps in exercises when users of PowerPoint 97 (instead of PowerPoint 2000) will see a different screen or will need to do the steps somewhat differently.

PREFACE

This book was written by trial lawyers for trial lawyers who want to use technology in the courtroom. The use of technology is an integral part of persuasive advocacy. This book gives you the skills to use basic presentation software in preparing displays for the courtroom and for mediation, arbitration, and appeal as well. You may prepare courtroom presentations infrequently. This book is designed so that you can always pick up where you left off, even if it was months ago and you have forgotten everything except the name of the software.

Why should busy trial lawyers learn PowerPoint? Those who make their own visual aids, or at least do a first draft before turning the job over to a specialist, find three important benefits.

> First, if the lawyer knows how to prepare visuals, this work can start during the early stages of trial preparation. The illustrative aids and demonstrative exhibits can be studied and changed as the case proceeds. Often these displays point up strengths or weaknesses in the case theory, so trial preparation is more effective.
>
> Second, it quickly becomes less expensive for the client if the lawyer can do this work rather than dictating, reviewing, making changes, having more drafts done, and so on.
>
> Third, visual displays are an integral part of the courtroom drama and, just as trial lawyers would not want to have other people writing their oral statements, they benefit from "writing" their own visual displays. Even a trial lawyer who has available skilled graphics and computer personnel will benefit from preparing drafts. Knowing how to create PowerPoint presentations allows a lawyer to direct the specialists more effectively.

Presentation software, such as Microsoft's PowerPoint, allows trial lawyers to outline opening statements and closing arguments, and present document and photo exhibits for direct and cross-examination. In addition, visual displays for the courtroom can be brought readily into briefs, memoranda, and correspondence. Because PowerPoint is fast and easy, this work can be done as other preparation work on the case proceeds. PowerPoint is not the only product suitable for these purposes. The techniques explained in this book are generally applicable to other software in this category.

The exercises in this book do not require extensive computer experience. Each chapter tells you what you are going to do, describes in detail the steps necessary to get there, and guides you through the process one logical step at a time.

Hardware: PowerPoint does not require sophisticated computer equipment. To do the exercises in chapters 2 through 10, you need:

1. A laptop or other computer, which has at least 16 MB of RAM (PowerPoint runs faster with 32 MB of RAM) and at least 10 MB of free storage space on your hard disk, which will be needed to save the PowerPoint visuals you make;

2. A mouse plugged into your computer (preferred even with a laptop); and

3. A CD-ROM drive in your computer or attached to it.

Software: You need this software on your computer:

1. Windows 95 or Windows 98; and

2. PowerPoint 2000 or PowerPoint 97. (PowerPoint 95 can be used for the exercises in Chapters 2 through 4.)

No other software is required. PowerPoint comes with certain versions of the Microsoft Office suite or can be purchased separately. This book focuses on PowerPoint 2000, which does not differ greatly from PowerPoint 97 for courtroom purposes. Adjustments for those of you using PowerPoint 97 are flagged.

Experience: This book is designed for lawyers who have no experience whatsoever with PowerPoint or other presentation software and who have relatively little general computer experience. You will need to know how to:

1. Operate the mouse;

2. Locate the SHIFT, CTRL, BACKSPACE, ENTER, ARROW, and DELETE keys and the SPACEBAR on your keyboard;

3. Put a CD into your CD drive;

4. Name and save files; and

5. Open and close files on your hard disk drive and on your CD drive.

To deal with files on a CD, you will also need to know the letter designation for the CD drive on your computer—perhaps D:\ or E:\. If you are missing any of these skills, consult a basic Windows manual or a manual about your computer.

This book explains only the aspects of PowerPoint directly related to trial advocacy. PowerPoint has a wealth of features, but only a few of them should be used in court. The same general rules apply to trial-related settings including mediation, arbitration and appeal. These materials pare down the PowerPoint features to those directly applicable to what lawyers do or should do. All too often, lawyers new to presentation software will use its capability to make exhibits that are flashy or even funny. The problem is, of course, that the jury's focus is on all the fancy things the software can do, rather than on the persuasive aspects of the case. PowerPoint should be used as an enhancement to persuasion. Because most of the frills available in the software distract from that purpose, they should not be used.

Bulleted lists, labeled photo exhibits, relationship charts, text document treatments, and annotated diagrams constitute about ninety percent of the demonstrative exhibits and illustrative aids used in most trials. This book equips any trial lawyer, within a very short time, to prepare each of these kinds of exhibits. Three representative case files provide a context for the course: a criminal case, a tort case, and a commercial case. In this way, trial lawyers can learn PowerPoint by working with general examples drawn from their own area of practice.

The book also provides guidance on moving up to the next level. Organization charts, video clips, statistical charts and graphs, and advanced time lines constitute most of the remaining ten percent of courtroom presentations, and these can also be done with PowerPoint. ANIX™, a new software product that works with PowerPoint, provides additional capabilities important for courtroom presentations. PowerPoint users can master ANIX readily.

The outstanding oral advocate has an important edge in a courtroom, but persuasive graphic presentations can level the playing field. Seeing the point while hearing it explained will engender a more complete understanding than just hearing it alone. Understanding is a hallmark of fairness.

The National Institute for Trial Advocacy
March 2000

ACKNOWLEDGMENTS

The authors are grateful for the assistance received from Sharon McGovern, a professional administrator who is proficient in PowerPoint. Sharon read drafts, found better ways to explain concepts, and helped edit the text of the entire manuscript.

The authors also received valuable suggestions from Mark McCurdy, Chantel Bland, Julie Clegg, Bob Blasco, Gerald Clay, and Hon. Carol Corrigan who beta tested the descriptions used in the book. They all took time from busy lives and careers to make a voluntary contribution to making the book a better product.

Tony Bocchino, NITA's Editor-in-Chief, helped shape the book and its balance of technical and tactical advice. Elizabeth Blakey, NITA's Copy Editor, edited the manuscript, and we appreciated greatly her ability to avoid techno-jargon and make the text relatively easy to read. Shelly Goethals, NITA's Publications Manager, handled the production and her skilled contribution made the book's design especially appropriate for the topic. Nick Croce and Gene Klimov of DOAR Communications, Inc. gave valuable guidance on technical matters and provided help on the illustrations.

The case files in this book were originally published in *Problems in Trial Advocacy*, by Bocchino, Beskind, Broun, Lubet, Maciejczyk, Natali, Seckinger, Stein, and Wolfson (NITA 1996).

SEND US YOUR COMMENTS

We would like to hear from you! Visit the NITA web site at *www.nitastudent.org* and give us your comments or send along the inventive new slides you have produced. Tell us what you like about the book or what should be changed. Your feedback lets us know whether we are meeting your needs.

ABOUT THE AUTHORS

Deanne C. Siemer is a trial lawyer who, as a partner in a large firm with a national practice, tried commercial cases in federal and state courts regarding contracts, business torts, patents, discrimination, and government administrative issues. Her office is in Washington, D.C. She wrote the text of the book based on experience in trials using computer-generated demonstrative aids over the past fifteen years. She teaches courses in trial practice and courtroom technology for NITA, and is the author of *Tangible Evidence: How to Use Exhibits at Deposition and Trial* (NITA 1996) and other books and articles on trial practice.

Frank D. Rothschild is a trial lawyer who has tried civil cases in private practice and criminal cases as a public defender and state prosecutor. He holds an appointment as a local court judge in Kauai, Hawaii, and also serves professionally as an arbitrator/mediator. He worked on the text of the book, upgraded the NITA case files contained in the appendices, and designed the CD-ROM that comes with the book. Rothschild teaches courses in PowerPoint for Litigators, trial practice, and specialized subjects for NITA. He also provides training for judges and law firms and consults on trial cases.

Edward R. Stein is a trial lawyer and founding partner of a small law firm with an active trial practice in Ann Arbor, Michigan. He specializes in medical and legal malpractice, personal injury, and fraud cases and represents a large state university in a variety of matters. He uses computer-generated demonstrative aids in trials in large and small matters. Stein pioneered the teaching of PowerPoint for Litigators with courses beginning in 1995, sponsored by NITA, and he created the teaching method used in this book. He teaches courses in trial practice, depositions, courtroom technology, and evidence for NITA.

Samuel H. Solomon is the founder and CEO of DOAR Communications, Inc., located in Rockville Centre, NY. The firm equips courts with technology and provides trial support for lawyers. As a consultant to trial lawyers, Solomon provides case analysis, jury research, graphics design, and on-site courtroom technology support. He has generated PowerPoint slides for use in opening statements, closing arguments, and expert witness presentations for trials on many subject matters over the past ten years. Solomon also teaches courses in courtroom technology for NITA and is a frequent lecturer on trial practice subjects.

Chapter 1

Litigation Uses for Presentation Software

Presentation software builds visual displays that can be shown in a courtroom on a monitor or projection screen. These displays are used to accompany opening statements, closing arguments, and witness examinations. One category includes all the illustrative aids—lists, labeled exhibits, charts, diagrams, time lines, and other graphics—designed to enhance understanding of the case. The other general category covers enlarged versions of demonstrative exhibits, such as video clips, x-rays, photos, statistical charts, maps, drawings, and documents. Jury instructions and transcripts can also be displayed on the large screen.

Even a basic list of points, without any artistic effort at all, can increase the power of your advocacy. Virtually every opening statement and closing argument can benefit from the support of a good bullet point list. Photographs can be enhanced with labels reminding jurors why the photo is important or pointing out the focus of the evidence. Documents, which are often difficult to present effectively in paper form, come alive when enhanced with boxes, circles, lines, and callouts.

Persuasion flows from both style and content. You will find basic suggestions on persuasive quality in the sections describing each kind of visual. For more on the admissibility of exhibits designed with PowerPoint and the persuasive use of these exhibits at trial, consult *Tangible Evidence* (NITA 1996).

Each chapter is self-contained so that you can go right to the topic you need. Chapter 1 explains the software, outlines the case files, and tells you about the special buttons and toolbars that allow you to work quickly toward a finished product. Chapters 2 through 4 explain basic displays you can create just by typing words. Chapters 5 through 8 cover ways you can enhance exhibits like photos, documents, and diagrams in order to display them more effectively. Chapters 9 and 10 explain how to add motion and special effects.

PowerPoint uses a number of specialized terms (such as slide, background, fill, and handle) which are defined in sidebar boxes when they first occur. Explanations about PowerPoint also require common terms associated with the Windows operating system (such as cursor, mouse pointer, toolbar, button, and drop-down menu). A glossary at the back of the book contains explanations.

All the common problems that lawyers face, particularly those who are just starting out with presentation software, are clearly marked. The book provides explanations of the best way to proceed. Chapter 12 contains a summary of all of the software's shortcuts and alternatives so that you can tailor your own practices to your personal preferences.

1.1 Versions of PowerPoint

There are three versions of PowerPoint in general use. This book is designed so you can make the fullest use of the version that you have.

PowerPoint 2000: This version was released in 1999. It comes with Microsoft's Office 2000 Suite and can also be purchased as a stand-alone product. If you have PowerPoint 97, you can get an inexpensive upgrade to the new version. For trial lawyers, PowerPoint 2000 is very much like its predecessor. Most of its new features were designed for creating a presentation for a web site or for presenting a slide show on the Internet. This book presents all of the material in a manner oriented to the PowerPoint 2000 user.

PowerPoint 97: This version was released in 1997. Most users acquired it automatically as a part of Microsoft's Office 97 Suite, but it also was available as a stand-alone product. PowerPoint 97 is entirely adequate for use by trial lawyers, and you do not need any upgrade to do all of the basic and advanced exercises in this book. PowerPoint 97 is easier to use for courtroom purposes in some ways because it is not encumbered with the new web and Internet functions and the screen display is more functional for the limited objectives that trial lawyers have.

97 When an instruction for accomplishing a particular task with PowerPoint 97 is different from the instruction for PowerPoint 2000, that item is flagged with an icon and the specific instructions applicable to PowerPoint 97 are provided. Illustrations of the screen displays for PowerPoint 97 are provided when they are different from what you would see on the screen when using PowerPoint 2000. Appendix D contains a supplement for PowerPoint 97 users.

PowerPoint 95: This version was released in late 1994. It was later bundled with some versions of Office 95. It was designed to handle text displays enhanced by color and clip art. It does not allow you to import photographs or other images unless it has been upgraded. For that reason, you can use PowerPoint 95 to do the exercises in Chapters 2, 3, and 4 following the same instructions for the later versions. If you want to work on the types of displays shown in Chapters 5, 6, 7, 8, and 9, you will need to upgrade.

1.2 The case files

This book guides you through PowerPoint by having you prepare materials for an actual case in the manner you would in any of your own cases. You have your choice of three case files.

Criminal case: The defendant, James Lawrence, is charged with larceny and assault as a result of an alleged purse snatching incident that occurred on October 1, YR-1.[1] The victim of the purse snatching was Gale Fitzgerald. Ms. Fitzgerald reported the crime to the police on the evening it happened and gave several statements to Officer James Wright.

Tort case: The plaintiff, Kenneth Brown, is suing for damages arising out of a car accident on April 20, YR-1. He claims that the defendant, Robert Byrd, was following too closely and failed to keep a proper lookout. Brown seeks $50,000 in damages for his neck and back injuries. Byrd denies liability and asserts that the impact, even if it was his fault, was not sufficient to cause any physical injury to Brown.

Contract case: The plaintiff, Roberta Quinlan, is a broker who arranges the purchase and sale of businesses. Quinlan claims that she is owed a commission of $300,000 on the sale of Kane Electronics. The defendant, Brian Kane, was the president and sole shareholder of Kane Electronics when it was sold. Kane admits that Quinlan had conversations with him about the sale and that Quinlan referred the buyer to him, but denies there was any agreement to pay a commission.

The examples in the text are from the contract case, and they illustrate how PowerPoint would be used for various kinds of tasks with the exhibits available in this case file, including photos, documents, and diagrams.

A Comparable examples for the tort case and the criminal case are in the appendices. Each case uses the same kinds of exhibits, so the work you will do in each chapter will be the same, no matter which case you decide to use in learning PowerPoint.

Digital files containing the documents, photos, video clips, and diagrams available as evidence in each case are on a CD that comes with this book or may be downloaded from the NITA web site, *www.nitastudent.org*. You will need these digital files for the exercises in Chapters 6 through 8. All of the sample illustrative aids and demonstrative exhibits appear in the digital files in full color and with animation where applicable (while this book is black and white), so look at the CD or the downloaded files to see the actual courtroom versions.

---

1. NITA uses a convention for dates as follows: YR-0 (this year), YR-1 (last year), YR-2 (two years ago) and so on.

1.3 The design of the exercises

All of the exercises in this book use the same format. The title of each exercise indicates what the finished product will be. Each exercise has a series of steps. Each step is a discrete operation in PowerPoint. Under each step, there are detailed instructions labeled A, B, C, and so on, telling you how to complete the step.

The first exercise in Chapter 2 starts with turning on the computer and covers every step you need from there onward to open the software, make adjustments to the screen display where necessary, and begin to work. Everything that comes up on the screen is pictured in the book, so you can tell exactly where you are.

As you become familiar with PowerPoint, you may not need the specific instructions included within each step pointing out which keys to press and buttons to use. If you read the description of a step and know how to do that operation, you do not need to read the A, B, C instructions included with that step. Just go on to the next step. If you read the description of a step and you are not sure how to do it, follow the A, B, C instructions immediately below it. Similarly, a few of the A, B, C instructions have subparts numbered 1, 2, 3, and so on. These are even more detailed instructions so there is no chance you will get lost. If you know how to do the work described at the A, B, C level, you can skip the numbered level below it.

The exercises progress from the easiest to the more complicated. No exercise is difficult, but it is more efficient to start at the beginning and work your way through each exercise before going to the next. The methods that you use in the chapters on basic illustrative aids, such as bullet point lists and relationship charts, are used in the same way in the chapters on the presentation of documents, photos, and diagrams. The cross-references in the text will take you back to the illustrations that help with each of the PowerPoint operations.

Each exercise is built around constructing a visual aid that works well in a courtroom setting, and that should not draw a sustainable objection under most circumstances. In this way, the book provides access to both the tools within PowerPoint and the techniques particularly useful to lawyers.

The book is designed so that you can pick it up and work efficiently even if you have not touched PowerPoint for months and have forgotten all of the routines that you learned when you first worked your way through the exercises. Each exercise is self-contained. When an exercise uses an operation that was described in detail in an earlier chapter, you will see a cross-reference to that more detailed explanation.

1.4 Using the keyboard and mouse

PowerPoint uses five keys on your computer keyboard: SHIFT, CTRL, BACKSPACE, ENTER, and DELETE. Each has the same function that it does when you work with other Windows programs.

PowerPoint also uses the SPACEBAR on your computer keyboard. This moves one space or step forward. For some operations, you will use the directional arrows—UP ARROW, DOWN ARROW, LEFT ARROW, RIGHT ARROW—also located on your keyboard. The references in the text to these keys are capitalized so that you will recognize them as instructions to use the keyboard.

In a few cases, you will use controls activated by a combination of keys. For example, CTRL+D (holding down the CTRL key while pressing the letter D key) causes a duplicate to be made. This is a handy shortcut used quite often in PowerPoint.

PowerPoint also provides keyboard alternatives for many of the operations that can be carried out with the mouse. The exercises in this book use the easiest of the mouse options and explain only one of PowerPoint's methods for accomplishing a particular task. If you prefer using the keyboard, please refer to the keyboard alternatives in Chapter 12.

Your mouse may have a variety of buttons and wheels. PowerPoint uses the left mouse button for most operations. The instructions will specify right mouse button for those few times when it is needed.

When the instructions say "click on" something, they mean that you should move your mouse pointer to that place and tap the left mouse button one time. When the instructions say "double click" on something, you need to tap the left mouse button twice in rapid succession.

When the instructions require you to "drag" the mouse over words or phrases to "highlight" them, you should place your mouse pointer at the start of the word or phrase, hold down the left mouse button, and move the mouse from left to right. Release the mouse button when you reach the end of what you want to highlight. When you drag the mouse across a word or phrase, it will be highlighted. The black letters on a white background become white letters on a black background when a word or phrase is highlighted. To "un-highlight" an item, move the mouse to another location and click once.

When you use presentation software, your mouse pointer changes shapes as you perform different tasks. After you click on buttons for specialized tasks, the shape of the mouse pointer will tell you what the software is ready to do.

The cursor, which appears on your screen as a blinking vertical line, is different from your mouse pointer. When your mouse pointer moves, the cursor, or insertion pointer, stays in one place and marks where text will start when you begin to type. When you click on the left mouse button, the cursor will move to the place where the mouse pointer is located. As you type, the cursor moves to the next blank space.

Mouse Pointer Shape Reference Guide

 One-arrow: Selects buttons and menu options

I-beam: Appears when you are where you can type

Two-arrow: Drags handles to change the shape of boxes

 Four-arrow: Drags things to another place

 Cross: Indicates where shapes will be placed (activated by buttons on the Drawing Toolbar)

 Crop: Cuts back the edges of pictures

1.5 Using bars and buttons

Presentation software requires you to use buttons to perform certain functions. Some buttons are labeled with words and others are marked by a little icon. Groups of buttons are arranged into bars. Once you get started, you will see that the buttons and bars are easy to use. Each chapter contains step-by-step instructions for the buttons and bars relevant to that chapter. To demystify the process, the next few pages lay out the bars and buttons you will need for litigation uses. You can use this section as a reference when working on particular exercises.

The PowerPoint 2000 screen layout has these principal features when you start it up for the first time.

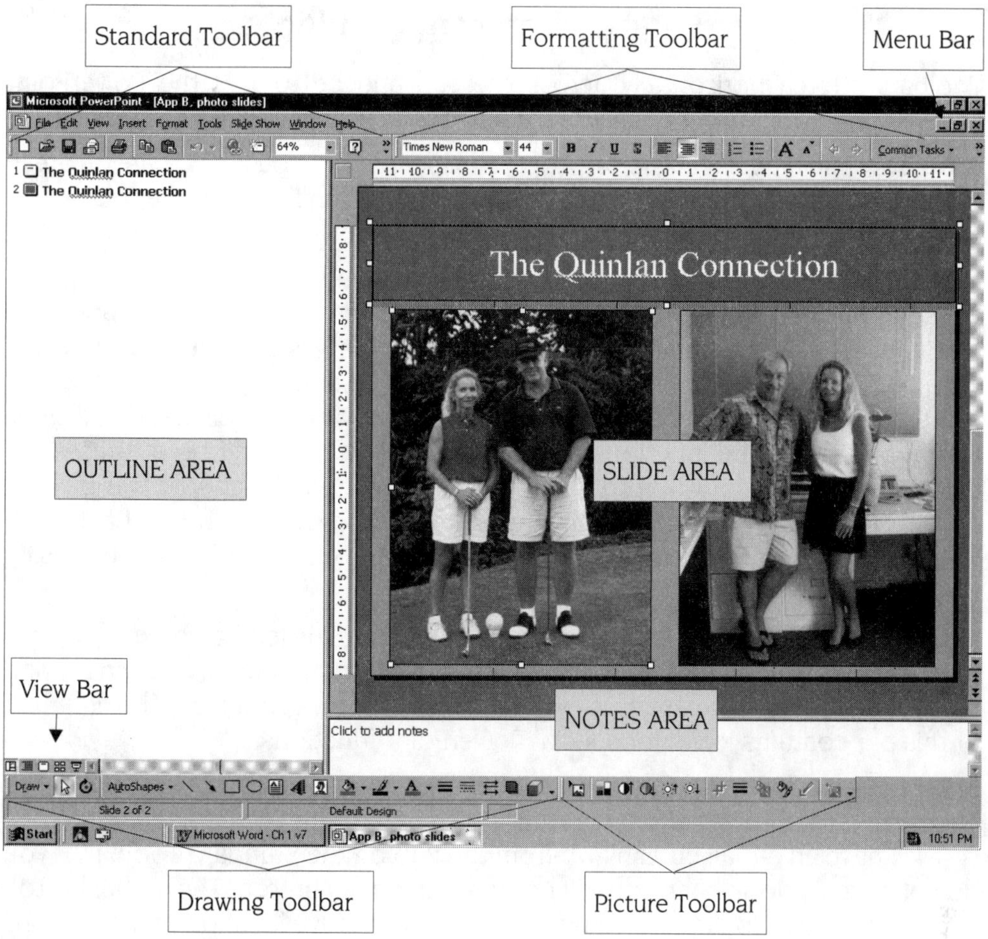

Standard Toolbar
Formatting Toolbar
Menu Bar
Microsoft PowerPoint - [App B, photo slides]
The Quinlan Connection
OUTLINE AREA
SLIDE AREA
View Bar
Click to add notes
NOTES AREA
Drawing Toolbar
Picture Toolbar

97 The PowerPoint 97 screen is set up differently. This layout is more convenient for the work done by lawyers. Nearly all of the buttons on the toolbars are the same in both versions of PowerPoint. The layout looks like this:

Standard Toolbar located above Formatting Toolbar
Drawing Toolbar and Picture Toolbar in same positions
No Outline or Notes areas

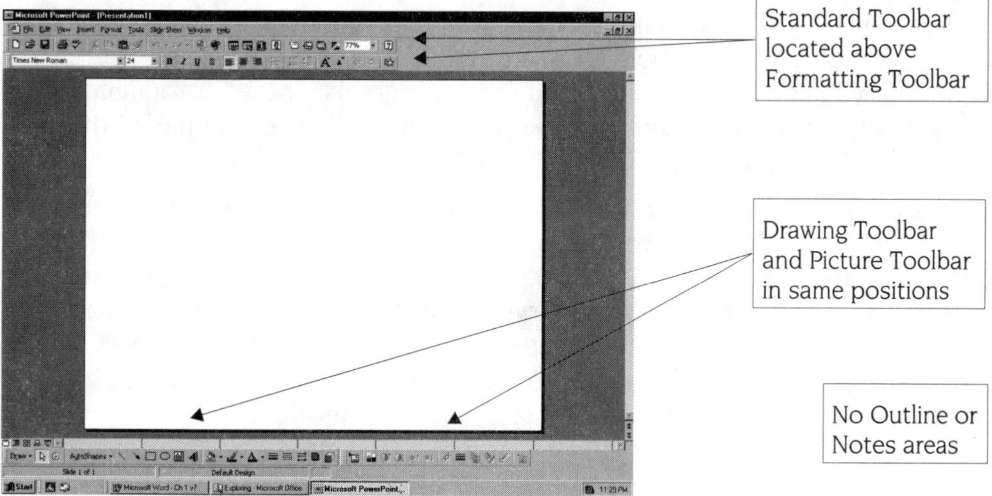

Toolbar Reference Guide

Toolbars stretch horizontally across the top and bottom of the PowerPoint screen. Each toolbar is a collection of buttons that have related functions.

Title Bar: The blue bar at the very top of the screen lets you know that you are in PowerPoint. At the far right corner, it provides the familiar Minimize, Maximize, and Close buttons. These are the same on all Windows programs.

Menu Bar: Located just below the Title Bar, the Menu Bar also contains familiar Windows buttons for the File, Edit, View, Insert, Format, Tools, Window, and Help functions. The buttons on the Menu Bar have word labels instead of icons. When you see the File button mentioned in the text, for example, you will know that it came from the Menu Bar because it has the printed word "file" instead of a small icon representing the function of the button. If you click on one of these buttons, a special menu will appear or "drop down" from which you will pick an option. These are known, logically enough, as "drop-down menus." Each contains a list of choices or options. The next step is to pick one of these options by clicking on it.

Standard Toolbar: This is just below the Menu Bar. The left half of this bar contains familiar Windows icons for open, save, print, cut, copy, paste, undo, and redo functions that operate as they do in other Windows programs. The right half of this bar contains icons for special PowerPoint functions.

In PowerPoint 2000, the Standard Toolbar has one quirk. If your computer has Microsoft Outlook loaded on it (perhaps as a part of the Microsoft Office Suite), you will have an e-mail button (4th from the left) on the Standard Toolbar. If you do not have Outlook, then you will not have an e-mail button. The e-mail button is irrelevant for purposes of this book except the relative location of the buttons on this toolbar. The examples in this book assume that you do not have the e-mail button.

Formatting Toolbar: In PowerPoint 2000, this toolbar is located at the top of the screen to the right of the Standard Toolbar. In PowerPoint 97 it is below the Standard Toolbar. The left half of this bar contains the familiar word processing buttons for font, type size, bold, italic, underline, and alignment (left, center, and right) that you use on most word processing programs. These buttons have the same functions in PowerPoint when you are typing text. The right half of this bar has special PowerPoint functions.

View Bar: This is the first (and very short) bar at the bottom left of the screen. It appears when you open an existing PowerPoint file or create a new one. The five buttons on this bar control the views of your work. You can see the full-size view of just one visual aid, thumbnail views of all the visual aids you created, an outline of the material in your bullet points, and any notes you made about individual visual aids. This bar also provides the control to move to the "show" mode so you can present your visual aids one after another.

Drawing Toolbar: This is the second bar at the bottom of the screen under the View Buttons. It contains special functions for adding labels and emphasis to text documents.

Picture Toolbar: This bar is also usually located at the bottom of the screen, to the right of the Drawing Toolbar. It contains special functions for importing, sizing, and adding emphasis to photos and other graphics.

Status Bar: Located at the bottom of the screen, this performs the same function as in other Windows programs. It shows the file name and where you are (on Slide #1, for example).

Ruler Bars: These appear on the top and at the left side of the screen. They show the distances from the center point. In PowerPoint 2000, when it first appears on the screen, the Ruler Bars are on the top and left side of the slide area.

Scroll Bars: These appear on the right side of the screen, going up and down, and on the bottom of the screen going left and right, and have about the same function as in other programs. Click on the small single arrow at each end of a scroll bar to move the screen display in the direction you want. The double arrow **page up** and **page down** buttons at the bottom take you from the current page (or individual visual display) slide to the preceding or succeeding one, and the slider on the vertical scroll bar takes you through your visual displays in the same way you can move through text in your word processor.

Illustrations showing the details for all the relevant bars and buttons are at the end of this chapter. Special terms used with bars and buttons are defined in the glossary at the end of the book.

Button Reference Guide

Buttons are the active areas on the bars. When you click on a button, the software will either execute a command or show you a drop-down menu or dialog box for selecting options. The buttons useful for litigation purposes are illustrated on the following pages. You can use these pages as a reference. You will quickly find that you do not need any written description because if you put your mouse pointer over any button and linger for a few seconds, PowerPoint will assume you want to know what it is and will display a little sign indicating what the button does. There are six kinds of PowerPoint buttons. They are described here so that you know what to expect.

Direct action buttons: Some buttons perform an action directly when you click on them. For example, when you click on the Undo button on the Standard Toolbar, PowerPoint will immediately reverse the last action you took. Direct action buttons do not display any choices or wait for you to do anything further. They act immediately.

Selected text buttons: Some buttons perform an action only on text that you have selected or highlighted on the screen. (See Exercise 2.2 for instructions on highlighting text.) For example, the Bold button on the Formatting Toolbar will put the text you have selected into bold face. Selected text buttons can also be activated before you start to type in text and all subsequent text will follow the button's format. Some buttons operate on shapes and pictures that have been "selected" or activated.

Next click buttons: These buttons activate a function that will appear or be performed when you move your mouse pointer to a place on the material with which you are working and click on the left mouse button. For example, when you click on the Rectangle button on the Drawing Toolbar, nothing happens immediately. But when you move your mouse pointer somewhere within your work area and click your left mouse button again, a rectangle will appear where you did the second click.

Menu buttons: Like the buttons on the Menu Bar, all of which produce drop-down menus, some buttons on the other toolbars also lead to drop-down menus. When you click on the button, the menu appears and you make your choice by moving the mouse pointer over the option you want and clicking on it.

Arrow-to-menu buttons: Multipurpose buttons display the current choice in a small white box on the toolbar and provide an arrow to the right of the box on which you can click to get to the menu. The typeface and type size buttons on the Formatting Toolbar are examples.

Dialog box buttons: Some buttons bring up dialog boxes that are more flexible than drop-down menus. They contain a number of mix-and-match choices to shape the operation you want the software to perform. For example, the Picture button on the Picture Toolbar brings up a dialog box that asks you about the location of the picture that you want to import. Once you identify the proper location, it goes there and imports the correct photo or graphic, and puts it directly on the visual aid on which you are working.

Extension button: Some toolbars and menus have more buttons or options than appear in the standard display. The rest are hidden until you need them. To extend the standard display to see the rest of what is available, the toolbar or menu will have an extension button that looks like this. When you click on it, the rest will appear. If you add a button it will automatically displace another button (the least used) on your toolbar. This displaced button can be accessed with the extension button.

Toolbar move handle: At the left end of each toolbar there is a handle marked with a rather faint vertical line. This handle is used to drag the toolbar to a new location. It also marks the beginning of the toolbar in places where one toolbar is on the same level as another.

There are many more buttons in PowerPoint than are used in this book. Some are duplicate ways of doing the same thing, as explained in Chapter 12. Others control functions not relevant to the kinds of visuals appropriate for trial work. They are all explained in the PowerPoint on-screen help system. Just go to the Menu Bar and click on the **Help** button.

2000 Standard Toolbar

	Save	Save your work in a designated file on your hard disk Dialog Box Button
	Copy	Copy material and hold for possible insertion elsewhere Selected Text Button
	Paste	Insert material that has been cut or copied Selected Text Button
	Undo	Go back one step and undo the last action; can go back twenty actions Direct Action Button
	New Slide	Bring up the screen display containing layout choices for the next slide Dialog Box Button
	Zoom	Enlarge or shrink the display so you can see more or less detail Arrow-to-menu Button
	Extension	Bring up rest of the buttons on the Standard Toolbar
	Redo	Put the last action back in place after it has been undone Direct Action Button
	Cut	Delete material and hold for possible insertion elsewhere Selected Text Button
	Format Painter	Copy color from one slide to another so the slides match exactly Next Click Button

PowerPoint 2000 displays only part of the toolbar. You will need to click on the Extension button to see the Redo, Cut, and Format Painter buttons. PowerPoint 97 displays all of the buttons at once.

The arrangement of the buttons on the Standard Toolbar in PowerPoint 97 is nearly the same and the functions of each of the buttons is the same. It looks like this:

2000 Formatting Toolbar

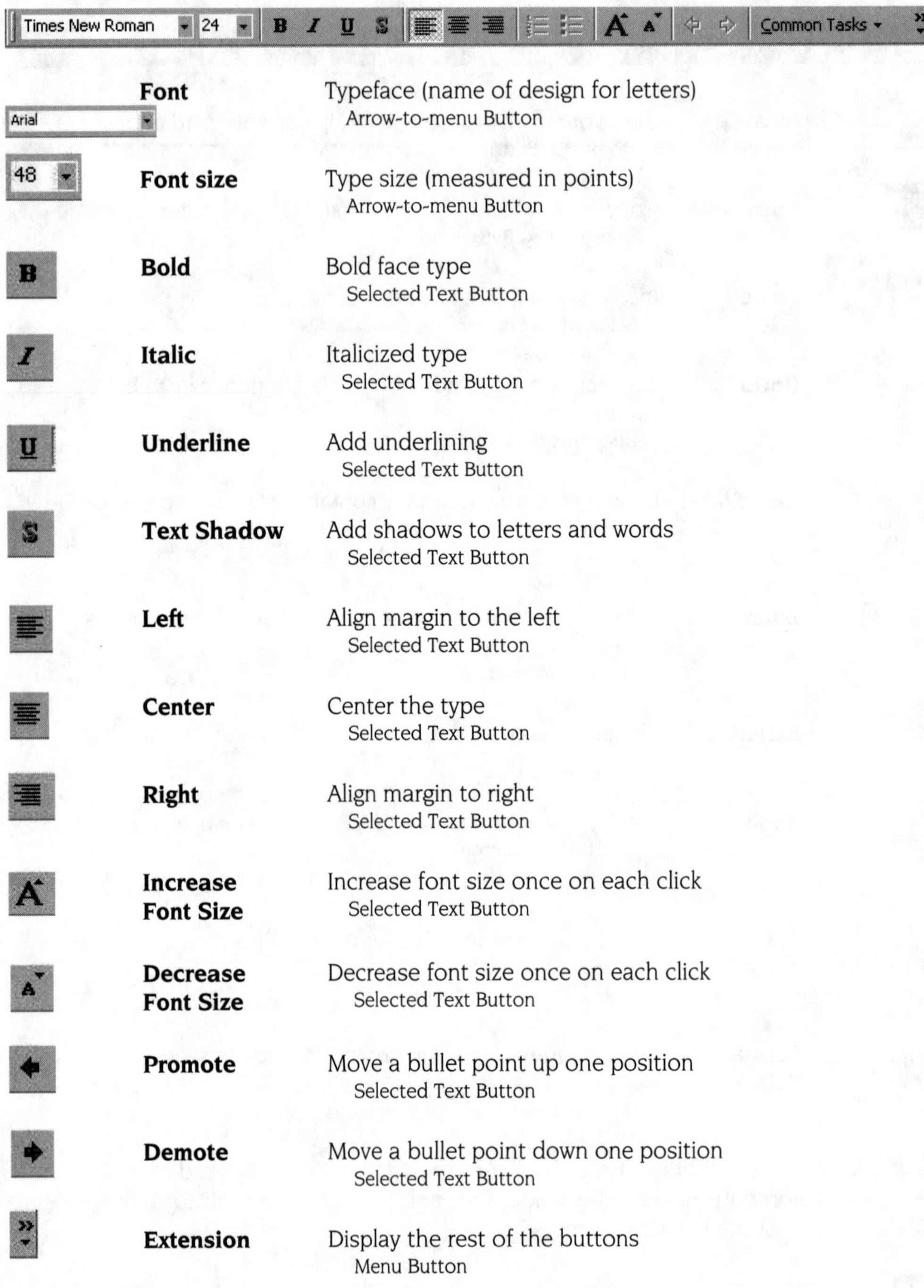

Button	Name	Description
	Font	Typeface (name of design for letters) Arrow-to-menu Button
	Font size	Type size (measured in points) Arrow-to-menu Button
	Bold	Bold face type Selected Text Button
	Italic	Italicized type Selected Text Button
	Underline	Add underlining Selected Text Button
	Text Shadow	Add shadows to letters and words Selected Text Button
	Left	Align margin to the left Selected Text Button
	Center	Center the type Selected Text Button
	Right	Align margin to right Selected Text Button
	Increase Font Size	Increase font size once on each click Selected Text Button
	Decrease Font Size	Decrease font size once on each click Selected Text Button
	Promote	Move a bullet point up one position Selected Text Button
	Demote	Move a bullet point down one position Selected Text Button
	Extension	Display the rest of the buttons Menu Button

The arrangement of the buttons on the Formatting Toolbar in PowerPoint 97 is nearly the same. The function of each of the buttons is the same. The toolbar looks like this:

2000 Drawing Toolbar

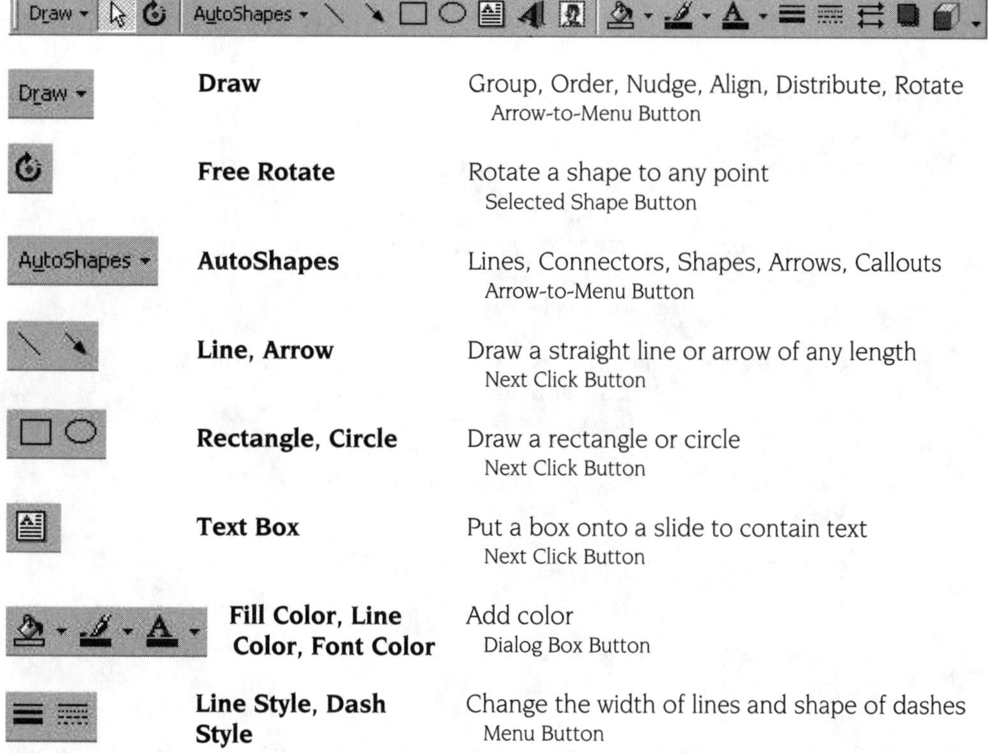

Button	Name	Function
Draw	**Draw**	Group, Order, Nudge, Align, Distribute, Rotate Arrow-to-Menu Button
	Free Rotate	Rotate a shape to any point Selected Shape Button
AutoShapes	**AutoShapes**	Lines, Connectors, Shapes, Arrows, Callouts Arrow-to-Menu Button
	Line, Arrow	Draw a straight line or arrow of any length Next Click Button
	Rectangle, Circle	Draw a rectangle or circle Next Click Button
	Text Box	Put a box onto a slide to contain text Next Click Button
	Fill Color, Line Color, Font Color	Add color Dialog Box Button
	Line Style, Dash Style	Change the width of lines and shape of dashes Menu Button

The Drawing Toolbar on PowerPoint 97 has one less button (the Insert Clip Art button has been added to PowerPoint 2000) and all the buttons have the same function. The toolbar looks like this:

2000 Picture Toolbar

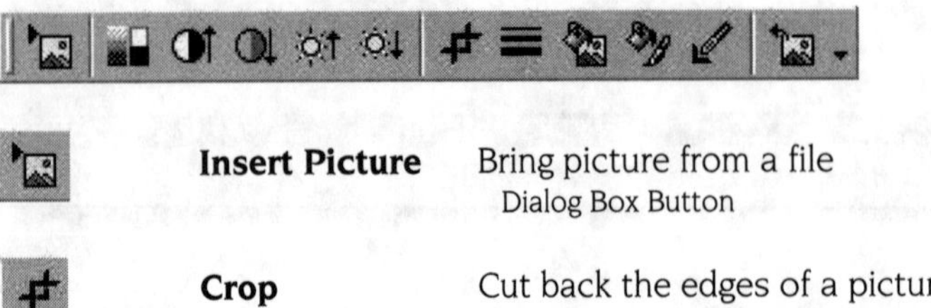

Insert Picture — Bring picture from a file
Dialog Box Button

Crop — Cut back the edges of a picture
Selected Picture Button

2000 View Bar

Full Screen View — Screen view with slide area, outline area, and notes area showing
Direct Action Button

Outline View — Rearranges the screen display so that the largest area is occupied by the outline
Direct Action Button

Full Slide View — One slide on the screen in full view
Direct Action Button

Slide Sorter View — Thumbnails of all the slides on the screen
Direct Action Button

Slide Show View — Runs the slide show
Direct Action Button

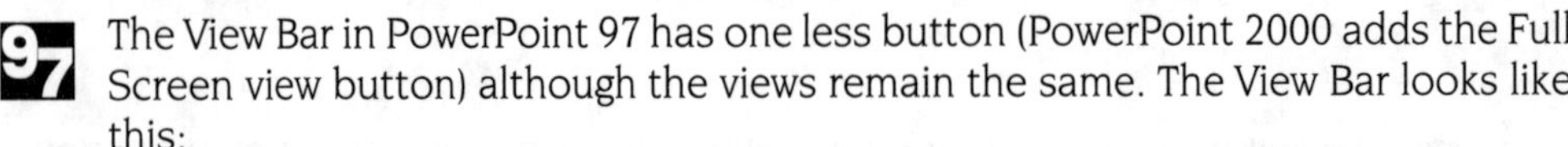

The View Bar in PowerPoint 97 has one less button (PowerPoint 2000 adds the Full Screen view button) although the views remain the same. The View Bar looks like this:

The Scroll Bar and Ruler Bar

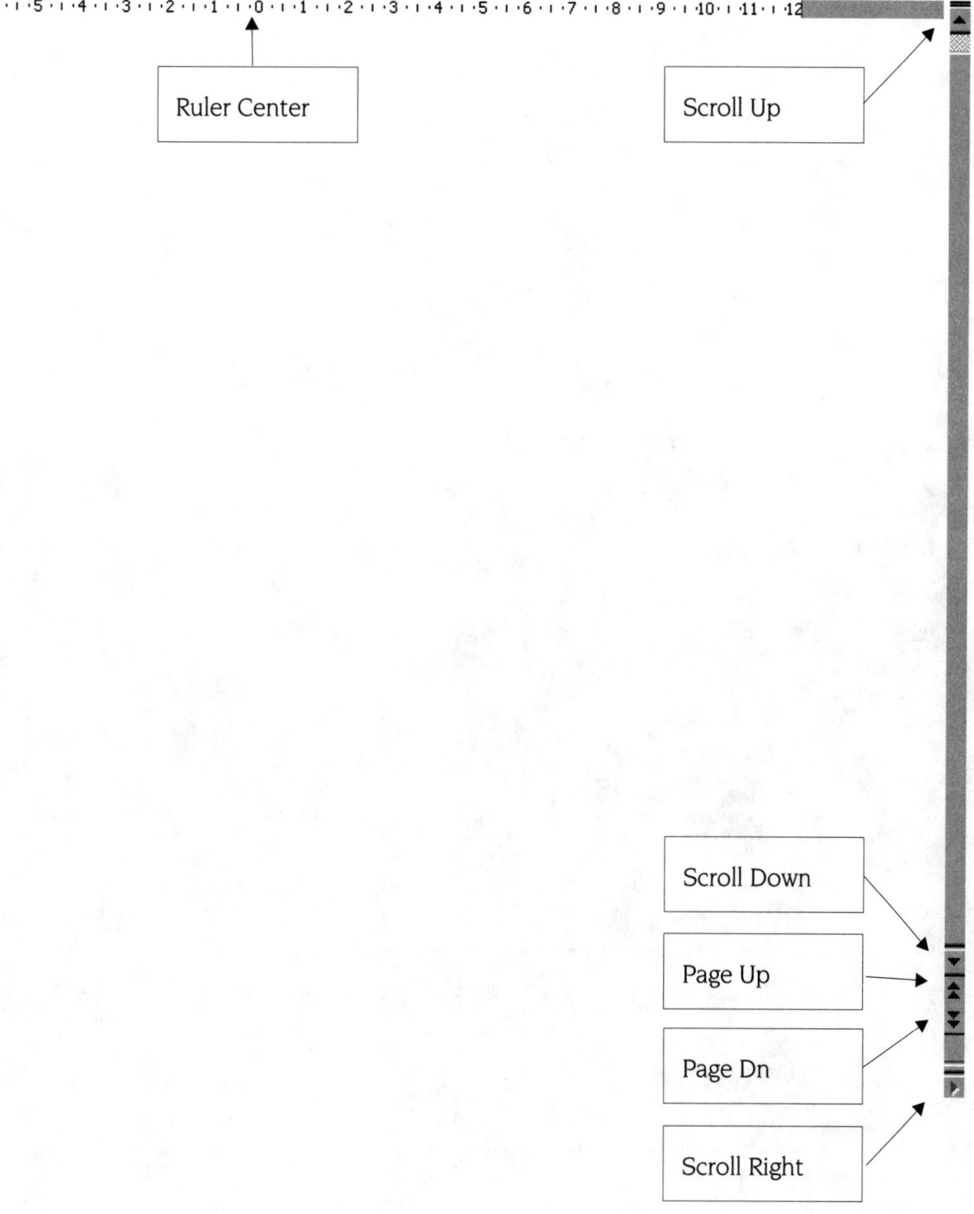

Chapter 2

The Basic Bullet Point List

A basic list of points, without any frills whatsoever, can increase the power of your advocacy. A list helps get across the logic of your presentation. It illustrates how one point is related to other points and makes the listener feel comfortable because the structure of the presentation is apparent. Working on a good list of points helps hone your own thinking about your presentation. Striking extraneous words keeps you focused on the essentials. Rearranging the order in which your points are made lets you examine alternative ways to persuade.

Virtually every opening statement and closing argument can benefit by coordination with a bullet point list. Although less common, the bullet point list may also be a good adjunct to witness examination. For example, an expert witness's method in arriving at an appropriate opinion can be illustrated effectively and made more persuasive by using a bullet point list. The bullet point list is usually less effective on cross-examination because the witness responses are less predictable.

A good bullet point list has a short title at the top and four to six evenly spaced one-line statements underneath the title. All of the points are directly related to the title. Each statement conveys only one thought. The text is stripped of extraneous words. All that remains are the minimum words necessary to make the point.

Simple bullet lists are effective exhibits even in very large commercial cases. This is an example:

Access to the Design

✓Design is on Apex's computer system
✓Only password holders can sign on
✓Jack Williams holds a valid password
✓Upwinger hires Williams
✓Design is on Upwinger's system

In matters of style, a bulleted list can be devoid of any special effects. It can work as a simple black and white display put together with the most basic tools that PowerPoint provides. No complicated steps are involved and no in-depth understanding of the software is required. When you read the slide, you know what the case is about.

This chapter has four exercises that allow you to start using visuals right away. You will:

1. Construct a basic bulleted list
2. Edit the text of the list
3. Resize the title and text to gain more space
4. Print the work product, close, and reopen the file and software program

Knowing how to create a list, edit the text, resize things, and print your work product is the foundation for the additional work covered in later chapters. As you go through the rest of the book, you can use this chapter as a reference on these basic PowerPoint skills.

Exercise 2.1: Construct a basic bullet point list

You can construct a functional bullet point list from start to finish with seven well-defined steps. The illustrations show what should be on your screen as you get started. Once you begin working with PowerPoint, each step should appear on your screen exactly the way you see it illustrated in this chapter.

Step 1: Turn PowerPoint on.

A. Turn the computer on.

B. Look at the very bottom of the screen. The small rectangles (or buttons) in the middle of that very bottom strip (or toolbar) tell you what programs are ready running. In this illustration, Outlook, America Online, and Word are running.

C. Click the START button (1st button at the far left on bottom of screen). The Start menu will appear above the button.

D. Move the mouse pointer to the PROGRAMS option on this menu. It will be highlighted. Your mouse pointer will have a one-arrow shape which is the general purpose pointer indicating that the system is ready to select options.

E. Click the left mouse button on the PROGRAMS option. Another menu will appear to the right listing all the programs available on your computer.

F. Move the mouse pointer over to this new menu and then up or down to the Microsoft PowerPoint option.

G. Click the left mouse button on the PowerPoint option. The PowerPoint logo will be displayed and then you will see the opening screen. It looks like this:

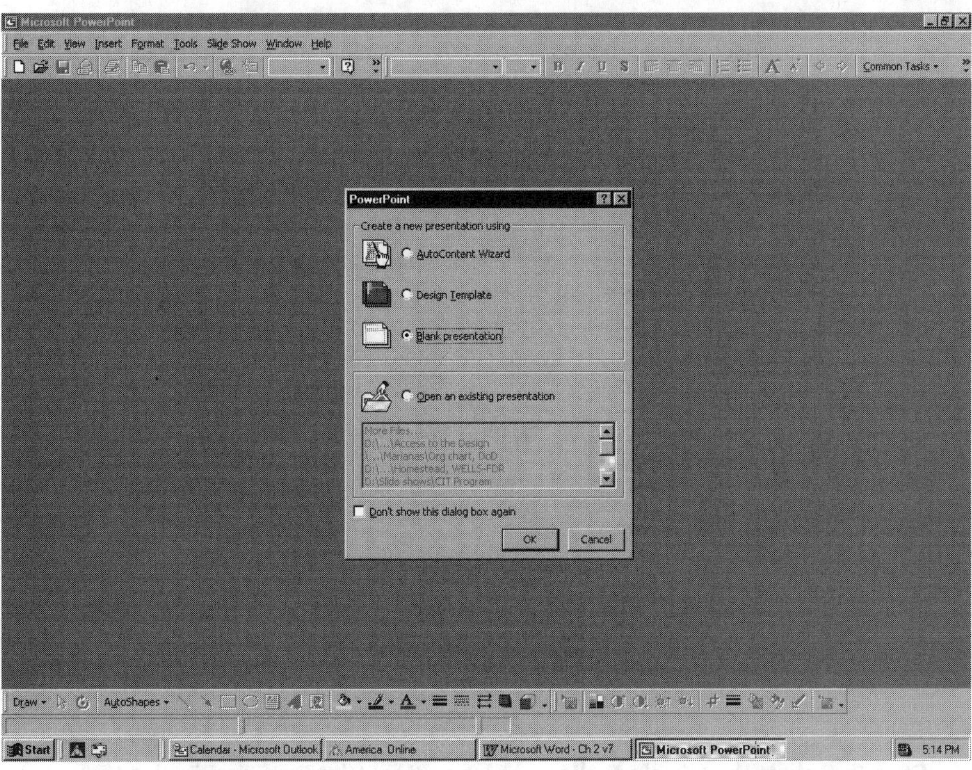

PowerPoint gives you four options on this screen: working with a wizard; using a template; starting from scratch with a blank presentation; or going to a presentation that you have already started. A *wizard* is an interactive script provided in the software that asks you questions to help you build a display. A *template* is a basic design for a bulleted list, complete with colors and typeface choices provided by the software. The wizards and the templates included in PowerPoint are geared toward business and sales presentations. For visuals to be used in the courtroom, it is easiest to start from scratch.

Step 2: Choose the Blank Presentation option (the 3rd one down).

A. Click on the circle next to this option.

B. Then click on the OK button in the lower right corner. The New Slide screen will appear showing you twelve possible layouts. Eleven of these are common designs often used in visual presentations and one is a blank so you can add all of the design elements yourself.

! Presentation software usually refers to "slides" (hence the "New Slide" screen). Just as computer keyboards adopted the familiar layout of a typewriter, presentation software uses the metaphor of camera-generated film exposures that have been made into individual slides and can be projected on a screen one by one using a projector and a slide carousel. A *slide* means a one-page visual display of some kind.

The New Slide screen looks like this:

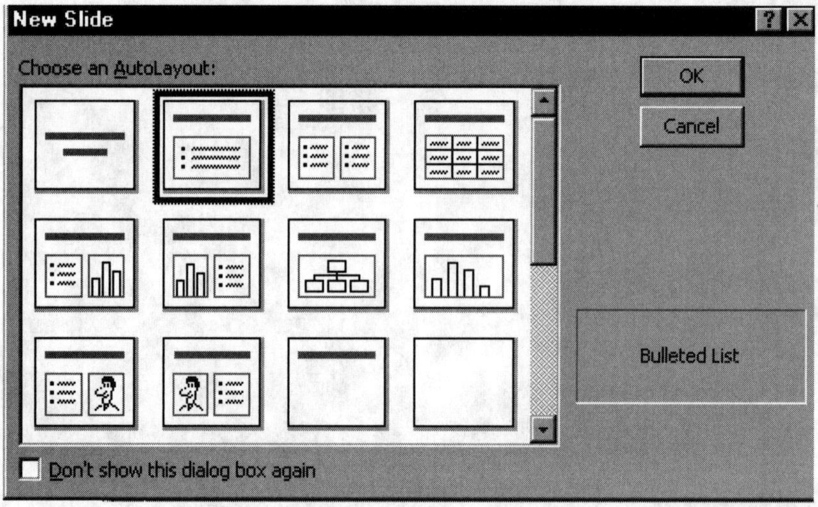

Step 3: Select the Single Bulleted List option (the 2nd one in the top row).

A. Click on the square illustrating the bulleted list layout and PowerPoint will highlight it.

B. Then click on the OK button in the upper right corner.

Now you have the layout for a bulleted list on your screen. It looks like this:

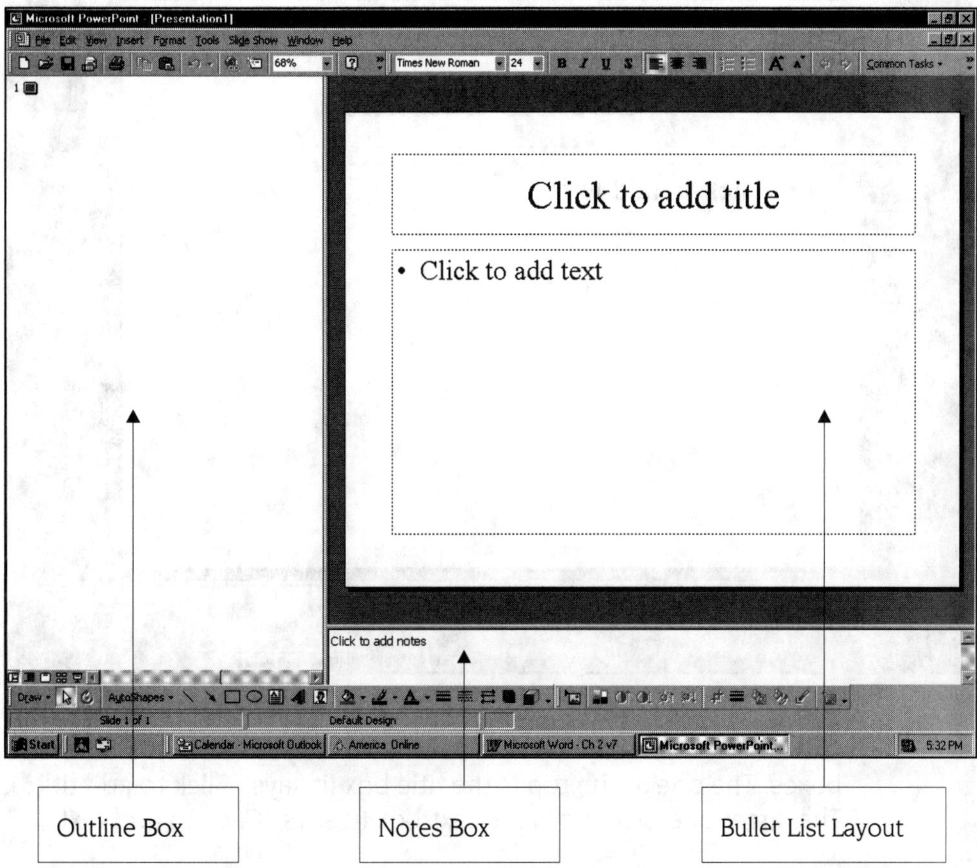

In PowerPoint 2000, there are three areas on this screen. The central area is Bullet List layout. It says "Click to add title" at the top. PowerPoint also provides an automatic outlining feature, which is the white box on the left, and a place to put notes about your slide, which is the white box at the bottom. Neither of these latter two help with tasks relevant to lawyers. They were added in the new version for other purposes. (For PowerPoint 97, skip Step 4.)

Step 4: Go to Full Slide View.

A. Go to the View Bar.

B. Click on the Full Slide View button.

C. Now the screen looks like this:

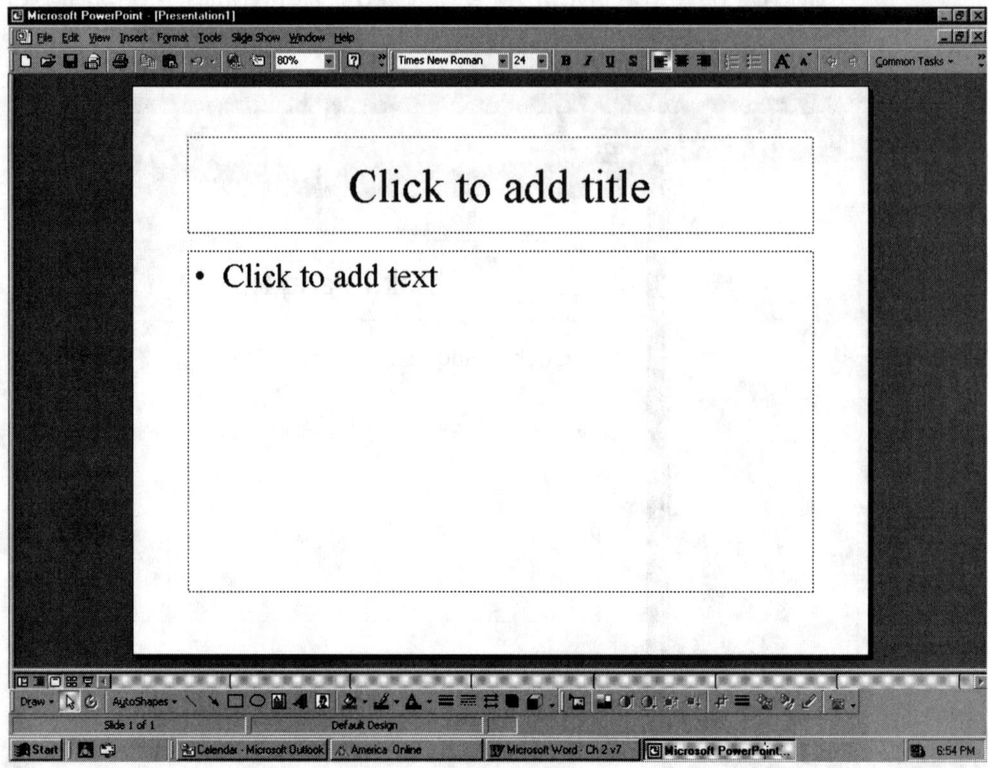

The Bulleted List layout that you have on your screen shows two boxes. The one at the top is the title box (it says "Click to add title"). The larger one below it is the text box (it says "Click to add text").

PowerPoint assumes you will want to control the title separately from the bullet point list. The title typically will be a larger type size, for example, and may have a different color scheme. PowerPoint makes this easy by having you put your title in one place and your text in another place.

97 PowerPoint 97 users do not need Step 4. Their main screen display will appear this way automatically, although the toolbars will be in slightly different positions as shown in the following illustration.

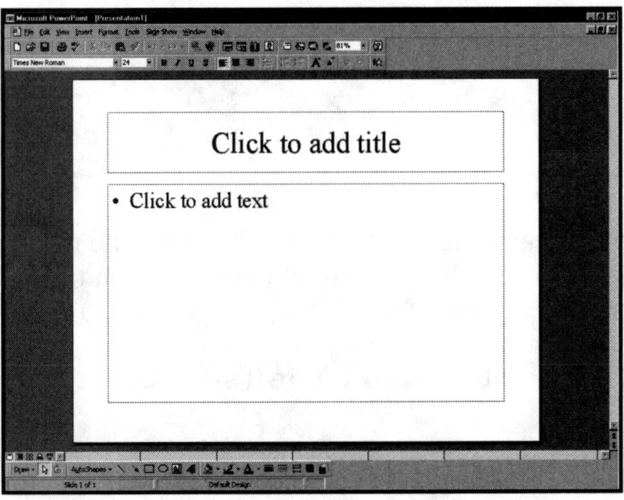

Step 5: Put a title into the title box.

A. Think about the major topics that you would cover in the opening statement for the case that you have selected. Pick a title that summarizes one of these topics.

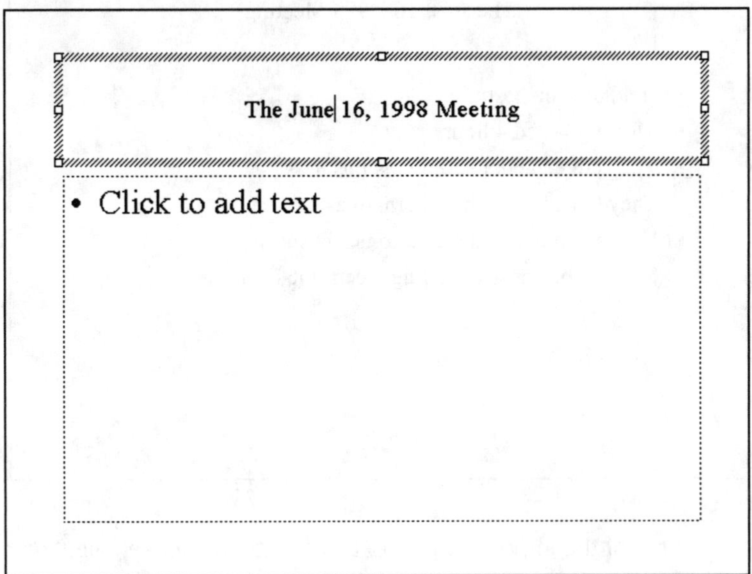

A A detailed statement of the facts in each case is in the Appendix for that case. The June 16 meeting is an important factor in the commercial contract case. If you are using the criminal case or the tort case, the Appendices for those cases also include sample slides that parallel those shown in the text for the contract case.

B. Put your mouse pointer inside the top box anywhere on the words "Click to Add Title." Click on the left mouse button. The pointer is now an I-beam shape.

C. Type your title in the title box.

D. Put your mouse pointer anywhere outside the title box. The mouse pointer now changes back to the one-arrow shape. Click on the left mouse button. Now you can see what your slide looks like so far.

Step 6: Type your list of points into the box where it says "Click to add text."

A. For the topic that is summarized by the title of the bullet list, think about the points that you want to make. You are going to display these visual aids as you speak, and you will talk about them in more detail than they are displayed on the screen.

The June 16, 1998 Meeting

- Held in Kane's study
- Meeting lasted 4 hours
- They talked about selling his business
- They talked about his alternatives
- He wanted to sell his electronics business
- She's in business of selling electronic businesses

A These are some of the important points the plaintiff's counsel might want to make about the June 16 meeting in the commercial case. Go to the Appendix for your case to see an example of bullet points that might be used in the criminal case or the tort case.

B. Put your mouse pointer anywhere in the lower box over the words "Click to add text." Click the left mouse button. The mouse pointer is an I-beam. A light bullet point appears to the left of your pointer.

C. Start typing. PowerPoint is now working like a word processor.

D. Hit the ENTER key on your keyboard when you finish a bullet point. PowerPoint will start the next bullet. If you make mistakes, just use the BACKSPACE key on your keyboard and type the text over again. The next exercise will show you how to edit the text.

E. Do not hit the ENTER key after creating the last bullet point.

F. Click anywhere outside the text box to see your slide in finished form. The first draft of the content of your first slide is done!

Your first draft will probably need improvement, as this slide does, but at least you have the material on the slide. You are now ready to consider how to make this slide more effective.

Lawyers differ about whether to use all capital letters, initial caps, or one initial cap for bullet point slides. If there is quite a bit of material on the slide, one initial cap and lowercase letters are generally easier to read.

Step 7: Save your work.

A. Click the mouse anywhere outside the box to tell PowerPoint that you are done.

B. Go to the Standard Toolbar.

C. Click the Save button (3rd from the left). When you save for the first time, PowerPoint delivers the Save As screen (or dialog box) that asks you to name the file. When you save this file on subsequent occasions, the Save button operates automatically.

PowerPoint assumes that you would like to save your slides in your My Documents directory, and it opens that one first. Your screen will look different from the one shown above depending upon what you currently have in your My Documents directory. To look at your options for saving your slides in some other place, click on the small arrow to the right of the box displaying the name of the My Documents directory. The screen will look like this:

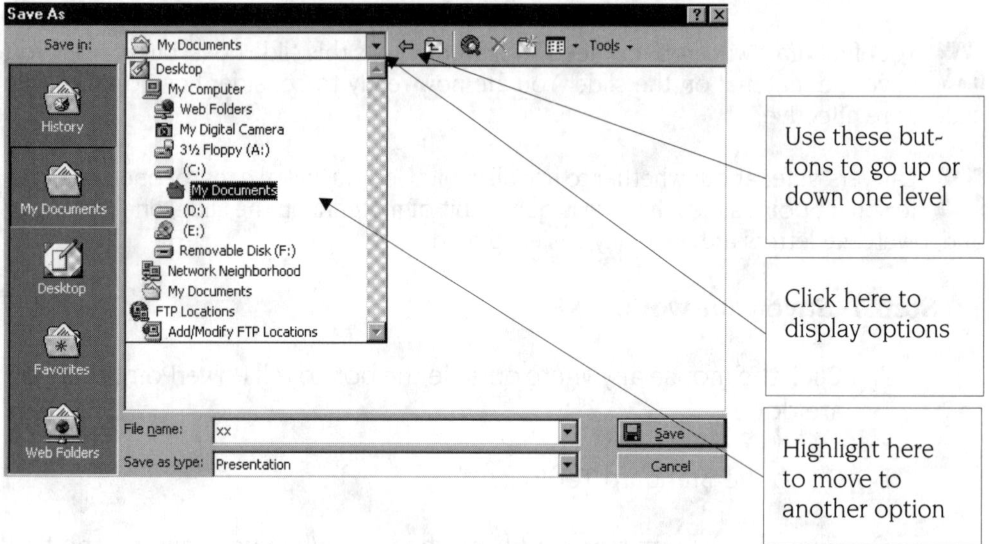

The actual display on your computer may be different from this one depending on whether you have an external disk, a setup for a digital camera, a network, and so on.

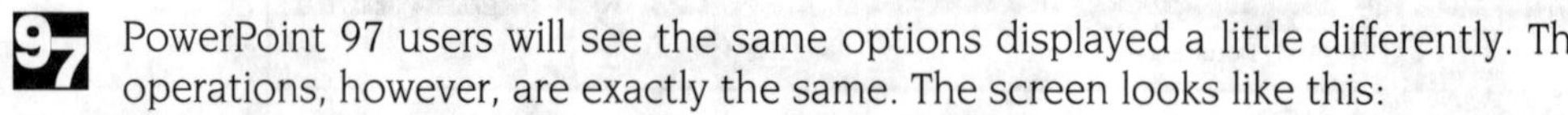

PowerPoint 97 users will see the same options displayed a little differently. The operations, however, are exactly the same. The screen looks like this:

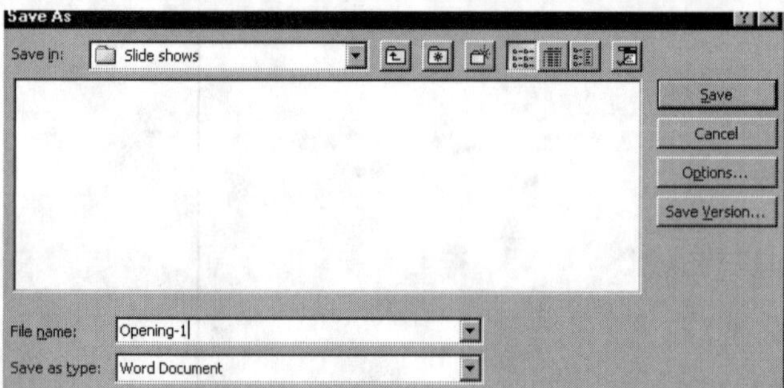

D. Go to the File Name box at the bottom left of the Save screen. Choose a name for this project and type it into this box.

E. Below the File Name box, you will see the Save As Type box. "Presentation" is the choice that should be showing. That is the right choice for working with your slides. If something else is showing, click on the arrow at the right side of the box to display a drop-down menu and pick the Presentation option.

F. Click on the Save button in the upper right corner of the screen.

The bullet point list that you have made in this exercise can be enhanced with better fonts, adding colors, and making other stylistic changes. These enhancements are explained in Chapter 3.

Bullet lists work better when they are animated so that the bullet points will appear one at a time. The directions for animating bullet lists are in Chapter 9.

You can make permanent the changes to your screen display so that it always appears in a form that saves steps for the particular way you work. See Ch. 12, Exercise 12.3.

Exercise 2.2: Edit the text

Editing slides is very similar to editing in word processing. The same commands are used in PowerPoint.

Step 1: Delete words you do not need.

A. Select (activate) the title box by clicking anywhere on the text in the box. Decide whether any of the words in the current title can be deleted.

B. Select (highlight) the word to be deleted by placing your mouse pointer at the beginning of the word, holding down the left mouse button, and dragging the mouse to the end of the word. Then release the mouse button.

C. Press the DELETE key on your keyboard.

PowerPoint Terms

Slide: A page or single screen display made with PowerPoint.

Select a box: When you "select" a box, you activate it by clicking on the text within it so you can work on it. When the box is active, it will have a fuzzy line border around the edges.

Select a word or phrase: When you "select" a word or phrase within text, you highlight it so you can work on it. Place the mouse pointer at the beginning of the word, hold down the left mouse button and drag to the end of the word. Release the mouse button when you reach the end of what you want to select. When the word or phrase is selected, it is highlighted as white lettering in a black box.

The Meeting

- Held in Kane's study
- Meeting lasted 4 hours
- They talked about selling his business
- They talked about his alternatives
- He wanted to sell his electronics business
- She's in business of selling electronic businesses

D. Do the same within the text box.

The Meeting

- Kane's study
- Four hours
- Subject: selling Kane's business
- Kane's choice
- Quinlan's business

★ Bullet points should be bare. Use words and phrases for your bullet points, not sentences. Pare down the words until you have the minimum that will serve as a marker for the thought or idea you want to convey. Get rid of pronouns, articles, and repetitive words and phrases.

Step 2: Delete a bullet item in the text for practice.

A. Select the bullet list box by clicking on the text inside the box.

B. Select (highlight) the bullet point phrase. The bullet itself will not be highlighted with the text.

C. Press the DELETE key on your keyboard. The text will disappear, and it will take the bullet along with it.

★ The items in your bullet point lists should be consistent, connected to one another, and at the same level of generality. Eliminate items that do not fit these criteria. They may belong in a subsidiary list or under another heading.

Step 3: Add words to consolidate or clarify.

A. Select (activate) the box that contains the text of your bullet list.

B. Place your mouse pointer on the line of text where you want to add the word. Click your left mouse button. The cursor will be blinking at this point.

C. Type the word.

The Meeting

- Four hours in Kane's study
- Talked about selling business
- Reviewed his alternatives
- Kane wanted to sell business
- Quinlan in business of selling

A The illustration above is one way to consolidate the points on this slide for the commercial contract case. Go to the Appendix for your case to see an example of a slide for which the text has been edited to make the bullet points more concise.

Step 4: Undo something that you have done when a mistake has been made.

A. Go to the Standard Toolbar.

B. Click on the Undo button (10th button from the left).

PowerPoint can undo up to twenty prior actions, so just keep clicking on the Undo button until you get back to where you want to be.

Step 5: Redo something you have mistakenly undone.

A. Go to the Standard Toolbar.

B. Click on the Redo button (the 11th button from the left).

Step 6: Save your work.

A. Go to the Standard Toolbar.

B. Click on the Save button. Once you have given PowerPoint the name for the file you are working on, (Exercise 2.1, Step 7) it will perform the entire "save" function automatically when you click on the Save button.

If you are working on bullet points for an opening statement, avoid adjectives and adverbs where possible. Remember that opening statements are not argument. Your opponent will look to your title and text to see if it is objectionable as argument. Stick to the facts.

This chapter (and others in the book) describes one way to do things. PowerPoint typically provides three or four ways to do the same thing. For example, if you want to save your work, one option is to go to the Standard Toolbar and click on the Save button; a second option is to go to the Menu Bar, click on the File button, and pick the Save option; and a third option is to go to the keyboard and press the CTRL key and the S key at the same time. All three methods produce exactly the same result. As you work with PowerPoint, you may decide that you prefer keyboard options for most operations or you may find that the Menu Bar (with its word descriptions for buttons) is easier for you than the various icons on the buttons on other Toolbars. Chapter 12 describes these options.

Exercise 2.3: Resize the boxes on the slide

Any box on your slide can be made larger or smaller, taller or shorter, fatter or thinner. This capability helps with many design tasks. For example, sometimes as you juggle the words in your slide, you realize that you need to make the text box a little wider so your bullet points can fit on one line, or a little taller so the spacing between your bullet points can be increased for ease of reading. In this exercise, you will see the mouse pointer change shapes as you ask the software to do different tasks. (See Chapter 1 for more details on your mouse pointer.) This is how to resize the title and bullet text.

Step 1: Select (activate) the title box.

A. Click on any text inside the title box. (Notice that when your mouse pointer is in an area of the slide outside the box, it has a one-arrow shape. When you move it inside the box over the text, it has an I-beam shape.)

B. A fuzzy border appears outlining the box. The box is now ready to be resized.

Step 2: Position the mouse pointer.

A. Locate the handle (small white box) in the middle of the bottom margin of the title box.

B. Put your mouse pointer over that handle.

↕ C. Make sure that the **two-arrow** pointer is showing. If the one-arrow, or I-beam, or four-arrow pointer is showing, move the mouse pointer slightly to the right or left over the handle until the two-arrow pointer appears.

> **PowerPoint Terms**
>
> **Cursor:** The stationary blinking vertical line after which text will appear when you type.
>
> **Mouse pointer:** The on-screen pointer that moves when the mouse moves. It has numerous shapes depending on work being done.
>
> **One-arrow pointer:** The shape used to select (activate) a box. If it is not showing, drop down to the Drawing Toolbar and click on the arrow pointer button.
>
> **Two-arrow pointer:** The shape used to move the margins to change the size and shape of a box. The two-arrow mouse pointer positioned over a handle moves the margin.
>
> **Four-arrow pointer:** The shape used to move the entire box from one place to another.
>
> **Handle:** A small white square in the border of a box that is the control point from which your mouse pointer can drag an edge or margin to a new position.

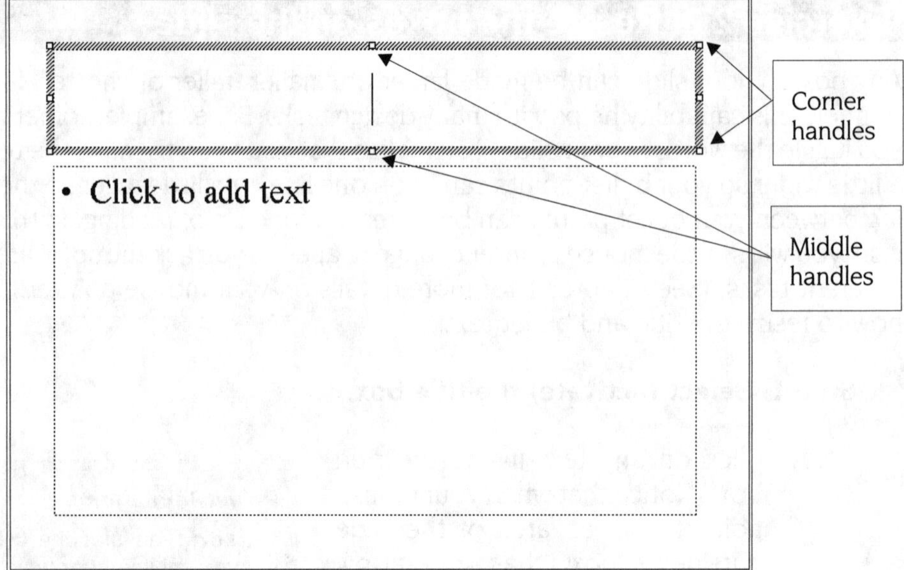

The handles in the middle of the top and bottom of the box change the height of the box. The handles in the middle of the right and left side change the width. The four corner handles change the height and width at the same time.

Step 3: Drag the bottom border up to make the title box narrower.

A. Hold down the left mouse button.

B. Drag this part of the border of the title box upward.

C. Release the left mouse button when you get where you want the margin to be.

! If you want to keep the box centered on the same place on the slide while you change its size, hold down the CTRL key while you drag the margin. If you want to maintain the box's proportions while you change its size, use the corner handles.

Step 4: Move the whole text box upward to fill the space you gained.

A. Activate the box that contains the text of your bullet points by clicking somewhere on the text in it. A fuzzy border will appear around the box.

B. Move your mouse pointer over one of the margins.

C. Hover or move slightly back and forth until the four-arrow pointer appears.

D. Click on the left mouse button. This will change the pattern of the fuzzy border. It is now ready for you to move.

E. Go to your keyboard. Click on the UP ARROW key several times. The whole bullet text box will move up one space at each click. You can use each of the keyboard's four arrow keys—UP, DOWN, LEFT, and RIGHT—in the same way. Alternatively, you can hold down the left mouse button and use the four-arrow pointer to drag the whole box upward. The arrow key method is more accurate than the drag method unless you have a very steady hand on the mouse.

Step 5: Enlarge the box containing the bullet points by dragging the bottom margin downward.

A. Move your mouse pointer over the handle in the center of the bottom margin.

B. Hover or move slightly back and forth until the two-arrow pointer appears.

C. Hold down the left mouse button and drag the bottom margin downward.

D. Release the left mouse button when you reach the position you want.

Step 6: Enlarge the text box sideways by dragging the side margins outward.

A. Move your mouse pointer over the handle in the center of the right side margin.

B. Hover or move slightly back and forth until the two-arrow pointer appears.

C. Hold down the left mouse button and drag the margin further to the right.

D. Release the left mouse button when you reach the position you want.

E. Do the same thing to move the left margin farther to the left.

Now that you have more space, add another line of text and see how it looks.

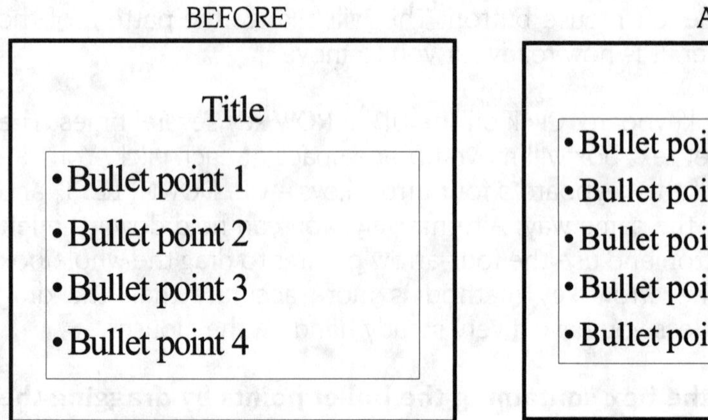

Step 7: Save your work

A. Go to the Standard Toolbar.

B. Click on the Save button.

If any of the boxes on the slide are still active, the Save option may be unavailable. It will appear in shadow form on the menu. If that happens, click outside the box to indicate you are finished with it before you click on the Save button.

Go to the CD and open the file for the case with which you are working to see examples of bullet slides with the boxes resized.

Exercise 2.4: Print, close, exit, and reopen

When you finish your work on a particular visual display, you may want to print it so that you can use the hard copy. You will also want to close the file and the software program, at some point, and reopen them again to do more work at a later time. Here's how to do these basic functions.

Step 1: Print the bulleted list.

With your slide on the screen—

A. Go to the Menu Bar.

B. Click on the File button. A drop-down menu will appear.

C. Click on the Print option. A Print screen will appear.

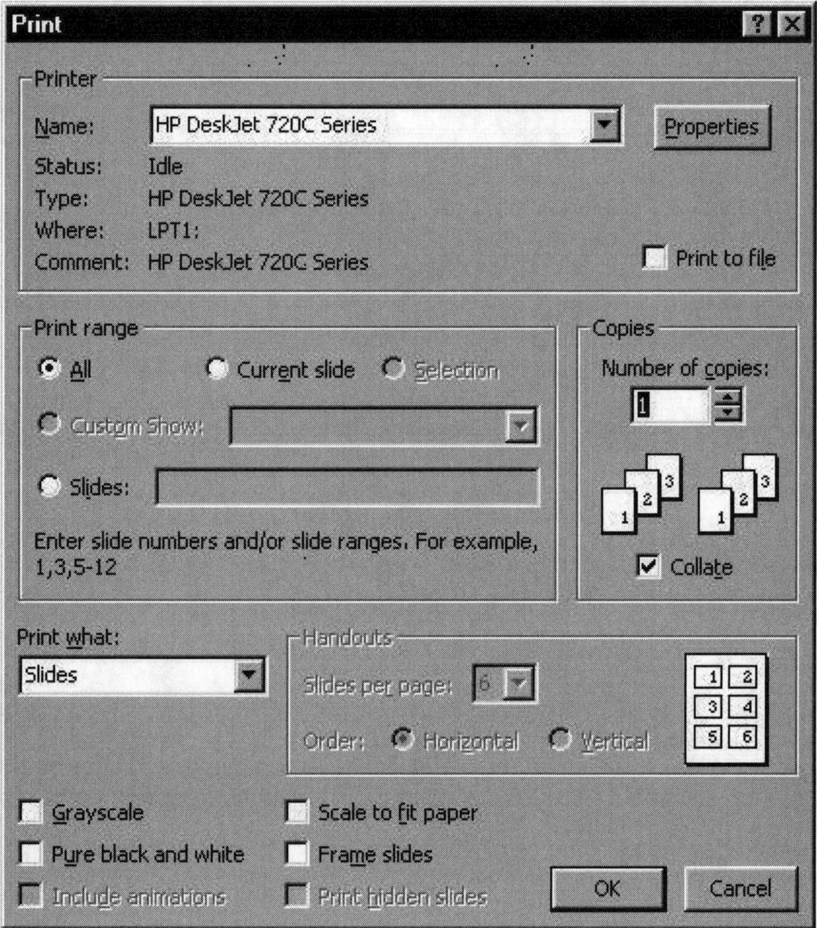

Your Print box may not look exactly this way, as PowerPoint will adapt to the type of printer you have, and will not display capabilities that your printer does not have.

D. In the Print Range box, choose the Current Slide option.

E. In the Print What box at the bottom of the screen, choose the Slides option.

F. Click on the small white box in front of the words "Frame slides," located just under the Print What box. A check mark will appear indicating that this function is active. This will draw a border around each of your slides.

G. Click on the OK button.

The Print screen for PowerPoint 97 looks slightly different, but the labeled boxes and buttons perform the same functions as described above.

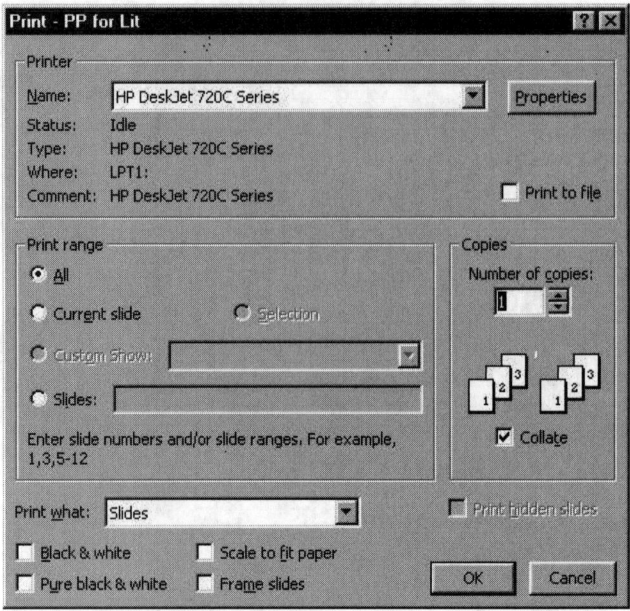

If you want to save paper, you can print more than one slide on each page. In the Print What box, click on the arrow to display a drop-down menu, and click on the Handout option. In the Handouts box (to the right) pick the number of slides to be displayed on each page. Click on OK.

When you print the first draft, even if you have a color printer, generally it is sufficient to look at a black and white version rather than using expensive color cartridges. To print a color slide in black and white, click on the Grayscale box in the lower left corner for PowerPoint 2000 and the Black & White box in the same place in PowerPoint 97. To switch back to color printing, click again on the small white box and the check mark will disappear. Now, if you have a color printer, your slide will be printed in full color. (Note: leave the box labeled "Pure black & white" unchecked. This is an alternative that converts all shades to either black or white, eliminating any grays.)

Step 2: Close the file.

A. Go to the Menu Bar.

B. Click on the File button. A drop-down menu will appear.

C. Choose the Close option. If you have made any changes since you last saved the file, PowerPoint will ask you if you want to save these changes before exiting the program. Choose Yes to save the file, or No to discard the changes.

Step 3: Exit the program.

A. Go to the Menu Bar.

B. Click on the File button. A drop-down menu will appear.

C. Choose the Exit option.

! Do not turn off the computer until after you have exited PowerPoint. To ensure that all of your files are safe, you need to exit the program first and then turn off the computer.

Step 4: Reopen the program.

This is the same as shown in Exercise 2.1, Step 1.

Step 5: Reopen the file.

A. When the opening screen for PowerPoint comes up, there are four options. The last option is Open an Existing Presentation. Click on this option. The screen displays (in the white box at the bottom) the names of the files with the most recent slides on which you have been working. For PowerPoint 2000, it looks like this:

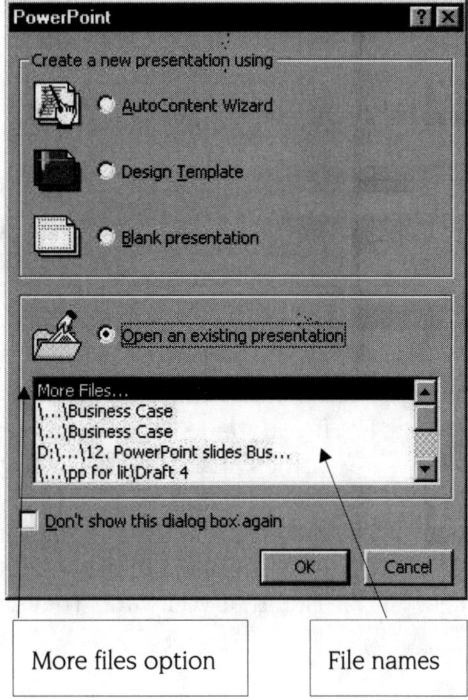

B. If the file you want is shown in the box, click on it. This highlights the file name. You may need to use the up and down scroll arrows to see all the file names. With the file name now highlighted, click on OK. The first slide in that file will be displayed automatically.

If the file is not listed there, click on the More Files option, which may already be highlighted. Click on OK. PowerPoint will display the Open dialog box. It looks like this.

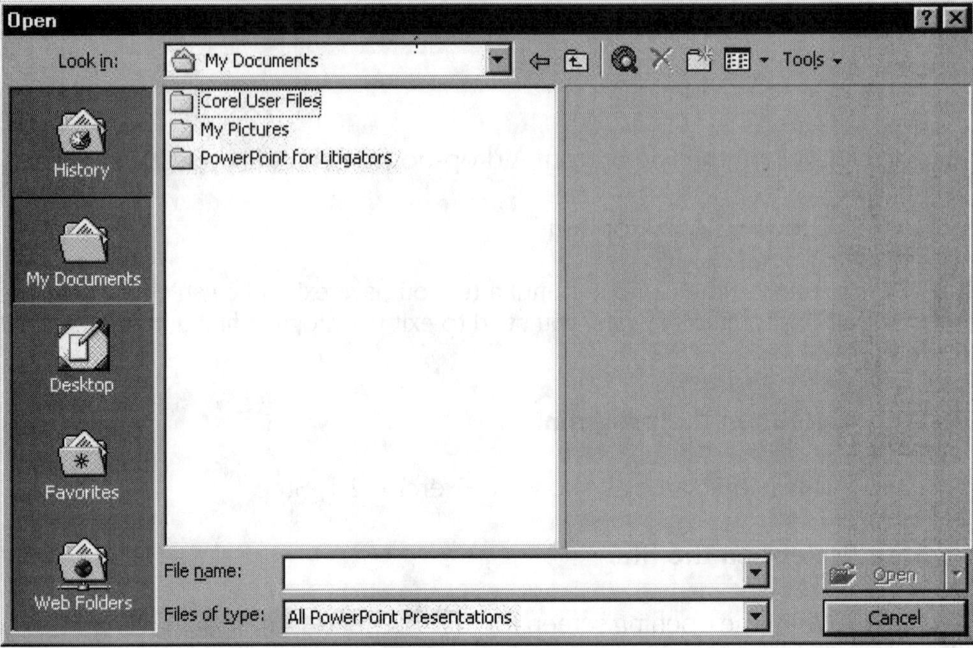

C. Look through the directory for the file name you want. Click on the file name to highlight it.

D. Click on the Open button. The first slide that you made under that file name will appear on the screen.

E. If you want to work on the slide that is displayed, click anywhere within it to activate it.

F. If you made more than one slide and you want to get to a slide that comes after the first one, go to the View Bar (Illustration, Ch. 1, Section 1.5), and click on the Slide Sorter button. The Slide Sorter screen shows you miniature pictures, or thumbnails, of each of your slides. (Illustration, Exercise 4.1, Step 1.) Double click on the thumbnail of the slide that you want. That slide will appear on the screen in full size.

The Open box in PowerPoint 97 looks slightly different but works in the same way.

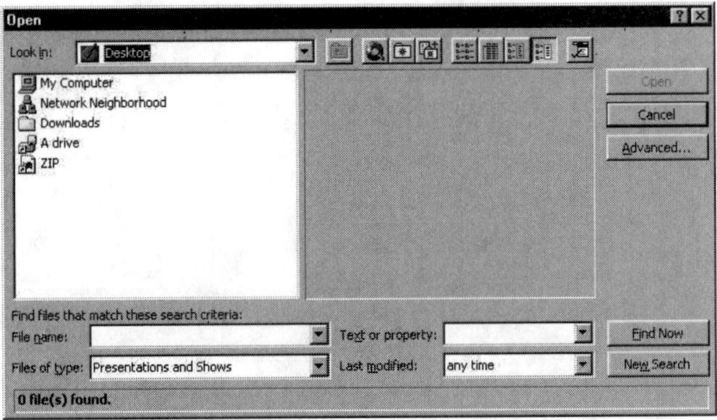

A glossary in the back of the book will help you with any specialized PowerPoint terms. The directions in these exercises are in plain English to the maximum extent possible, but some use of key PowerPoint terms is unavoidable.

Chapter 3

Enhancing Basic Lists

The slide that you made in Exercise 2.1 is composed of black letters on a white background. That is perfectly appropriate for a courtroom. However, there are some things you can do to make your visual aids more attractive and easier to read.

This chapter includes five useful ways to make slides easier to comprehend. These techniques can be used alone or in combination.

1. Adjust the shape, size, and alignment of the lettering
2. Put a box around your text
3. Add color to the elements of the slide
4. Adjust the shape, size, and spacing of the bullets
5. Use subheadings

As you dress up your slides, you will come to appreciate the enormous range of tools included in the software. Relatively few of these are applicable to courtroom use unless you have had a lot of experience using PowerPoint slides in actual trials and have found particular things that work well for you. Most of the splashy special effects, such as PowerPoint's huge array of colors, clip art selections, sound effects, and special renditions of text, do not work well in the courtroom. They raise potential objections or detract from the listener's ability to pay attention to the substance of what is being said.

★ Slides should enhance persuasion, not become the focus of the trial. If a juror or judge can think of nothing other than how interesting, clever, or amusing a slide or special effect is, the slide has crossed the line from an aid to persuasion to a distraction.

Enhancing your slides requires the use of toolbars. This is where you will go when you want to give PowerPoint a command to do something. The PowerPoint toolbars used in this book are illustrated in Chapter 1, Section 1.5. Before you start this exercise, check your screen to see which toolbars are displayed. For the exercises in this chapter, you should have these toolbars showing:

At the top of your screen—

Title Bar
Menu Bar

Standard Toolbar
Formatting Toolbar

At the bottom of your screen—

View Bar
Drawing Toolbar
Status Bar

If other toolbars are present, that is okay. They will be used in other exercises.

Sometimes one or more toolbars have been turned off on a particular computer. If any of the toolbars are missing, do this:

A. Go to the Menu Bar.

B. Click on the View button. A drop-down menu will appear.

C. Choose the Toolbars option. A second drop-down menu will appear. The toolbars that are active will be indicated by a check mark in the box in front of their names.

D. Click on the Standard, Formatting, and Drawing toolbars if any of these are not active. Click anywhere outside the menu to return to your main screen.

PowerPoint Terms

Toolbar: Toolbars are the long narrow strips on the top, bottom, and sides of the screen. Each toolbar displays a collection of related software functions that help you work with the slides you are making. Toolbars are activated by using the View button on the Menu Bar and selecting the Toolbars option.

Button: Buttons are the small rectangles or squares that appear on the bars and toolbars. Each button represents a different software function. Buttons are activated by putting the mouse pointer over the button and clicking on it with the left mouse button.

Drop-down menu: Drop-down menus are subsidiary lists of closely related software functions that appear when some kinds of buttons are activated. Options on the menu lists are selected by clicking with the mouse pointer.

Exercise 3.1: Set the typeface, size, and alignment

The typeface, type size, and alignment that you use for the words on your slides affect how readable they are. In most courtrooms, the jury is at least ten feet away from the monitor or screen where your slides will appear. That means you need to ensure that the letters are crisp and clear with sufficient spacing. Before trial, slides should be checked for clarity in the courtroom in which they will be used. (Some courtrooms have built-in small, high resolution monitors in front of each juror that will produce displays similar to your computer screen.)

The screen on which you display your slides in court usually will be bigger than the computer screen on which you design them. The big screen corrupts many stylistic choices that looked great on the computer screen. Always test with the screen or monitor you will be using at approximately the distance required in the courtroom where you will be working.

The typeface for a bulleted list should be one of the clean sans serif typefaces. **Arial** is a good choice. **Tahoma** is another good choice. These typefaces scale up well so that at large sizes they are still easy to read. Other typefaces such as Times New Roman or Courier may look good on your computer screen or on an 8½ x 11 sheet of paper, but when they are enlarged many times on the display screen in the courtroom, they are not crisp enough.

The type sizes for the title and text should be proportional to each other and readable at the distance your display screen will be from the judge and jury. The title is usually set in a size larger than the text. The choice depends on the display screen you will be using.

The sizes appropriate for a ten-foot projection screen are different from the sizes appropriate for a fifty-inch digital monitor.

Consider these combinations for title and text sizes:

Title	**Text**
54 point	44 point
54 point	36 point
48 point	36 point
46 point	36 point
36 point	28 point
32 point	24 point

PowerPoint Terms

Typeface: A typeface is a design for the letters in the alphabet which has been given a name like Courier or Times New Roman. Some designs are decorative and do not work in a courtroom.

Type size: Each typeface comes in a number of sizes, which are described in points. Low numbers describe small sizes. Most typefaces have a range of sizes, but only a few sizes in which they look their best.

Font: A combination of typeface and type size, e.g. 32 point Arial. The buttons for font selection are located on the Formatting Toolbar.

Bold: A thickened version of the typeface used for emphasis. The button for bold facing is located on Formatting Toolbar.

Italic: A slanted version of the typeface that is the same size but stands out because it leans to the right. The button for Italic facing is located on the Formatting Toolbar.

Underlining: A regular version of the typeface with a matching sized line drawn under it. The button for underlining is located on the Formatting Toolbar.

When making a series of bullet point slides, consistency is key. Once you pick a combination of title and text sizes, it is best to stick with that combination throughout your series. Your goal is to make the format of the slides as consistent as possible, so that attention will be focused on your message.

Step 1: Set the typeface for the title.

With your slide on the screen—

A. Select the title box by clicking anywhere on the text within it.

B. Select (highlight) all of the text of your title.

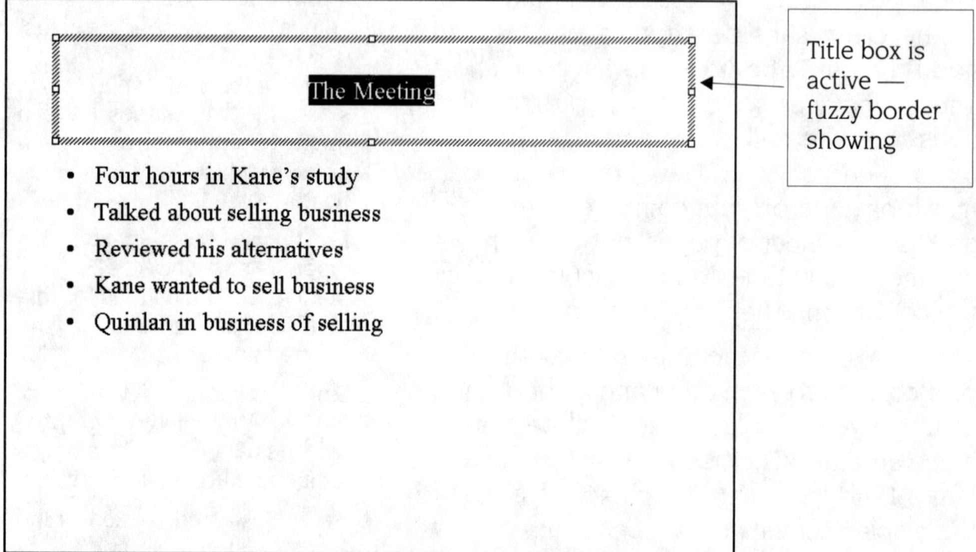

C. Go to the Formatting Toolbar. The name of the currently active typeface is displayed in the white box at the far left of this toolbar.

D. Put your mouse pointer on the small arrow immediately to the right of the white box and click on it. A drop-down menu will show you a list of typefaces. In PowerPoint 2000, each typeface name shows you how it actually looks.

E. Scroll up or down (using the small arrows at the right of the menu) to get to Arial. The typefaces are listed in alphabetical order. Click on that option. The name Arial will appear in the box as the active typeface.

Step 2: Set the type size for the title.

With the text of the title still highlighted—

A. Go to the smaller box just to the right of the box and arrow for the typeface. The white box will display the size of the type currently selected.

B. Put your mouse pointer on the small arrow at the right.

C. Scroll down to the 48-point size. Click on that option. The size 48 will appear in the box as the active type size. The lettering in your title will increase in size to 48 points.

! PowerPoint provides a way to see how type size changes look on the screen while you are working. Highlight the text for which you want to change the size, and click on the Increase Font Size button on the Formatting Toolbar (13th from the left). The Decrease Font Size button right next to it works the same way.

The Meeting

- Four hours in Kane's study
- Talked about selling business
- Reviewed his alternatives
- Kane wanted to sell
- Quinlan in business of selling

When you set the typeface for the title, it will remain selected for the title box only, as shown above. You will need to set the typeface for the bullet points separately as shown in Step 6 below.

A The illustration above shows how the screen will look in the commercial contract case. Go to the Appendix for your case to see an example.

Step 3: Set the alignment for the title.

Titles normally should be centered on the slide. PowerPoint should center the title automatically. If it does not, do this.

With the text of the title still highlighted—

A. Go to the Formatting Toolbar.

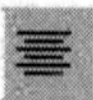

B. Click on the Center Alignment button (8th from the left). The title will center itself equidistant from the two sides of the title box.

Step 4: Add bold face for the title.

With the text of the title still highlighted—

A. Go to the Formatting Toolbar.

B. Click on the Bold button (3rd from left). The words that you have highlighted will switch to bold face.

Bold face for the title sets it off somewhat from the text. Bold face may be useful in this regard, but it is not necessary for all types of slides.

If you use bold, it will take up more space. Usually this is not a problem with titles because they are only a few words. Generally bold face is not used in the bullet points or bullet point text. If you use bold face on the text of the bullet points it might take up considerably more space, and perhaps run from one line of text to two.

Step 5: Add shadow to the title.

With the text of the title still highlighted—

A. Go to the Formatting Toolbar.

B. Click on the Text Shadow button (6th from the left). This applies a shadow to the text you selected.

C. Click outside the box to see if you like it.

D. To undo the shadow, go to the Standard Toolbar and click on the Undo button. You can also go to the Formatting Toolbar while the text is highlighted and click on the Shadow button again, which will turn off the shadow.

Shadowing is just an option for your title. Shadowing is used only for titles, never for the text of bullet points. Adding bold to the title is usually enough, and shadowing should not be used. It depends on the wording of the title, the color combination, and the way the letters look with shadowing. If in doubt, leave it out.

Step 6: Set the typeface, size, and alignment for the text of the bullet points.

A. Click anywhere on the text within the box containing the bullet points to activate it.

B. Select (highlight) all of the text of your bullet points. They are probably still in the Times New Roman font, which is PowerPoint's default setting.

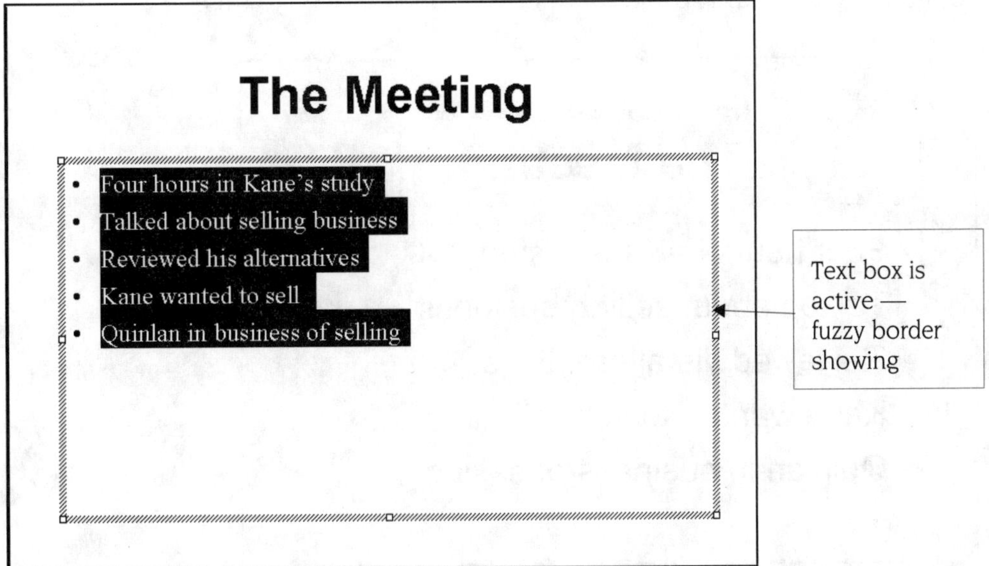

C. Check the typeface by looking at the Formatting Toolbar. The name of the currently active typeface appears there. Normally you will use the same typeface for the title and the text. This gives the bullet points a neat appearance. If the typeface is not Arial, which was used for the title, change it.

D. Set the type size to 36-point Arial. (Steps 1 and 2 above.) The bullet point text will enlarge on the screen.

E. PowerPoint should automatically align your bullet points to the left margin. If it does not, highlight the text, go to the Formatting Toolbar, and click on the left alignment button.

Step 7: Save your work.

A Go to the Standard Toolbar.

B. Click on the Save button.

Exercise 3.2: Put boxes around the title and text

It is usually helpful to create boxes around the title and text. This assists the viewer to focus easily on the two parts of the slide and makes each part more comfortable to read. The slide with boxes added looks like this:

The Meeting

- Four hours in Kane's study
- Talked about selling business
- Reviewed his alternatives
- Kane wanted to sell
- Quinlan in business of selling

Step 1: Put a box around the title.

With your slide on the screen—

A. Select (or activate) the title box.

B. Go to the Drawing Toolbar.

C. Click on the Line Style button (15th from the left) which brings up a menu of the primary line width choices.

PowerPoint Terms

Line style: The thickness of the line or whether the border has one, two, or three parallel lines.

Dash style: Whether the line is dotted or dashed, instead of continuous, and the appearance of the dashes.

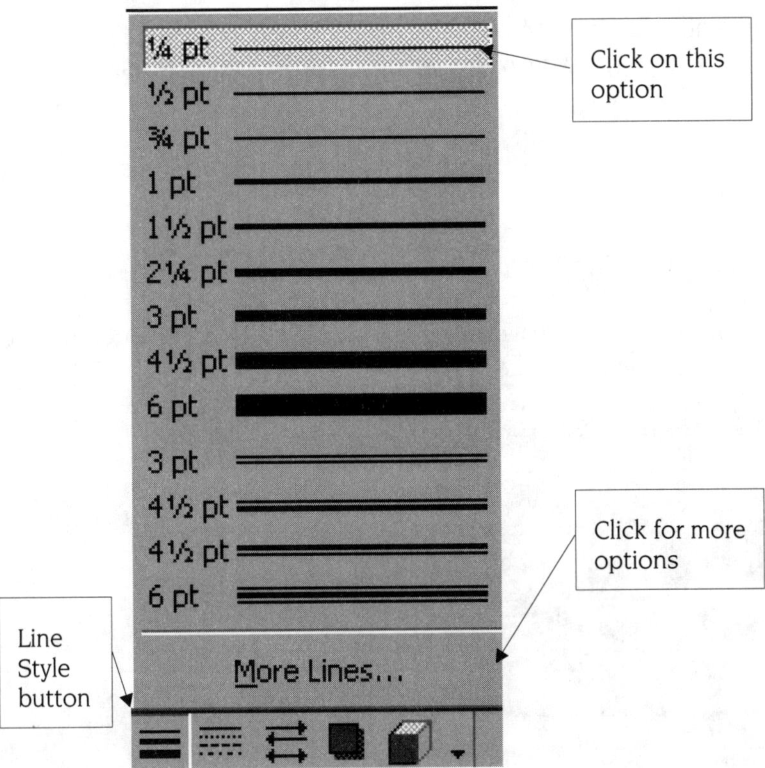

D. Click on the ¼-point size. A border will appear around your box.

E. Click outside the box to see that the border is now in place.

Step 2: Put a box around the text.

A. Select (or activate) the box containing the bullet point list.

B. Follow the same steps as in Step 1 above.

★ When you use lines, follow the principle of "least visual difference." Use the smallest width of line that will get the point across. If your slides will be shown on a large screen, you may need a wider line (depending somewhat on the capability of your projector).

★ When you pick a line size, stay with that selection for the boxes around titles and text throughout your slides.

Step 3: Add shadow to the title box.

A. Select (or activate) the box containing the title.

B. Put some fill color in the box (even white). (If there is no fill in the box, the shadow will appear on the lettering in the box as well as on the box itself.)

1. Select (activate) the title box by clicking anywhere on the text within it.

2. Go to the Drawing Toolbar.

3. Click on the small arrow to the right of the Fill Color button (12th from the left). This will take you to the Color Options box.

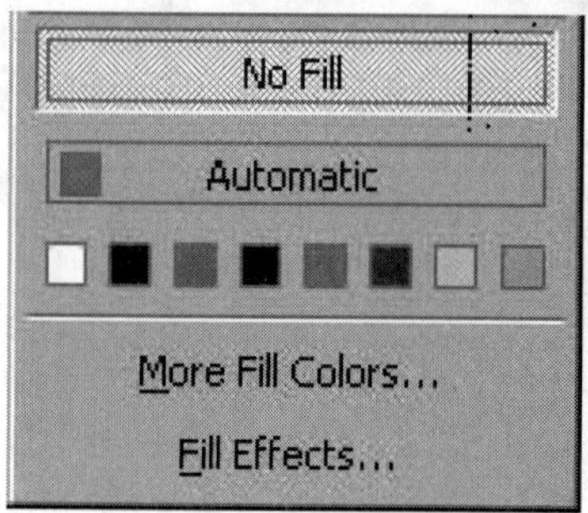

4. Click on the white square.

C. Activate the shadow.

1. Go to the Drawing Toolbar.

2. Click on the Box Shadow button (18th from the left). A dialog box will appear above the button showing you all the variations of shadowing available for your title box.

3. Click on the lower right shadow (2nd row from the top; 2nd icon from the left). A shadow will appear around the right and bottom margins of the box.

4. The depth of the shadowing can be changed by clicking on Shadow Settings at the bottom of the box. Another dialog box appears giving you four options.

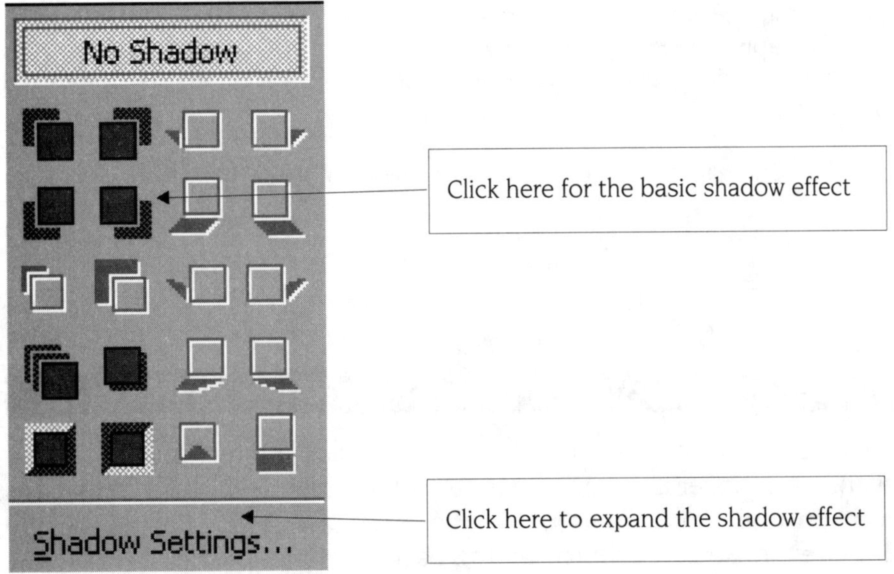

Your slide now looks like this:

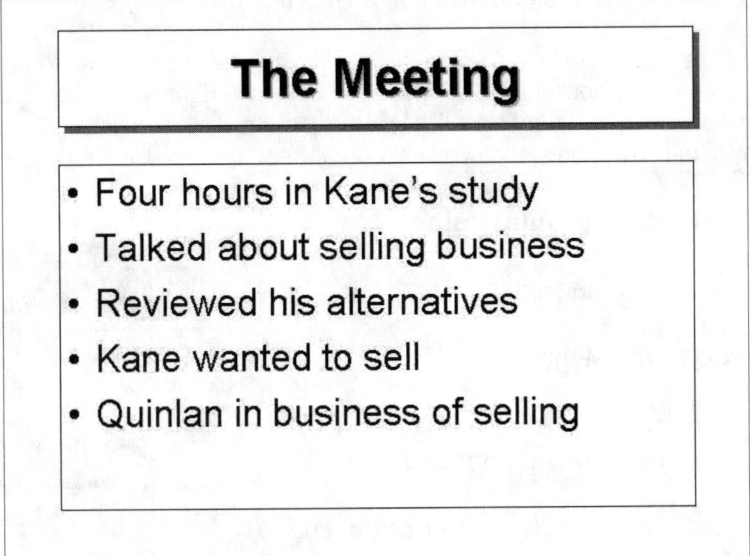

Step 4: Save your work.

Shadowing should not be used with every title box. It is a helpful emphasis by making the box appear to come off the page. However, it works best with short titles and simple formats. Adding shadowing to an otherwise somewhat "busy" slide would not help its effectiveness.

A Go to the Appendix for your case to see examples of these slides.

Exercise 3.3: Add color to the components of the slide

You can add color to all of the parts of your slide to add interest or emphasis to your presentation. Generally you will want to consider first your color selections for the **background** of the slide, which is the space on the slide behind the title box and the text box. This will provide the basic contrast for the title and text boxes that sit on top of this background. Next consider the **fill** (color within the title and text boxes). The **font** (lettering), **line**, and **bullet** color normally is black, although this exercise shows you how to color those elements as well. You do not need to color everything on every slide. It is a good idea to exercise restraint.

! Colors wash out quickly as the size of the display is enlarged. What looks best on a sharp 21-inch computer monitor will be much less bright on a 42-inch courtroom display monitor and quite faded on a 12-foot projection screen. Always test your slides on the monitor or projection screen you are actually going to use for your presentation.

Step 1: Add background color.

With your slide on the screen—

A. Go to the Menu bar.

B. Click on the Format button. A drop-down menu appears.

C. Click on the Background option. The Background screen appears in the middle of the slide on which you are working.

It looks like this:

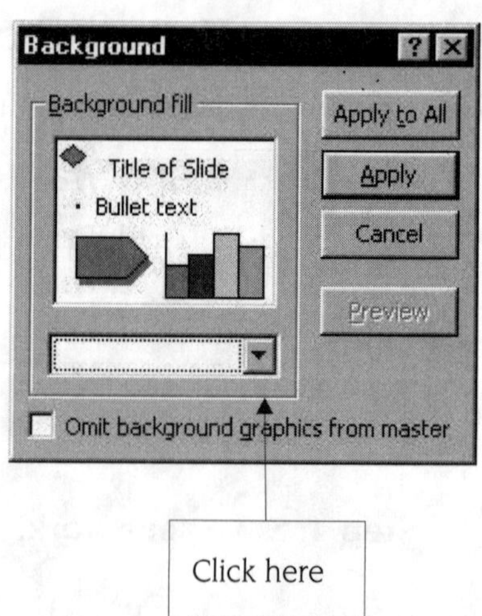

D. Click on the small arrow next to the box that shows the current color of the fill. The Color Options box appears.

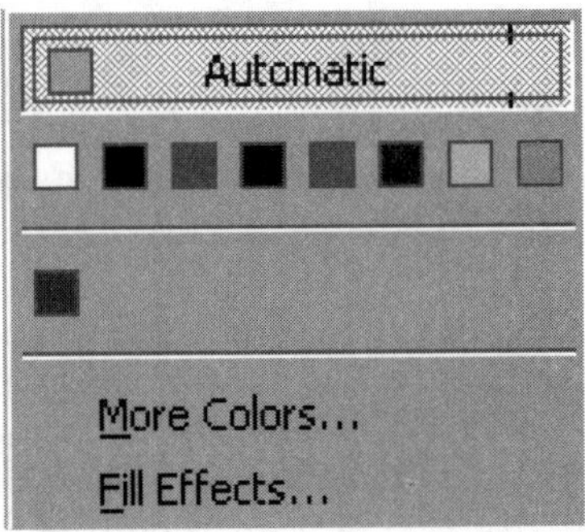

E. If the exact color you want is on the row of colors displayed at the top of the box, click on it. Otherwise, click on the More Fill Colors button. A palette of colors will appear and you can select any of those colors by clicking on one.

F. Click on a solid dark blue color for the background. PowerPoint will highlight your choice.

G. Click on the OK button if you are at the color palette screen. That takes you back to the Color Option box

H. Click the Apply button on the Color Option box.

I. Your slide will reappear on the screen and the background of your slide is now blue.

The Meeting

- Four hours in Kane's study
- Talked about selling business
- Reviewed his alternatives
- Kane wanted to sell
- Quinlan in business of selling

J. If you do not like the color you picked, go back through these steps again and pick another one.

K. Save your work.

Normally you will want to choose dark colors for the background of your slides. Dark grays, greens, and blues work well. Lighter colors will wash out when you project them on a larger screen.

When you pick a background color, stay with your selection for all of the slides in that part of the case. Constantly changing background colors is distracting. You can use the Apply to All button on the Background screen for this purpose.

PowerPoint 2000 provides a special button on the Formatting Toolbar for coloring backgrounds. It is shown in the illustration in Exercise 3.5 of the extension of the Formatting Toolbar. This very useful button can be added permanently to the toolbar as it is displayed on your screen. See Chapter 12, Exercise 12.3.

Step 2: Add color to the title box and the text box (fill color).

A. Select (activate) the title box by clicking anywhere on the text within it.

B. Go to the Drawing Toolbar.

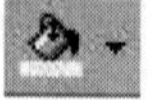

C. Click on the small arrow to the right of the Fill Color button (12th from the left). This will take you to the Color Options box.

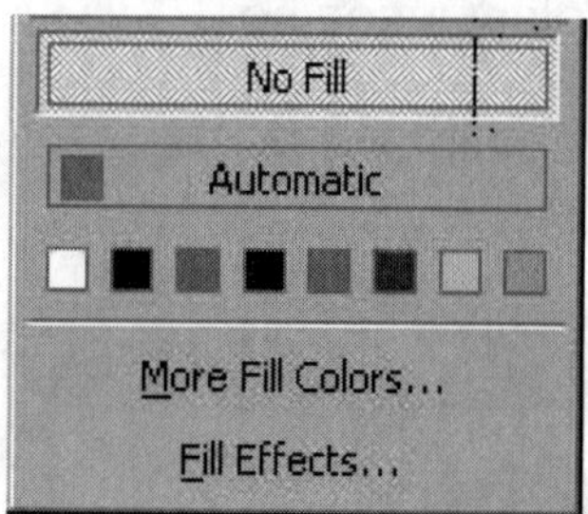

D. If the color you want is there, click on it. If not, click on the More Fill Colors button. A palette of colors will appear. (The Custom tab at the top of the screen button displays even more colors.) The screen looks like this:

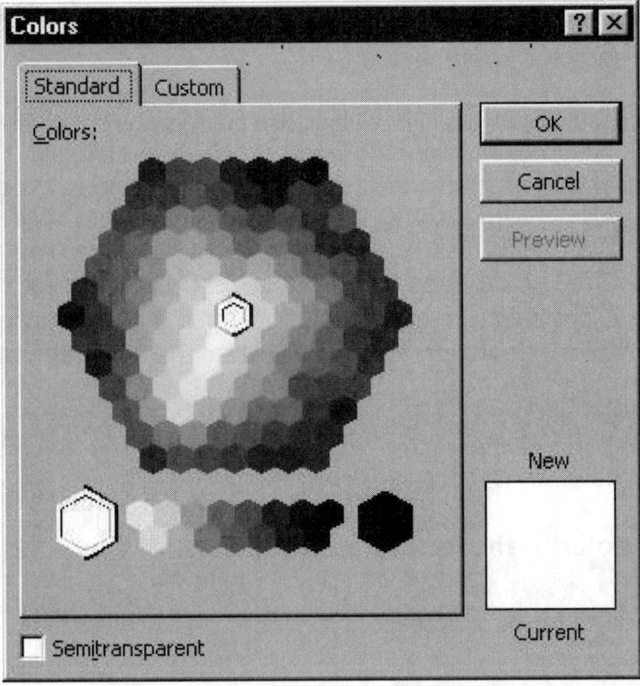

E. Click on a light yellow color for the fill within the title box. PowerPoint will highlight your choice.

F. Click on the OK button.

G. Your slide will reappear on the screen and the fill for your title box is now yellow.

The Meeting

- Four hours in Kane's study
- Talked about selling business
- Reviewed his alternatives
- Kane wanted to sell
- Quinlan in business of selling

H. If you do not like the color you picked, go back through these steps again and pick another one.

★ The fill color should be white, light yellow, or a quiet pastel. This will contrast well with the dark background of the slide (behind the text box and title box) and provide a good setting for the lettering of the bullet points. Both improve the readability of the slide.

I. Activate the box that contains the bullet points. Repeat these steps. Pick a slightly lighter color of yellow for that one. Having a slightly lighter color below separates the title from the text in yet another way.

A The Appendices contain examples for the criminal case and the tort case. To see the illustrations for all three cases in full color, go to the CD and open the PowerPoint file for the case that you are working on.

Step 3: Add color to the lettering (font color).

A. Activate the title box by clicking in it. Select (highlight) the text of the title.

B. Go to the Drawing Toolbar.

C. Click on the small arrow to the right of the Font Color button (14th from the left). This will take you to the Color Options box.

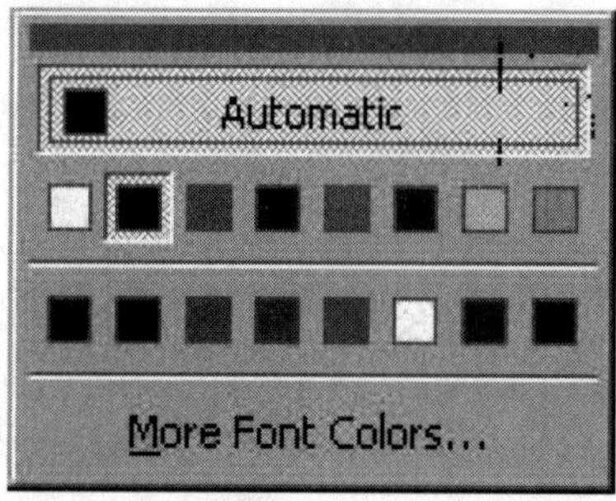

D. If the color you want is in the Color Options box, click on it. Otherwise, click on the More Font Colors button. A palette of colors will appear. (Illustration in Step 2 above.) If the precise color you want is not there, click on the Custom button to see even more colors.

E. Click on a dark blue color for the lettering of the title. PowerPoint will highlight your choice.

F. Click on the OK button.

G. Your slide will reappear on the screen but the lettering will be in a different color than the one you chose. Click anywhere outside the lettering that you selected to see the true color. The lettering of your title is now blue. If you do not like the precise shade you have picked, go back through these steps again and pick another one.

H. Activate the text box that contains the bullet points. Select (highlight) the text of the bullet points. Repeat the step above. Pick a slightly darker color of blue than you used for the title.

★ It is also possible to use white or yellow letters on a black or dark blue or dark green background. This does not work well with more than a line or two of text, but is an alternative for emphasis and highlighting.

★ The steps for adding color to lettering are included here for your information. Usually you will want to leave the letters in black. A multitude of colors will make the slide too busy and less persuasive.

Step 4: Add color to the lines (line color).

A. Activate the title box by clicking anywhere on the text within it.

B. Go to the Drawing Toolbar.

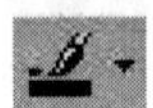

C. Click on the arrow to the right of the Line Color button (13th from the left). This will take you to the Color Options box.

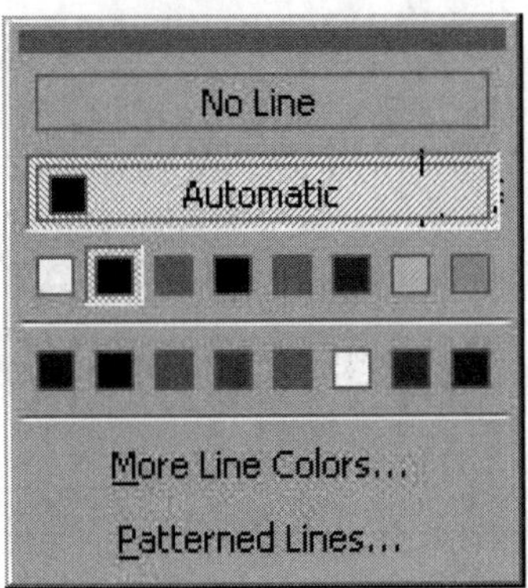

D. If the color you want for your box is on the screen, click on it. Otherwise, click on the More Line Colors button. A palette of colors will appear. If the precise color you want is not there, click on the Custom button to see even more colors.

E. Click on a light red color for the lines in the box around the title. PowerPoint will highlight your choice.

F. Click on the OK button.

G. Your slide will reappear and the box around your title is now highlighted lightly in red. If you do not like the color you picked, go back through these steps again and pick another one.

H. Activate the box that contains the bullet points. Pick the same color of red for the lines in the box around that one.

! The blue color that comes up as the default on the color palette when the Line Color button is activated makes a good choice in many kinds of slides.

★ You might want to skip a separate color for the lines in the title box and text box and leave them black. This gives the slide a dignified appearance and increases its persuasive impact.

Step 5: Add color to the bullets.

PowerPoint 2000 automatically changes the color of the bullets to match the color of the text. If you want black bullets with colored text, you have to change the bullet color to black. PowerPoint 97 leaves the bullets black when you change the color of the text, and if you want colored bullets, you have to change them. In both versions, the process of changing the color works like this:

A. Select (activate) the box containing the bullet point list by clicking anywhere on the text within that box.

B. Select (highlight) the text associated with the bullets you want to change. The highlight will not cover the bullets themselves. (You may have to try a few times to get off the four-arrow mouse pointer shape and onto the I-beam shape. Just click outside the box containing the bullet points and try again.)

C. Go to the Menu Bar.

D. Click on the Format button. A drop-down menu will appear.

E. Choose the Bullets and Numbering option. In PowerPoint 2000, the Bullets and Numbering screen will appear.

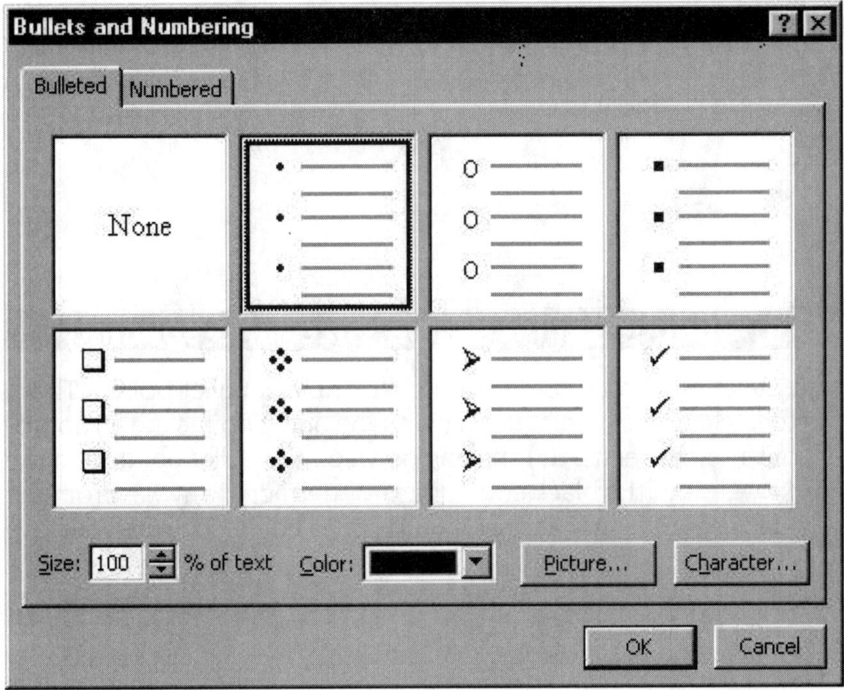

F. Click on the arrow next to the box at the bottom labeled "Color." This will take you to the Color Options box.

G. If one of the colors shown in the box is what you want, click on that color. Otherwise, click on the More Colors button at the bottom of the box. A palette of colors will appear. (Illustration, Step 2.)

H. Click on a color for the bullets. PowerPoint will highlight your choice.

I. Click on the OK button. You should now be back at your slide and the bullets should be changed to the new color.

Step 6: Save your work.

97 The layout of the Bullet screen in PowerPoint 97 is different. The box for choosing a color appears in the upper middle area of the screen. The function is the same.

★ It is not often that you will use color with bullets themselves. Black bullets make the slide appear more businesslike. Occasionally, in a photo or diagram for example, there may be a color that you want to replicate with the color of the bullet point that explains it.

! As a shortcut for Fill Color, Line Color, and Font Color, when you choose a color the first time, PowerPoint puts that color in the small bar underneath the icon on the button. After that, if you want the same color again, you can just click on the button.

Bullet points often need animation so that only one point appears at a time. The animation of bullet points is discussed in Chapter 9, Exercise 9.1. The same material for PowerPoint 97 is covered in Appendix D. PowerPoint 97 is somewhat different in this regard. Examples of these slides in color and with animation are on the CD.

Exercise 3.4: Change bullet shape, size, and spacing

The PowerPoint bullet list layout comes with circular black bullet points. These are an excellent choice for most courtroom uses. The bullet points are an appropriate size for courtroom screens, the spacing between the bullet points and the text usually works well, and the black color does not detract in any way from the message. If you decide to change these standard bullet points, be sure you have a good reason.

Step 1: Change the shape of the bullets.

A. Select the bullets to be changed.

1. Select (activate) the text box containing the bullets you want to change.

2. Select (highlight) all of the text for which the bullet points are to be changed. Although the highlighting as it appears on the screen does not seem to include the bullets, they are in fact included.

B. Go to the Bullet style screen.

1. Go to the Menu bar.

2. Click on the Format button. A drop-down menu will appear.

3. Click on the Bullets and Numbering option. The Bullets and Numbering screen will appear. (Illustration, Exercise 3.3, Step 5E.)

4. Click on the Character button at the lower right. The Bullet style box will appear. It looks like this:

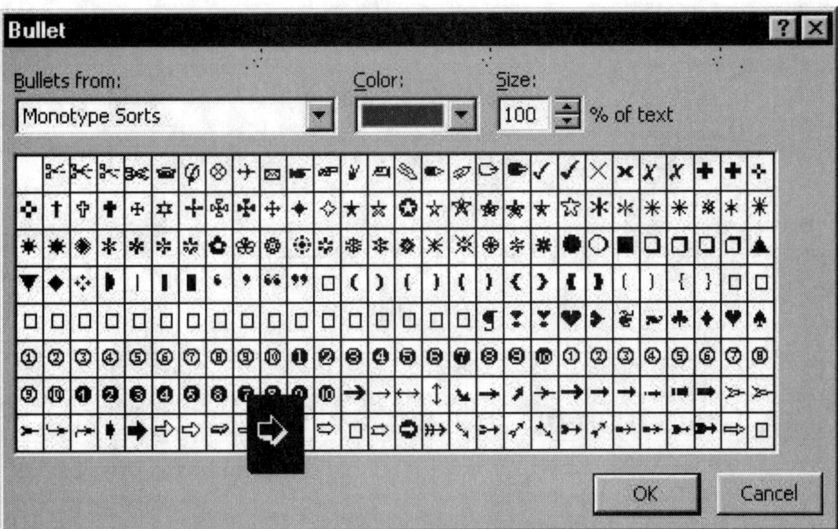

In PowerPoint 97, the option on the format button drop-down menu is called Bullet. The same Bullet style box will appear.

C. Pick the bullet style you want to use.

1. Click on the arrow next to the white box labeled "Bullets from." A drop-down menu will list many sources for shapes. Choose the option called Monotype Sorts. The options are listed in alphabetical order.

2. Click on the arrow bullets box (bottom row, 10th box from the left). The square bullet (3rd row from the top, 6th box from the right) is also a good choice.

3. Click on the OK button. You should now be back at your slide, and the solid round bullets should be changed to arrow-shaped bullets.

The Meeting

- Four hours in Kane's study
- Talked about selling business
- Reviewed his alternatives
- Kane wanted to sell
- Quinlan in business of selling

! PowerPoint 2000 automates the option of numbering or lettering your points instead of using bullets. Go to the Menu Bar, click on the Format button, choose the Bullets and Numbering option. When the Bullets and Numbering screen appears, click on the Numbered tab. The screen will show options for numbering and lettering. Click on the one you prefer. Click on OK. The bullet points will change to numbers or letters.

★ PowerPoint provides hundreds of alternatives for bullet shapes. Look at the Normal, Wingding, and Monotype Sorts options as good sources. PowerPoint also offers smiley faces, fingers pointing, and other alternatives for bullet points. These forms can raise objections. It is safer to stick to the traditional shapes.

Step 2: Change the size of the bullets.

A. Select the bullets to be changed.

1. Select (activate) the text box containing the bullets you want to change.

2. Select (highlight) all of the text for which the bullet points are to be changed. The highlighted area that shows your selection will not include the bullet points.

B. Go to the Bullets and Numbering screen.

1. Go to the Menu bar.

2. Click on the Format button. A drop-down menu will appear.

3. Choose the Bullets and Numbering option. The Bullets and Numbering screen will appear.

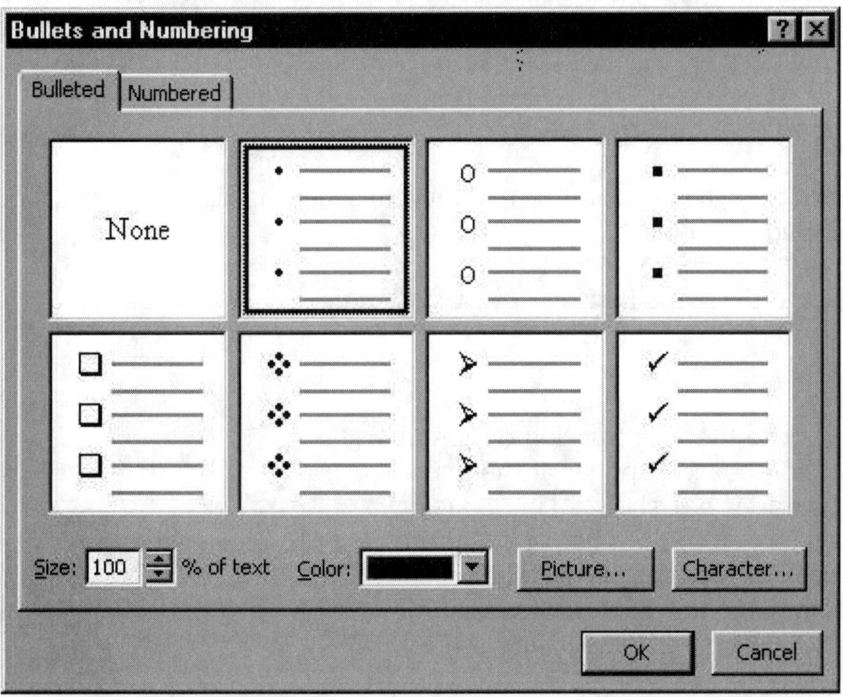

! In PowerPoint 2000, the normal bullet shape you started with is on the Bullets and Numbering screen just to the right of the box that says "None." See above. In PowerPoint 97, the normal bullet shape is in the [Normal Text] option, fifth row down, sixth from the left.

C. Click on the arrow next to the Size box in the lower left corner of the screen. The up arrow will increase the size of the bullets, and the down arrow will decrease their size.

D. Click on the OK button. You should now be back at your slide with the new size bullets.

! When you change the size of your typeface, the software automatically will adjust the size of the bullets so they will continue to be proportional to the text size. If you change the shape of the bullets, however, the new shape may not be proportional to your text, and you may need to adjust the size of the bullets. If you change the size of the bullet points to make them larger, you will probably need to increase the amount of space between the bullet point and the text that follows it. (See below.)

Step 3: Change the spacing between the bullet points.

The PowerPoint layout for a bullet point chart is ideal for five lines. If you have less than that, or occasionally more than that, you may need to adjust the spacing between the lines so that the slide looks well proportioned.

With your slide on the screen—

A. Select (highlight) all of the text on your slide. The highlighting will not include the bullets.

B. Go to the Menu Bar.

C. Click on the Format button.

D. Choose the Line Spacing option. A dialog box will appear. If the dialog box does not show a Line Spacing option, go to the small arrow at the bottom of the box, which will expand it to show more options, including the Line Spacing option.

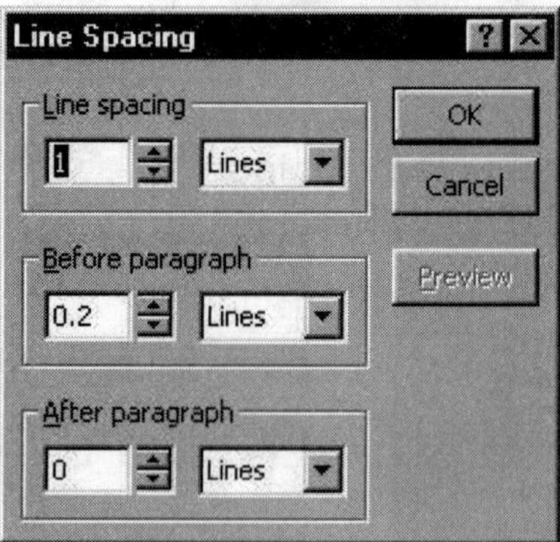

E. The top two options in the dialog box control line spacing for your slide. The box on the left will show the amount of space that you now have between the bullet points. The box on the right will say "Lines."

F. Use the up arrow next to the left button to increase the amount of space between each bullet point. Use the down arrow to decrease the amount of space. You do not need to change the button on the right side. (PowerPoint gives you the option to measure space by lines or points. Use the line option.)

G. Click on the OK button. This will take you back to your slide.

H. Your slide still has the text highlighted. Click anywhere and the highlighting will disappear. The new spacing will be in place.

Step 4: Save your work.

! In PowerPoint, you normally have the option of double-clicking with the left mouse button on the option you have chosen instead of clicking once on the option and then clicking on the OK button.

If you have a two-line bullet point on a slide with several one-line bullet points, you may need to adjust the spacing so that the amount of space between the lines of the two-line bullet point is less than the amount of space between the points. To do this, highlight just the lines of the two-line bullet point, go to Line Spacing, and create the correct spacing.

PowerPoint 2000 has special buttons on the Formatting Toolbar for Increasing Paragraph Spacing and Decreasing Paragraph Spacing that perform the spacing function more quickly. See Chapter 12, Exercise 12.3. A glossary of terms at the back of the book will help with any unfamiliar terms.

The CD that comes with the book shows animations (Exercise 9.1) and transitions (Exercise 10.2) for these slides. It also shows examples of different types of bullet shapes in the three case files.

Exercise 3.5: Create subordinate points

PowerPoint provides tools for indenting subordinate points and for switching the order of the points on your slide. This facilitates experimentation with the order in which you are making your points, and is an easy way to try out different ideas.

Step 1: Create subordinate points.

With your slide on the screen—

A. Put your mouse pointer anywhere in the text of the bullet point that is to be made a subordinate point to another bullet point.

B. Click the left mouse button once to activate the cursor at that point.

C. Go to the Formatting Toolbar.

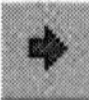

D. Click on the Demote button (15th from the left).

The arrow pointing to the right is the Demote button and the arrow pointing to the left is the Promote button. The Promote button will not be active unless your cursor is on a subordinate point that can be promoted to be a main point.

The Demote button will automatically indent the bullet text, with a new and smaller bullet, under the preceding point.

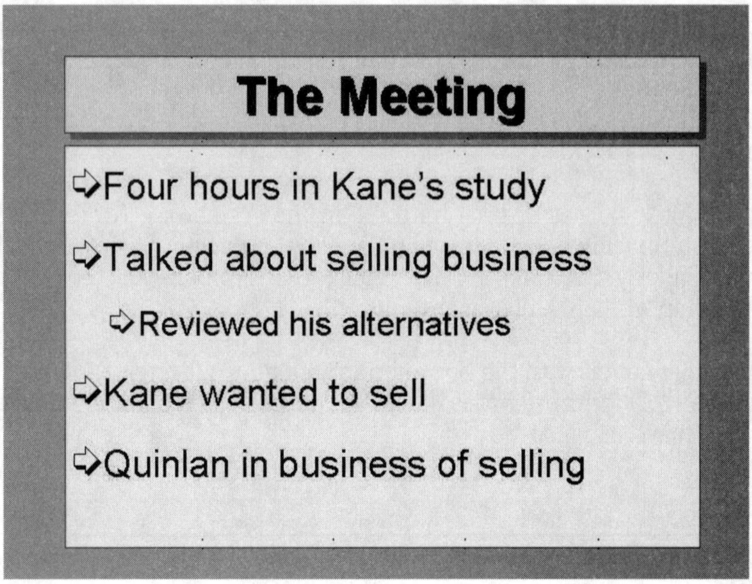

The Meeting

- ➪Four hours in Kane's study
- ➪Talked about selling business
  - ➪Reviewed his alternatives
- ➪Kane wanted to sell
- ➪Quinlan in business of selling

E. To add another indented point, with your cursor at the end of the point that you just indented, hit Enter and type in the text for the next indented point.

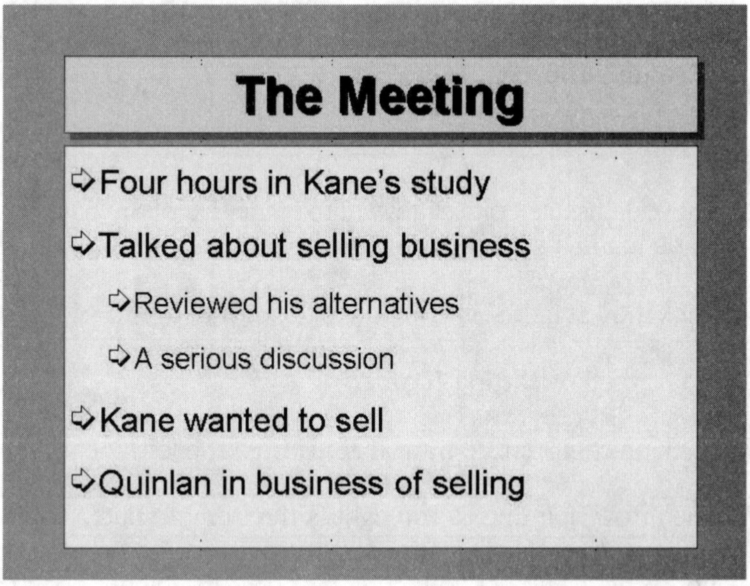

The Meeting

- ➪Four hours in Kane's study
- ➪Talked about selling business
  - ➪Reviewed his alternatives
  - ➪A serious discussion
- ➪Kane wanted to sell
- ➪Quinlan in business of selling

If you change your mind and want to make the subordinate point back into a main point, put your cursor anywhere in the text of the subordinate point and click on the Promote button.

Step 2: Reorder lines of text.

If you are working in PowerPoint 2000, the reordering function has been automated with special buttons. This is described below. If you are working in PowerPoint 97, you have to cut and paste.

A. Add the Move Up and Move Down buttons to the Formatting Toolbar.

1. Go to the Formatting Toolbar.

2. Click on the Extension button at the righthand end of the toolbar. A drop-down menu will appear.

3. Click on the button marked Add or Remove Buttons. A second drop-down menu will appear listing all of the buttons available on the Formatting Toolbar. The buttons currently visible on the Toolbar will have a check mark in the small box in front of their names. The menu is shown below.

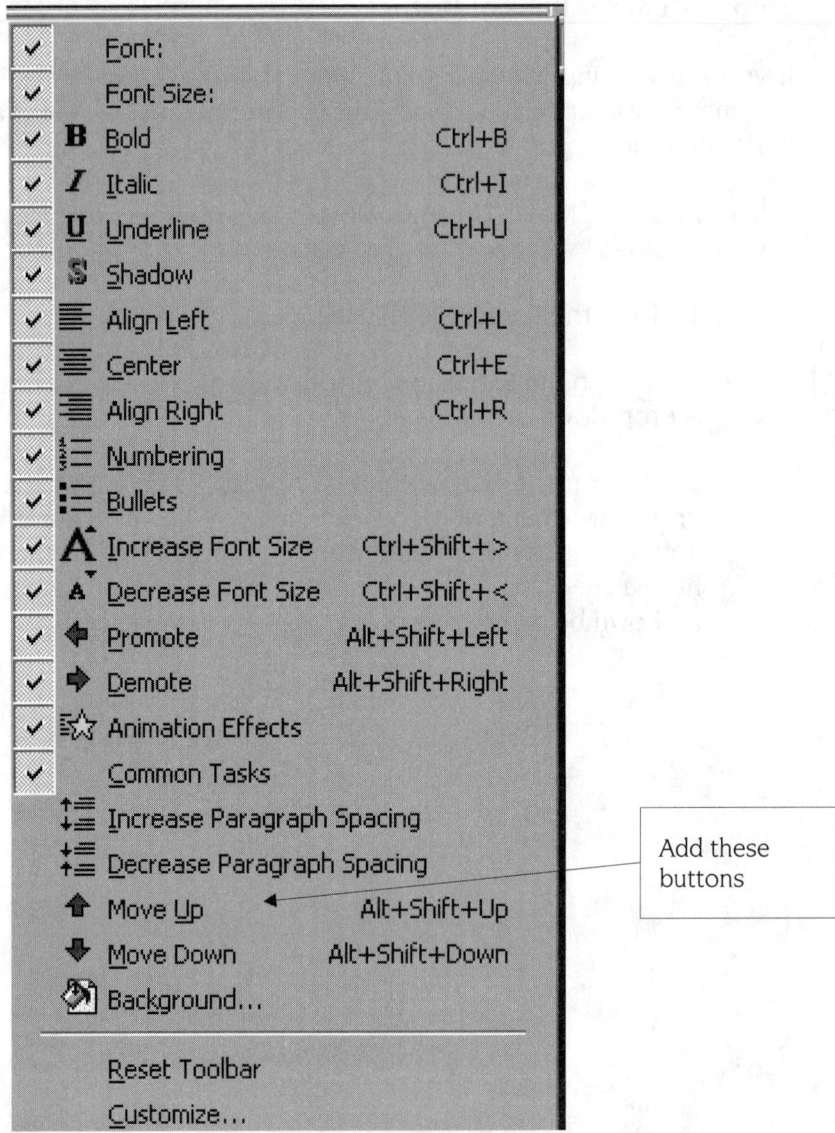

4. Click on the Move Up and Move Down options. Check marks will appear in small boxes in front of the listings for these two buttons.

5. Click anywhere outside the box. These two buttons will be added to the Formatting Toolbar at the top of your screen just to the left of the Extension button at the very end of the Toolbar. They will replace other buttons formerly occupying an equal amount of real estate on the Toolbar. (PowerPoint selects buttons you use infrequently.) The displaced buttons can be found by clicking on the Extension button again.

B. Put your cursor on the line of text within your slide that you want to move up one level.

C. Click on the Move Up button. The line of text will automatically switch places with the line above it. Click on the Move Up button again, and the line will move up one more place.

D. The Move Down button operates in the same way.

Step 3: Change the indicator for the subordinate point.

You can substitute a dash or other symbol for the bullet shape that indicates a subordinate point.

A. Select (highlight) the subordinate point.

B. Go to the Menu Bar.

C. Click on the Format button. A drop-down menu appears.

D. Click on the Bullets and Numbering option. A dialog box appears. The Bulleted tab should be active within the box. If not, click on it.

E. Click on the Character button. A dialog box appears. Go to the arrow next to the Bullets From box and scroll down to the Symbol option.

F. Click on the dash, which is the 14th in the top row.

G. Click on OK. The bullet shape for the subordinate point will now be a dash.

Step 4: Save your work.

★ If you find yourself using subordinate points, think about whether the slide or the series of slides should be reorganized. Subordinate points sometimes make it more difficult for the reader to keep in mind the overall structure of the presentation.

The CD that comes with the book shows animations (Exercise 9.1) and transitions (Exercise 10.2, Step 1-2) for this slide. It also contains, in each of the three case files, examples of various ways to use subordinate points.

Chapter 4

Sets of Matching Bullet Lists

Most points illustrated at trial using the bullet list approach require more than one slide. When you use multiple slides in sets, perhaps one set for your opening and another for the closing, you need to use a consistent style and format.

Consistency in style requires you to use the same typefaces and sizes, the same line styles, and the same color arrangements on successive slides in the same series.

Consistency in format means using the same shape and size of bullet points, the same way of boxing the title and text, and generally the same spacing for margins, lines, and other arrangements.

A matching set of bullet point slides might have a very simple layout. For example, the four slides shown below were created for the defense closing argument in a murder case where the government had tried and eventually discarded several theories on how the death occurred, because they did not square with the facts.

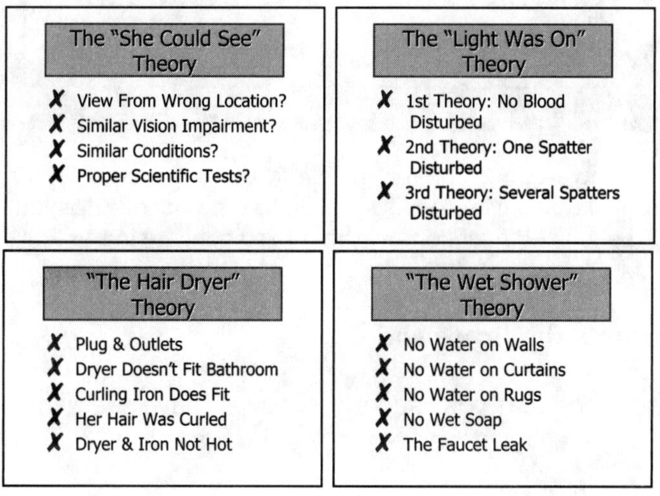

This chapter has two exercises:

1. Make a companion slide to your first bullet point slide
2. Make a no-title slide in the same style as your other two slides

These exercises illustrate the principal areas where you need to be concerned about consistency in style and format.

Exercise 4.1: Make a companion slide

A companion slide is another bulleted list that follows logically from the first slide that you created. For this exercise, we will use the slide you created in Exercise 2.1. The companion slide you create will also have a title and bullet points related to the subject matter of the title. The color scheme, font, and style will be the same.

For example:

The Duck

- She writes to confirm deal
- He says he never got it
- She calls to confirm deal
- He tells secretary to avoid call
- She has Fuller call Kane to deal
- Kane says she didn't do the deal

A This is an example of a companion slide in the commercial contract case that matches the slide shown in Exercise 3.4. Go to the Appendix for your case to see a similar example. The full color versions of these examples are in the PowerPoint file on the CD.

Step 1: Create a duplicate slide.

Follow these steps and your second slide will have the same background color, fill color, line styles, and format as the first slide.

A. Go to the View Bar.

B. Click on the Slide Sorter button (4th from the left). The Slide Sorter screen will appear. It displays miniature pictures (thumbnails) of all of the slides in the set on which you are currently working. If you had completed three slides, it would look like this:

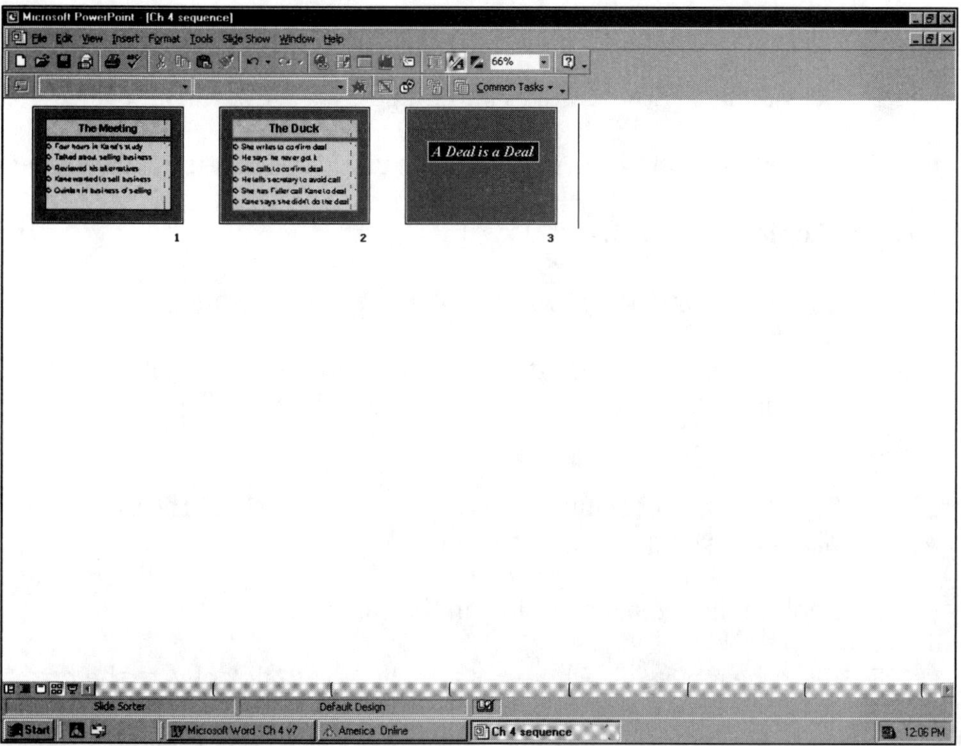

The Slide Sorter screen will automatically add the Animation Effects Toolbar at the top of the screen underneath the Standard Toolbar. You do not need this toolbar for this exercise. It is explained in Chapter 9.

C. Select the slide you want to duplicate by putting your mouse pointer on it and clicking with the left mouse button. PowerPoint will highlight the slide.

D. Hold down the CTRL key on your keyboard and press the D key. A duplicate of your slide will appear on the screen right along side the original.

E. Double click on the thumbnail of the duplicate slide to bring it up on the screen in full size so you can work on it.

! You can get any slide shown on the Slide Sorter screen into working mode by double-clicking on the thumbnail of the slide you want. The full size slide will appear on the screen and you are ready to work.

Step 2: Replace the title.

With the duplicate slide on the screen—

A. Select (activate) the title box.

B. Select (highlight) the words in the title.

C. Type in your new title. As you start to type, the old title will disappear.

Step 3: Replace the text.

A. Select (activate) the box containing the bullet points.

B. Select (highlight) the text of the bullet points. The highlighting that appears on the screen seems not to include the bullets, but they are included.

C. Type the text of the first point for your second slide. The old text will disappear when you start to type.

D. Replace the remaining points in the same manner.

E. Click the mouse anywhere outside the box to de-activate the box.

If you maintain a consistent style and format, the judge and jurors will concentrate on the substance of what you are saying, instead of trying to figure out why you used a fat typeface for that slide and a thin one for this slide and what kind of subliminal message you might be trying to send them.

Step 4: Go back and look at your previous slides.

A. Go to the vertical Scroll Bar. (Illustration, Ch. 1.)

B. Click on the Page Up button. Each click will take you to a previous slide. The Page Down button works the same way.

Step 5: Consider variations on the theme that may make the companion slide more persuasive.

Maintaining a consistent style and format helps the viewer stay oriented to the series of points you are making. However, varying the way the bullets are presented may help make the point. For example:

The Duck

Confirms in writing

"Never got it"

Calls to confirm deal

Avoids call

Has Fuller call Kane

"She didn't do the deal"

In this companion slide, the same layout (typeface, type size, box size) is used for the title and bullet boxes on the background, and the same background color is used. But the actions of the plaintiff are summarized in lines that reach the margin without bullet points (select "None" in the Bullets & Numbering screen) and the actions of the defendant are indented to emphasize that these were the defendant's responses. Go to the CD to see this slide in color. The plaintiff points are in black and the defendant points are in red.

Step 6: Save your work.

Some lawyers like to use one style of slide, with a blue background, for example, for points about liability issues and another style, with a green background, for points about damages. Similarly, you could use one background color for compensatory damages and shift to another for punitive damages. If you have an extremely powerful exhibit or summary slide, you may want to enhance its importance by a noticeable departure from your otherwise consistent style and format.

The title of this slide "The Duck" is an example of something that could be objected to as argumentative. However, in this case, one of the documents, the outgoing phone log, uses the phrase "ducking me" and would be admitted into evidence. The title is close enough to the wording of the document to survive an objection.

When working with quotes, it is sometimes effective to have each word appear separately, one after another. This type of animation is covered in Exercise 9.1, Step 3 and is shown on the CD that comes with this book.

Exercise 4.2: Construct a no-title slide

There are occasions when you will want to use a slide with a single word, phrase, or sentence on it. These are called no-title slides. Here is an example of a no-title slide in the commercial contract case.

A Go to the Appendix for your case to see a similar example. The full color versions are on the CD.

Step 1: Set up a blank slide.

A. Go to the Standard Toolbar.

B. Click on the New Slide button (10th from the left). This brings up the New Slide Screen. (Illustration, Ch. 2, Exercise 2.1.)

C. Click on the Blank option (bottom row, last on right).

D. Click on the OK button. You now have a blank slide on the screen that has no boxes on it.

Step 2: Activate the Ruler Bars.

If the Ruler Bars are not already displayed on your screen (Illustration, Ch. 1)—

A. Go to the Menu Bar.

B. Click on the View button. A drop-down menu will appear.

C. Click on the Ruler option.

D. A horizontal white ruler bar will appear at the top of your screen just below the Formatting Toolbar, and a vertical ruler bar will appear at the left side of your screen. Each ruler bar has a zero in the middle that indicates the center of your slide. (Illustration, Ch. 1.)

! You will probably want to leave the rulers on your screen when you finish working on this exercise, as they are useful for a number of purposes. However, you can make the ruler bars disappear clicking on the View button and clicking on the Ruler option again, which turns off the display.

Step 3: Create a text box in the center of the slide.

A. Go to the Drawing Toolbar. (Illustration, Ch. 1, Section 1.5.)

B. Click on the Text Box button (9th from the left). This creates a text box that can be placed anywhere on the slide. In order to put any text on a slide, you need a box into which to put that text. You cannot type directly on the slide.

C. Move your mouse pointer toward the center of the slide. As you move it, you will see a marker on each ruler that also moves. When the marker gets to the zero point, your pointer is equidistant from the margins of your slide.

D. Click once at the location you have chosen. A small box appears on your slide with your blinking cursor in the middle. It has a fuzzy border and handles in each margin. You have created an expandable text box into which you can type whatever you need.

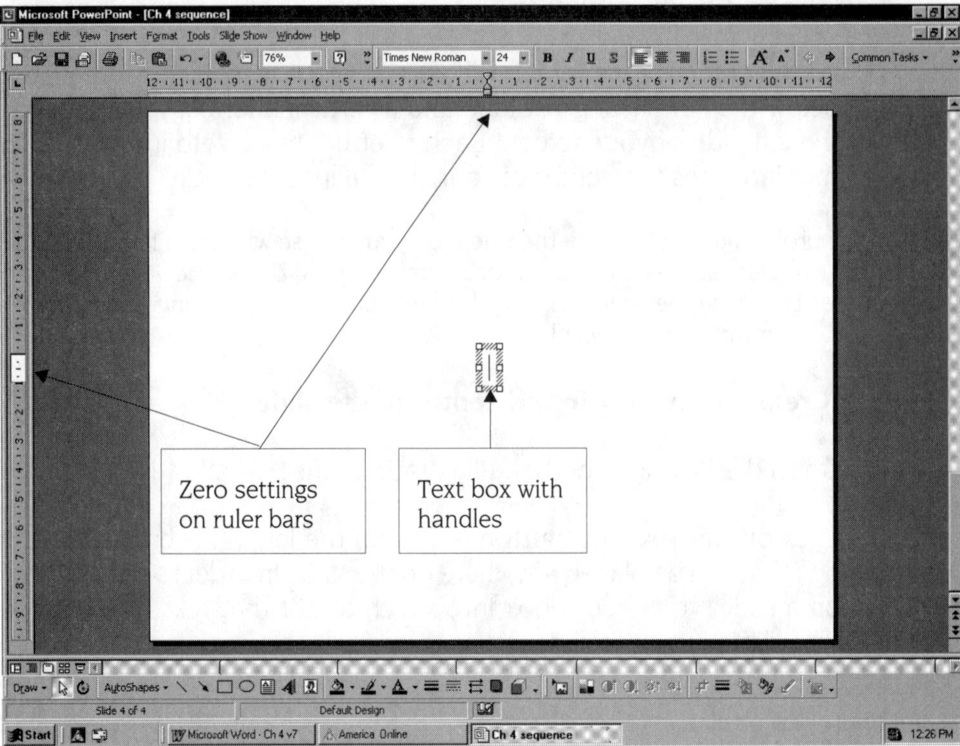

Step 4: Check the font setting.

A. While you have the mouse pointer inside the text box, look at the typeface box. It is the first box on the Formatting Toolbar. The white box should say "Arial" or whatever typeface you selected for your previous slides. Sometimes PowerPoint reverts to the default setting, perhaps Times New Roman or Courier, when it is asked to do a new task.

B. If the correct typeface is not there, move your mouse pointer to the small arrow to the immediate right of the white box. Click there to find the right typeface.

C. Also check the type size in the box immediately to the right of the typeface box.

Step 5: Check the alignment.

A. Go to the Formatting Toolbar. Check which of the alignment buttons is active. The text should be centered in the box. For that result, the Center Alignment button should be active.

B. Click on the Center Alignment button (if it is not already active).

Step 6: Type in the text.

A. Without moving the mouse pointer out of the text box, start typing. Your box will expand as you type.

B. You can make corrections in the same way as you did with the title and text boxes in Exercise 2.2.

Step 7: Adjust the size of the type if necessary.

With the text of your slide still highlighted—

A. Go to the Formatting Toolbar.

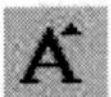

B. Click on the Increase Font Size button (12th from the left end of the toolbar). This will increase the type size with each click. The Decrease Font Size button right next to it does just the opposite.

Step 8: Adjust the position of the box up or down if necessary to center it on the slide.

With the box still active—

A. Put your mouse pointer on one of the margins of the box.

B. Move the pointer gently until the four-arrow pointer appears.

C. Hold down the left mouse button and drag the entire box up or down to the location you want. Release the mouse button.

D. For more precise positioning, with the four-arrow pointer active, click the left mouse button once. The pattern of the fuzzy border will change. Go to the UP ARROW or the DOWN ARROW key on your keyboard and press it one or more times. The whole box will move one space with each click. The LEFT ARROW and RIGHT ARROW keys work the same way.

E. Use the Ruler Bars to check that the box is centered exactly.

1. Put your mouse pointer over the middle handle on the top border of the box.

2. Look at the top Ruler Bar. There is a vertical line marker on the Ruler Bar that moves with your mouse pointer. When your mouse

pointer is over the middle handle, the vertical line marker on the top Ruler Bar should be at zero.

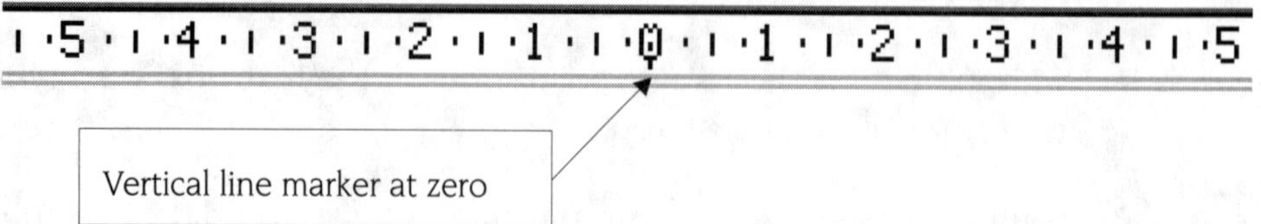

3. Put your mouse pointer over the middle handle on the left border of the box.

4. Look at the left Ruler Bar. When your mouse pointer is over the middle handle, the vertical line on the left Ruler Bar should be at zero.

5. If it is not, move the box slightly to get it there.

97 The Ruler Bars do not always display automatically in PowerPoint 97. If they are not on your screen, go to the Menu Bar, click on the View button, choose the Toolbars option. A drop-down menu will appear showing the active toolbars. (A check mark appears before each active toolbar.) Click on the Ruler Bar option to activate them.

Step 9: Add color if useful. Sometimes a no-title slide is best left in black and white.

A. Background color. (Exercise 3.3, Step 1.)

B. Fill color. (Exercise 3.3, Step 2.)

C. Special adaptations for a black and white slide.

1. White lettering on black fill.

Change the lettering to white. Highlight the lettering. Go to the Drawing Toolbar. Click on the Font Color button (14th from the left). Select the white color. (The letters will temporarily disappear because they are now white on a white fill color. If you click about where you think the box is, they will reappear.) Click outside the box to deactivate the highlighting.

Change the fill to black. Click inside the box to make it active. Go to the Drawing Toolbar. Click on the Fill Color button (12th from the left). Select black for the fill. (The letters should now reappear as white on black.)

2. White border around a box with black fill.

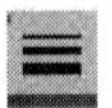

Put a border around the box. With the box active (fuzzy border showing), go to the Drawing Toolbar. Click on the Line Style button (15th from the left). A menu of line sizes will appear. Pick the 1 point size.

Make the border white. With the box still active, go to the Drawing Toolbar. Click on the Line Color button (13th from the left). Select the white color for the border.

Step 10: Save your work.

Making a no-title slide can also be done by selecting the slide format from the New Slide dialog box that has only one box on it. You can fill in the words, and then move the box around on the slide to the proper position.

A no-title slide is often used when discussing the burden of proof. A slide explaining the phrase "preponderance of the evidence" helps the jurors focus on what you are saying. Having the legal standard, standing alone, before the jurors while you explain it during your closing argument could differentiate your case from what jurors have seen on television.

For example:

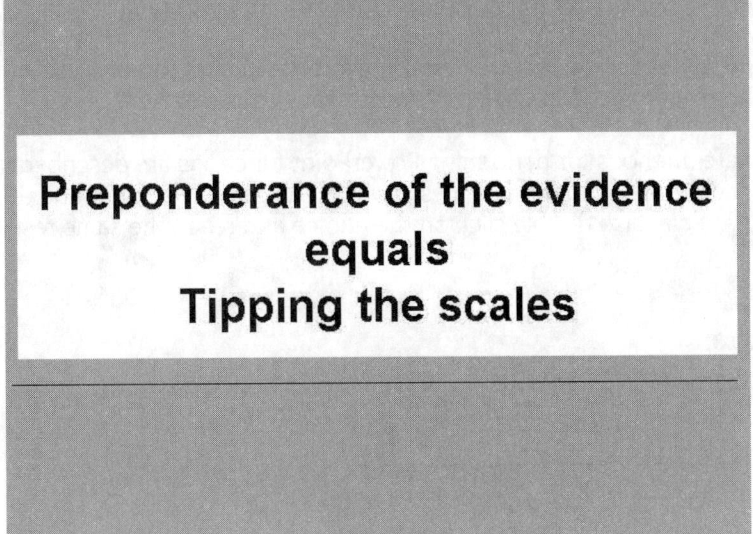

Preponderance of the evidence
equals
Tipping the scales

The tipping of the box in the second slide is done using the Free Rotate button on the Drawing Toolbar. See explanation in Exercise 6.2.

You have now completed three slides. To add motion and special effects to these slides, go to Chapter 9, Exercise 9.1. (PowerPoint 97 users should go to Appendix D.) To learn how to run the slide show consisting of these three slides, look at Chapter 10. The CD shows examples of all of these slides in full color and motion.

No-title slides can be constructed using a rectangle instead of a text box. See the Box Reference Guide in Chapter 7 for relevant considerations.

Alternate methods for performing PowerPoint functions are described in Chapter 12. For example, in some instances in which you click on a choice and then click an OK button, you can also double click on the choice and reach the same result.

Chapter 5

Labeled Photo Exhibits

Photos are often very important exhibits, but using them effectively in the courtroom presents challenges. When a photo is handed from one juror to another, their collective attention is scattered. Even on an 8 x 10 enlargement, it may be difficult to see relevant details. PowerPoint makes it easy to display any photo on a large courtroom monitor or projection screen. This emphasizes the importance of the exhibit and allows you to talk about particular details while having everyone's attention focused at the same spot.

When used with PowerPoint, a photo can be labeled, put side-by-side with another photo or a document, or enhanced with annotations or directional arrows to make the persuasive impact much greater.

You have in the file one or more photos that would help make important points. Your photos are on the CD-ROM provided with this book or can be downloaded from the NITA web site.

This chapter has four exercises for photo exhibits.

1. Construct a slide that can hold a photo and a title
2. Import the photo into the slide
3. Create a title
4. Dress up the slide

These four operations will enable you to use many kinds of photographs, as well as drawings, maps, charts, graphs, tables, and diagrams that come from other sources and are available in digital format.

Photo Reference Guide

Working with photos requires attention to a few more technical details. None of these are difficult or complicated.

Cameras: Photos taken with traditional cameras can be used in PowerPoint slides if they have been scanned into digital format. This can be done with a small office scanner. Most photo shops and copy shops also provide this service. They will put all of your photo exhibits onto a CD that you can use like you are using the CD that comes with this book.

Photos taken with digital cameras are already in digital format and, once loaded from the camera to the computer, are ready for use with PowerPoint. The resolution provided by your digital camera should match the capability of the computer that you will use to work with the resulting photos. For example, a digital camera with a resolution of one million (1152 x 864) pixels takes great photos but it requires a very fast laptop to work with the very large files these cameras produce. If you have an older laptop, then you will be better off with a lower resolution. Otherwise, when you bring up your PowerPoint slides, the photos will be very slow to appear on the screen. For most kinds of photos, you will not lose much clarity in the final product by using a lower resolution.

Format: Scan photos in JPEG format if possible. Some services provide photos in TIF format. You may also be offered GIF, PDD, PDF, BMP, and other file formats. All of these will work in one context or another. JPEG is preferable for PowerPoint work for two reasons. First, the file sizes are much smaller without resulting loss of clarity. This means your slide show will run better (no long waits for photos to appear) and will take up less storage space. Second, the JPEG format will fit onto your slides much better. JPEG photos will load onto a slide by automatically scaling down to the size of the slide or the box within the slide. TIF format produces the same quality image, but it is harder to work with. When you import the file containing the photo, you will need to reduce the size of the photo substantially because TIF format produces very large images.

If your images are scanned in another format, you can convert to JPEG using photo software (Adobe PhotoDeluxe or Microsoft Photo Editor, for example). Click on File, Save As, and select JPEG on the drop-down menu. See Chapter 12, Exercise 12.14 for additional information on scanning.

Resolution: Scan photos at a minimum of 200 dpi (dots per inch). The number of dots per inch determines the *resolution* of the image (how sharp and detailed it is). If you scan photos at 300 dpi, they will have better resolution, but the files will be much bigger in size. The size of the file determines how fast the photo will appear on the screen. If the file size is large, and your computer is slow, when you call up a slide containing a photo it will take a long time for the photo to get to the screen. Fast computers can handle large files, but it is often not necessary to go above 200 dpi for slides to be used in a courtroom in any event.

Color: Scan photos in 24 bit color.

Naming files: Be sure to name each photo in some way that you can recognize what it is from its name.

Exercise 5.1: Build a slide for a photo and a title

This exercise shows you how to put a title on a photo. If you want to display a photo with a title, the slide needs a title box. You have already done a title box for the bullet point slide in Exercise 2.1, and the title box for a photo slide is just the same. The slide also needs a box for the picture. This is different from the text box that you created with the bullet point lists but it operates in much the same way.

Step 1: Set up the slide.

A. Go to the Standard Toolbar.

B. Click on the New Slide button (10th from left). This brings up the New Slide screen that shows the 12 basic slide formats. (Illustration in Ch. 2, Exercise 2.1.)

C. Choose the Title Only format (bottom row, 2nd from right) by clicking on it.

D. Click on the OK button. Now you have a slide with a title box, where you can label your picture, and a space below the title where you can add a picture box.

Step 2: Activate the Picture Toolbar, if it is not already displayed.

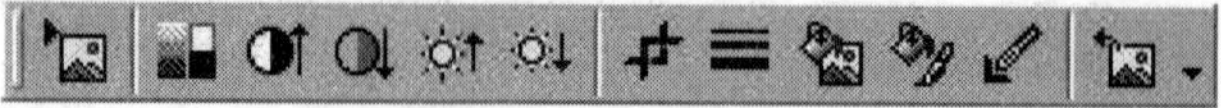

A. Go to the Menu Bar.

B. Click on the View button. A drop-down menu will appear.

C. Move your mouse pointer to the Toolbars option. A drop-down menu will appear.

D. Click on Picture. A small box will appear to the left with a check mark in it indicating that the Picture Toolbar is active.

E. The Picture Toolbar probably will appear just to the right of the Drawing Toolbar at the bottom of your screen. If it pops up elsewhere, put your mouse pointer on it, hold down the left mouse button, and drag it to the right spot.

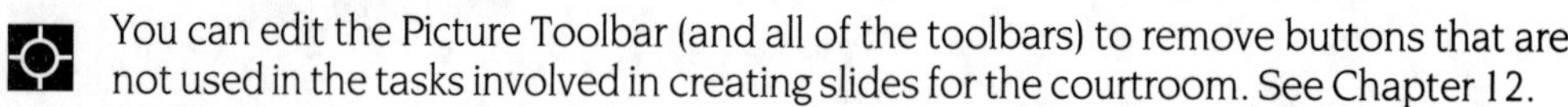

You can edit the Picture Toolbar (and all of the toolbars) to remove buttons that are not used in the tasks involved in creating slides for the courtroom. See Chapter 12.

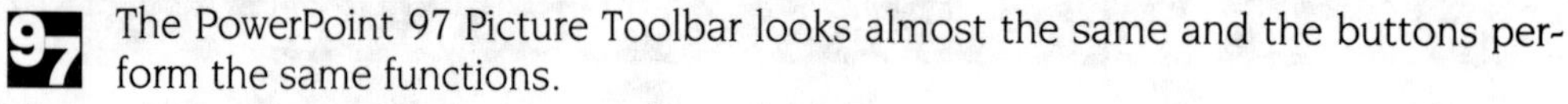

The PowerPoint 97 Picture Toolbar looks almost the same and the buttons perform the same functions.

Step 3: Color the background of the slide.

A. Go to the Menu Bar.

B. Click on the Format button. A drop-down menu will appear.

C. Click on the Background option. A Background screen will appear. (Illustration in Ch. 3, Exercise 3.3.)

D. Click on the small arrow next to the color box. The Color Options screen appears. (Illustration in Ch. 3, Exercise 3.3.)

E. Click on your background color. Click on the OK button. (If the color you want is not one of the immediate options, choose the More Colors option and you will find it there.)

F. Click on the Apply button.

! Sometimes it is difficult to see where you are on the slide while you are working with a picture. If you color the background first, you will be able to tell where the margins of the slide are located.

Step 4: Save your work.

Exercise 5.2: Add the photo

The photos that are potential exhibits for each case file are on the CD that came with this book or can be downloaded from the NITA web site, *www.nitastudent.org*. If you are using the CD, be sure that it is in the CD drive on your computer. You are going to locate the file that contains all of the photos for the case and import one of the photos into your slide. You can use this same process to import any kind of graphics (clip art, diagrams, charts, and graphs) from floppy disks, your hard disk drive, or other CDs.

Step 1: Import the photo.

With the slide on the screen—

A. Go to the Picture Toolbar.

B. Click on the Insert Picture button (1st one on the left). The Insert Picture screen will appear. In PowerPoint 2000 it looks like this:

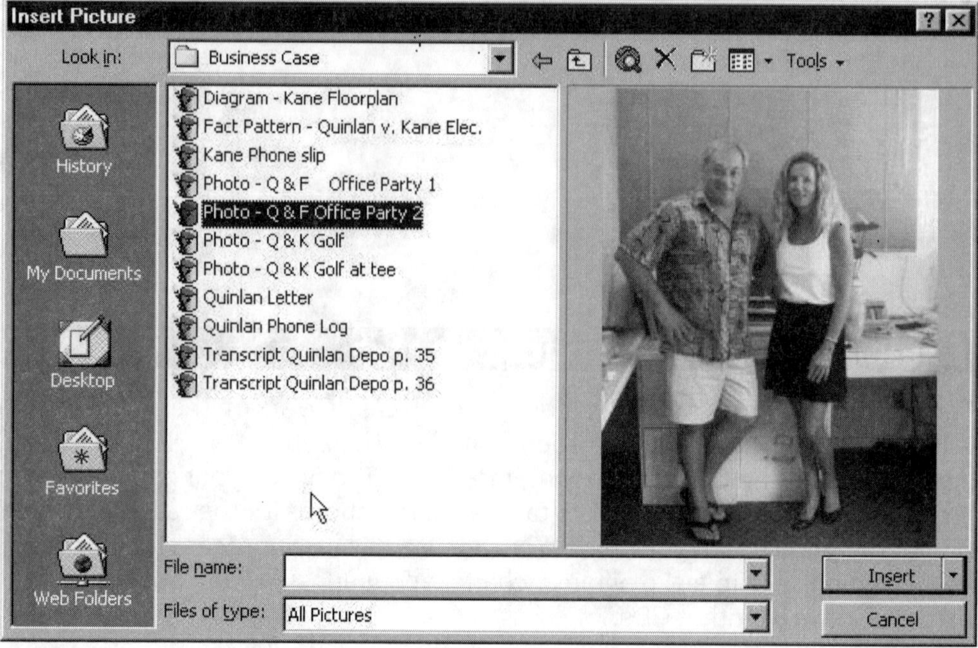

C. Click on the small arrow next to the "Look in" box at the top left. This displays the places where the photo might be—your hard disk drive, your CD drive, and an external hard drive if you have one.

D. Click on the letter for your CD drive (or your hard disk drive if you downloaded this files from the NITA web site). In the large white box below, you will see all the folders on the CD. The names of the folder and the file containing the photo are in the Appendix for your case. (See illustration in each Appendix.)

E. Click on the file name of the photo. A small version of the entire photo will appear in the viewer box to the right so that you can check to be sure you have the photo you want.

F. Double click on the icon to the left of the file name of the photo. The photo will appear on your screen.

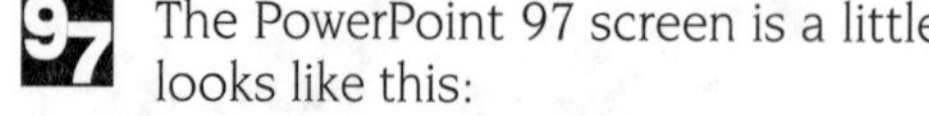
The PowerPoint 97 screen is a little different but performs the same functions. It looks like this:

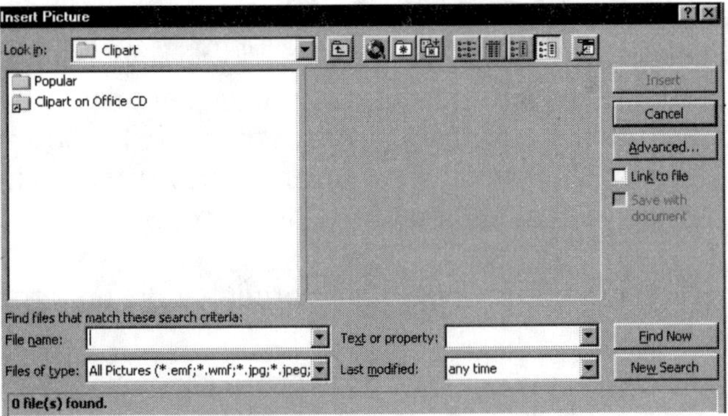

Step 2: Resize the photo to fit the slide.

The photo may be too large for the slide and therefore it will cover the entire screen. Sometimes the photo is so large that only a small part of it (greatly enlarged) is showing. This is not a problem. It is caused by the method by which the photo was scanned. Different methods produce different results. The slide is still there under the photo, and you can resize the photo to fit the space available on the slide.

For example, your slide may be this size (on the screen):

And due to the scanning process, your photo is this size:

So when you put the photo on top of the slide, it does not fit.

You need to shrink the photo down quite a bit to get it where you want it on the slide. It will of course be enlarged again when you display the slide on a large screen or monitor.

A. Find the handle in the upper right corner of the photo. (Illustration, Ch. 2, Exercise 2.3.)

   1. Use the horizontal scroll arrow at the bottom right corner of the horizontal scroll bar to click to the right one space at a time until you find the right edge of the photo. (Illustration, Ch. 1, Section 1.5.)

2. Now use the vertical scroll arrow at the top right corner of the vertical scroll bar to click up one space at a time until you find the top edge of the photo. Sometimes the scroll bar will accidentally move you to the previous slide. You can easily get back to the slide you are working on by clicking on the Page Down button in the bottom right corner of the vertical scroll bar. (Illustration, Ch. 1, Section 1.5.)

B. Move the mouse pointer over the upper right corner handle until the two-arrow pointer appears.

C. Drag the pointer diagonally toward the bottom left to make the whole photo smaller. Let up on the mouse button.

D. Put your mouse pointer over the top margin of the photo and move it until the four-arrow pointer appears. Hold down the left mouse button and drag the reduced-size photo back into place on the slide. You may have to repeat these operations several times to get the photo where you want it.

E. Click anywhere outside the picture to view the finished work.

! WHEN SIZING PHOTOS, YOU SHOULD USE ONLY THE CORNER HANDLES, **NEVER** THE MIDDLE ONES. The corner handles will resize the photo without distortion. (They resize horizontally and vertically while maintaining proportionality.) The middle handles will cause distortion. (They resize in only one direction and "stretch" or "shrink" so that proportionality is lost.)

★ It is very important not to distort the photo unintentionally. If the photo has been admitted separately, as a fair and accurate depiction of something, then normally you will want to keep the photo undistorted when you use it on a slide. If the photo has not been admitted as an exhibit, but is being used as an illustrative aid, it must be qualified as helpful to understanding the testimony. If it is distorted, it may be misleading, and will not qualify.

★ If the photo becomes distorted by mistake while you are working with it, use the Undo button (Standard Toolbar, 8th from the left) or, in the alternative use the CTRL key and the Z key (at the same time) to undo and start over.

Step 3: Crop the photo to focus on the portion you need.

Cropping is different from sizing, which you did in Step 2. Cropping cuts away portions of the photo to reduce the margins of the photo or to focus on one aspect of the original photo.

A. Click anywhere in the picture.

B. Go to the Picture Toolbar.

C. Click on the Crop button (7th from the left).

D. Put your mouse pointer over one of the MIDDLE handles. The crop icon (same as on the button) should appear at the handle.

E. Hold down the left mouse button and drag the handle in the direction you want to crop.

F. The margins of the picture will be reduced in the direction you drag.

G. Click anywhere to de-activate the cropping tool.

! The software's cropping tool does not affect proportionality. Unlike the resizing in Step 2, you do not have to worry about this kind of distortion of the photo. However, USE THE **MIDDLE** HANDLES TO CROP (NOT THE CORNER ONES), which will work on one margin at a time. It is easier to control the result this way.

! The cropping tool works both ways—in and out. If you crop too far, you can drag the margin back and try it over again. This allows you to look at various ways of cropping a photo without having to make multiple copies.

★ Cropping a photo may lead to an objection that showing just a portion of the original photo is unfair in some respect—perhaps in emphasizing one detail at the expense of others. This objection usually can be overcome by showing the whole photo first, and then the cropped version.

Step 4: Resize the photo to make it larger if necessary (after cropping) to fit the area available on the slide. Use Step 2 above for this process. Drag the corner handle outward.

A Examples of these uses of photos for the tort and criminal cases are in the appendices. Full color versions of these slides are in the PowerPoint slide show for each case file on the CD.

Step 5: Center the photo on the slide.

A. Activate the photo by clicking on it. A fuzzy border with handles indicates that the box is active and ready to be worked on.

B. Move your mouse pointer to the handle on the top at the middle. Look at the Ruler Bar. A marker on the Ruler Bar lines up with the mouse pointer and tells you how far you are from center (the zero point).

C. Click on the LEFT ARROW or RIGHT ARROW key on your keyboard to move the photo one space at a time to the left or right until the middle handle is lined up with the zero on the Ruler Bar. (Exercise 4.2, Step 8.)

D. You can align the photo vertically in the center by using the middle handle on the left margin as the reference point, and using the UP ARROW and DOWN ARROW on the keyboard in the same way as above.

E. If you have only a short distance to go, try the Nudge function. (Drawing toolbar, Draw button, Nudge option.) This moves very small increments up, down, left, or right. See explanation in Chapter 12.

Step 6: Save your work.

★ It is sometimes helpful to gather several photos on a single slide. The animation features described in Chapter 9 allow you to introduce each photo separately as you or a witness talk about them.

For example:

In making a slide with multiple photos, if there is overlap and you want one photo to sit behind another, use the Order function which is explained in Chapter 12, Exercise 12.10. Examples of single and multiple photo slides are on the CD.

Exercise 5.3: Add the title

This is the same process as described for creating a title for a bullet list. (Ch. 2, Exercise 2.1.)

Step1: Select (activate) the title box by clicking anywhere on the text within it.

Step 2: Choose the typeface and type size for your title.

Step 3: Type your title into the title box.

If you decided that you want to have the title or caption below the photo, then activate the title box and drag it to the bottom of the slide. Activate the picture box and move it up on the slide to create enough room for the title at the bottom. Then readjust the placement of the title box.

Step 4: Click anywhere outside the title box to view the finished product.

Step 5: Save your work.

You need not title every photo. Some photos are excellent exhibits standing alone. Titles may be impermissibly argumentative for use in opening statements and leading in direct examination, provoking objections where the photo by itself would be unobjectionable.

The label for a photo can be constructed with a rectangle rather than a text box. See the Box Reference Guide in Chapter 7 for relevant considerations.

Exercise 5.4 Dress up your slide

This is the same process as described in Chapter 3 for dressing up a bulleted list.

Step1: Box the title and the photo. (Ch. 3, Exercise 3.2.)

Step 2: Apply color to the slide background. (Ch. 3, Exercise 3.3, Step 1.)

Step 3: Give the title box of this slide the same color as the titles to your bullet point slides.

A. Click on the Page Up button in the lower right corner of your Scroll Bar to get one of your bullet point slides on the screen.

B. Click in the title box of that slide to activate it.

C. Move your mouse pointer to the border of that box, and click again. This ensures that the entire box is activated, not just one part.

D. Go to the Standard Toolbar.

E. Click on the Format Painter button (Standard Toolbar, extension box on PowerPoint 2000, 9th from the left on PowerPoint 97).

F. Click on the Page Down button of your Scroll Bar to return to the slide you are currently working on.

G. Click anywhere in the title box to activate it.

Step 4: Save your work.

Using the same color for the background (fill) of all the titles on your slides avoids confusion and creates a consistent look for your slide presentation. If this slide relates to a very special point and needs to be distinguished from other slides, you may want to change the color. Look at the colors used on the slides on the CD for examples.

If you use a title with a photo, you may want the title to come onto the screen after you first display the photo. Motion and special effects for photo exhibits are covered in Exercise 9.2. PowerPoint 97 users should consult Appendix D.

Chapter 6

Relationship Charts

A relationship chart shows the connection between one fact, person, entity, or event and another or how a process works. The connection does not have to be causal. It can be a logical progression, a time progression, or steps in a process. The relationship chart can be used effectively while you are explaining to the jury the logic of your position.

PowerPoint makes relationship charts easy by providing the shapes you need and allowing you to type text into the shapes.

This chapter has three exercises:

1. The Zap-Zap-I-Win relationship chart
2. The All-Roads-Lead-to-Rome relationship chart
3. The basic time line

Relationship charts are by their nature argumentative. If used in closing argument, there are fewer restrictions on the wording put on the chart. When used for opening statements or witness testimony, be careful to make the wording as non-argumentative as possible. The argument should rest in the shape of the display itself.

Exercise 6.1: The Zap-Zap-I-Win relationship chart

The principal idea for this kind of relationship chart is to extract key facts and show how they lead inexorably to the conclusion you are urging. The layout for this kind of relationship chart looks like this:

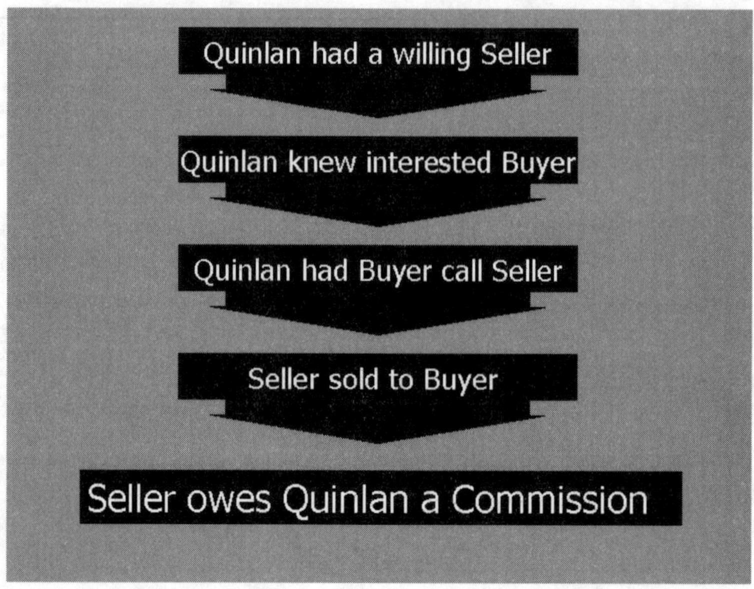

Here's how to put this chart together.

Step 1: Set up the underlying slide.

A. Get a blank slide on the screen.

1. Go to the Standard Toolbar.

2. Click on the New Slide button (10th from the left). The New Slide screen will appear. (Illustration, Ch. 2, Exercise 2.1.)

3.Click on the Blank Slide option (bottom row, last on right).

4. Click on the OK button. Now you have a blank slide.

B. Color the slide background. (If you previously chose the Apply to All option for background color, your slide background is ready.)

1. Go to the Menu Bar.

2. Click on the Format button. A drop-down menu will appear.

3. Choose the Background option. This brings up the Background screen. (Illustration Ch. 3, Exercise 3.3.)

4. Click on the arrow next to the color box (it may be white). This brings up the Color Options box. (Illustration, Ch. 3, Exercise 3.3.)

5. Choose the same blue you used for your other slides.

6. Click on the Apply button. The background on your slide should now be in blue.

Step 2: Isolate the two to four facts that lead to a conclusion in favor of your client.

Step 3: Add the first relationship arrow to display the fact that has the most text.

A. Put a down-pointing block arrow on the slide.

1. Go to the Drawing Toolbar.

2. Click on the AutoShapes button (4th from the left). A drop-down menu will appear.

3. Choose the Block Arrows option. A drop-down menu will appear with twenty-eight arrow shapes.

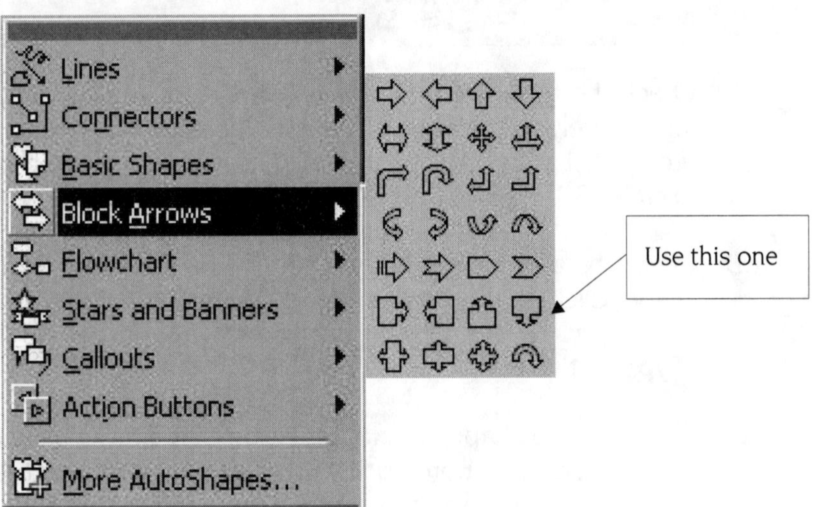

4. Click on the down-pointing block arrow option. The menu shows seven rows of options. The one you want is the last shape on the right in the sixth row.

5. Move your mouse pointer back to the slide. The pointer will have a cross shape. Place the pointer where you want the block arrow shape to appear.

6. Click the left mouse button. The block arrow will appear with a default color, with eight white handles and three yellow handles.

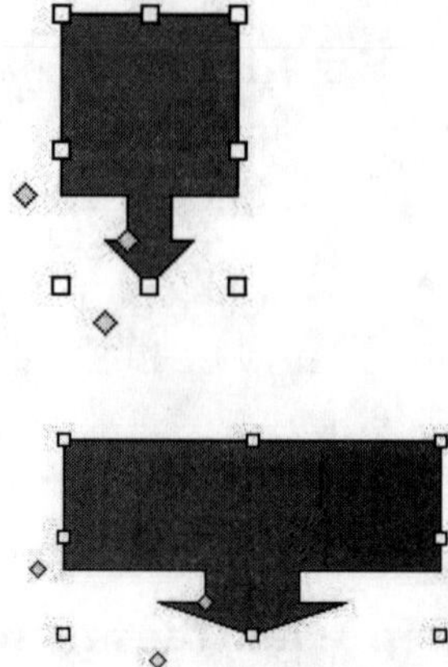

B. Expand and re-shape the block arrow as necessary, using its handles. The white handles change the shape of the block arrow in the usual ways. (Ch. 2, Exercise 2.3.) The yellow handles change the shape of the arrowhead, the block body, and the distance between the two.

Step 4: Set the typeface, type size, and alignment. (Exercise 3.1.)

A. Put your mouse pointer inside the arrow and click to activate it.

B. Check the typeface box in the Formatting Toolbar (1st white box at the left end of the toolbar) to see if the correct typeface is active. If not, select the correct typeface and click on it so that its name shows in the box. (See Exercise 3.1.)

C. Check the type size box in the Formatting Toolbar (2nd white box immediately to the right of the typeface box). If not, select the correct type size and click on it so that its number shows in the box. (See Exercise 3.1.)

D. Check the alignment. The type should be centered within the arrow shape. Click on the Center Alignment button if it is not active.

Step 5: Type in the text.

A. The arrow is a shape and not a text box, so although it will allow you to type beyond its borders, it will not expand its shape to contain the text you type. You will need to use the handles for that.

B. Use the ENTER key on your keyboard when you want to start a second line.

C. Edit the text within the arrow shape if necessary to balance the display and eliminate unnecessary words. (Exercise 2.2.)

Step 6: Add duplicate arrows to display the other facts that have less text.

With the first block arrow still active—

A. Hold down the CTRL key on your keyboard and press the D key at the same time. This will create the second block arrow (a duplicate of the first block arrow) slightly below and to the right of the first one. While still holding down the CTRL key, press the D key again to create the third block arrow, and again for the fourth.

B. Use the four-arrow mouse pointer to drag the second, third, and fourth arrows down into place under the first arrow. They do not have to be aligned exactly at this point. There's another step that will align all the arrows automatically.

Step 7: Type the text into the second, third, and fourth arrows.

Check the typeface, size, and alignment so that it is the same as the first arrow.

Step 8: Get the arrows in the right order and aligned with each other.

A. Use the four-arrow mouse pointer to drag the arrow that makes the first point to the top. Drag other arrows into the right order.

B. Align all the block arrows so they are in a straight line.

1. Hold down the SHIFT key on your keyboard and click on each of the block arrows in succession, activating them all.

2. Go to the Drawing Toolbar.

3. Click on the Draw button (1st on the left). A drop-down menu will appear.

4. Click on the Align or Distribute option. Another drop-down menu will appear.

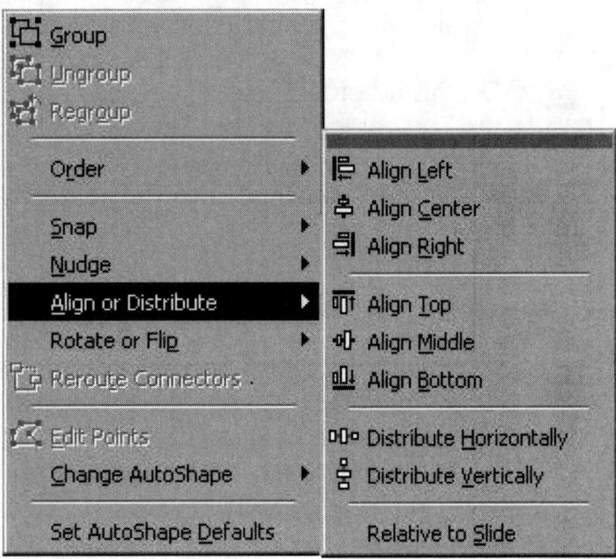

5. Click on Align Center. This lines the block arrows up in a row with their centers one above the other.

C. Space the block arrows so they are an equal distance apart.

With all four of your objects still activated—

1. Go back to the Drawing Toolbar.

2. Click on the Draw button (1st on the left). The drop-down menu will appear.

3. Click on the Align or Distribute option. Another drop-down menu will appear.

4. Click on Distribute Vertically. This provides an equal amount of space between the block arrows.

D. Click anywhere outside the block arrows to deactivate them all.

Step 9: Add a text box to display the conclusion drawn from facts #1-4.

A. Go to the Drawing Toolbar.

B. Click on the Text Box button (9th from the left). This activates the text box and changes the mouse pointer to a cross shape.

C. Move the mouse pointer to the place on the slide where you want the text box to go. Click on the left mouse button. A box with a fuzzy border will appear at that place. Your cursor will be blinking in the box.

D. Put a border around the text box for emphasis. Go to the Drawing Toolbar, click on the Line Style button, pick a line size.

Step 10: Type your text into the text box.

A. Center your type by highlighting it and clicking on the center alignment button. (Ch. 3, Exercise 3.1, Step 3.)

B. Adjust the type size if necessary. Use the font size buttons on the Formatting Toolbar. (Ch. 4, Exercise 4.2, Step 7.) A text box will not expand vertically beyond the size or amount of type you put in it. If this is a problem for the design of your chart, use a rectangle instead. (Exercise 7.1, Steps 6-10.)

C. Center the text box under the arrows if necessary using the ruler bars. (Ch. 4, Exercise 4.2, Step 3.) PowerPoint centers the text box automatically as you type, so it should be all right.

Step 11: Choose a fill color for each of the relationship arrows and perhaps a different fill color for the text box at the bottom.

A. Select (activate) the arrow shape by clicking on it.

B. Go to the Drawing Toolbar.

C. Click on the small arrow to the right of the Fill Color button (12th from the left next to the tilted A button). This will take you to the Color Options screen. (Illustration, Ch. 3, Exercise 3.3.)

D. Click on the More Fill Colors button. A palette of colors will appear.

E. Choose the color you want by clicking on it. PowerPoint will highlight your choice.

F. Click on the OK button.

G. The fill (interior background) of the arrow shape will now be colored.

Step 12: Save your work.

Relationship charts for the criminal case and the tort case are in the appendices. The full color versions of these slides are in the PowerPoint slide show for each case file on the CD.

It is not necessary to limit yourself to a top-to-bottom design for your relationship chart. Block arrows that go from left to right work equally well. PowerPoint provides block arrows for all four directions (up, down, right, and left) so that you can construct relationships for many different fact patterns. You can also use other arrow designs to connect different boxes containing information about relationships.

Relationship charts can be made more powerful using animation tools that allow you to reveal one arrow at a time. That way, the jury concentrates on the fact that you are explaining rather than reading ahead to see what the rest of the chart says, and perhaps missing part of the points you are making. The methods for adding motion and special effects to the zap-zap relationship chart are explained in Exercise 9.3. (PowerPoint 97 users should go to Appendix D.)

Exercise 6.2: The All-Roads-Lead-to-Rome chart

This model of relationship chart uses the familiar metaphor that all the principal facts in the case point to a central conclusion.

For example:

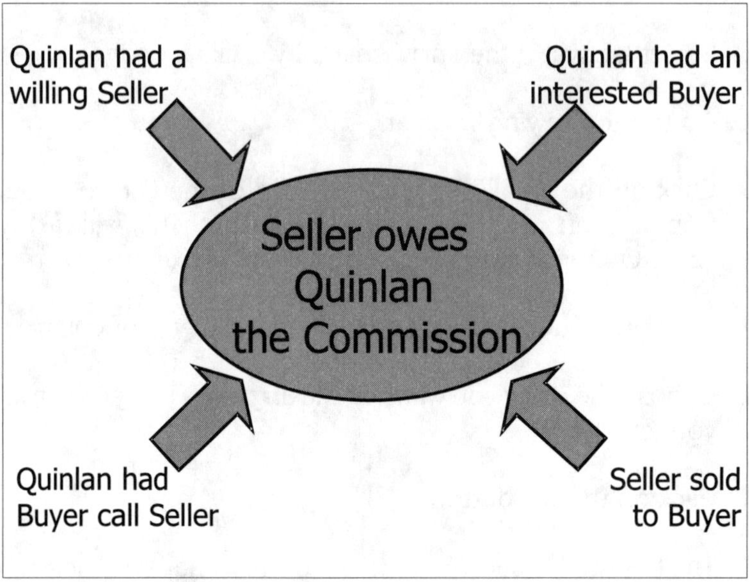

Here's how to put together this type of chart.

Step 1: Set up the underlying slide.

A. Get a blank slide on the screen.

1. Go to the Standard Toolbar.

2. Click on the New Slide button (10th from the left). The New Slide screen will appear. (Illustration, Ch. 2, Exercise 2.1.)

3. Click on the Blank Slide option (bottom row, last on right).

4. Click on the OK button. Now you have a blank slide.

B. Color the slide background.

1. Go to the Menu Bar.

2. Click on the Format button. A drop-down menu will appear.

3. Choose the Background option. This brings up the Background screen. (Illustration, Ch. 3, Exercise 3.3.)

4. Click on the arrow next to the color box (it may be white). This brings up the Color Options box. (Illustration, Ch. 3, Exercise 3.3.)

5. Choose the appropriate color, perhaps a very light background.

6. Click on the Apply button. The background on your slide should now be colored.

Step 2: Create a central shape to house the conclusion in favor of your client.

A. Create an oval shape. (A circle will work as well but may take up more space.)

1. Go to the Drawing Toolbar.

2. Click on the Oval shape button (8th from the left).

3. Move your mouse pointer to the center of the slide.

4. Click the left mouse button to locate the shape. A circle shape with green temporary fill will appear at the spot where you clicked.

B. Enlarge the shape (using the handles) as necessary to contain the text.

C. Type in the text.

D. Reduce the height of the shape (creating more of an oval) to fit the text without much extra space left over.

E. Center the shape on the slide.

1. Put your mouse pointer on the center handle of the top of the shape.

2. Look at the zero point on the top ruler bar. A line on the ruler will correspond to the location of your mouse pointer. Move the shape until the center top handle lines up with the zero point on the ruler.

3. Put your mouse pointer on the center handle at the left.

4. Look at the zero point on the left ruler bar. Move the shape until it lines up.

Step 3: Create text boxes to contain the facts leading to the conclusion.

A. Get the first text box on the slide. (Exercise 4.2, Step 3.)

1. Go to the Drawing Toolbar.

2. Click on the Text Box button (9th from the left).

3. Move your mouse pointer to the place where you want one of the text boxes to be located.

4. Click the left mouse button. A small text box will appear with the cursor blinking in the center.

B. Put a border around your text box so you can keep track of it on the screen.

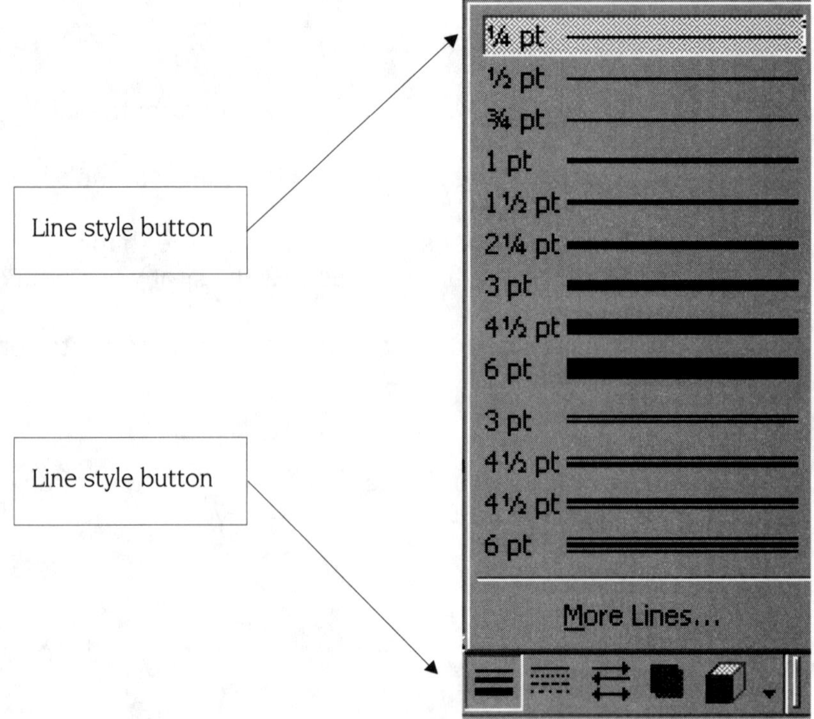

1. Go to back to the Drawing Toolbar.

2. Click on the Line Style button (15th from the left). A menu will appear listing line sizes.

3. Click on the ¼-point size to put a border around your text box.

C. Create duplicate boxes to house the rest of your points.

1. Put your mouse pointer on any part of the new border.

2. Click to activate the box. A fuzzy border will appear.

3. Press the CTRL key and the D key on your keyboard.

4. A duplicate box will appear slightly below and to the right of your first box.

5. Press the CTRL key and the D key again for each of the boxes that you need.

D. Move the boxes to the locations where you want to put them on the slide.

1. Activate the box by clicking on one of its borders.

2. Move your mouse pointer slightly until the four-arrow shape appears.

3. Hold down the left mouse button and drag the box to the place where you want to put it.

E. Match the center handles to the Ruler Bar both horizontally and vertically to set each box in a spot that matches exactly the locations of the other boxes. (Exercise 5.2, Step 5.) Just doing it by eye is usually not enough if you want the slide to be perfectly balanced and look just right.

F. Type in the text into each box. The boxes will expand as necessary.

G. Remove the borders on your text boxes if they make the slide too busy.

1. Activate the text box by clicking in it. Go to the Drawing Toolbar.

2. Click on the small arrow to the right of the Line Color button. A menu will appear. At the very top of the menu is a button labeled "No Line."

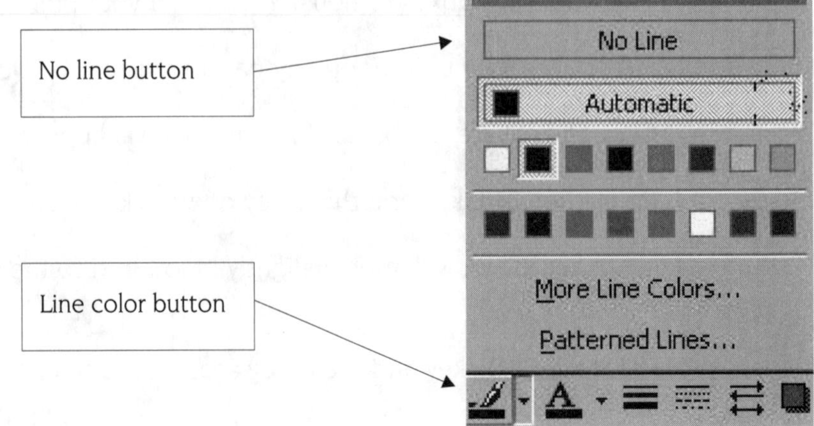

3. Click on the No Line button. The border will disappear.

Step 4: Create the arrows pointing from the facts to the conclusion.

A. Get the first arrow onto the slide.

1. Go to the Drawing Toolbar.

2. Click on the AutoShapes button (4th from the left). A menu will appear.

3. Click on the Block Arrows option. Another menu will appear.

4. Click on the arrow shape that is the last one in the top row.

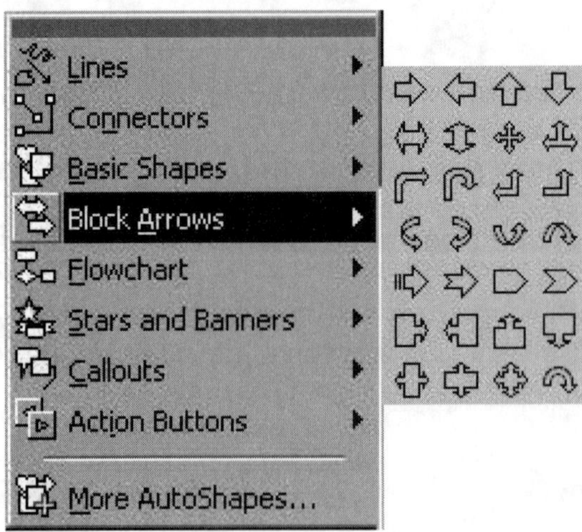

5. Put your mouse pointer on the slide near where you want one of the arrows to be.

6. Click the left mouse button. The arrow shape will appear on the slide. It will have eight white handles and one yellow one.

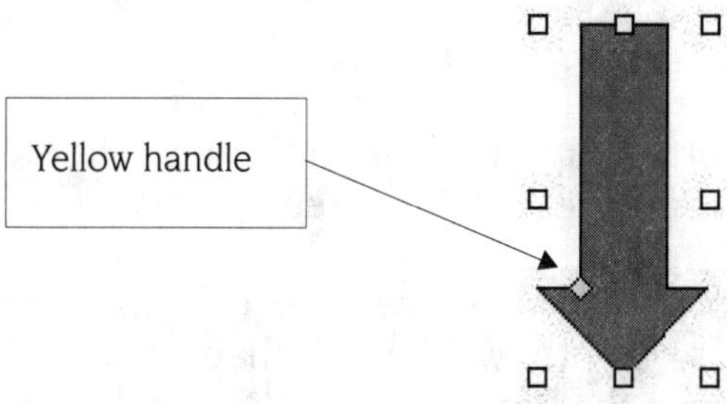

B. Shape the arrow so that it fits the purpose.

1. Use the white handles at either end of the arrow to make it longer or shorter.

2. Use the white handles on the sides to make it wider or narrower.

3. Use the white handles in the corners to make it proportionally larger or smaller.

4. Use the yellow handle to change the arrow's shape.

C. Create duplicate arrows.

With the handles showing around the arrow—

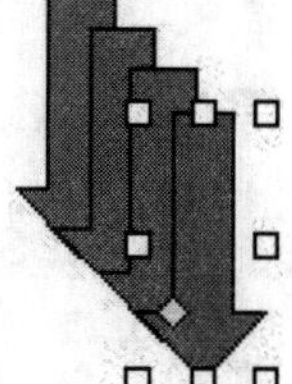

1. Press the CTRL key and the D key on your keyboard.

2. A duplicate arrow shape will appear slightly below and to the right of your first box.

3. Press the CTRL key and the D key again for each of the arrows that you need.

D. Position the arrows near the text.

With the handles showing around the arrow—

1. Move the mouse pointer over the arrow until the four-arrow pointer shape appears.

2. Hold down the left mouse button and drag the arrow to the location where you need it. It may be pointing in any direction at this stage.

E. Rotate the arrows to point from the text to the conclusion.

1. Click on the arrow that you want to rotate. The handles will appear.

2. Go to the Drawing Toolbar.

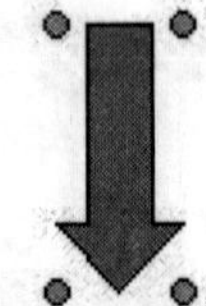

3. Click on the Rotate button (3rd from the left). The handles around the arrow will turn into green points.

4. Move your mouse pointer over one of these green points. The mouse pointer will have a shape that is the same as the icon on the Rotate button. Center the circle on the green point.

5. Hold the left mouse button down and drag the arrow in any direction you need. It will rotate on an axis.

6. Check the Ruler Bars to be sure you have each arrow in the right position. The arrows should be aligned vertically and horizontally with each other and with the central oval shape.

7. Click outside the arrow shape when you are done.

Step 5: Add color.

A. Color the fill of the oval shape in the middle of the slide using the Fill Color button (12th from the left) on the Drawing Toolbar. (Exercise 3.3.)

B. Color the arrows using the Fill Color button on the Drawing Toolbar.

Step 6: Save your work.

★ You can use more or fewer arrows. There is no magic about the design with four. Use as many as you have good points. Just be certain that the chart is easy to read and understand.

Exercise 6.3: The basic time line

A basic time line shows a picture of the order in which events occurred and supports the argument that because the events occurred in this order, a particular conclusion should be reached.

The layout of a time line looks like this:

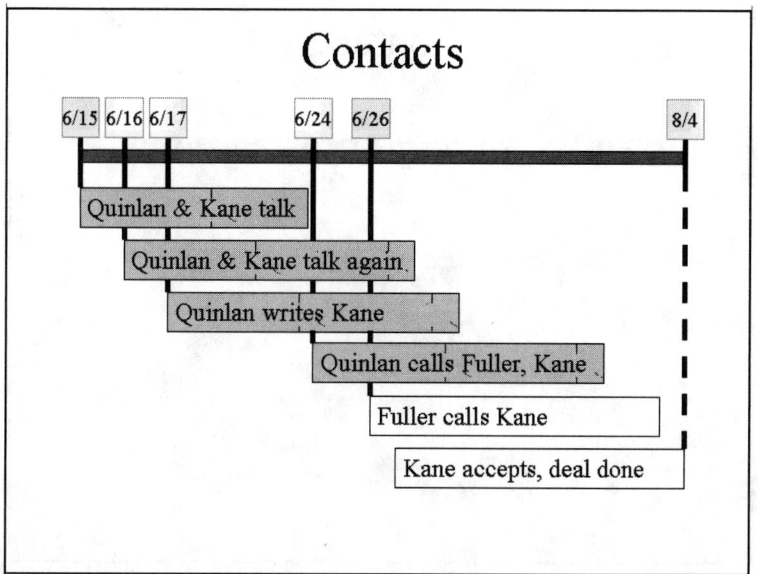

To create a basic time line, do this:

Step 1: Create a slide with a title box. (Standard Toolbar, New Slide button, Title Only option.)

Step 2: Type in the title and move the title box to the top of the slide. This allows the maximum room for the time line. (Ch. 3, Exercise 3.1.)

Step 3: Create the time references.

A. Create a horizontal time reference line across the width of the slide.

1. Go to the Drawing Toolbar.

2. Click on the Rectangle button (7th from the left).

3. Move your mouse pointer to the approximate spot on the top of the slide (under the title box) where you want the time line to go. Click there. A green square box appears with handles. (The color is temporary.)

4. Use the handles to shape the time line.

5. Go to the Drawing Toolbar.

6. Click on the Fill Color button (12th from the left). Choose a color for the time line. (See Exercise 3.3.) Your slide now looks like this:

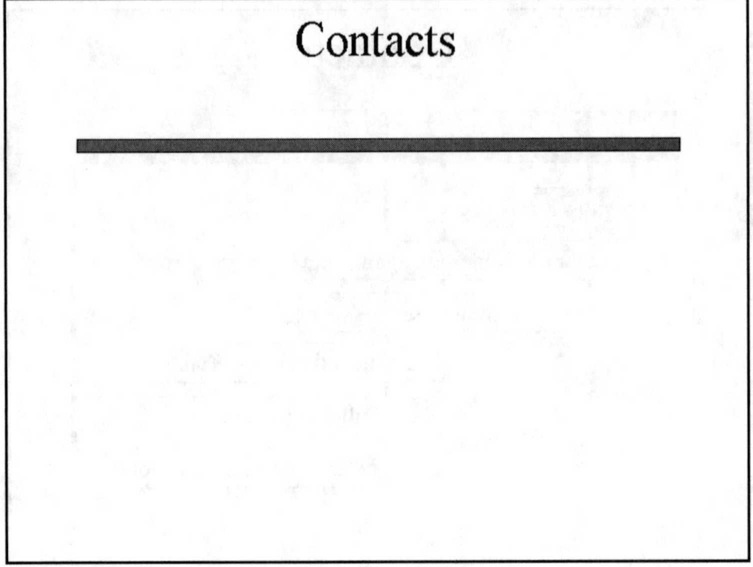

B. Make small text boxes for the key dates.

1. Go to the Drawing Toolbar.

2. Click on the Text Box button.

3. Move your mouse pointer to the approximate place above the time line where you will put the dates. Click there. A small box with a fuzzy border will appear. Your cursor will be blinking in the middle of the box.

4. Type in the date. The box will expand as you type. (Check the font and change if necessary. See Exercise 3.1.)

5. Put a border around the box using the Line Style button. (Go to the Drawing Toolbar. Click on the Line Styles button. A drop-down menu will appear. Click on the ¼-point size line for the border of your box. A line will appear around the box.)

6. Resize the box to make sure it is no larger than necessary. (Activate the box and use the handles.)

7. Add the fill color. (Drawing Toolbar, Fill Color button. See Exercise 3.3.)

8. Now that you have one box the way you want it, create as many duplicates as you need. Activate the box, hold down the CTRL key on your keyboard, and press the D key as many times as you need boxes. Drag the boxes to space them out along the time line.

9. Align the boxes along their tops. (Activate each of the boxes so that all are active at once. Go to the Drawing Toolbar, click on the Draw button, click on the Align or Distribute option, pick the Align Top alternative.) Your slide now looks like this:

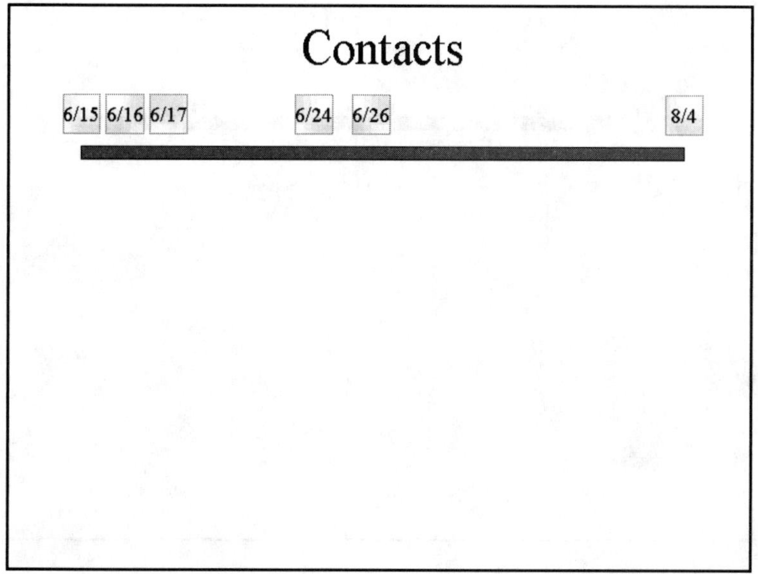

C. Make short vertical lines across the horizontal time reference line to mark the relative position of the key dates.

1. Go to the Drawing Toolbar.

2. Click on the Line button (5th from the left).

3. Put your mouse pointer over the place on the time reference line where you want the first date to be, hold down the left mouse button, and draw a short vertical line by dragging your mouse and releasing the mouse button at the desired spot.

4. Size the line to 4½ points using the Line Style button. (See Exercise 3.2.)

5. Create as many duplicates as you need for the reference points on the time line. (Activate the line, CTRL + D.)

6. Drag the lines into position indicating the relative dates.

7. Align the lines at the top. (Activate all the lines. Go to the Drawing Toolbar, Draw button, Align and Distribute option, Align at Top. See Exercise 6.1, Step 6.)

8. Drag the date boxes over the lines. Now your time line looks like this:

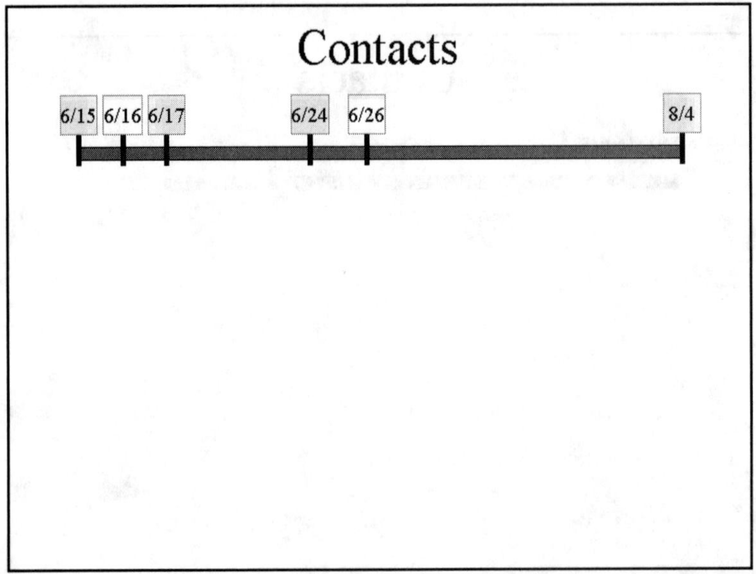

Step 4: Create the event references.

A. Create six duplicate text boxes for the key events. Place them under the time line. Distribute the boxes vertically so they are evenly spaced (Drawing Toolbar, Draw button, Distribute option, vertical). Type in the descriptions. Choose a fill color. (Exercise 3.3.)

B. Move the event reference boxes under the time reference lines. Line up the end of each box with the appropriate date on the time reference line. The time line now looks like this:

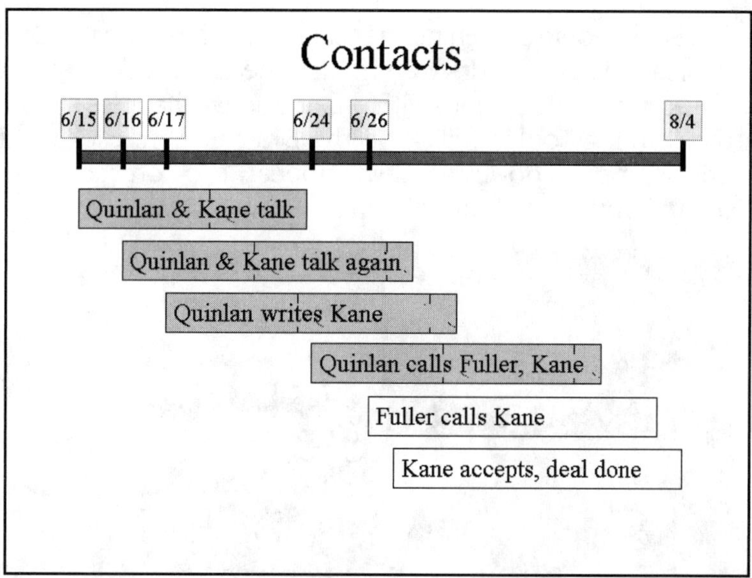

Step 5: Connect the event references to the time references with lines.

A. Activate each vertical line by clicking on it. Handles will appear at each end.

B. Put your mouse pointer over the bottom handle. The two-arrow pointer shape should appear. Hold down the left mouse button and drag the line down to meet the corner of the event box to which it should be attached.

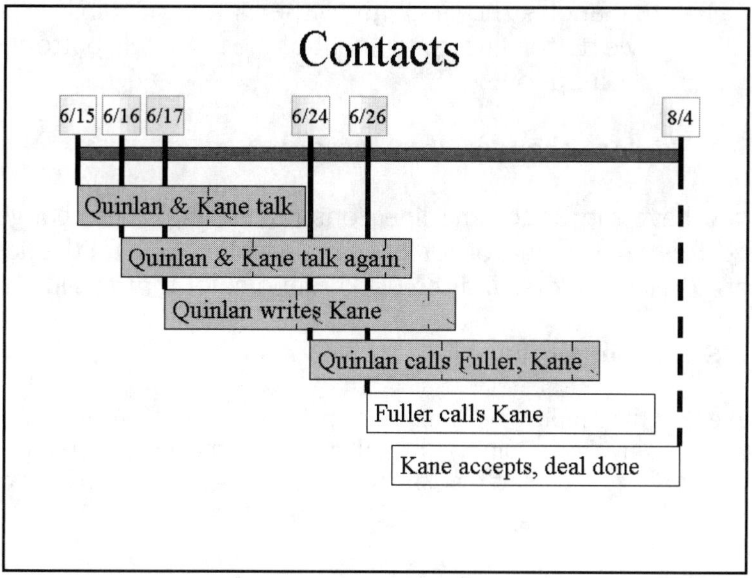

C. The lines should go behind the text boxes. If they do not do this automatically when you draw them, use the Order command to put the boxes in the foreground. With the box active (handles showing), go to the Drawing Toolbar, click on the Draw button, click on the Order option, a drop-down menu will appear, click on the Bring to Front option. This menu looks like this:

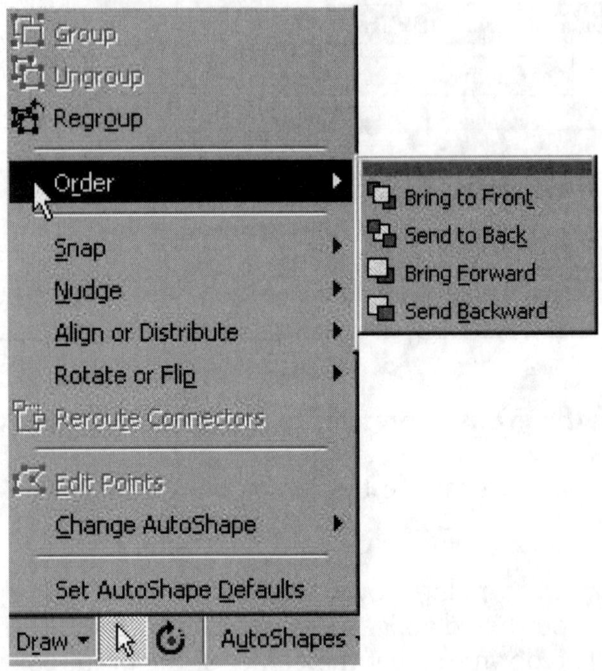

D. To make the last line into dashes instead of a solid line, with the line activate (handles showing), go to the Drawing Toolbar, click on the Dash Style button (just to the right of the Line Style button), and pick a long dash option.

Step 6: Make font changes, if necessary.

Once you have the basic time line constructed, consider changes to the typeface (to Arial, Tahoma, or some other suitable choice for the design), the fill colors, the line colors, and the background color for the slide.

Step 7: Save your work.

In the case of the simple time line, you might want to use the same fill color for all of the actions involving Quinlan (the golf game, the meeting, the phone calls, and the letter) to emphasize the point that she was the driving force behind the deal.

The time intervals measured on a time line do not have to be exact because the chart is used as an illustrative aid (and is usually not admitted into evidence). However, if you distort the time intervals by a large amount, there may be an objection based on fairness and misleading the jury. You can get the alignment exactly right this way: when you place the marker vertical lines on the horizontal time reference line, use the keyboard arrows to move them rather than dragging them. If one tap on a keyboard arrow equals one day, one week, or one month, you will arrive at the correct spacing by just counting the taps.

The text boxes used in a basic time line can also be rectangles if particular circumstances require. The relevant considerations are explained in the Box Reference Guide in Chapter 7.

Time lines such as this one benefit from being animated. Go to Chapter 9, Exercise 9.3 for directions on animating relationship charts. For PowerPoint 97 users, go to Appendix D for these directions. You can see these time lines in color, with animations, in the PowerPoint slide show for each case file on the CD that accompanies this book.

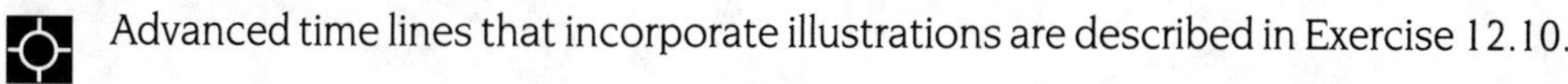

Advanced time lines that incorporate illustrations are described in Exercise 12.10.

Chapter 7

Text Document Treatments

Nearly every text document that is an exhibit can benefit from a "treatment" that points out or extracts its significant portions. Long text documents are difficult to use effectively as exhibits. They take a lot of time for jurors to read thoroughly; most disputed documents need some interpretation; and dense lines of words and numbers do not display well, even on very large screens.

PowerPoint slides are an efficient way to present text documents. The judge and jury will have hard copies of the exhibits, but you will not need to spend time handing the exhibit to your opponent, handing it to the judge, passing it out to the jury, and then trying to get everyone on the same page.

★ Displaying documents in an enlarged format on a big screen improves juror comprehension significantly. Because everyone's attention is drawn to the screen, it is much easier to focus the attention on the word or phrase highlighted on the screen. Jurors can look and listen at the same time. If they are using hard copy only, they likely will be hunting for the place on the document in the exhibit book while, at the same time, trying to listen to the questions and answers about it. Under these circumstances, some jurors will never find the word or phrase being discussed and may also miss the entire discussion while hunting for it.

Your case file includes several text documents. These documents have been scanned, and they are on the CD that came with this book or can be downloaded from the NITA web site, *www.nitastudent.org*. Think about slides for possible direct or cross-examination of a witness in your case using these documents.

This chapter has exercises with respect to six text document treatments.

1. Box
2. Circle
3. Line link
4. Split screen with bullet points
5. Re-keyed callouts
6. Direct callouts

In this chapter, some of the steps in each exercise involve operations you learned in earlier chapters. If you know how to do the operation described in the A, B, C headings, you can skip reading the 1, 2, 3 subheads underneath.

! Documents are usually in an 8½ by 11 format. PowerPoint slides are in a 4½ by 3½ ratio, which is called *the aspect*. Because the display size does not match the document size, documents fit only if reduced significantly in size. This reduces readability, and is another reason why document treatments—boxes, circles, lines, split screens, and callouts—are necessary.

Box Reference Guide

Working with text document treatments involves two kinds of PowerPoint boxes: text boxes and rectangles. They can perform some of the same functions, but have different characteristics. You will choose one or the other depending on the task at hand.

TEXT BOX	RECTANGLE
Appears with no border; if needed, a border is added with the Line Styles button	Appears with a border; if required, the border can be deleted with the Line Color button (no line option); size can be changed with the Line Styles button
Appears with no fill; if needed, fill color can be added with the Fill Color button	Appears with a default color; if necessary, this color can be changed with the Fill Color button or deleted by selecting the No Fill option
Can be used to put text onto a slide	Can be used to put text onto a slide
Text is aligned at the left margin	Text centers automatically when entered
Size expands automatically with text	Size does not expand automatically; use of handles is required to resize
Can be expanded with the middle handles horizontally beyond text, but not vertically; to expand vertically, a larger text size must be selected or the Enter key must be used to create spaces	Can be expanded with middle handles both horizontally and vertically regardless of the amount or size of the text
When resized using corner handles, text alignment adjusts automatically; this limits the flexibility of the shape	When resizing using corner handles, text is not affected; this requires a separate operation to re-position the text if necessary
Cannot be used to box text in a document treatment	Can be used to box text in a document treatment

The other PowerPoint shapes—circles, basic shapes, block arrows, and callouts—work in generally the same way as the rectangle.

Exercise 7.1: Use a box for focus

PowerPoint will draw a box around any word or phrase on the face of the document. Boxing is usually used to point out the identifying features of the document—the date, address, signature, or exhibit number. You may want to box more than one such feature depending on the testimony you intend to elicit from the witness.

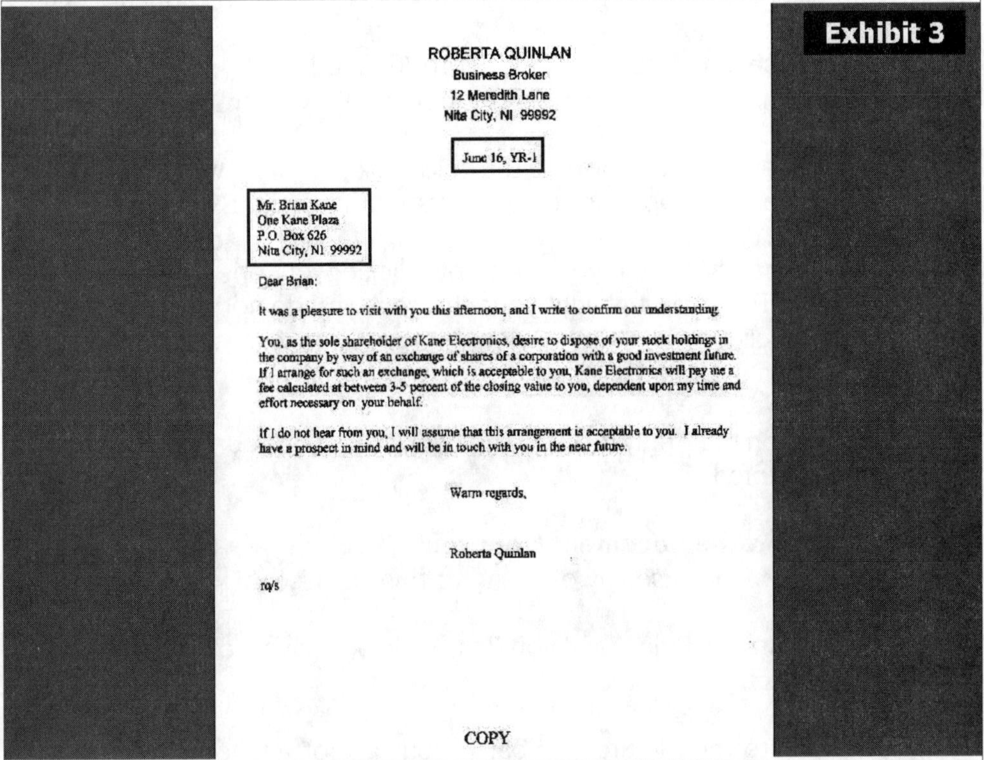

ROBERTA QUINLAN
Business Broker
12 Meredith Lane
Nita City, NI 99992

June 16, YR-1

Mr. Brian Kane
One Kane Plaza
P.O. Box 626
Nita City, NI 99992

Dear Brian:

It was a pleasure to visit with you this afternoon, and I write to confirm our understanding.

You, as the sole shareholder of Kane Electronics, desire to dispose of your stock holdings in the company by way of an exchange of shares of a corporation with a good investment future. If I arrange for such an exchange, which is acceptable to you, Kane Electronics will pay me a fee calculated at between 3-5 percent of the closing value to you, dependent upon my time and effort necessary on your behalf.

If I do not hear from you, I will assume that this arrangement is acceptable to you. I already have a prospect in mind and will be in touch with you in the near future.

Warm regards,

Roberta Quinlan

rq/s

COPY

Go to the Appendix for your case for an example.

The box directs the eye to a particular spot on the document, making spoken words about the document easier to follow. The box adds emphasis but does not change the underlying document; therefore this technique seldom raises an objection.

Step 1: Get a blank slide on the screen.

A. Go to the Standard Toolbar.

B. Click on the New Slide button (10th from the left). The New Slide Screen will appear. (Illustration, Ch. 2, Exercise 2.1.)

C. Click on the Blank Slide button (bottom row, last on right).

D. Click on the OK button. Now you have a blank slide on the screen.

Step 2: Color the slide background. This makes it easier to work with the document that you are going to put on the slide.

A. Go to the Menu Bar.

B. Click on the Format button. A drop-down menu will appear.

C. Choose the Background option. This brings up the Background screen. (Illustration, Ch. 3, Exercise 3.3.)

D. Click on the arrow next to the color box (it may be white). This brings up the Color Options screen. (Illustration, Ch. 3, Exercise 3.3.)

E. Choose the color you want by clicking on one of the squares. PowerPoint will highlight your choice. If you do not see the color you want, click on the More Colors button. Choose a color by clicking on it, then click on OK.

F. Click on the Apply button. The background on your slide should now be colored.

Step 3: Import the document from your CD. Each case has several documents, and you may use any of them for this exercise.

A. Activate the Ruler Bar if you do not already have it on the screen. (Ch. 4, Exercise 4.2, Step 1.)

B. Activate the Picture Toolbar if you do not already have it on the screen. (Ch. 5, Exercise 5.1, Step 2.)

C. Click on the Insert Picture button to import your document to your slide. (Ch. 5, Exercise 5.2, Step 1.)

! Because your document is in image format, PowerPoint treats it like a picture. When you click on the Insert Picture button, you will be asked where the picture is located. The directory and file names for the documents are in the Appendix for your case.

Step 4: Resize the document to fit on the slide. (Ch. 5, Exercise 5.2, Step 2.)

Step 5: Put a border around the document.

A. Select (activate) the box containing the document by clicking anywhere within it.

B. Go to the Drawing Toolbar.

C. Click on the Line Style button (15th from the left). A drop-down menu appears.

D. Click on one of the line styles for the border. A ¼-point size is sufficient for a document that has a white background. The border will appear around the document.

Step 6: Move the document to the center of the slide.

A. Select (activate) the box containing the document by clicking anywhere within it.

B. Put your mouse pointer on one of the margins of the box. Move the pointer gently until the four-arrow pointer appears. (Illustration, Ch. 1, Section 1.4.)

C. Click on the left mouse button once. The pattern of the fuzzy border will change.

D. Go to the UP ARROW key or the DOWN ARROW key on your keyboard and press it one or more times. The document will move one space each time you press the key.

E. When you get to the center, the handle at the top center will be directly under the zero on the ruler bar at the top, and the handle at the left center will be directly across from the zero on the ruler bar on the left side.

Step 7: Place a rectangle on the document.

A. Go to the Drawing Toolbar.

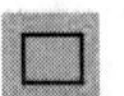

B. Click on the Rectangle button (7th from the left). This activates a cross-shaped mouse pointer. (Illustration, Ch. 1, Section 1.4.)

C. Move your mouse to the position on the document where the date is located. Click there. A solid colored rectangle with handles in the border now obscures the text at the point you picked.

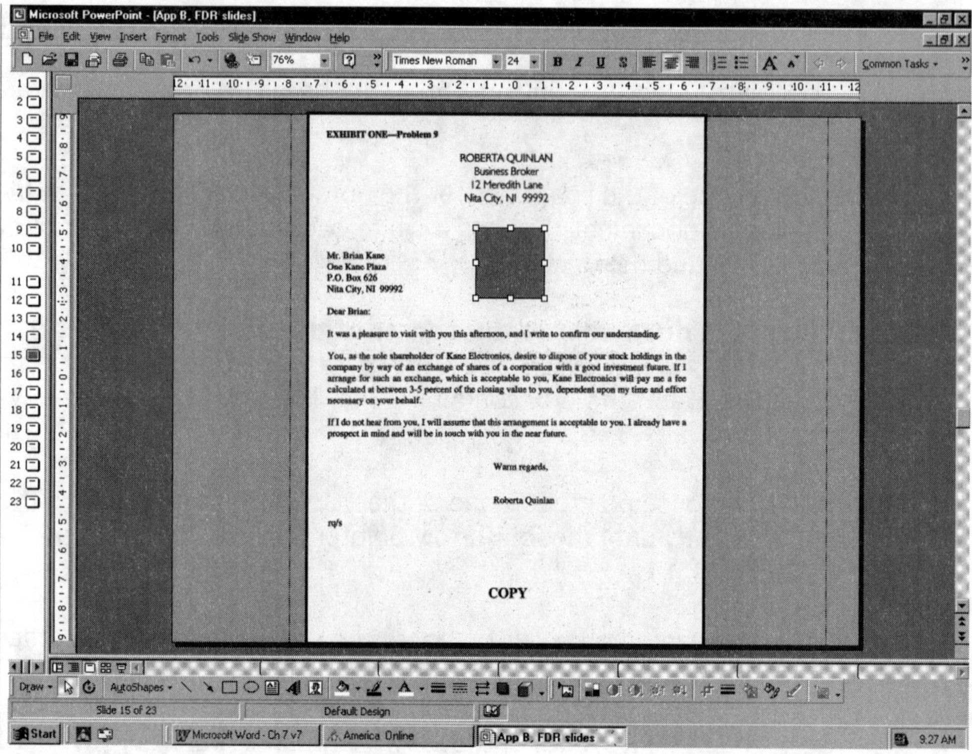

Step 8: Remove the fill color so you can see the text underneath.

A. Go to the Drawing Toolbar.

B. Click on the arrow next to the Fill Color button (12th from the left). This brings up the Color Options box. (Illustration, Ch. 3, Exercise 3.3, Step 2.)

C. Click on the No Fill button at the top of the screen. The color disappears and you can now read the text underneath.

Step 9: Position the rectangle to surround the text you want to emphasize.

A. Put your mouse pointer on the border indicating the rectangle is active and hold it there or move it slightly until the four-arrow pointer appears.

B. Hold down the left mouse button and drag the rectangle to the general location you want.

Step 10: Size the rectangle so that it covers only the text you want to emphasize.

A. Put the two-arrow pointer over one of the middle handles.

B. Hold down the left mouse button and drag the line to the specific location you want.

C. Repeat this operation with each side of the rectangle until it is where you want it.

Step 11: Adjust the thickness of the lines forming the box around the text.

A. With the box still active, go to the Drawing Toolbar.

B. Click on the Line Style button (15th from the left). A drop-down menu will appear.

C. Choose the three-point size for your line by clicking on it.

Step 12: Color the lines forming the box.

A. Go to the Drawing Toolbar.

B. Click on the arrow next to the Line Color button (13th from the left). The Color Options screen will appear. (Illustration, Ch. 3, Exercise 3.3.)

C. If one of the colors shown in the box is what you want, click on that color. Otherwise, click on the More Line Colors. A palette of colors will appear. Choose a blue color by clicking on it.

Step 13: Repeat steps 7-12 to place a rectangle around the address portion of the document.

Step 14: Create a label for the exhibit number by adding a rectangle in the upper right corner of the slide. Use a contrasting fill color. For white lettering on a dark background, see Exercise 4.2, Step 9.

★ Every text document needs to be identified for the viewer on every slide. Normally you will want to make sure the exhibit number or the name of the document (sometimes both) plus the date are made clear on your slide, either in a title or with other labeling. A small label, located in a consistent position on the slide, will serve this purpose very well.

Step 15: Save your work.

! These text treatments can be made more effective for courtroom presentation by animating them so that the boxes around important features of the document appear one at a time. Go to Exercise 9.4 for directions on motion and special effects. (PowerPoint 97 users should consult Appendix D.) In animating slides that have text treatments, be consistent. If you have one slide in which the exhibit number is given first and then the date, use the same order (number, date) throughout. Examples of slides with animations are on the CD.

Exercise 7.2: Circle words and phrases for emphasis

The software provides a circle or oval that you can put on a document for emphasis. The circle marks a significant word or set of words about which you will be questioning the witness. It is less formal than the box, which identifies the document, but focuses attention on something that is important about the substance of the document.

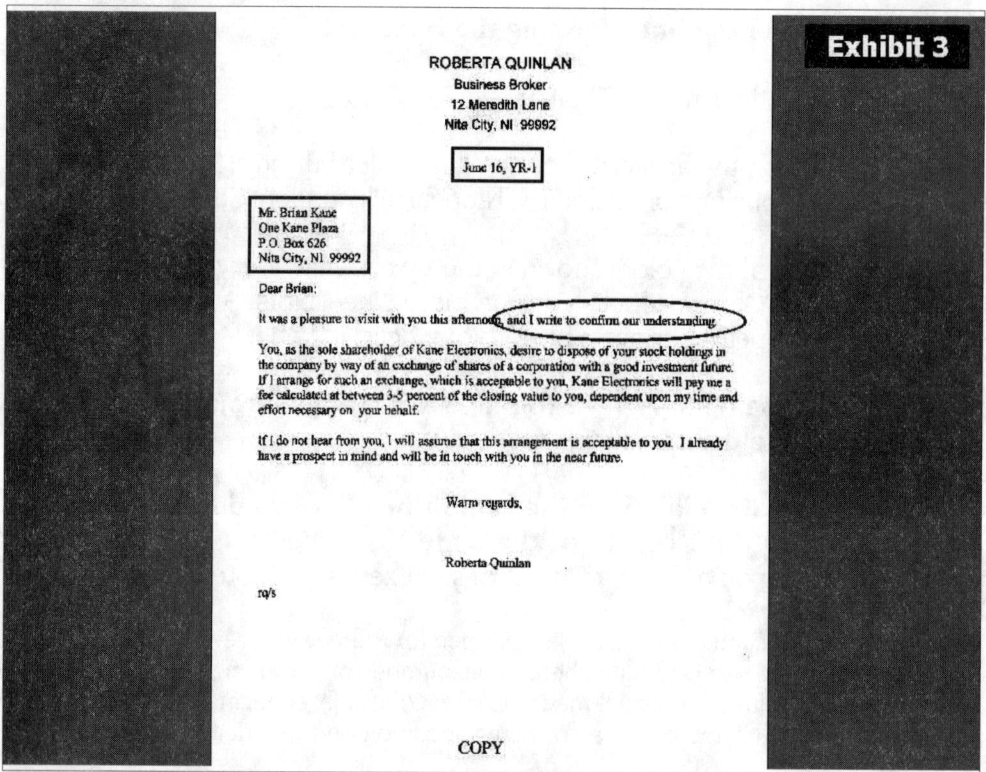

Exhibit 3

ROBERTA QUINLAN
Business Broker
12 Meredith Lane
Nita City, NI 99992

June 16, YR-1

Mr. Brian Kane
One Kane Plaza
P.O. Box 626
Nita City, NI 99992

Dear Brian:

It was a pleasure to visit with you this afternoon, and I write to confirm our understanding.

You, as the sole shareholder of Kane Electronics, desire to dispose of your stock holdings in the company by way of an exchange of shares of a corporation with a good investment future. If I arrange for such an exchange, which is acceptable to you, Kane Electronics will pay me a fee calculated at between 3-5 percent of the closing value to you, dependent upon my time and effort necessary on your behalf.

If I do not hear from you, I will assume that this arrangement is acceptable to you. I already have a prospect in mind and will be in touch with you in the near future.

Warm regards,

Roberta Quinlan

rq/s

COPY

A Go to the Appendix for your case to see a similar example.

Step 1: Bring up a circle.

With the slide from the Box exercise on the screen—

A. Go to the Drawing Toolbar.

B. Click on the Oval button (to the right of the Rectangle button). This activates a cross-shaped mouse pointer.

Step 2: Put the circle on the document.

A. Move your mouse pointer to the document and click over the phrase you want to highlight. A solid color oval now obscures the text at the point you picked.

B. Remove the fill color. (Exercise 7.1, Step 7.)

C. Use the handles to position the oval exactly over the text. If you have trouble moving the oval with the mouse, select the oval and move it to the desired spot using the ARROW keys on the keyboard.

This way of marking document content mimics the action of drawing a circle on the face of the document for emphasis, a format familiar to most people, and is readily understood. Like the box, the circle (or oval) does not change the substance of the document and therefore usually draws no objection.

Step 3: Use the Zoom function to enlarge the area you are working on if the size of the image is too small for you to be sure you have the oval in the right place.

A. Go to the Standard Toolbar.

B. Look at the Zoom box, a small white box on the far right. It will say 50% or 66% or 75% depending on the method of scanning used to produce a digital copy of the document.

C. Click on the arrow to the right of the box. A drop-down menu will appear.

D. Choose the 100% option by clicking on it. Your screen will resize and the document will be enlarged. This may take a little time, depending on the speed of your computer.

E. Use the scroll bar arrows (vertical and horizontal) to adjust the image if the enlargement is not centered where you need it. (Illustration, Ch. 1, Section 1.5.) Be sure to use these arrows one click at a time because your computer will have to readjust the screen display every time you click. If you go too fast, it may just give up and quit.

Step 4: Choose a line size for your circle. (Exercise 7.1, Step 10.)

Step 5: Choose a line color for your circle. (Exercise 7.1, Step 11.)

Step 6: Save your work.

To be effective, you should use the same shape (such as the rectangle) for the same purpose (such as pointing out the date) in all of your slides. Once you use a red rectangle to point out a date, do not use the same color and shape to highlight words in the text. A circle might be better. When you come to the date of a document on another slide, use the red rectangle there too. Your audience will know what to look for.

These text treatments can be made more effective for courtroom presentation by animating them so that the circle draws itself around the words or phrases to be emphasized. Go to Exercise 9.4 for directions on motion and special effects.

PowerPoint has many shape alternatives listed under the AutoShapes button. Resist the temptation to use them all. Simplicity in presentation helps your audience appreciate the facts more readily.

Exercise 7.3: Link key terms with a line

When you want to make a connection between two words or phrases in a document that are not adjacent to one another, you can box or circle them and draw a line between them. Line linking can be particularly effective when you have two or more documents you are going to treat in the same way.

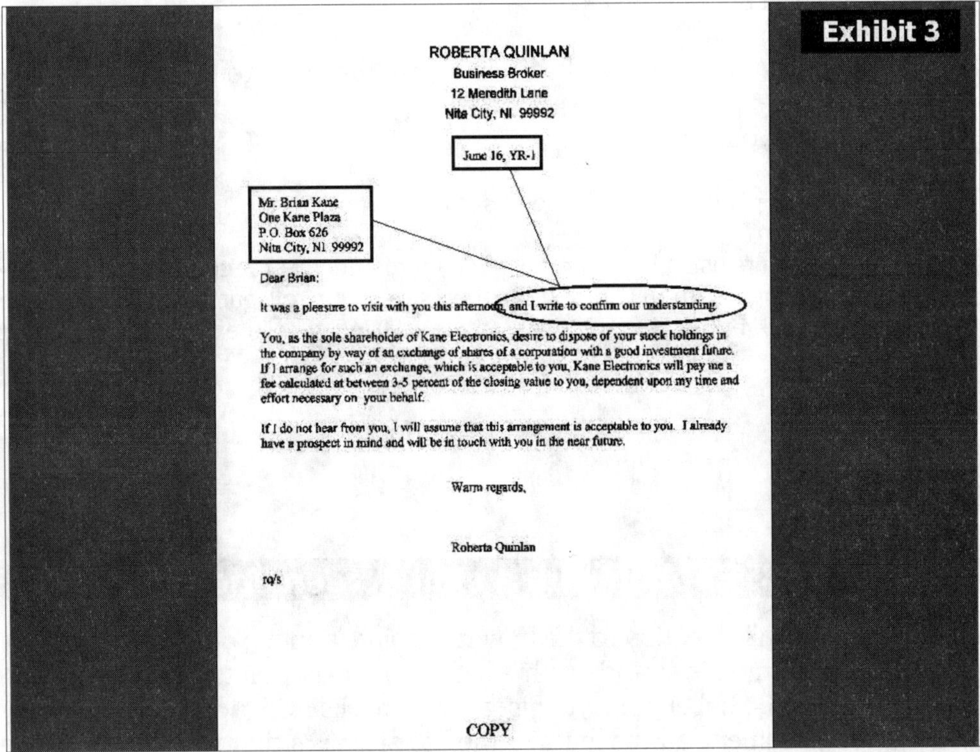

ROBERTA QUINLAN
Business Broker
12 Meredith Lane
Nita City, NI 99992

June 16, YR-1

Mr. Brian Kane
One Kane Plaza
P.O. Box 626
Nita City, NI 99992

Dear Brian:

It was a pleasure to visit with you this afternoon, and I write to confirm our understanding:

You, as the sole shareholder of Kane Electronics, desire to dispose of your stock holdings in the company by way of an exchange of shares of a corporation with a good investment future. If I arrange for such an exchange, which is acceptable to you, Kane Electronics will pay me a fee calculated at between 3-5 percent of the closing value to you, dependent upon my time and effort necessary on your behalf.

If I do not hear from you, I will assume that this arrangement is acceptable to you. I already have a prospect in mind and will be in touch with you in the near future.

Warm regards,

Roberta Quinlan

rq/s

COPY

With the document containing the box (Exercise 7.1) and the circle (Exercise 7.2) on the screen—

A. Go to the Drawing Toolbar.

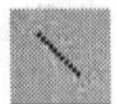

B. Click on the Line button (5th from the left, next to AutoShapes). This activates the line drawing function.

C. Put your mouse pointer on the document at the bottom center of the box shape that you have drawn around the date.

D. Hold down the left mouse button and draw the line from that point to the top center of the circle shape that you have drawn around the phrase.

E. Release the left mouse button.

F. Click anywhere on the document to indicate that you are finished drawing the line.

! The line you drew works just like the text boxes and picture boxes from prior exercises. If you need to adjust the line, put your mouse pointer over it and click on it. Two handles will appear, one at either end. Put your mouse pointer over the handle until the two-arrow pointer appears. Hold down the left mouse button and move that end of the line in any direction.

G. Repeat steps A-F to draw a line from the circle to the address.

H. Save your work.

A Go to the Appendix for your case to see an example.

Text treatments using lines can be made more effective for courtroom presentation by animating the lines so that they stretch or roll out from one point to another. Exercise 9.4 provides directions on motion and special effects. Examples are on the CD.

Exercise 7.4: Explain with a split screen and bullets

Another way to call attention to the principal points about a document is to display the document side-by-side with a list of summary points about the document. These can be bullet points or just an informal list with no bullets. Normally you put the document on the left and the list of points that you want to make about the document on the right.

This layout shows how a document slide looks with boxes. A split screen layout can be done with overlapping when there is adequate white space at the right margin of the document and when the wording of the bullet points is long and requires more space. The overlap helps connect the bullet points visually with the document. Bullet point boxes without overlapping are the usual choice and have less risk of a cluttered look.

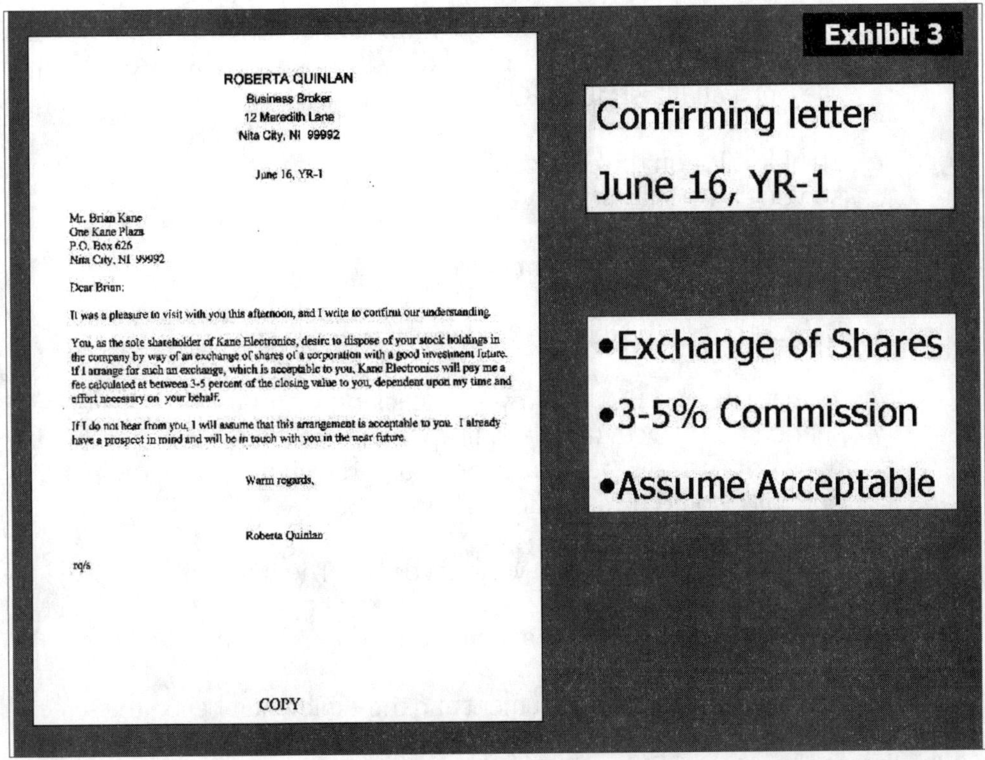

ROBERTA QUINLAN
Business Broker
12 Meredith Lane
Nita City, NI 99992

June 16, YR-1

Mr. Brian Kane
One Kane Plaza
P.O. Box 626
Nita City, NI 99992

Dear Brian:

It was a pleasure to visit with you this afternoon, and I write to confirm our understanding.

You, as the sole shareholder of Kane Electronics, desire to dispose of your stock holdings in the company by way of an exchange of shares of a corporation with a good investment future. If I arrange for such an exchange, which is acceptable to you, Kane Electronics will pay me a fee calculated at between 3-5 percent of the closing value to you, dependent upon my time and effort necessary on your behalf.

If I do not hear from you, I will assume that this arrangement is acceptable to you. I already have a prospect in mind and will be in touch with you in the near future.

Warm regards,

Roberta Quinlan

rq/s

This layout is best used when you need to summarize what a document says because you cannot readily extract words, phrases, or sentences from the document itself to use as callouts. (Exercise 7.5, re-keyed callouts; and Exercise 7.6, direct callouts.) This may be the case when the importance of the document is an inference to be drawn from or an action that was taken because of the document. It may also be useful when the words in the document themselves require explanation.

In doing this exercise, work with the document you already imported unless you prefer to create a new slide with a different document.

Step 1: Create a duplicate slide.

A. Go to the View Bar.

B. Click on the Slide Sorter button (4th from the left). The Slide Sorter screen will appear. (Illustration, Ch. 4, Exercise 4.1.)

C. Select the slide you want to duplicate by putting your mouse pointer on it and clicking with the left mouse button. PowerPoint will highlight the slide.

D. Hold down the CTRL key on your keyboard and press the D key at the same time. A duplicate of your slide will appear on the screen next to the original. (Illustration, Ch. 4, Exercise 4.1.)

E. Double click on the duplicate slide to bring it to the screen in full size so you can work with it.

Step 2: Clean up the document.

A. Delete the two boxes, the circle, and the two lines.

1. Activate the first box by first clicking on one of its margins. A shaded border with handles will appear indicating that it is active. If it does not activate, get your mouse pointer where one of the handles normally would be and click again.

2. Hit the DELETE key on your keyboard. The box will disappear.

3. Do the same for the remaining box, the circle, and the lines.

B. Now you have just the document and the exhibit number on the screen.

Step 3: Move the document to the left side of the slide.

A. Click anywhere in the document to activate it.

B. Go to the LEFT ARROW key on your keyboard and press it one or more times. The document will move one space to the left each time you press the key. Leave a small margin on the left.

Step 4: Crop the unnecessary portions (or margins) of the document to maximize the available space for your points.

With the document still active—

A. Go to the Picture Toolbar.

B. Click on the Crop button (7th from the left).

C. Put your mouse pointer over the middle handle in the top margin.

D. Hold down the left mouse button and drag the margin down to eliminate most of the white space around the top edge of the document's text.

E. Release the mouse button.

F. Do the same thing for each of the other margins.

G. Click anywhere to de-activate the cropping tool.

Step 5: Resize the cropped document so that it is as large as possible given the available space on the slide. (Ch. 5, Exercise 5.2, Step 2.)

Go to the Appendix for your case to see an example.

Step 6: Create a text box for additional identification of this document.

A. Go to the Formatting Toolbar.

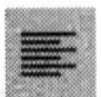

B. Click on the Left Alignment button (7th from the left). This will allow you to type from left to right in your text box.

C. Go to the Drawing Toolbar.

D. Click on the Text Box button (next to the oval shape button).

E. Put your mouse pointer on the background of your slide in the blank area to the right of your document where you want the identification of your document to go.

F. Line it up by looking at the Ruler Bar at the top. The marker on the Ruler Bar will be at the same place where your mouse pointer is.

G. Click when you get to the location you want. A small text box will appear and your pointer will be inside the box.

H. Type the additional identification information.

I. Increase the type size, if necessary, using the Increase Font Size button on the Formatting Toolbar. (Ch. 4, Exercise 4.2, Step 7.) Use the Decrease Font Size button if it is already too large.

When you use a split screen layout with the document on one side and bullet points about the document on the facing side of your slide, you can use a separate text box, above the bullet points and to the right of the document to identify the document if the exhibit number is not enough. This text box may contain the date or some other identifying information about the document so the jurors are clear about what the document is.

Step 7: Create a text box for your summary points about the document.

A. Go through the same process as in Step 6 above to create the text box.

B. If you want this text box to be lined up with the text box in which you put the identification, be sure to line up the right margin of this box on the Ruler Bar at the same marker. Alternatively, you can activate both text boxes at the same time. Go to the Drawing Toolbar, click on the Draw button, choose the Align or Distribute option, and use the Align Left function. (Exercise 6.1, Step 6(C).)

★ The summary points about the document normally are positioned in a separate text box underneath the text box that contains the identification of the document. The summary points provide information drawn from the document.

Step 8: Type in the text of your summary points.

Step 9: Put in bullets.

A. Highlight the text for which you want to add bullets.

B. Go to the Menu Bar.

C. Click on the Format button. A drop-down menu will appear.

D. For PowerPoint 2000, click on the Bullets and Numbering option. The Bullets and Numbering screen will appear.

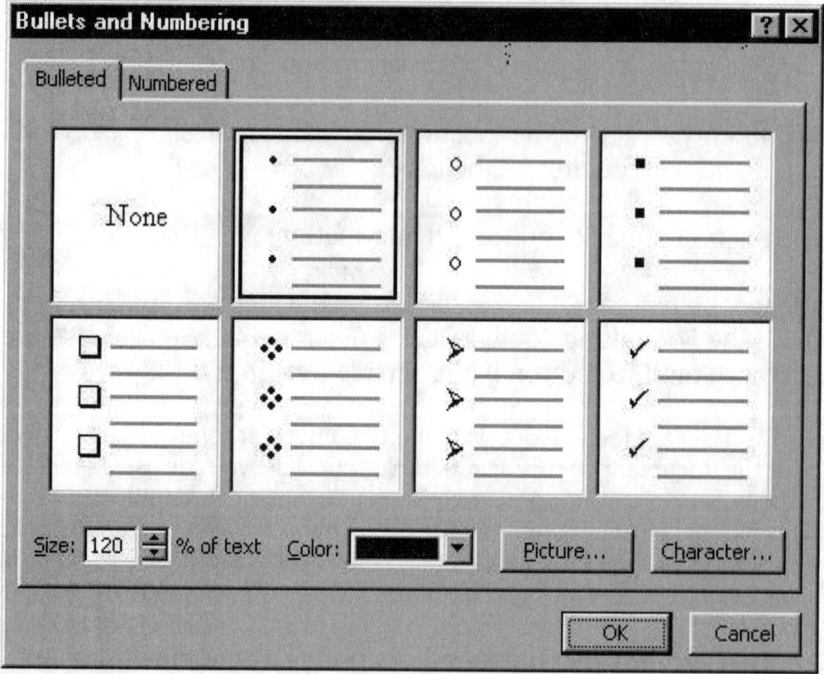

E. Set up the bullet shape and style.

1. Click on the Bulleted tab at the top of the screen if that one is not already displayed.

2. Click on the round bullets option in the top row (2nd from left),

3. The Color box should show a black bar. If it does not, click on the small arrow to the right of the box and select black as the color for the bullets.

4. The Size box should show 100%. If it does not, click on either the up arrow or down arrow to the right of the box to get to 100%.

5. For other shapes, use the Character button at the bottom right. (Ch. 3, Exercise 3.4.) For numbers, use the Numbered tab at the top.

6. Click on the OK button at the bottom. A bullet point should now appear in front of each line of text in your box.

97 To set up bullet style and shape in PowerPoint 97, go to the Menu Bar, click on the Format button. Click on the Bullet option which leads to the Bullet screen. On that screen use the Bullets From box for style, the Color box for color, and the Size box for relative size.

F. Adjust the spacing between the bullet points and the text if necessary. (Ch. 3, Exercise 3.4.)

Step 10: Dress up your slide. (Ch. 3, Exercise 3.2, 3.3.)

! Remember to add borders to the text boxes containing your summary points if you need to set the box off from the rest of the slide. Borders on this kind of text box sometimes make the slide look more neat and crisp. With the text box active, go to the Drawing Toolbar, Line Style button (pick a size), and Line Color button (pick a color).

Step 11: Save your work.

Text treatments can be made more effective for courtroom presentation by animating them so that the boxes and bullet points appear one at a time. Exercise 9.5 explains special effects for split screens with bullet points.

Exercise 7.5: Construct re-keyed callouts

Often the best way to make a point about a document is to highlight a phrase or sentence with a callout. This is a method of copying a phrase or sentence from a document, enlarging it, putting it in the margin ("calling it out" of the document) so that it is easier to see, then connecting it to the appropriate point in the original document with one or more line pointers.

Callouts are particularly useful with long text documents. It is always difficult to get this kind of exhibit on a screen in the courtroom in a readable size.

A *re-keyed callout* is one in which you use a callout box, which is a special shape provided by PowerPoint, and re-type the text into the box in a font size large enough to accomplish your purpose.

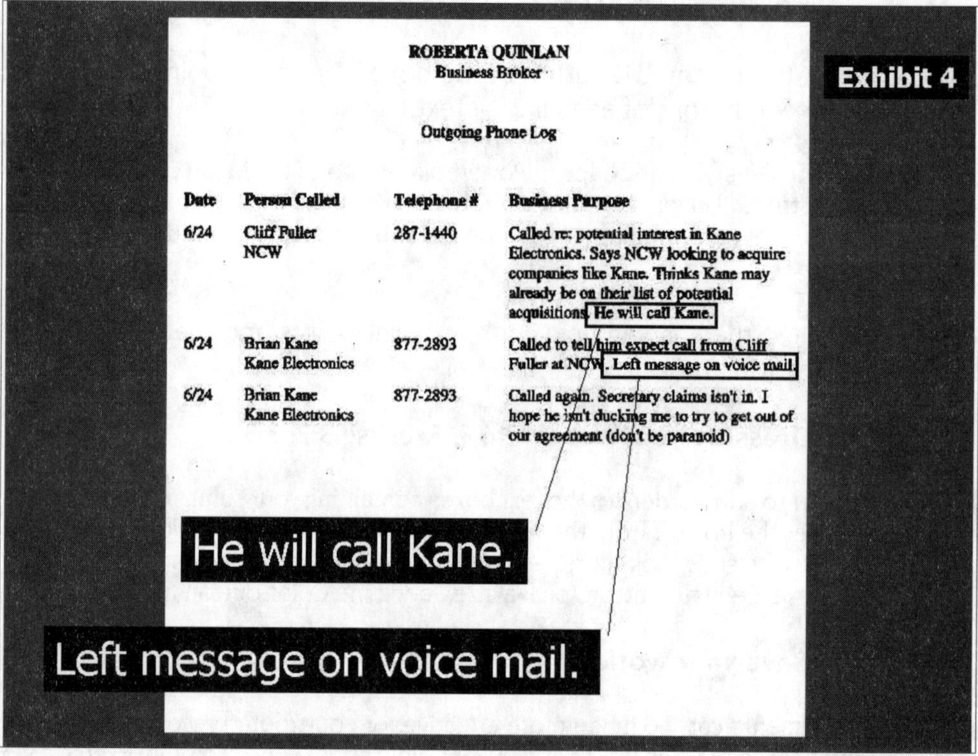

ROBERTA QUINLAN
Business Broker

Outgoing Phone Log

Date	Person Called	Telephone #	Business Purpose
6/24	Cliff Fuller NCW	287-1440	Called re: potential interest in Kane Electronics. Says NCW looking to acquire companies like Kane. Thinks Kane may already be on their list of potential acquisitions. He will call Kane.
6/24	Brian Kane Kane Electronics	877-2893	Called to tell him expect call from Cliff Fuller at NCW. Left message on voice mail.
6/24	Brian Kane Kane Electronics	877-2893	Called again. Secretary claims isn't in. I hope he isn't ducking me to try to get out of our agreement (don't be paranoid)

This type of callout usually is used when the underlying document has poor legibility or its type size would not enlarge very clearly, so that a direct callout, as described in Exercise 7.6, is not practical. Re-keyed callouts are also used where most of the called-out text occurs on one line of the document and a short piece goes over to a second line, making it difficult to use a direct callout.

★ You probably do not need the jury to read the whole document. Most document exhibits contain a lot of material that does not add anything to the issue you are pursuing. Use a callout rather than a circle when you want to focus on more than a few words, need better readability, or want to make several points on a single page.

At this point, most of the steps involve operations you performed in earlier exercises. If you know how to do the operation, skip the detailed numbered instructions, and go on to the next step.

Step 1: Get the document on a slide.

A. Get a blank slide on the screen.

1. Go to the Standard Toolbar.

2. Click on the New Slide button (10th from the left). The New Slide Screen will appear. (Illustration, Ch. 2, Exercise 2.1.)

3. Click on the Blank Slide button (bottom row, last on right). Now you have a blank slide on the screen.

B. Color the slide background to make it easier to work with the document that you are going to put on the slide.

1. Go to the Menu Bar.

2. Click on the Format button.

3. Choose the Background option. This brings up the Background screen. (Illustration, Ch. 3, Exercise 3.3.)

4. Click on the arrow next to the color box (it may be white). This brings up the Color Options screen. (Illustration, Ch. 3, Exercise 3.3.)

5. Choose the background color.

6. Click on the Apply button. The background on your slide should now be in color.

C. Import the document from your CD.

1. Activate the Picture Toolbar if you do not already have it on the screen. (Ch. 5, Exercise 5.1, Step 2.)

2. Go to the CD and identify the document you want. Because your document is in image format, PowerPoint treats it like a picture. The folder and file names for the document are in the Appendix for your case.

3. Resize the document to fit on the screen. (Ch. 5, Exercise 5.2.)

D. Crop as necessary to create more space for the callouts and to make the document larger and easier to read. (Exercise 5.2, Step 3.)

1. Click anywhere in the document so that it is active.

2. Go to the Picture Toolbar.

3. Click on the Crop button (7th from the left).

4. Put your mouse pointer over the middle handles on each of the margins in turn.

5. At each margin, hold down the left mouse button and drag the margin to eliminate most of the white space in the document's margins.

6. Release the mouse button.

7. Click anywhere to de-activate the cropping tool.

E. Resize the document within the available space to make it larger.

1. Click anywhere in the document so that it is active.

2. Put your mouse pointer over the right corner handle and drag the margin up and to the right to enlarge the document. Use the corner handles to resize the document (instead of the middle handles) to avoid distortion.

3. Move the whole document to the left (Exercise 7.1, Step 5), if necessary, and resize it again to use the available space efficiently.

Step 2: Create the identification box. Each document that is displayed for jurors should be clearly identified. Usually the exhibit number will be put in a small box in the upper right part of the slide, above the callouts.

A. Put a small rectangle box in the upper right corner of the slide.

1. Go to the Drawing Toolbar.

2. Click on the Rectangle button (7th from left).

3. Move the mouse pointer to the upper right corner where the box displaying the exhibit number is to be located. Click there. A solid colored rectangle with handles in the border is now on the slide.

4. Shape the rectangle to the size you need using the handles.

B. Type in the exhibit number and adjust the font as necessary. For white lettering on a dark background, see Exercise 4.2, Step 9.

C. Position the identification box in relation to the document. Usually you will want to leave some background showing around the top and left borders.

Step 3: Create an anchor box. This serves as a point of reference in the document pointing out where the callout came from. (Exercise 7.1, Steps 6-11.)

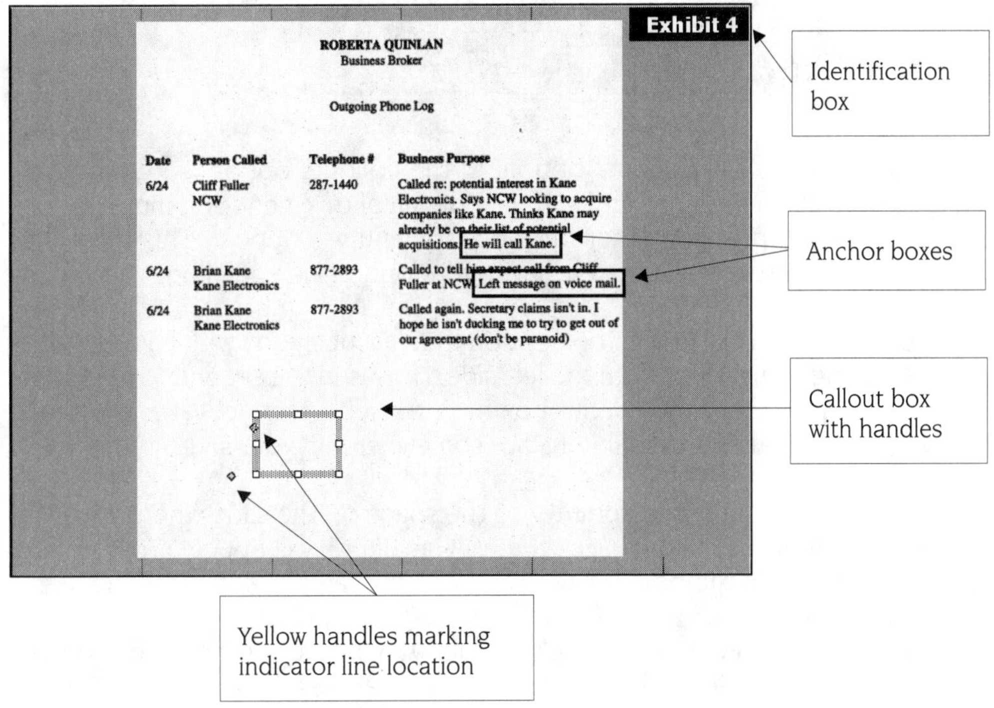

Step 4: Create the callout box.

A. Go to the Formatting Toolbar. Click on the Left Alignment button (7th from the left) so the text in your callout box will be justified on the left margin.

B. Go to the Drawing Toolbar. Click on the arrow next to the AutoShapes button (4th from left). A drop-down menu will appear.

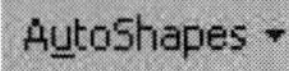

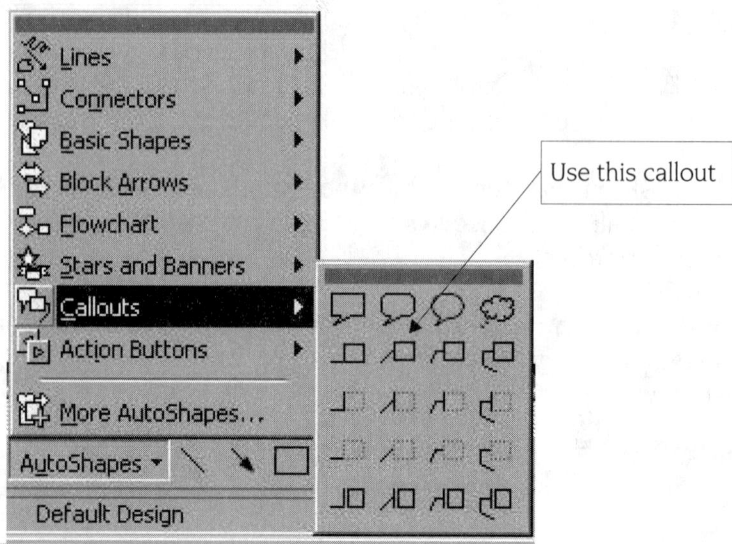

C. Choose the Callouts option. (If the Callouts option is not showing, click on the small arrow at the bottom of this menu and more options will appear.) Another drop-down menu will appear. This menu has five lines of callout styles with four options in each line.

D. Click on the callout box option that is a plain box with a line extending straight out from the left side. (This is in the second row from the top, the second callout box from the left.) This activates the shape and makes it available to put somewhere on your slide.

E. Move your mouse pointer to the space on the slide where you want to put the callout. Click there. A small box will appear. Your pointer will be in the box.

F. In PowerPoint 2000, click on the fuzzy border of the callout box so that you will be able to see the yellow handles marking the location of its indicator line. (Not necessary in PowerPoint 97.)

Step 5: Type the text in the callout box.

Step 6: Choose a font for the text. (Ch. 3, Exercise 3.1.) Consider using a font that is close to the font used in the document so that the text in the callout box looks as if it came from the document.

Step 7: Pick a location for the callout box. Resize it if necessary so that the box looks good in the space. Use the handles in the fuzzy border around the box and the two-arrow mouse pointer. (Ch. 2, Exercise 2.3.)

★ The location of your callout box on the slide, relative to the underlying document, should give the impression of not hiding anything. When you put a callout box over a part of the document that contains text or markings, even if jurors cannot read the document on the screen they may feel uneasy that something is not visible. You can locate the box above or below and to the left or right of the anchor box in the text. One standard approach is to put the document as far to the left on the slide as possible making room for the callouts on the right. If there is empty space at the bottom of the document, as in this example, that may also be a good location for the callout boxes.

Step 8: Connect the indicator line.

A. The callout box has a small line hanging off the left side. This is a separate shape that you can extend. Click on the line to activate it. You will see a handle (small yellow box) at the end of the line.

B. Put your two-arrow mouse pointer on the handle, hold down the left mouse button, and drag the line to the nearest corner of the anchor box in the text of the document. Release the mouse button.

C. The indicator line and its box are connected so that when you move one, the other also moves. Adjust them both to get the callout where you want it.

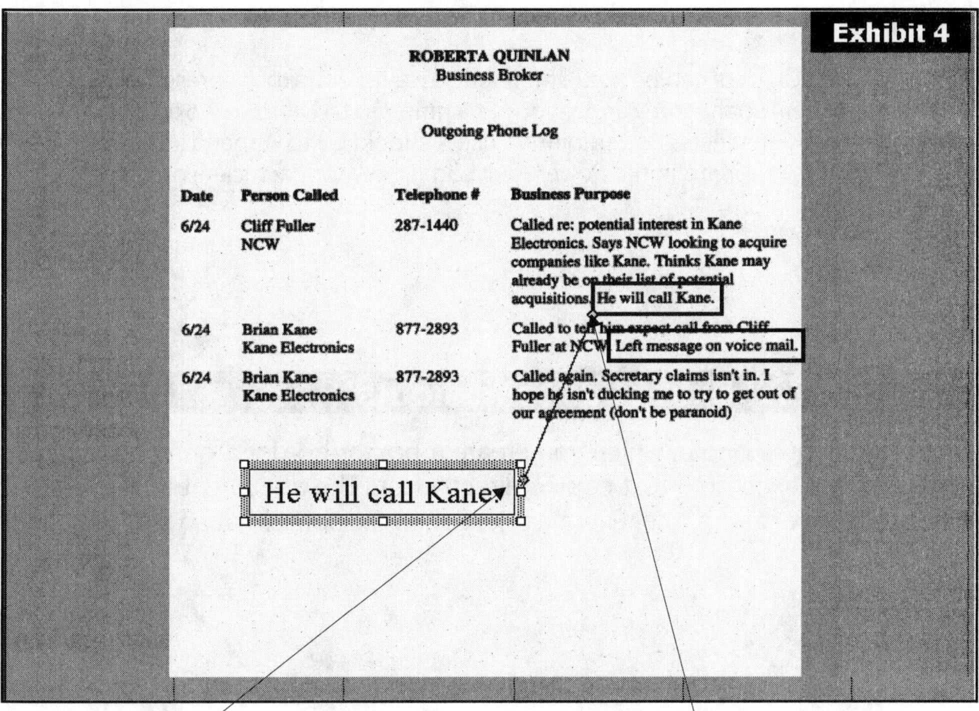

This yellow handle relocates automatically to the proper side of the callout box

Drag this yellow handle on the indicator line to connect with the anchor box

Step 9: Add a second anchor box on the document.

Step 10: Add matching callout. This callout should be placed in a logical relationship, often below, the first callout. Use the horizontal Ruler Bar to line up the two callouts where necessary. (Exercise 7.2, Step 4.) Alternatively, activate both callout boxes, go to the Drawing Toolbar, click on the Align or Distribute option, and line up the boxes that way.

It is easy to make mistakes in this area, so remember the helpful Undo button on the Standard Toolbar (8th from the left). Click on the Undo button to go back one or more steps and start over.

Step 11: Put in the colors.

A. Add slide background color. (Ch. 3, Exercise 3.3, Step 1.)

B. Add callout fill color. (Ch. 3, Exercise 3.3, Step 2.)

C. Add line color where useful. (Ch. 3, Exercise 3.3, Step 3.) The blue color that comes up as the default on the color palette when the Line Color button is used makes a good choice for callout boxes.

Step 12: Save your work.

Re-keyed callouts can be made more effective for courtroom presentation by animating them so that they appear one at a time. Go to Exercise 9.6 for directions on motion and special effects. PowerPoint 97 users should go to Appendix D. Examples of these callouts in color are in the PowerPoint slide show for each case on the CD.

Exercise 7.6: Extract direct callouts

A direct callout is one in which you create a box or border around an enlarged version of the excerpted text copied directly from the document itself. This has the advantage of being "the real thing" just enlarged somewhat so that it is easier to read.

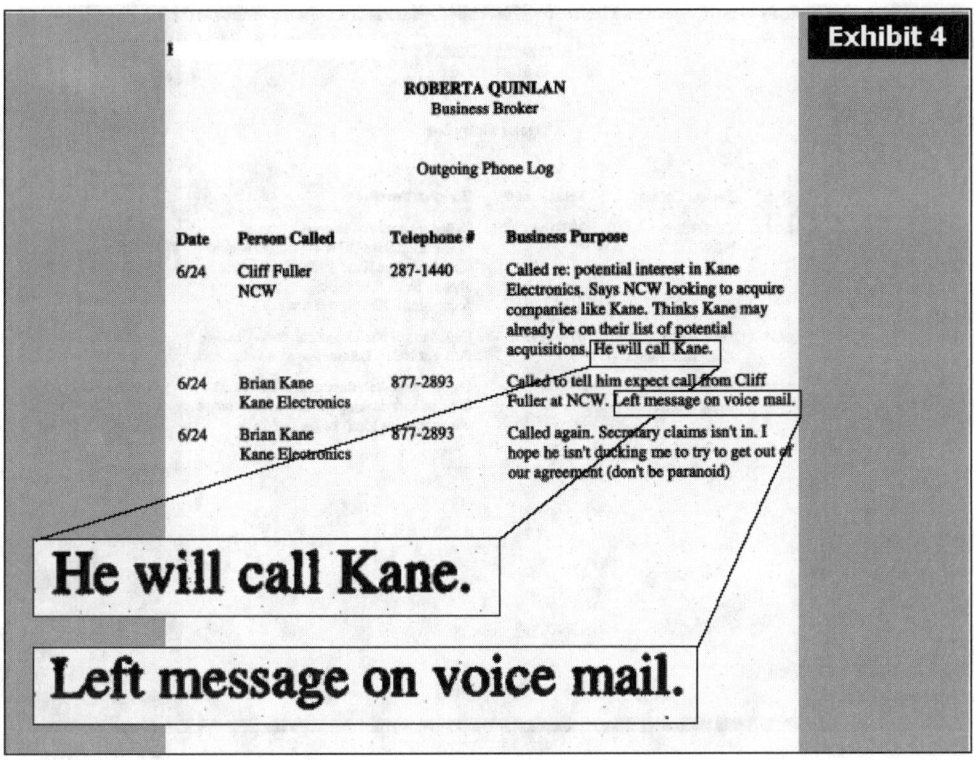

ROBERTA QUINLAN
Business Broker

Outgoing Phone Log

Date	Person Called	Telephone #	Business Purpose
6/24	Cliff Fuller NCW	287-1440	Called re: potential interest in Kane Electronics. Says NCW looking to acquire companies like Kane. Thinks Kane may already be on their list of potential acquisitions. He will call Kane.
6/24	Brian Kane Kane Electronics	877-2893	Called to tell him expect call from Cliff Fuller at NCW. Left message on voice mail.
6/24	Brian Kane Kane Electronics	877-2893	Called again. Secretary claims isn't in. I hope he isn't ducking me to try to get out of our agreement (don't be paranoid)

A direct callout is often more difficult to set up because the shape of the text you are copying dictates the size and usually the position of the box. Sometimes you will need to make the document considerably smaller to have space for the box.

Step 1: Create the slide with the document on it.

A. Create a duplicate of the slide from Exercise 7.5. (Exercise 7.4, Step 1.)

B. Delete the re-keyed callouts and their anchor boxes.

1. Activate the callout by clicking on one of its lines. A shaded box with handles will appear indicating that it is active. (If it does not activate, try to get your mouse pointer at the point where one of the handles normally would be and click again.)

2. Hit the DELETE key on your keyboard.

3. Repeat for the second callout and both anchor boxes.

C. Now you have just the document and the exhibit identification box on the screen. It looks like this:

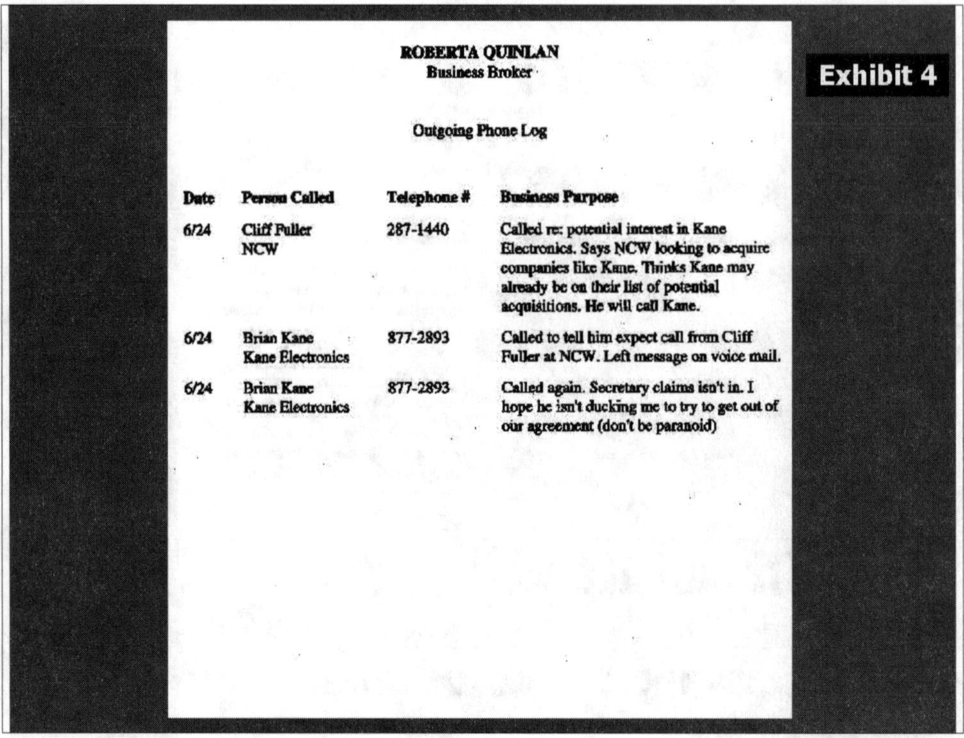
Exhibit 4

ROBERTA QUINLAN
Business Broker

Outgoing Phone Log

Date	Person Called	Telephone #	Business Purpose
6/24	Cliff Fuller NCW	287-1440	Called re: potential interest in Kane Electronics. Says NCW looking to acquire companies like Kane. Thinks Kane may already be on their list of potential acquisitions. He will call Kane.
6/24	Brian Kane Kane Electronics	877-2893	Called to tell him expect call from Cliff Fuller at NCW. Left message on voice mail.
6/24	Brian Kane Kane Electronics	877-2893	Called again. Secretary claims isn't in. I hope he isn't ducking me to try to get out of our agreement (don't be paranoid)

Step 2: Prepare the first callout.

A. Create another duplicate of your slide. (Exercise 7.4, Step 1.) Because the direct callout is a duplicate of what is on the slide, only enlarged, you need to have another slide that you can crop to get there.

B. Crop this duplicate down to the precise area you want to include in the callout.

1. Click anywhere in the document so that the document is active.

2. Go to the Picture Toolbar.

3. Click on the Crop button (7th from the left).

4. Put your mouse pointer over the top middle handle.

5. Hold down the left mouse button and drag the pointer down to the top of the line of the text that you want in the callout. Release the mouse button.

6. Put the mouse pointer over the bottom middle handle.

7. Hold down the left mouse button and drag the margin up to the bottom of that line of text. Release the mouse button.

8. Click anywhere to de-activate the cropping tool.

When you are extracting a phrase from a document, it is easier to crop fairly close to the text you want, but not as close as you ultimately would like to be.

tions. He will call Kane.

De-activate the cropping tool, resize the cropped area to make it larger (Ch. 2, Exercise 2.3), then crop the bigger image again. You can be more accurate this way. You can leave the final cropping until you have the callout in place on your slide.

C. Copy the box that includes the cropped area.

1. Click anywhere within the box to activate it.

2. Go to the Standard Toolbar.

3. Click on the Copy button (6th from the left). This puts the box into the clipboard, from which you can paste to another slide.

D. Go back to the slide you are building by clicking on the Page Up button at the bottom of the vertical Scroll Bar to bring the previous slide to the screen.

E. Paste the box that includes the cropped area onto that slide.

1. Put your mouse pointer on the document. Click on the left mouse button.

2 . Go to the Standard Toolbar.

3. Click on the Paste button (7th from the left). This puts the box on your document.

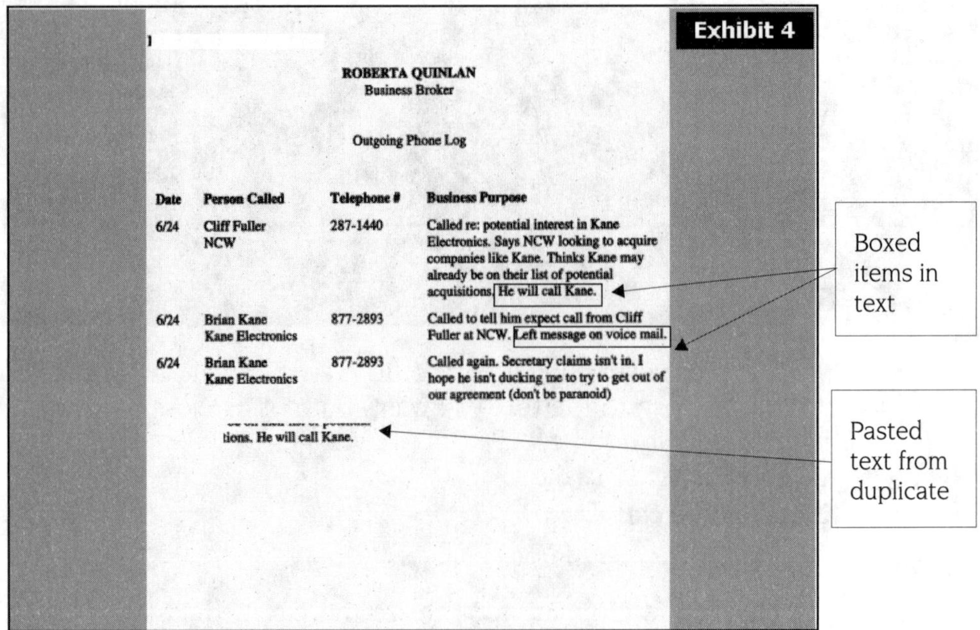

ROBERTA QUINLAN
Business Broker

Outgoing Phone Log

Date	Person Called	Telephone #	Business Purpose
6/24	Cliff Fuller NCW	287-1440	Called re: potential interest in Kane Electronics. Says NCW looking to acquire companies like Kane. Thinks Kane may already be on their list of potential acquisitions. He will call Kane.
6/24	Brian Kane Kane Electronics	877-2893	Called to tell him expect call from Cliff Fuller at NCW. Left message on voice mail.
6/24	Brian Kane Kane Electronics	877-2893	Called again. Secretary claims isn't in. I hope he isn't ducking me to try to get out of our agreement (don't be paranoid)

tions. He will call Kane.

F. Position the callout.

1. You may have to look to find where PowerPoint pasted your cropped words. You should be able to see the handles around the box.

2. Drag this box to a spot on the slide where it will not cover up any text and where it can be read easily.

G. Enlarge the callout and crop further as necessary.

1. Use the two-arrow mouse pointer and the corner handles to enlarge the box containing the cropped words so it stretches across more of the width of your slide. This will enlarge the text. Make sure that the text of the callout is large enough to be easily readable.

2. Use the cropping tool to trim away remaining text from above, below, or either side of the phrase that you want in the callout.

Step 3: Put a border around the callout box.

A. Click inside the callout box and activate it so the fuzzy border with handles is showing.

B. Go to the Drawing Toolbar.

C. Click on the Line Style button (15th from left). A drop-down menu will appear containing nine line sizes.

D. Choose the three-point size. Click on it.

E. Your callout will be surrounded by a black box.

Step 4: Color the border around the callout box.

A. Select (activate) the line by clicking in it.

B. Go to the Drawing Toolbar.

C. Click on the small arrow to the right of the Line Color button (13th from the left). This will take you to the Color Options screen. (Illustration, Ch. 3, Exercise 3.3.)

D. Click on a dark red for the lines around your callout.

E. Your slide will reappear and the lines around the callout will be colored red.

Step 5: Add an anchor box in the text for the callout. The anchor box surrounds the text that appears in enlarged form in the callout box. (Exercise 7.1, Steps 6-11.)

Step 6: Add two indicator lines from the callout box to the anchor box.

A direct callout which has a long narrow shape usually needs two indicator lines to indicate the place in the text from which the callout came. One line goes from the left side of the callout to the left side of the anchor box in the document, and the other line goes from the right side of the callout to the right side of the anchor box in the document.

A. Go to the Drawing Toolbar.

B. Click on the Line button (5th from the left, next to AutoShapes). This activates the line drawing function.

C. Put your mouse pointer on the upper left corner of the callout.

D. Hold down the left mouse button and draw the line from that point to the upper left corner of the place in the text of the document from which the callout came. Release the mouse button.

E. Go to the upper right corner of the callout and do the same thing.

It is easy to make mistakes in this area, so remember the helpful Undo button on the Standard Toolbar (8th from the left). Click on the Undo button to go back one or more steps and start over.

Step 7: Create the second callout by repeating Steps 2-6.

If there are two callouts to be anchored to boxes in the text, and an indicator line for one of the callouts crosses the box in the text for the other callout, you should use the Order function so that it looks like it goes under the box. See explanation in Chapter 12, Exercise 12.2. Bring the box to the forefront over the line.

Lines generally look better on direct callouts than arrows. The effect is cleaner and the arrow head is unnecessary in this design to get the point across. If there are two callouts, and using two indicator lines for each callout would make the slide look too busy, anchor one callout with two lines, and use a single line with the other, as in the example shown at the beginning of this exercise.

Step 8. Save your work.

If a sentence or long phrase you want to call out starts in the middle of one line and runs to a second line, you can white out the text you do not need. To create a rectangle shape to cover the unwanted text, make the fill color white (which blocks out everything underneath it), and stretch it to cover all of the unwanted text. Then proceed with your callout.

These text treatments can be made more effective for courtroom presentation by animating them so that the anchor boxes are drawn around the text they mark, the lines stretch to the callout box, and the callouts appear one at a time. Go to Exercise 9.7 for directions on motion and special effects. PowerPoint 97 users should go to Appendix D. For examples of these callouts in color and with animations, go to the PowerPoint slide show for each case file on the CD.

Chapter 8

Annotated Diagrams

Annotations help jurors understand a graphic display like a diagram, drawing, map, chart, or graph. Annotations can place people, mark routes, and measure distances.

Annotations can be word labels like START ... STOP; BEGIN ... END; RED LIGHT, SKID MARK, IMPACT; W-1 (for a particular witness), W-2, W-3; or a number label like 1, 2, or 3. If you use number labels, you may want to have a list on the display of what the numbers stand for.

This chapter has three exercises.

1. Add annotations to the diagram
2. Use dotted lines to show action
3. Layered annotations

The most important aspect of using annotations with underlying diagrams is to come up with a design that helps but does not overwhelm the diagram. Every annotation must have an important purpose. Not everything on a diagram or map needs a separate label. Some diagrams need a title as well as labels. Others, such as maps and statistical charts benefit from a legend that identifies the source of the information.

Exercise 8.1: Add annotations to the diagram

Pick the places on the diagram on which it is important to focus attention. For example, annotated diagrams can be used effectively in the direct examination of witnesses. As a witness testifies about a particular action or event, you can picture it on the diagram. Each of these places will get an annotation (or label) so that it is easy to direct attention to the precise spot.

The layout of a simple annotated diagram marking a location looks like this:

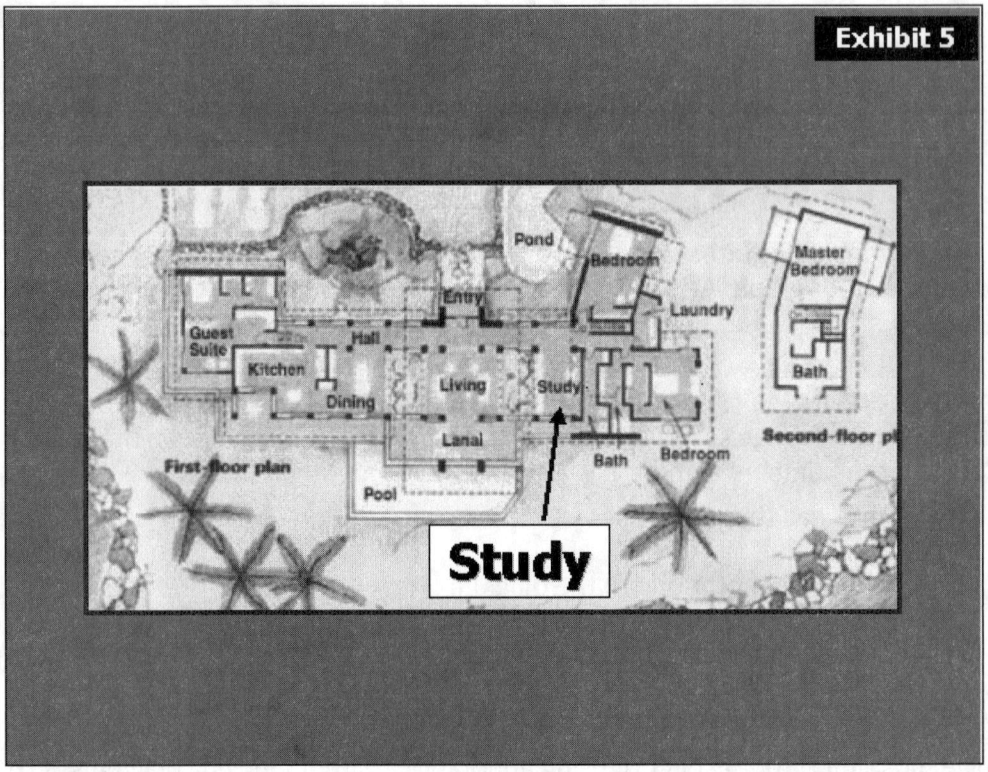

Step 1: Set up the underlying slide.

A. Get a blank slide on the screen. (Standard Toolbar, New Slide button, Blank Slide button.) (Ch. 2, Exercise 2.1.)

B. Color the slide background. (Menu Bar, Format button, Background option.) (Ch. 3, Exercise 3.3.)

Step 2: Get the diagram on the slide.

A. Insert the picture (the diagram image). (Picture Toolbar, Insert Picture button From File option, identify the directory location for the diagram.) (Exercise 5.2.)

B. Resize the diagram to fit the slide. (Ch. 2, Exercise 2.3.)

Step 3: Add one or more shapes to contain the annotations.

A. Go to the Drawing Toolbar.

B. Click on the AutoShapes Menu button. A drop-down menu will appear.

AutoShapes ▾

C. Choose the Basic Shapes option. A second drop-down menu will appear showing the choices of shapes.

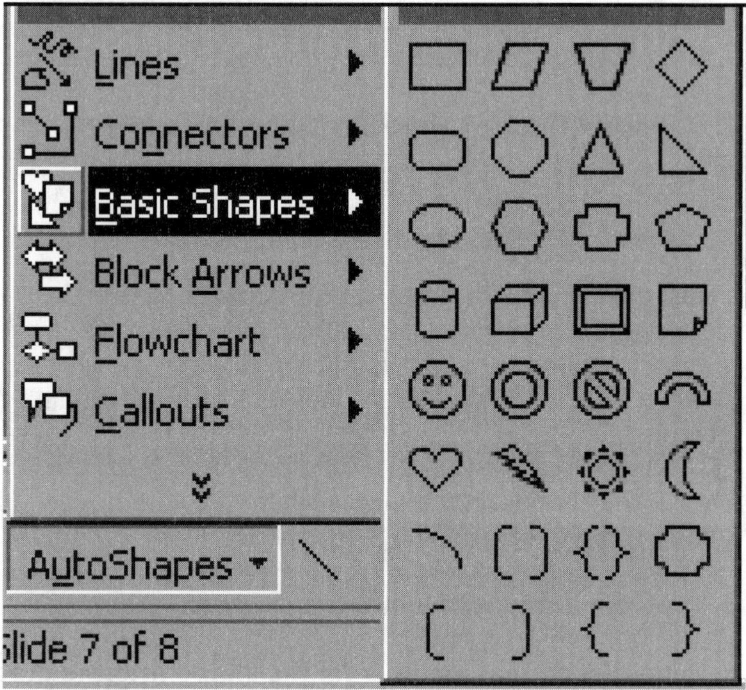

D. Click on one of the shapes. In the example above, the rectangle shape is used. (The rectangle also has a special button on the Drawing Toolbar because it is used frequently.) Your mouse pointer will turn to a cross shape. (Illustration, Ch. 1.)

E. Move your mouse pointer to the place on the diagram where you want to put the shape. The middle of the cross on the mouse pointer will be at the upper left corner handle of the shape when it is placed on the diagram.

F. Click the mouse button to place the shape. The shape will appear with a temporary color in it. Your mouse pointer may be in a two-arrow shape. You need to glide it gently over the shape until it changes to the four-arrow shape.

G. With the four-arrow mouse pointer showing, hold the left mouse button down and drag the shape to the point on the diagram where you want it to be. If you need more precise placement, put the four-arrow mouse pointer over one of the margins of the shape and click the left mouse button. Now the arrow keys on your keyboard will be able to move the shape one space in any direction when you press one of the arrow keys.

H. Enlarge the shape if necessary to contain the words that you plan to put in it. (Ch. 2, Exercise 2.3.)

Step 4: Duplicate the first shape as many times as you need for your diagram.

With the first shape active—

A. Hold down the CTRL key on the keyboard and press the D key. (If you press the D key twice, this will produce two more versions of the shape in the same size.) If you tweaked the shape while it was on the screen, this process will produce exact duplicates including your tweaks.

B. Move the shapes to the places where they are needed for annotations, using the process in Step 3 above.

Step 5: Type the annotations into the shapes.

Step 6: Put a directional arrow from the shape into the diagram.

A. Go to the Drawing Toolbar.

B. Click on the Arrow button (6th from the left).

C. Move your mouse pointer to the approximate place on the diagram where the bottom of the arrow is supposed to be. Hold down the left mouse button and draw the arrow. Let up on the mouse button.

D. Position the arrow. The arrow will have handles on both ends. Move your mouse pointer over a handle until the two-arrow shape appears. Move the arrow into position.

E. Adjust the thickness of the arrow to 3 pt. (Ch. 7, Exercise 7.1, Step 10.)

Step 7: Create an exhibit identification box for your diagram. (Exercise 7.5, Step 2.)

Step 8: Save your work.

★ If you think your opponent's diagram is inaccurate in any respect, you could mark and annotate the inaccuracies. Almost any graphic with enough contrast to be copied legibly can be scanned into digital form and used with PowerPoint. See Chapter 12, Exercise 12.14 on scanning.

Exercise 8.2: Use dotted lines to show action

It is often useful to use a dotted or dashed line between annotations. Sometimes this marks the route that someone walked from point A to point B. Other times this line can be labeled with the distance between two points, or the forces that were exerted on a surface.

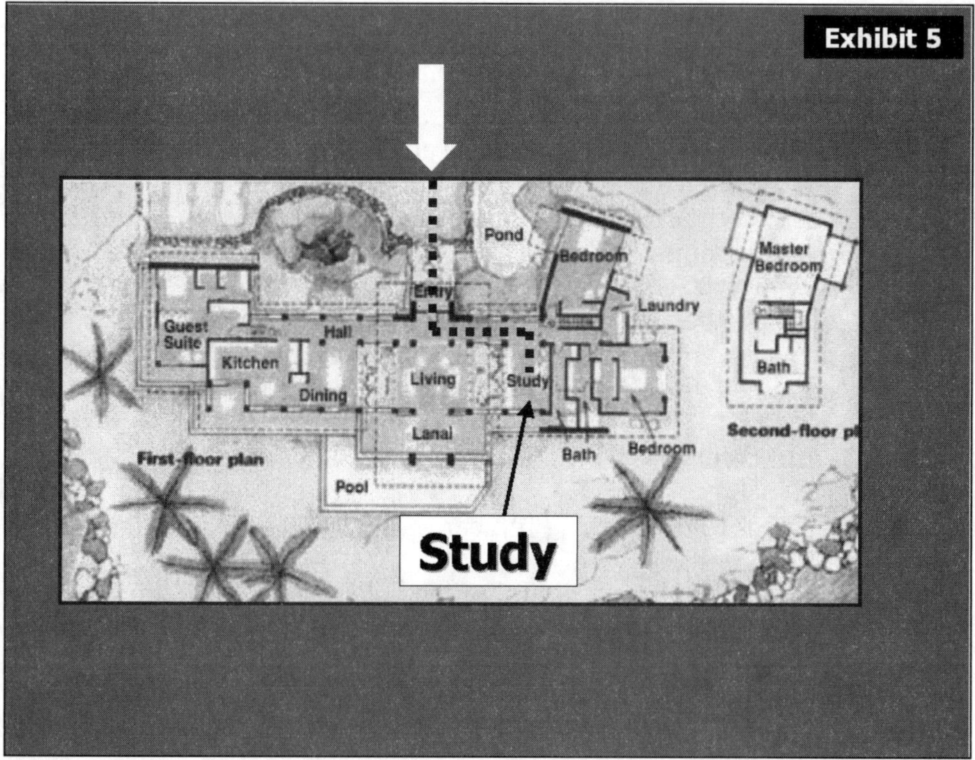

This annotation of the diagram of the house layout from the commercial case shows the path from the entryway directly to the study. It is intended to help emphasize the point that this was a business meeting, as plaintiff claims, rather than a social get-together as defendant claims. This is quite a busy diagram, which includes small black squares marking support structures. To make the dotted line effective, it needs to be emphasized by a different color and the starting point is marked with a white arrow. Go to the CD to see this diagram in color.

Step 1: Add lines between points on the diagram.

A. Go to the Drawing Toolbar.

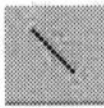

B. Click on the Line button (5th from the left, next to AutoShapes). This activates the line drawing function.

C. Put your mouse pointer on the point on the diagram where the dotted line should start.

D. Hold down the left mouse button and draw the line from that point to where the line either ends or turns in another direction.

❗ The lines drawn on a diagram with the Line button go from one point to another. To turn a corner, you need to end one line and begin another. The AutoShapes button has a freehand line drawing function that will go around corners.

Step 2: Make the solid lines into dotted lines.

A. Go to the Drawing Toolbar. (Make sure that the line you have drawn is active with handles still showing at either end.)

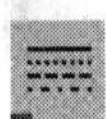

B. Click on the Dash Styles button (16th from the left). A drop-down menu will appear. Choose a dotted line style.

C. Click on the Line Styles button (15th from the left). A drop-down menu will appear. Choose a thick line style. Dashes often need to be fat to be effective.

Step 3: Add color.

A. Go back to the Drawing Toolbar.

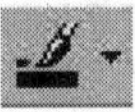

B. Click on the arrow next to the Line Color button (13th from the left). This will take you to the Color Options box. (Illustration, Ch. 3, Exercise 3.3, Step 4.)

C. Click on a color that will give the dotted line a good contrast with its surroundings.

★ If you need to use two lines for different purposes, for example one line indicating the path taken by Person A and another line indicating the path taken by Person B, use different dash styles and colors for the two lines to make the diagram clearer. A legend with each person's name and a short sample of the colored dotted line associated with each is another alternative.

Step 4: Add the directional arrow.

A. Go to the Drawing Toolbar. Click on the AutoShapes button (4th from the left). A drop-down menu will appear. Click on the Block Arrows option. Pick the down arrow.

B. Move your mouse pointer to the place on the diagram where the arrow should appear. Click at that spot. The block arrow will appear with a default green color.

C. Drag the arrow to the correct spot.

D. Color the arrow white. (Drawing Toolbar, Fill Color button.) (Exercise 3.3, Step 2.)

It is sometimes useful to have an arrow to get the viewer oriented to the direction represented by the dotted lines on a diagram. Here, the arrow shows where Kane and Quinlan came in through the door of the house.

Step 5: Save your work.

Both the annotations and the lines connecting them can be animated so that the annotations will be revealed one by one and the lines will "walk" across the diagram from one point to another. These features are discussed in Exercise 9.8, and they are shown on the slides on the CD. PowerPoint 97 users should consult Appendix D.

Exercise 8.3: Layered annotations

Annotations can be layered to achieve a quick transmission of the message. For example, crossing out something emphasizes the point that it did not happen, or did not happen the way the opposing side claims.

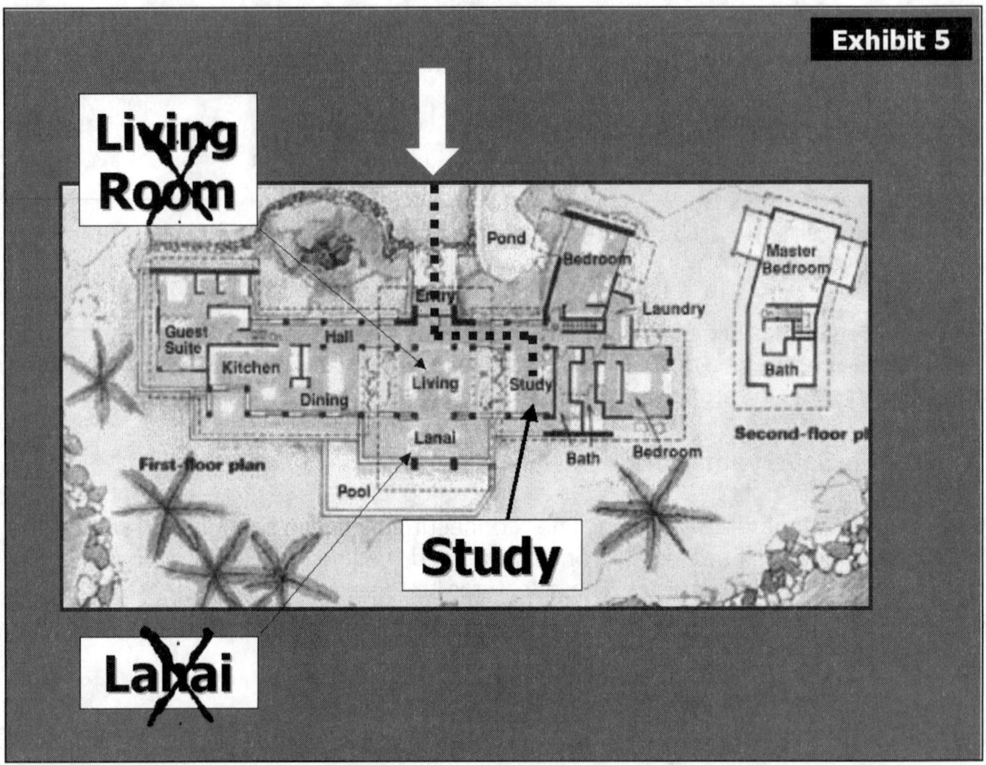

In this annotated diagram, the lawyer plans to make the argument that the location of the meeting between Quinlan and Kane supports Quinlan's position that this was a business meeting. The get-together did not happen in the living room, or out on the lanai, which in the setting of this home would be logical places to entertain social guests. It happened in the study, which is a logical place for a business meeting. The diagram is intended to show that Kane took Quinlan directly there.

To make this slide with layered annotations, do this:

Step 1: Add the labels and arrows pointing out the lanai location and the living room location. (Exercise 8.1.)

Step 2: Create large X marks to put on the labels.

A. Create a text box. (Drawing Toolbar, Text Box button, mouse pointer on approximate place on slide, click left mouse button.)

B. Set the font. (Formatting Toolbar, arrow immediately to the right of the Font box.) In this example, the font name is Chiller. The splashes are a part of the font. (Not found in PowerPoint 97.)

C. Type an X in the box.

D. Color the X red using the Font Color button.

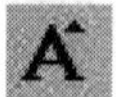

E. Enlarge the X to a size big enough to be effective when put on top of the label. Highlight the X. Go to the Formatting Toolbar, click on the Increase Font Size button as many times as necessary. Each click increases the font size. The current size at each step will be shown in the Font Size box (immediately to the right of the Font box on the Formatting Toolbar.) The text box will expand as the font size increases. In this example, the font size is 117 point.

F. The text box should have no fill color and no border at this point. If it has either one, get rid of them by clicking on the No Fill option at the top of the menu displayed by the Fill Color button or the No Line option at the top of the menu displayed by the Line Color button, both of which are on the Drawing Toolbar.

G. Duplicate the X box (CTRL + D) so that you have one for the second label.

Step 3: Put the X marks on top of the labels.

A. Drag the box containing the X into position over the label.

B. Align the X marks by activating both boxes (click on the first one, hold down the SHIFT key and click on the second one), click on the Draw button, choose the Align Center option.

C. Click anywhere outside the box. The fuzzy border on the text box containing the X will disappear, leaving the X superimposed on the label underneath it.

Step 4: Save your work.

Go to the Appendix for your case to see examples of the layout in layered annotations. Sample slides are on the CD.

Chapter 9

Motion and Special Effects

PowerPoint has built-in tools that help some kinds of slides achieve maximum potential in the courtroom. This chapter deals with individual slides—the motion and special effects that move from one bullet point to the next or one object to the next within one slide. The next chapter deals with groups of slides and the transitions when you move from one slide to the next.

The software allows you to reveal portions of a slide one by one. In this way, with a single slide, you can have four, eight, ten, or even thirty separate displays to show on the screen in the courtroom.

There are eight exercises in this chapter covering motion and special effects for each of the types of displays created in chapters 2 through 8.

1. Bulleted lists
2. Photo exhibits
3. Relationship charts
4. Text documents—box, circle, line
5. Text documents—split screen
6. Text documents—re-keyed callouts
7. Text documents—direct callouts
8. Annotated diagrams

Each exercise includes suggestions for effective ways to animate these types of slides.

★ Motion and special effects control the order in which you let the jury see things. This may create an impression with the jury about the relative importance of one thing versus another, and it has an effect on your pacing. Both are very important to the overall presentation of your case, so you may want to try out several plans for animation to see which works best and practice coordinating your oral presentation with the timing of the appearance of things on your slides.

In applying the guidance in this chapter on motion and special effects, distinguish between your direct case (opening, direct examination of your witnesses) and your attacks on your opponent's case (cross-examination, some parts of closing argument). What is inappropriate for your direct case because of the negative imagery conveyed may work perfectly well for your attack on your opponent's case.

The full motion versions of each of the slides described in this chapter, and comparable examples for the tort and criminal cases, are on the CD that accompanies this book or can be downloaded from NITA's web site, *www.nitastudent.org*. By examining these models, which incorporate the special effects described in the text, you can see how animation changes the slide and its impact.

Useful Terminology

The special terminology involved in using PowerPoint's motion and special effects that facilitates the description of these functions is set out here. This applies to the entire chapter.

Animation: The word *animation* is used in this context to describe the directions to the software with respect to an object that will appear separately, after the slide is displayed. This is quite different from the more common use of the word animation in connection with cartoons. In the PowerPoint context, it just means making some movement on the slide. For example, if you had a slide with a photo and a caption, and you want the photo to appear when the slide first comes up, but the caption to appear later (perhaps after the witness identifies the photo), then you would designate animation (motion—the later appearance) for the caption but not the photo. PowerPoint has two kinds of animation: preset and custom. The preset animation features do not work well in a courtroom setting, so you will need to build your own animations with the custom animation capability.

Object: A defined area on a slide. Types of objects include the boxes that contain text, photographs, clip art, and drawings as well as the lines and shapes available on the Drawing Toolbar. An object can be activated and de-activated. It has handles for resizing and moving it from one place to another on the slide.

Naming of objects: All of the special effects discussed in this chapter work on individual objects on your slide. To keep things simple, PowerPoint automatically names each object and you use these names to tell the software what you want. The software uses "Text" for text boxes, like bullet charts, relationship charts, and re-keyed callouts. The software uses "Picture frame" for images, like photos, documents, and diagrams imported into a "frame" within your slide. Lines, rectangles, and ovals are called, logically enough, "Lines," "Rectangles," and "Ovals." If you grouped anything (Exercise 9.4, Step 3), the software uses "Group" to refer to all of the elements grouped together.

Numbering of objects: To differentiate between several objects with the same name, the software assigns a number to each object indicating the order in which the object was created when you were building the slide. Thus, if you put a document on the slide first, that object will be called "Picture frame 1." If you put two text boxes on the slide right after you finished with the document, they will be called "Text 2" and "Text 3" indicating that they are text boxes that are the second and third objects you created.

Grouping of objects: Defining a number of separate objects on a slide (such as two lines and a text box) as a "group" so that the software will work with them all at once when it animates or moves them. This is useful, for example, when you want the two indicator lines to a direct callout to move toward the box simultaneously or when you want a label and its pointer arrow to appear on the slide simultaneously.

Entry: When you animate an object, it will appear on the screen at a defined point in your presentation. This is its *entry*. For example, if you have four bullet points on a list, you might have each one come up separately as you talk about these points. The entry for bullet point #1 is first, the entry for bullet point #2 is second, and so on. PowerPoint has a number of special effects that you can use for the entry of a bullet point, a photo, a title, or any other object. They can be revealed slowly from the top down, they can move across the screen from left to right, or they can appear in dozens of other ways.

Entry effect: The way that an object makes its entry is known as its *entry effect*, which means the special effect operational at the time the object makes its appearance to make it move or place itself on the screen in a particular way. Each type of courtroom display has one or more types of special effects that work well under most circumstances, and many that are only rarely useful in a courtroom setting. This chapter concentrates on those generally applicable effects that are effective for courtroom use.

Effects icon: When you designate any special effect or motion for any object on a slide, the software puts a small icon below the slide indicating that some kind of special effect is included in this slide. You can see these icons when you are in the Slide Sorter view. They look like this:

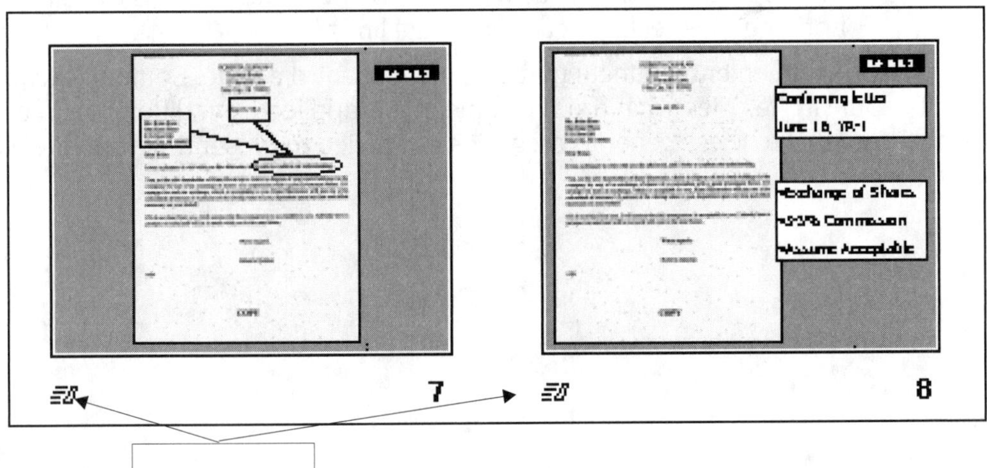

Useful General Rules

WHEN TO ANIMATE: The most important consideration is when to use animation for a slide or group of slides. Not every slide benefits from animation. Too much animation makes a presentation seem jumpy or jerky to the viewer.

	Always	**Usually**	**Occasionally**
Bulleted lists		X	
Relationship charts	X		
Labeled photos			X
Text treatments		X	
Annotated diagrams		X	
Statistical charts			X
Time lines		X	

Even in categories for which animation is usually applied, there will be instances in which you should elect to display a plain slide with no animation. Always articulate a specific reason why the animation you chose will make the advocacy point.

WHAT TO USE: Three basic types of motion are safe for most litigation uses.

> **In place:** These effects do not make the object appear to come from anywhere or go anywhere. They are the safest types of effects for litigation use.
>
> **Down motion**: Motion that moves the viewer's eye down the page feels natural because that is the way English speakers read a page.
>
> **Left to right motion**: Motion that moves from left to right on a page, when associated with text, is easy to follow because that is the direction English speakers read individual lines.

There are seventeen entry effects that can be applied to a slide. Some of these effects come in "families" that are the same effect applied from different directions. They fall into these general categories as applied to presenting your direct case.

Effects for Opening and Direct Case

Generally Okay	Sometimes Okay	Generally Not Okay
Appear	Blinds, horizontal/vertical	Checkerboard, across/down
Box, in/out	Crawl, bottom/left/right/top	Dissolve
Wipe, down/right	Split, all varities	Flash, fast/medium/slow
Zoom, in/in slightly	Stretch	Fly, all varities
	Strips, right-down	Peek, top/bottom/left/right
	Wipe, up/left	Random bars
	Zoom, out slightly	Spiral
		Strips, left-up/rt-up/left-down
		Swivel
		Zoom, out/screen ctr (both)

The effects in the "generally okay" category are those with which the fewest mistakes are likely to be made. The "No effect" choice is always okay. By the time you get to the step of choosing an effect, you already will have made the object appear separately on the slide. That may be emphasis enough. The other three effects in this category are not strong or overstated effects that are likely to detract from the persuasiveness of the substantive material on the slide. They have a focusing effect that is easy on the eye.

The effects in the "sometimes okay" category make a stronger appearance and, although suitable for some kinds of slides, can be counter-productive with others. These effects can contribute to making specific points, but need a stronger justification before they are added to a slide.

The effects in the "generally not okay" category all have strong negatives when applied to making points in an opening statement or direct examination of witnesses. These negatives almost always outweigh the positives. The justification should be particularly strong for using any of these instead of one of the choices in the first two categories.

There are, of course, exceptions to each category. Some things listed in the Generally Okay group might be inappropriate under special circumstances. Others listed in the Generally Not Okay group might work well in a particular instance because of a specific effect you are hoping to create in the viewer's mind. In addition, this categorization for purposes of your direct case has considerably more flexibility when it comes to taking apart your opponent's graphics. Dissolve, Flash, and Spiral, all of which are in the "generally not okay" category can do effective things to undermine a point being made by the opposing side. Their best image can be made to crumble with Dissolve, disappear with Flash, rotate suggestively with Swivel, or appear to fly from left field by using one of the Fly options.

The illustrations in this chapter use animations that are suitable for general purposes. They are not the only choices that might be used. Sometimes several alternatives could work equally well. The principal rule is to be conservative and to use effects only for a purpose you can articulate.

Special Effects Reference Guide

Blinds: The blinds family has two members: vertical blinds and horizontal blinds. Both mimic the action of Venetian blinds on windows and doors in which the angle of the individual slats can be changed to let in more or less light. The vertical blinds open gradually to reveal the text or object underneath as if vertical Venetian blinds were being turned from full shut (in which none of the text is visible) to full open in which all of it is visible. The horizontal blinds do the same thing stretching from left to right across the screen. Either horizontal or vertical blinds are okay.

Box: The box family also has two members: box in and box out. The box in option reveals things on the slide from a square or rectangle in which the material on the outside appears first and gradually the material toward the center of the square or rectangle follows to fill in the whole picture. The box out option works just the opposite. The material at the center of the rectangle appears first building outward to the edges.

Checkerboard: The checkerboard family is a variant of blinds. Instead of a pattern of vertical or horizontal lines stretching all the way across the slide when revealing text or objects, this is a series of little squares. There are two options: checkerboard across, in which the little squares appear in a horizontal pattern, and checkerboard down, in which the little squares appear in a vertical pattern. Neither one works for courtroom presentations. It looks like the image is made up of crumbly pieces that could fall apart at any moment.

Crawl: This is a slower version of the fly family (see below). It comes in four variations: bottom, left, right, and top. Crawl is not a good choice for litigation purposes unless you are trying to emphasize how slowly the other party acted, to your client's detriment.

Dissolve: This is a worse variation of checkerboard. The pieces that assemble themselves to form the letters and objects on the screen are much smaller, so the image is even more distracting. This connotation is not useful when you are trying to convey solid, dependable points. It is sometimes applied effectively to give an unstable feeling to your opponent's points when you are commenting on them in your presentation. It makes a point seem to be drawn out of thin air. Photographs brought up on a dissolve are particularly slow to display.

Flash once: This family has three members: fast, medium, and slow. This option brings the text or object to the screen, holds it there for a time, and then makes it disappear. The second piece of text or object then appears, stays for a time, and disappears. This is almost never useful for presenting your own case, but can be used to comment on your opponent's exhibits. Points about disappearing arguments and evidence can be made quite graphic in this way.

Fly: The fly family brings words and objects onto the screen by moving ("flying") them from offstage to onstage in eight ways. Your choices are: bottom (material enters at the bottom of the slide and moves vertically to its assigned position), left (material appears at the center of the left margin and moves horizontally to its assigned position), right, top, bottom-left, bottom-right, top-left, and top-right. Fly is usually not a good choice in the courtroom context. It raises the question "Where did this come from?" because the object or words are flying in from off the screen. With groups of words, such as bulleted lists, the "fly" animation can be very distracting and hard on the eyes when viewed on a large screen.

Peek: The peek feature is a close relative of the fly feature. Fly appears from off screen and comes all the way across the screen to its intended spot. Peek appears from a slot on the screen and comes the rest of the way across the screen to its intended spot. There are four varieties of peek: top, bottom, left, and right. Peeks are usually no more useful than flys.

Random Bars: Random bars are like the blinds. There are two types: vertical and horizontal. Where the blinds reveal the underlying material in an orderly progression from top to bottom or left to right, the random bars reveal it from bottom to top, then from the middle to the ends, then from top to bottom, and so on in random order. These have somewhat less utility than blinds.

Random Effects: This option, located at the very bottom of the menu, is for the person who cannot make up his or her mind. This displays items on the slide with random choices from all the effects. It is not useful for litigation purposes.

Spiral: This is another close relative of the fly feature. Fly appears from off screen and moves in a straight line to its intended spot. Spiral appears from off screen and loops around the screen in a right-to-left spiral before landing at the intended spot. This will be useful in your next case about tornadoes, but is otherwise of limited utility in presenting a direct case. Some lawyers like it for commentary on particular points of an opponent's case. The analogy to flushing down the drain is obvious.

Split: The split is another variation of blinds that operates somewhat like the box feature. There are four types: horizontal in, horizontal out, vertical in, and vertical out. With the splits, the material is revealed starting at the center (for the "in" variations) or the edges (for the "out" variations). Split horizontals work well on bulleted lists, and split verticals may be useful for short points on a list.

Stretch: The stretch family has five members: across, from top, from bottom, from right, and from left. This effect presents material on the screen by beginning at a point and moving (or "stretching") the text or object out of that point until it reaches its full size. This can be used for presenting the lines on diagrams or charts. Wipe is often a better choice because it is smoother and works better under all conditions and angles. The Stretch can be effective for callouts where a line and text box have been grouped.

Strips: The strips feature reveals text by moving along lines (or "strips") until the whole item is on the screen. There are four of them: right-down, right-up, left-down, and left-up. The right-down strips work well because this is the direction in which English speakers read. This effect is effective with photos and documents. With simple text lines, it looks pretty much like a Wipe Right. The "up" strips and the left-down strips go counter to the way people read and sometimes look like effects that were added for a purpose other than to help the viewer understand the material.

Swivel: The swivel effect starts at the middle of the text or the object, moves out to either side to reveal the entire item, then swings it around and displays it again, then swings it around and displays it a third time, when it comes to rest. It would be a rare slide that could use this effectively in a litigation context.

Wipe: There are four variations of wipe: down, left, right, and up. The wipe effect looks like a blank sheet is covering the material underneath and it is gradually being pulled away to reveal the text or object. With a wipe down effect, it looks like the sheet is being pulled from the top to the bottom, gradually revealing the material on the slide. Wipe right goes from left to right, the way most people read. They work particularly well on text boxes and relationship charts. Wipe left and wipe up are useful for lines that need to proceed in those directions, but are counter to the way most people read, and therefore are not as useful for text slides.

Zoom: The zoom starts at a point and enlarges the text or object so that it looks like it is emerging from the point and being magnified at the same time. There are six variations: in, in slightly, in from screen center, out, out slightly, and out from screen bottom. With zoom in, the point is positioned in the center of the area where the text or object ultimately will be located. With zoom in slightly, the item appears in place in reduced size and is expanded somewhat to full size. With zoom in from screen center, the point is positioned in the center of the screen and the text or object, as it is enlarged, moves to its proper place. The zoom outs all start large and reduce to the proper size and location. The zoom in slightly and zoom out slightly work well. For example, zoom out slightly grabs attention for boxes and ovals and places the eye directly where you want people to look. The zoom outs and zoom from screen center do not usually work well in a courtroom context. The Zoom animation effects can appear jerky depending on the age and speed of your computer.

97 PowerPoint 97 uses animation screen displays that are different from PowerPoint 2000. Although the basic functions are the same, PowerPoint 2000 has enhancements as well as different displays. For this reason, the explanation with respect to PowerPoint 97 is in Appendix D. PowerPoint 97 users should now turn to Appendix D.

Exercise 9.1: Bulleted lists

The most useful special effect for bulleted lists is some kind of motion that brings the bullet points to the screen one after another so that the viewer is concentrating on the same point that the speaker is making instead of reading ahead. You can also dim previous points so that the current point is highlighted on the screen to command attention while the preceding points are less commanding yet still visible.

Step 1: Display bullet points one at a time.

With the full slide on the screen—

A. Click on the text in the box containing the bullet points to activate it.

B. Click the right mouse button. A drop-down menu will appear. It looks like this:

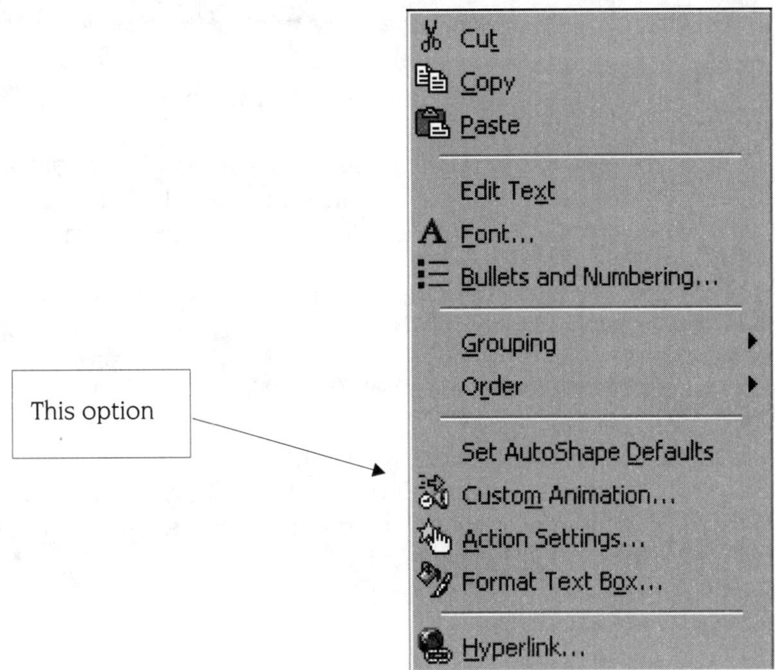

C. Click on the Custom Animation option. The Custom Animation screen appears. The screen looks like this:

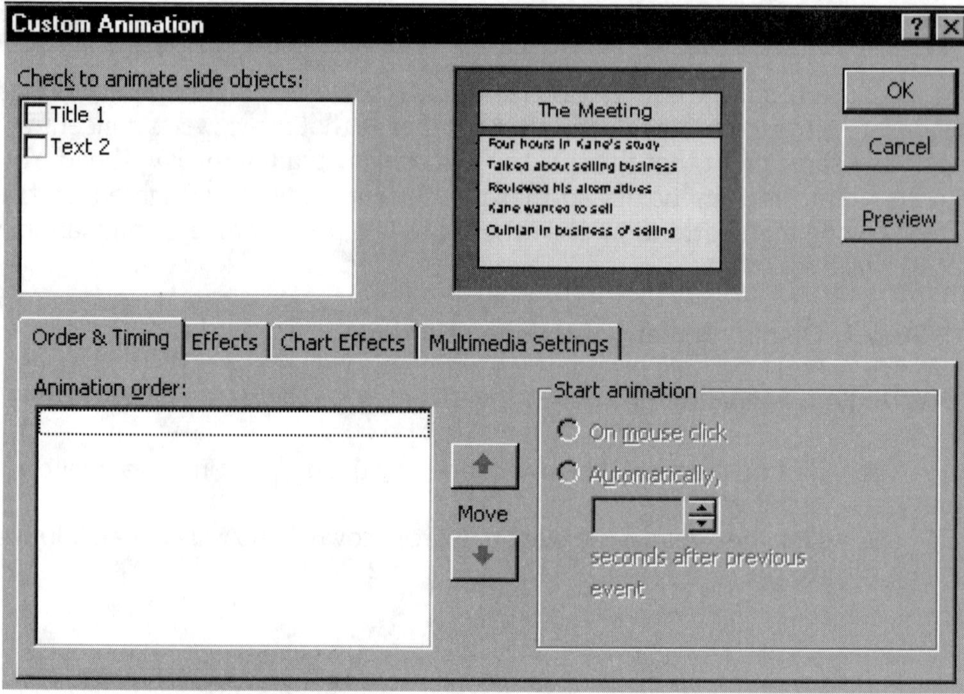

A thumbnail of your slide appears in the top middle of the screen.

The two objects or boxes on your slide—one for the title and one for the bullet points—are listed in the white area at the top left of the screen. They will be listed in the order you created them.

! If you click on one of the items listed in the top left hand box, without checking the box next to it, the item will be highlighted in blue and it will also be identified in the thumbnail to the right. This helps identify items for ordering animations when you have a long list of items and are not sure which is which.

D. Click on the Effects Tab. (There are four tabs across the middle of the screen—Timing, Effects, Chart Effects, and Multimedia Settings.) When you click on the tab it will come to the foreground.

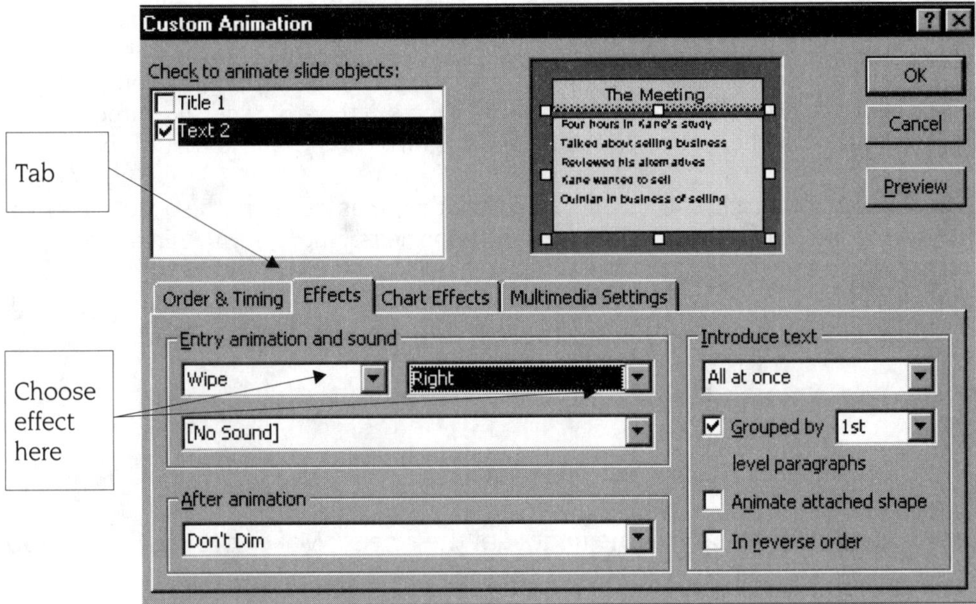

E. Click on the small box to the left of the label "Text 2." A checkmark will appear. In the preview box, handles will appear around the box containing the bullet points. This selection tells the software that the special effect you are about to designate belongs to this object.

F. Go to the Entry Animation and Sound area at the left side of the Effects box. The name in the top box indicates the animation effect that is currently active. The box may say "No Effect." The name in the second box indicates the sound effect that is currently active. That box may say "No Sound."

G. Click on the arrow next to the box to display the options.

H. Scroll down and click on the Wipe option.

I. Then, in the direction box immediately to the right, scroll down and click on the Right option.

J. Click on the Preview button in the upper right area of the screen to see if you like the animation. It will run on the small thumbnail of your slide that appears in the adjacent box.

K. Go back and make changes if the animation is not what you wanted. Keep testing until it looks right.

L. Click on the OK button in the upper right corner.

Animate any bulleted list where you do not want the viewer reading ahead of your oral presentation. If you want the viewer to see everything on the bullet chart at once, then pass up animations. Normally, animating the bullet list is sufficient, and you should allow the title to appear with no special effects. If there is a specific purpose to be achieved, add only the motion to the title that is directly relevant to that purpose.

To add motion and special effects to the title box as well as to the bullets, click on the item labeled Title 1 in the box in the upper left of the Custom Animation screen and follow the same steps as above.

Step 2: Dim prior points so the current point is highlighted.

With the full slide on the screen—

A. Go back to the Custom Animation screen. (Step 1, A, B, C above.)

B. Go to the tabs in the middle of the screen. Make sure the Effects Tab is still active. If not, click on it.

C. Go to the check boxes in the upper left part of the screen. The item called Text 2 should be checked and highlighted in blue.

D. Go to the After Animation box in the bottom left corner. It probably displays the option Don't Dim.

E. Click on the small arrow to the right of the box. A drop-down menu will appear. It looks like this:

F. Click on a gray color if one is displayed; otherwise go to More Colors and find one. The option box will now display the gray color you selected. The gray color will dim the text of a preceding bullet point (turning the letters from black to gray) when the next bullet point is selected.

G. Click on the Preview button in the upper right area of the Custom Animation screen to see if the dimming works well.

H. Click on the OK button.

If you choose gray, keep it a medium to dark gray because a very light gray will nearly disappear from the screen. If you choose a color other than gray for your special effect, the text of the previous bullet point will change to this color when you move to the next bullet point.

★ If you choose the Hide After Animation option, your text will appear on the screen and then immediately disappear. This is never useful because the time interval is very short.

★ If you choose the Hide On Next Mouse Click option, the bullet point text will appear on the screen and stay there until you choose the next bullet item by clicking your mouse. (Chapter 10, Running Your Slide Show.) Then it will disappear. This is almost never useful for your direct case because jurors worry about things that disappear from the screen. They do not trust their ability to remember and wonder why you are taking away things they are supposed to retain.

★ It is sometimes quite effective in dealing with your opponent's best points to create a new slide containing those points, or copy one of your opponent's bullet point slides, and add the Hide On Next Mouse Click option. After you finish explaining why that point is wrong, it will disappear from the screen and the next point will come up. You can demolish the points one by one and end up with a blank screen summarizing the effect of your opponent's main arguments. This is much the same as the practice of making such a list on a blackboard and erasing the points one by one.

Step 3: Bring up bullet points one letter or one word at a time.

With the Custom Animation screen in front of you (Step 1, A, B, C above) and the Effects tab active—

A. Go to the Introduce Text box at the bottom right part of the screen. The white box should display the All At Once option.

B. Click on the small arrow to the right of the box. A drop-down menu will appear displaying two more options—the By Word option, and the By Letter option.

C. Click on the By Letter option. If you want the material to appear word-by-word instead of letter-by-letter, when you go to the Introduce Text box, pick the By Word option.

D. Preview this to see if it works by clicking on the Preview button at the top right of the Custom Animation screen.

E. Click on the OK button.

★ Emphasizing bullet points by spelling them out one letter at a time can be an effective way of introducing short key quotes to your audience. For example, a bulleted list of critical phrases in a contract might benefit from this treatment because it reminds jurors that your opponent wrote this language. When you choose this effect, it will apply to the whole slide. This effect should be used sparingly because jurors get impatient waiting for the letters to spell out.

Step 4: Add a typing sound to the material introduced letter by letter.

With the Custom Animation screen in front of you (Step 1, A, B, C above) and the Effects tab active—

A. Go to the Entry animation and sound area in the lower left of the screen. There are two white boxes in this area. The first is for effects and the second is for sound. The Sound box should display the message "No sound."

B. Click on the small arrow to the right of the Sound box. A drop-down menu will appear.

C. Scroll down to the Typewriter option, listed in alphabetical order, and click on it.

D. Click on the OK button.

It is not often that a lawyer can get away with any of the sound effects that the software makes available—camera clicks, drive by, several variations of whoosh, and typewriter clicks—or that are available on CDs that augment the software. However, when you elect to spell something out letter by letter, emphasizing the fact that someone sat down and wrote this prose while thinking about it, you can sometimes use the typewriter click, which is sort of fun.

Using any kind of sound in a courtroom immediately raises the problem of producing sound that everyone can hear. The sound on most laptops with their very inexpensive speakers is usually not sufficient for juries. In a relatively quiet courtroom with the laptop volume turned all the way up, the jury may be able to hear the sound. For anything important you will need sound amplification. It is easy to hook up a laptop to a set of computer speakers.

Step 5: Preview all the animations for your slide using the full slide view.

A. Go to the View Bar.

B. Click on the Slide Show button (5th button from the left). The slide title should appear with a blank space below where the bullet points will go.

C. Click once with the left mouse button. The first bullet point should appear.

D. Click again. Each time you click, another bullet point will appear displaying the entry effect and sound effect that you chose.

E. To end the slide show at any time, click the right mouse button. A drop-down menu will appear. Click on the End Show option.

Step 6: Save your work.

A. Go to the Standard Toolbar.

B. Click on the Save button.

! The default action for animations in PowerPoint is to have the animations appear one by one on individual mouse clicks. This default is indicated on the Order & Timing tab, at the right under the heading Start Animation. The other option is to have objects appear automatically. This is often used for kiosk displays and for sales presentations, but is not an option for litigation uses.

Exercise 9.2: Photo exhibits

When you use a labeled photograph slide, you may want to consider having the photo appear with the slide and then adding the title. Alternatively, you can bring the title up first, then add the photograph. If you want to add basic animation to your photograph slide, do this:

Step 1: Designate the photo to be displayed without animation.

With the full slide on the screen—

A. Go to the Menu Bar.

B. Click on the Slide Show button. A drop-down menu will appear.

C. Click on the Custom Animation option. The Custom Animation screen will appear.

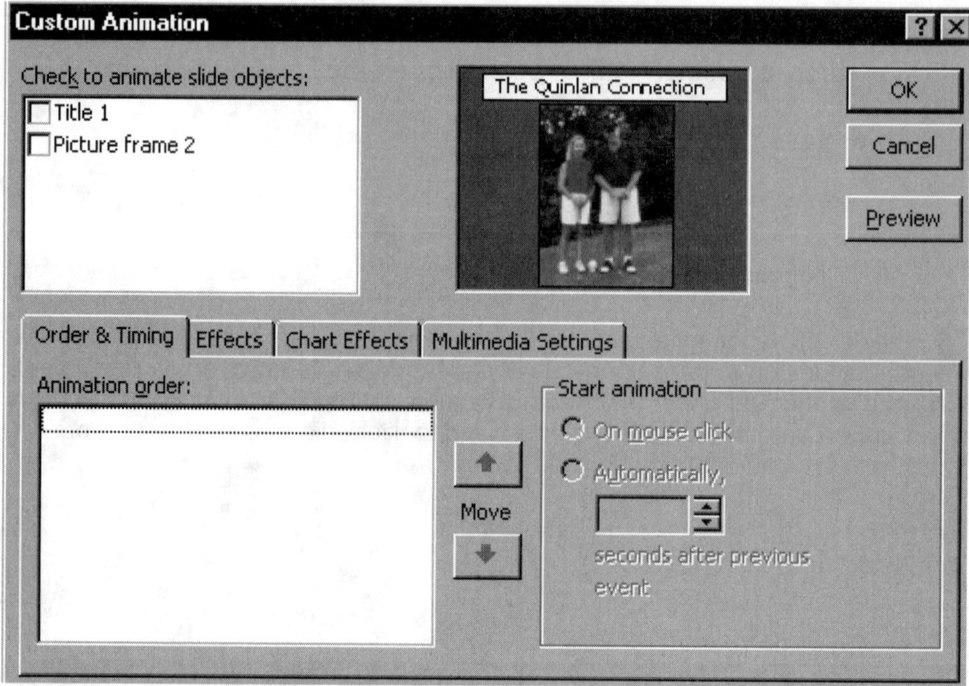

The two objects on this slide—the title box (called Title 1) and the photo (called Picture frame 2)—are listed in the white box in the upper left. Your slide appears in the preview box in the upper middle part of the screen.

! If you click on the name of an item (and not in the check box), it will be highlighted in blue, and it will also be identified in the thumbnail to the right. This helps identify items for ordering of animations when you have many objects listed and are not sure which is which.

D. Leave the photo (Picture frame 2) unchecked. This means that it will not be animated. If it has no animation, it will appear with the slide when the slide is called up.

Step 2: Designate the title for animation.

While still on the Custom Animation screen—

A. Click on the small box in front of the label "Title 1" in the box at the upper left of the screen. A check mark will appear, and the title will be listed below in the Animation order box.

★ In addition to animating the title, occasionally it makes sense to introduce the photo with animation as well. To do this, designate the photo (Picture frame 2) by checking it. The most useful animation for a photo is to reveal the photo gradually rather than presenting it all at once. Use the Wipe Down, Strips Right Down, or similar effects.

Step 3: Choose the special effect for the title.

While still on the Custom Animation screen—

A. Click on the Effects tab in the middle of the screen. A new box will appear at the bottom of the screen. It looks like this:

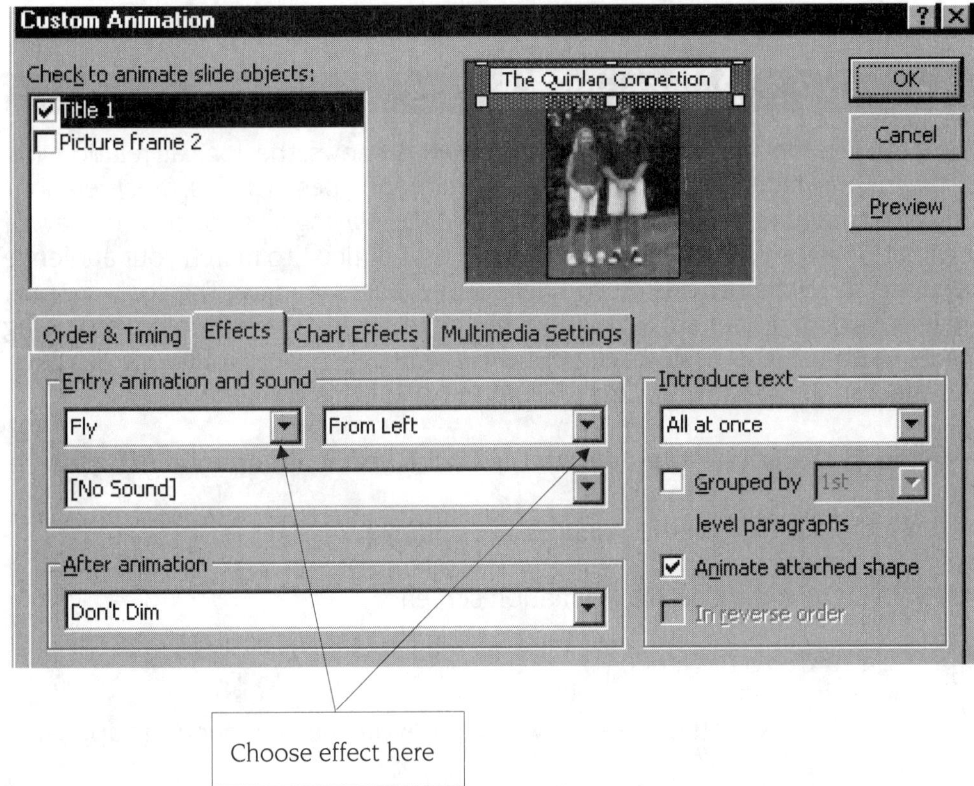

When you switch to the Effects tab with one of the objects highlighted, the Entry animation box normally shows the "Fly From Left" effect as the default.

B. Click on the arrow to the right of the name of the effect to see the list of options. Choose Zoom. Then go to the direction box immediately to the right. Click on the arrow to see the list of directions. Choose In Slightly.

Step 4: Preview your work to be sure it operates properly. Click on the Preview button in the upper right part of the Custom Animation screen.

Step 5: Click on the OK button if the Preview looks all right. This stores your work but does not save it.

Step 6: Save your work.

 None of these effects is necessary for labeled photographs. These slides work perfectly well in their un-animated state.

Exercise 9.3: Relationship charts

The first relationship chart built in Chapter 6 shows the logical relationship between three facts and a conclusion. Unlike other types of slides, most relationship charts require animation to be effective. Displaying all at once your view of the relationships you want to point out makes it difficult to march your audience persuasively to the conclusion you believe the facts mandate. The software provides ways to hide parts of a relationship chart while different points are being made, or to use the basic background elements for several different displays. Use the Zap-Zap-I-Win chart from Exercise 6.1 for this animation.

Step 1: Designate the objects for which you want special effects.

With the full slide on the screen—

A. Open the Custom Animation screen.

1. Go to the Menu Bar.

2. Click on the Slide Show button. A drop-down menu will appear.

3. Click on the Custom Animation option. The Custom Animation screen will appear.

! There are two ways to get to the Custom Animation screen. One is to use the Menu Bar, as above. The other is to right click on an object on the slide and pick Custom Animation from the menu that appears.

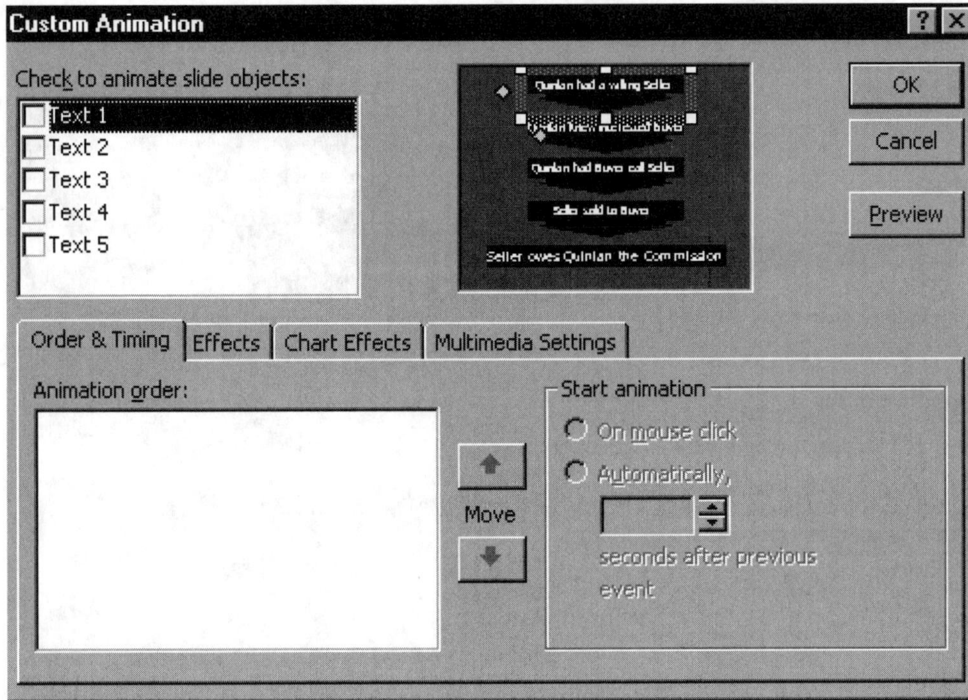

A thumbnail of the relationship chart is in the box at the top middle of the screen. All of the objects on the relationship chart should be listed in the box at the upper left. There are four block arrows and a rectangle on the slide. The software calls them all text boxes and labels them Text 1, Text 2, Text 3, Text 4, and Text 5.

B. Click on the Order & Timing tab if it is not already active.

C. Click on the box in front of the names of all five objects in the box at the upper left in order to add a special effect to each of them. A check mark will appear in each box. The names will also be listed in the Animation Order box in the lower left. The screen now looks like this:

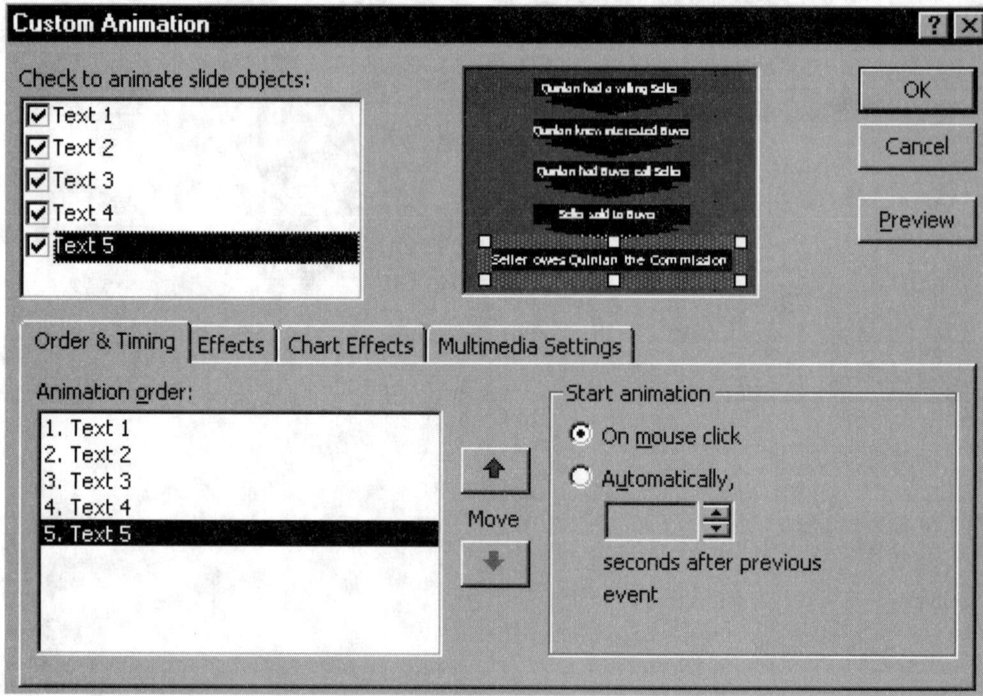

Step 2: Get the objects in the right order.

With the Custom Animation screen still in front of you, and the Order & Timing tab still active—

A. Go to the Animation Order box in the lower left corner. Your five objects should be listed there. They will be called Text 1, Text 2, Text 3, Text 4, and Text 5. The numbering reflects the order in which you created them, but it makes no operational difference. If your numbers are different, just use them as they are.

B. If you cannot remember which object goes with which name, click on the name (not the box) and it will be highlighted on the thumbnail of your slide in the small preview box in the top middle of the screen.

! The display of a relationship chart requires a logical order. You need to show the viewer the block arrow with Fact #1 first, so that must be first in order. The next object must be the block arrow with Fact #2. In this particular relationship chart, the first two objects are followed by Fact #3, Fact #4, and then the conclusion. The numbering assigned to each arrow by PowerPoint makes no difference so long as you have them in the order you need.

C. If the objects are in the correct order in which you want them to appear, you do not need to do anything.

D. If any object is out of order, click on the name of the object that is out of order. The name will be highlighted. Then go to the Move arrow buttons to the right of the Animation Order box and click on the Up Arrow button or the Down Arrow button to get it into the right order. Each click will move the name up or down one place in the list.

E. Make sure that the On Mouse Click option is active. The button is located in the Start Animation box on the right side of the lower half of the screen.

Step 3: Choose the effect to be used with each object.

A. Click on the Effects tab. This displays the Effects Box in the lower half of the screen.

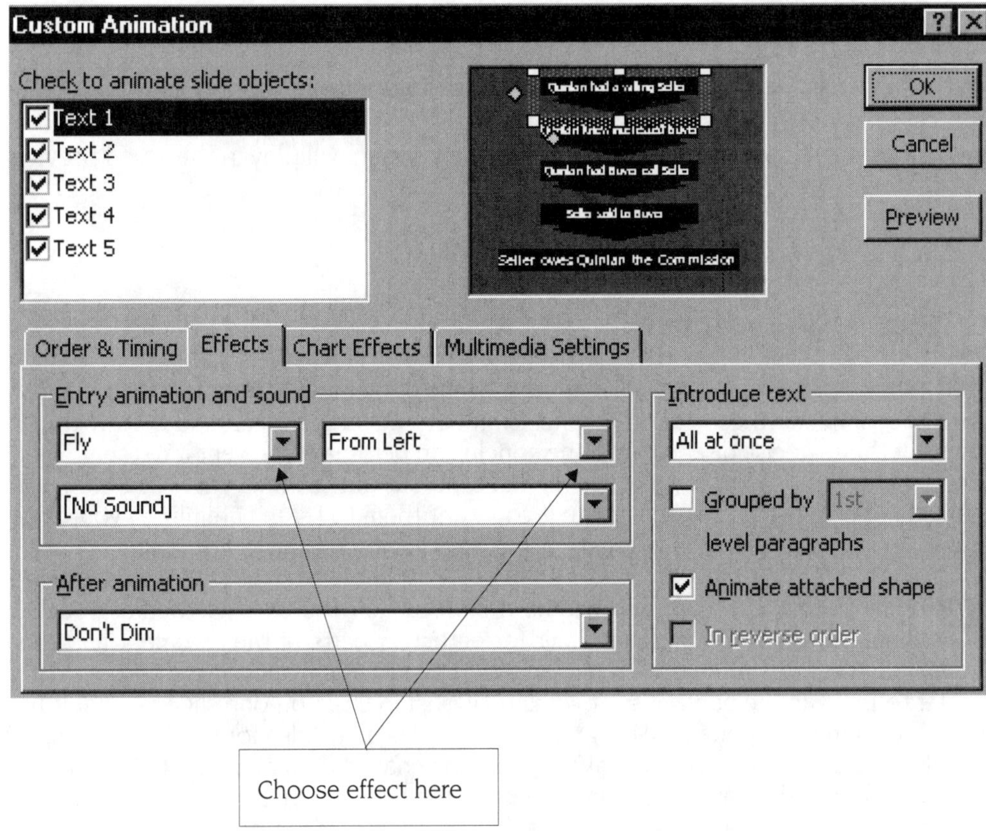

B. Go to the top left box and highlight the Text 1 item by clicking on it. The preview box which displays a thumbnail of your relationship chart will show that Text 1 is the first block arrow. It will be marked by a fuzzy border and handles.

C. Go to the Entry animation and sound box. The default choice for a special effect is Fly From Left. The Fly option will be showing in one of the rectangular white boxes and From Left will be showing in the other.

D. Click on the arrow to display options. Click on the Stretch option in the first box and the From Top option in the direction box next to it.

E. Repeat these steps for each of the other objects.

F. Click on the OK button at the top right to store your selections.

The OK button stores your work but does not save it. You still need to perform a Save in order not to lose what you have accomplished.

Step 4: Preview your work.

A. Click on the Preview button in the upper right corner of the screen.

B. The special effects that you have chosen will play in the small preview box.

C. Go back and make changes if necessary.

Step 5: Save your work.

If the jury sees the slide in its entirety at the outset, most jurors will read the relationship chart, consider the conclusion before you get there, and quickly decide whether they agree or disagree with the conclusion before you present it to them. Then, no matter which result they reach, they will tune out of the remaining discussion until something else comes on the screen. If you want them to listen carefully to your argument, you need to build the chart step by step until you reach the conclusion.

Relationship charts often become a summary of the case. Sometimes several small relationship charts are built for particular parts of the argument and then combined to demonstrate the overall force of the logic. For management purposes, it is better to build all the parts of the overall relationship chart on one slide, even if it has twenty or thirty components. Using successive slides in a series for this kind of display usually means that you need to make conforming changes in a number of places whenever you change the design. This increases the opportunity for error.

Exercise 9.4: Text treatments—box, circle, and line

Exercises 7.1, 7.2, and 7.3 involve the construction of a slide with two boxes to identify the date and addressee of the document, an oval (extended circle) to emphasize important words, and two lines to connect the boxes and the important words. This exercise assumes you constructed the slide described in Chapter 7 and are now ready to animate it.

Step 1: Display box, circle, and line objects one at a time.

With the box-circle-line slide on the screen in full slide view—

A. Designate the two boxes, the oval, and the two lines (but not the document) for animation.

1. Go to the Menu Bar.

2. Click on the Slide Show button. A drop-down menu will appear.

3. Click on the Custom Animation option. The Custom Animation screen will appear.

4. Click on the Order & Timing tab in the middle of the page if it is not already active (in the foreground).

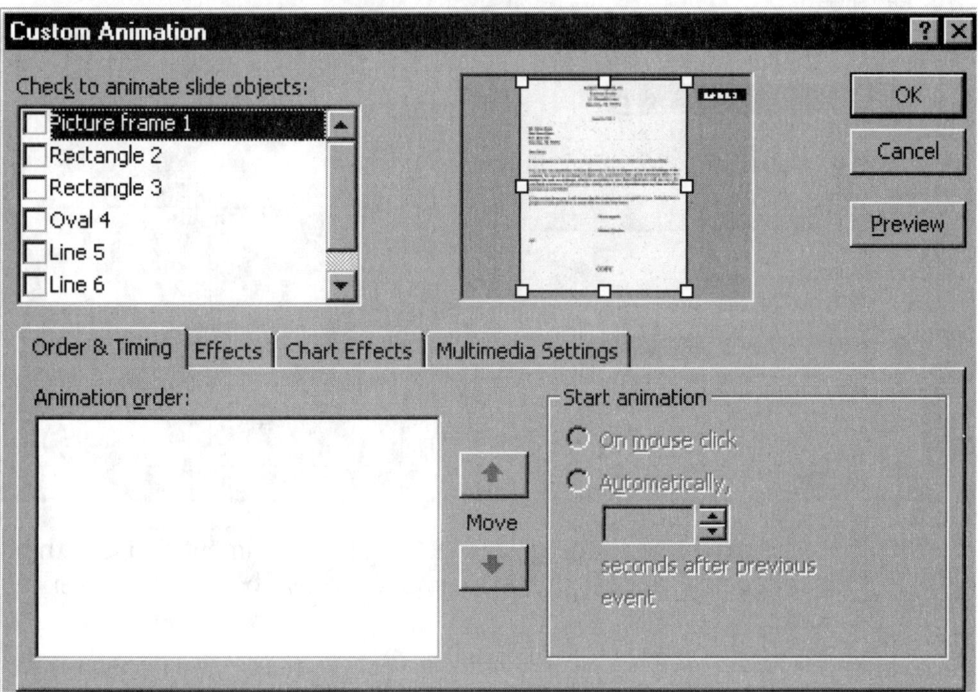

The box at the upper left of the screen should contain the names of the objects in the order you created them.

5. If you cannot remember which name goes with which object on your slide, click on the name (not the box) and the object will be highlighted in the preview box in the upper middle part of the screen. In the example pictured above, the objects are "Picture frame 1" (the document); Rectangle 2 (the box around the date), Rectangle 3 (the box around the address), Oval 4, Line 5 (the line between the circle and the date), Line 6 (the line between the circle and the address), and Text 7 (the box containing the exhibit number). The Text 7 object is out of sight because of limited space in the box and would be reached using the scroll bar at the right of the white box.

6. Click on the check boxes in front of all the objects except Picture frame 1 (the document) and Text 7 (the box containing the exhibit number). This will designate all the objects for animation except the document and its exhibit identifier. The screen looks like this:

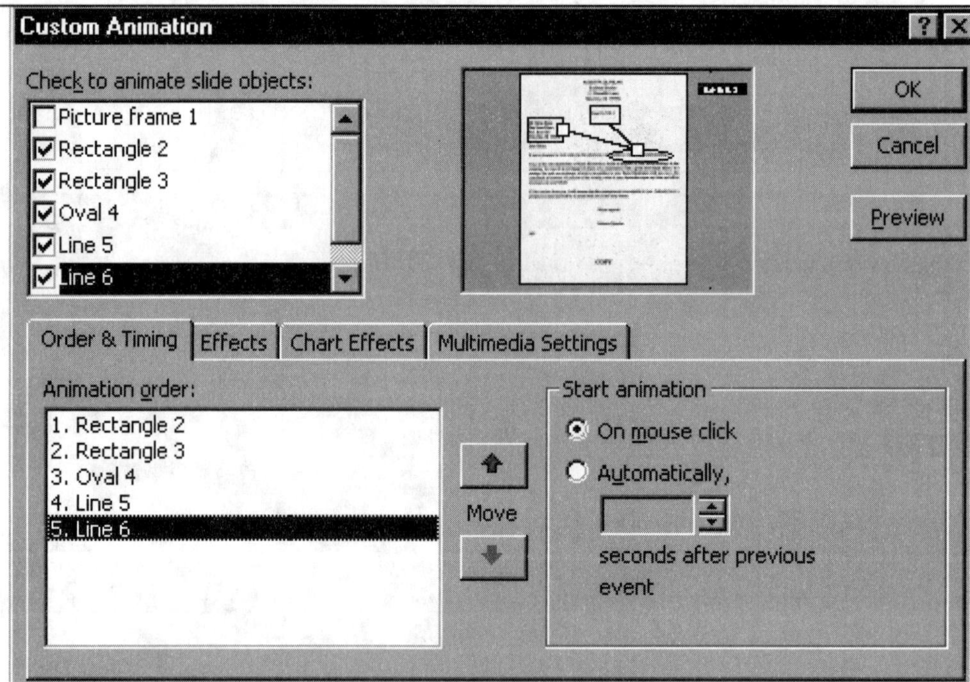

7. The names of all the objects except the document and its exhibit number now appear in the Animation order box in the lower left corner.

B. Specify the order in which the objects should appear.

With the Custom Animation screen still in front of you, and the Order & Timing tab still active—

1. Click on each of the names in the Animation order box in turn. Watch the preview screen to see if they are in the right order for the sequence in which you want them to appear on the screen.

2. If you need to change the order of any of the objects, click on it so that its name is highlighted in blue. Then use the up and down arrows next to the Animation order box to change its relative position.

★ This type of illustrative aid is sometimes used in the examination of a witness. Because you want the document to appear solid and dependable, normally you will have the document and its identifying exhibit number appear with the slide. Then, if you will be making the point brought out by the date of the document first, you will want to have the box around the date appear on the document first, without the circle and the line. If you will be making the point about the addressee of the letter next, you will want the box around the address to come up second. In this example, the circle is next, followed by the line from the circle to the date and then the line from the circle to the address.

Step 2: Add appropriate effects on entry.

With the Custom Animation screen still in front of you—

A. Get the Effects box on the screen.

1. Click on the Effects tab in the middle of the screen (2nd from left).

2. A new box will appear in the lower half of the screen.

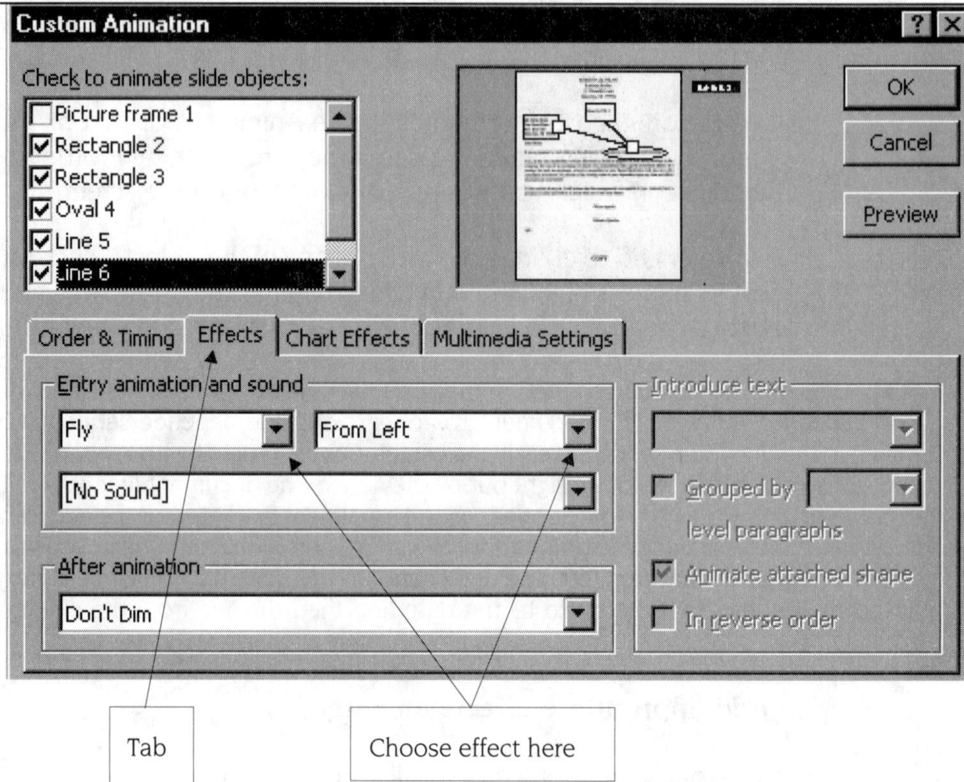

B. Select the effect that you want for each of your objects.

1. Go to the Entry animation box. (It says "Fly" in the example above because that is normally the default choice.) Click on the small arrow to the right of this box to see the list of all the options. Click on your choice.

2. Go to the direction box just to the right of the Entry animation box. (It says "From Left" in the example above.) Click on the small arrow to the right of this box to see the list of all the options as to direction. Click on your choice.

For the two rectangles: Use Wipe and Down.

For the oval: Use Wipe and Right.

For the lines: Use Stretch and From Bottom.

3. Click on the OK button at the upper right.

Step 3: Group the lines.

As an alternative for the lines, consider using the Group feature to have them both move simultaneously from the oval toward the boxes. Here's how to do this.

A. Go back to the full slide view. (After you click on the OK button, you should be back at the full slide view.)

B. Put your mouse pointer over the first line and click on it to activate it. The handles should be showing at each end.

C. Keep the first line active while you activate the second line by holding down the SHIFT key on your keyboard, putting your mouse pointer over the second line, and clicking on it.

D. Go to the Drawing Toolbar.

E. Click on the Draw button (1st on the left). A menu will appear.

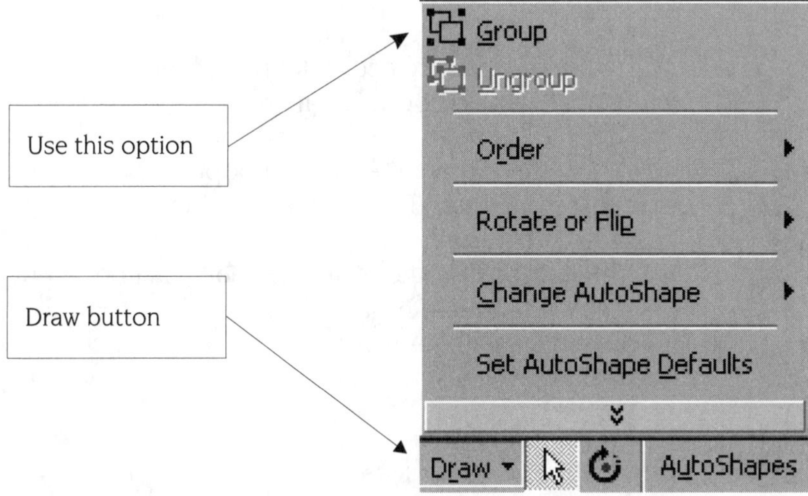

F. Click on the Group option. A new box with handles will surround the two lines. This is the "group." Once you have "grouped" objects together, they all move together.

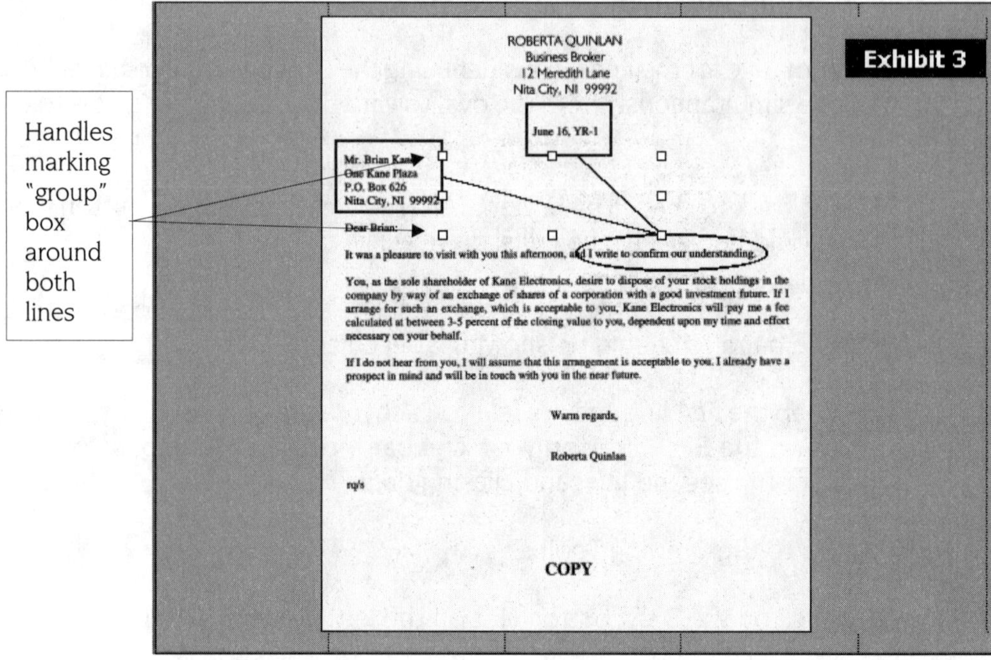

ROBERTA QUINLAN
Business Broker
12 Meredith Lane
Nita City, NI 99992

June 16, YR-1

Mr. Brian Kane
One Kane Plaza
P.O. Box 626
Nita City, NI 99992

Dear Brian:

It was a pleasure to visit with you this afternoon, and I write to confirm our understanding.

You, as the sole shareholder of Kane Electronics, desire to dispose of your stock holdings in the company by way of an exchange of shares of a corporation with a good investment future. If I arrange for such an exchange, which is acceptable to you, Kane Electronics will pay me a fee calculated at between 3-5 percent of the closing value to you, dependent upon my time and effort necessary on your behalf.

If I do not hear from you, I will assume that this arrangement is acceptable to you. I already have a prospect in mind and will be in touch with you in the near future.

Warm regards,

Roberta Quinlan

rq/s

COPY

G. With the Group box active (handles showing), click on the right mouse button. A drop-down menu will appear.

H. Click on the Custom Animation option. The Custom Animation screen will appear. The names for Line 5 and Line 6 will now be replaced with Group 5. Any items below this on the list (in this example the text box for the exhibit number) will be re-numbered.

I. Click on the small box in front of Group 5. A check mark will appear in the box.

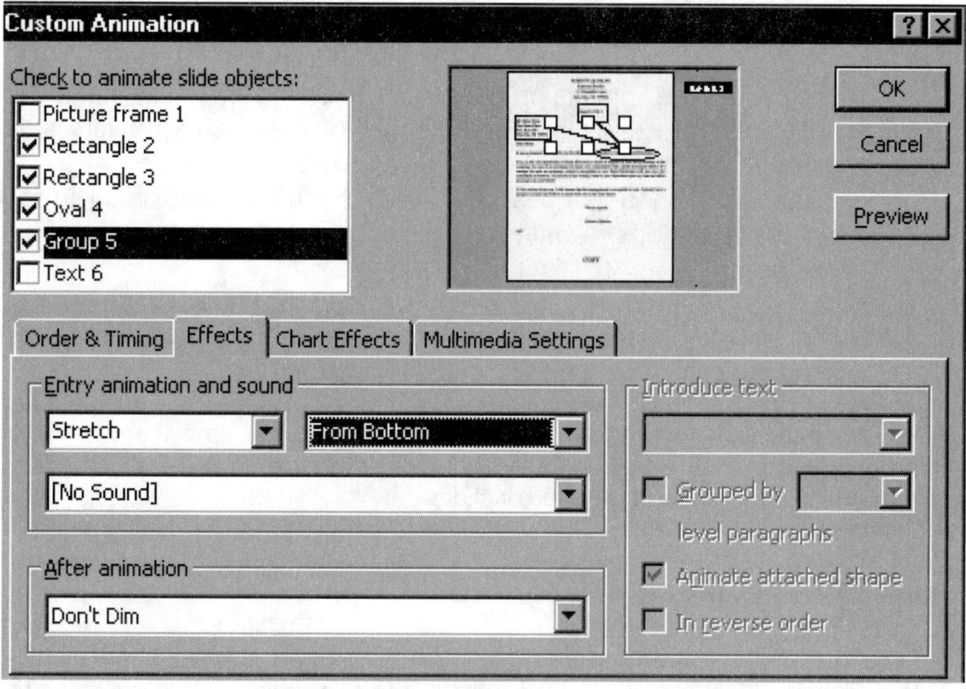

J. Click on the Effects tab if it is not already active.

K. Select the Stretch effect with the From Bottom direction.

L. Click on the Preview button to see the animation. Now, both lines will stretch toward the boxes simultaneously.

M. When you are finished, click on the OK button.

If you have Grouped items in order to animate them together, you will need to Ungroup them before you can work on them individually again. Click anywhere within the Group so that the outer handles are showing. Go to the Drawing Toolbar, click on the Draw button, and choose the Ungroup option. Click outside the group to de-activate the items within the Group. Now you are back to where you started.

When you animate lines, use the direction in which the line moves to emphasize your point. For example, if you are making the point that X caused Y, then you would want the line to stretch from X to Y. If the point to be made is that the event or item that is circled happened on the date that is in the box, you might want to have the line go from the box to the circle. In that case, you would use the Stretch from Top option.

Step 4: Preview your work in full size.

A. Go to the View Bar.

B. Click on the Slide Show button (5th from the left).

C. When your slide appears on the screen, it should show just the document and the exhibit number. Neither of these objects were animated. Click your left mouse button. The box around the date (Rectangle 2) should appear next. Click the mouse button again for successive actions, displaying the second rectangle, the oval, and the lines.

D. When you are finished, click the right mouse button and a drop down menu appears. Click on the End Show option.

! You do not need to go through the entire slide show. You can stop at any point by right clicking and using the End Show option or simply press the Escape key. That will take you back to the view of the slide or slides that you had just before going to the Slide Show view.

Step 5: Save your work.

★ Because documents are a serious subject matter for jurors, be careful with animation. Too much animation can lead to a juror to conclude that you are trying to fool them about the document. For this reason, some lawyers have two slides for each text document treatment. One slide has just the document on it in a size as large as can be fit on the slide. The other slide has the document in smaller form with all of the treatments (like the box, circle, and line) on it animated to make certain points about the document.

Exercise 9.5: Text—split screens with bullet points

Exercise 7.4 involves the construction of a slide that uses a reduced-size version of the document on the left side of a split screen and an expanded identification of the document plus explanatory bullet points on the right side of the split screen. Use the slide you prepared in Exercise 7.4 for this animation.

Step 1: Designate the box containing the bullet points for animation.

With the full slide on the screen—

A. Click on the object containing the bullet points to activate it.

B. Click with the right mouse button. A drop-down menu will appear. (Illustration, Exercise 9.1, Step 1B.)

C. Click on the Custom Animation option. The Custom Animation screen will appear.

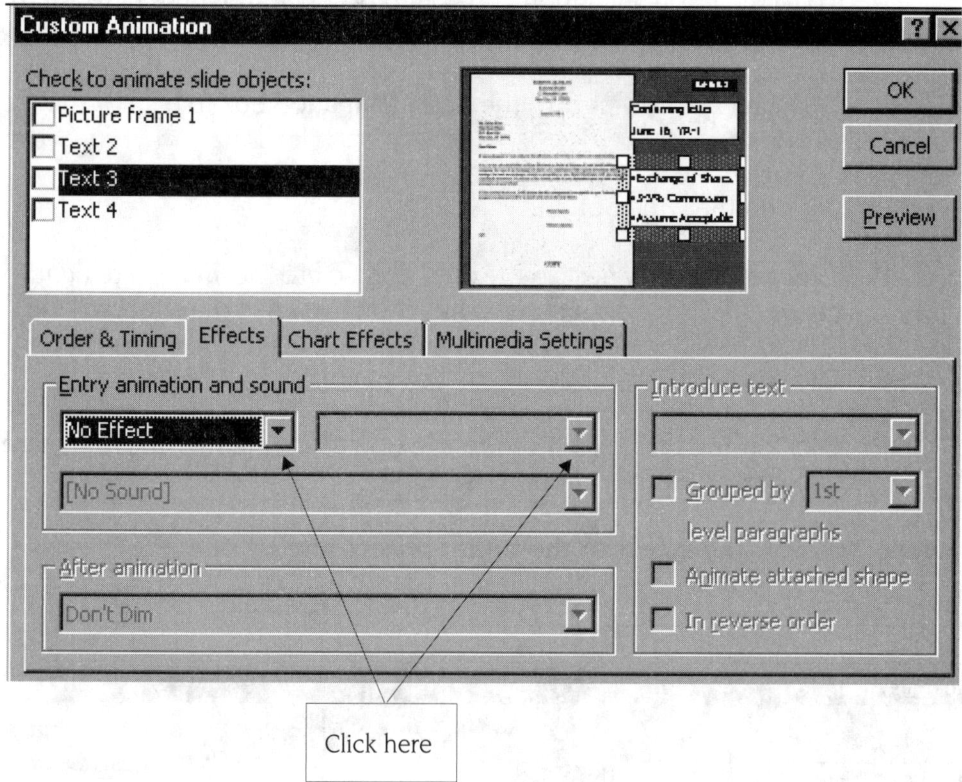

The name for the box containing the bullet points (Text 3 in this example) will be highlighted in blue in the box in the upper left corner of the screen. A thumbnail of your slide will be showing in the box in the upper middle of the screen. The box containing the bullet points will also be highlighted there.

There are three other objects on this slide: (1) the document, called Picture frame 1; (2) the box containing the exhibit number (Text 4); and (3) the box containing the expanded identification of the document (Text 2). None of these are animated, therefore they will all come up when the slide is first displayed.

★ Normally you will want the document and its exhibit number on the screen when the slide comes up, and then the bullet points will come up one by one. Because the identification is an "anchor" for the bullet points, it is a good idea to have no effects when that object appears, but to have the bullet points enter with an appropriate effect for contrast.

Step 2: Select the effect that you want to use for the bullet points.

A. Go to the Entry animation and sound box just under the Effects tab. The label "No Effect" will be showing, highlighted in blue.

B. Click on the arrow next to the Entry animation box to display the list of options.

C. Click on the Wipe option.

D. Click on the arrow next to the direction box to the immediate right to display the list of options as to directions in which the effect will run.

E. Click on the Down option.

F. Click on the Preview button in the upper right corner to make sure this works well for your purpose.

Step 3: Apply the effect to the bullet points one by one.

A. Go to the Introduce Text box at the lower right portion of the screen.

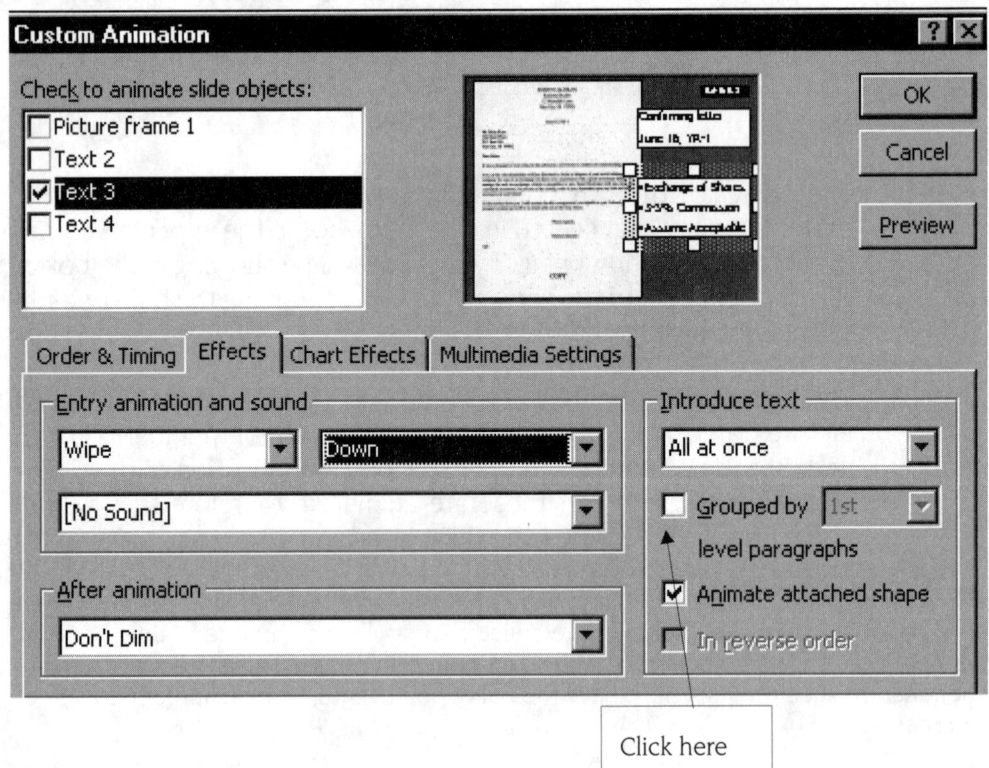

The box will say "All at once."

B. Click on the small box in front of the label "Grouped by." A check mark will appear.

C. Just to the right of that label, a small box should display "1st." If it does not, use the arrow to the right of the box to get to 1st. This will make the bullet points appear separately.

D. Click on the OK button in the upper right corner.

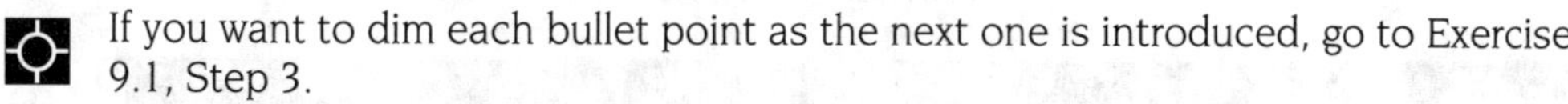

If you want to dim each bullet point as the next one is introduced, go to Exercise 9.1, Step 3.

Step 4: Preview your slide in full size.

A. Go to the View Bar.

B. Click on the Slide Show button (5th from the left). The slide will appear with the document, the exhibit number, and the identification box.

C. Click your left mouse button to see the effects. The box for the bullet points will appear on the first mouse click and then the bullet points will each appear in turn on succeeding mouse clicks.

D. Right click when you want to end the show. A drop-down menu will appear. Pick the End Show option.

If after previewing your slide, you decide to animate the identification box as well as the bullet point box, repeat Steps 1 and 2 for that box. The "Appear" option is a simple effect that allows you to put the identification box on the screen separately from the document and its exhibit number.

Step 5: Save your work.

Exercise 9.6: Text—re-keyed callouts

Exercise 7.5 covers re-keyed callouts that use a callout shape from the AutoShapes menu with the text re-typed inside the box. Use the slide that you constructed in that exercise to add the special effects described here.

Step 1: Designate the objects that you want animated.

With the full slide on the screen—

A. Go to the Menu Bar.

B. Click on the Slide Show button. A drop-down menu will appear.

C. Click on the Custom Animation option. The Custom Animation screen will appear. The names of all the objects on the slide are listed in the box in the upper left corner of the screen.

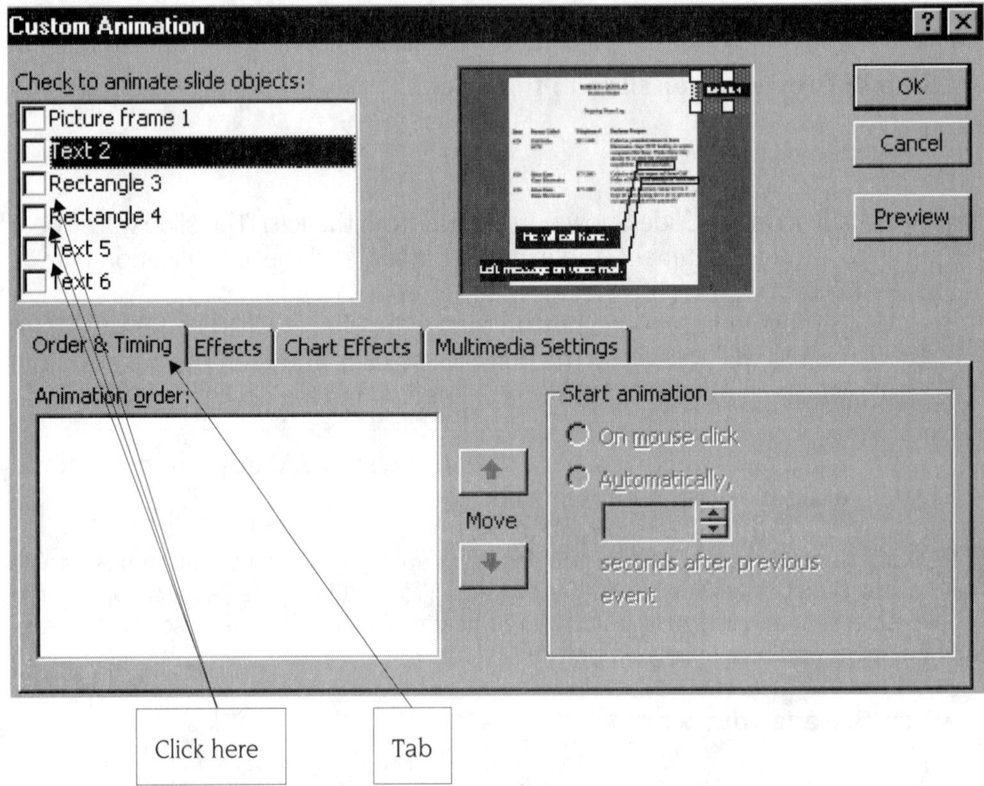

D. Click on the Order & Timing tab if it is not already active.

E. Click on the small check boxes in front of all the objects that will be animated (all but Picture frame 1, the document, and Text 2, the exhibit number). A check mark will appear in the small box and the name of the object will appear in the Animation order box in the lower left.

F. If you cannot remember which name goes with which object, click on the name (not the box) and the object will be highlighted on the thumbnail of your slide that appears in the preview box in the top middle part of the screen. In the example above, Picture frame 1 is the document and Text 2 is the Exhibit number. The first anchor box in the text (pointing out the words "He will call Kane") is Rectangle 3. The second anchor box in the text (pointing out the words "Left message on voice mail") is Rectangle 4. The callout box used in a re-keyed callout consists of a box with a line attached to it. The first callout box is called Text 5. There is no separate name for the line because it is treated as a part of the callout box. The second callout box is Text 6.

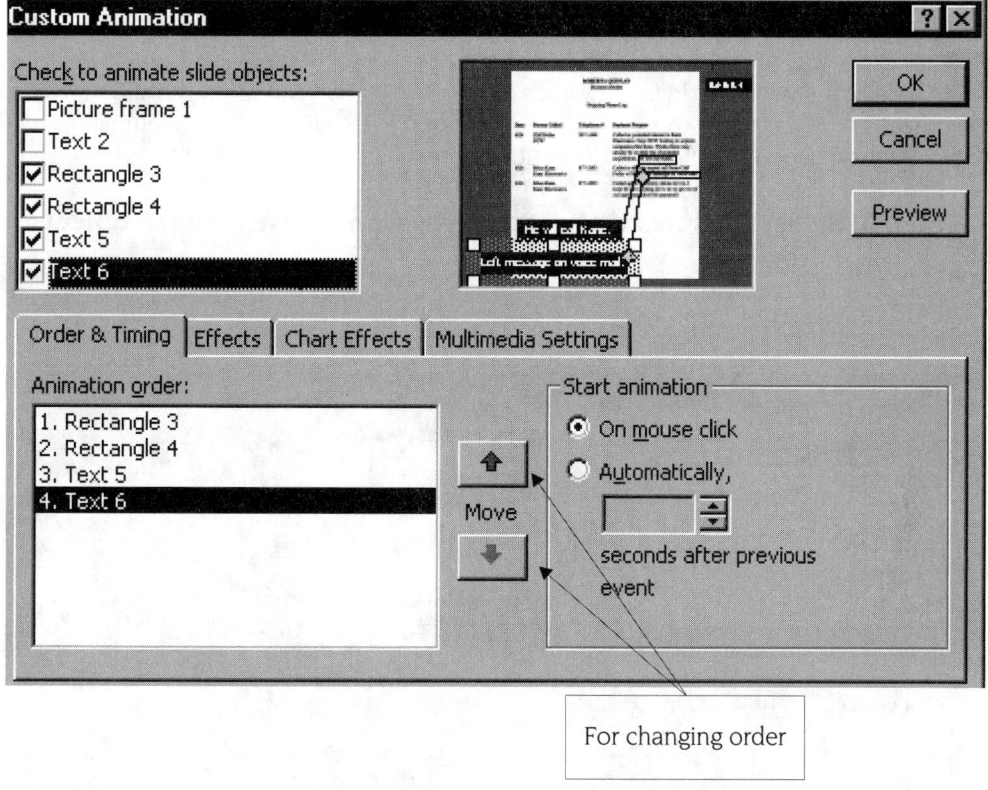

If there are more objects on your slide than there is space in the box in the upper right of the screen, you will need to use the arrow at the right side of the box to scroll down to the remaining names. Remember that the numbers assigned by the software make no difference to you. They are just for identification. Yours may be different. That is okay.

Step 2: Put the objects in the order in which you want them to appear.

A. Go to the Animation order box in the lower left. Look at the order in which the objects are listed (the order in which you created them).

B. If this is not the order you want, click on an object to highlight its name and use the Move arrows at the right of the box to change the relative order of that object.

C. If you need to see which object is represented by a particular name in the list, click on the name of the object and it will be highlighted on the thumbnail of your slide in the preview box.

To animate this kind of callout, you will bring up the document and its identification box first, then the first anchor box in the text followed by its callout box, and then the second anchor box in the text followed by its callout box. You will animate each of the two callouts in the order you intend to use them in examining the witness or arguing the point.

Another way to emphasize the importance of the document is to have a separate slide that shows the document in as large a size as you can fit on the slide with its identification box. Display this first. Then you can follow that with the callout slide that has a much smaller copy of the document used for displaying the callouts.

Step 3: Select the special effect that you want to use for each object.

A. Click on the Effects tab. This will bring a box to the bottom of the screen. It looks like this:

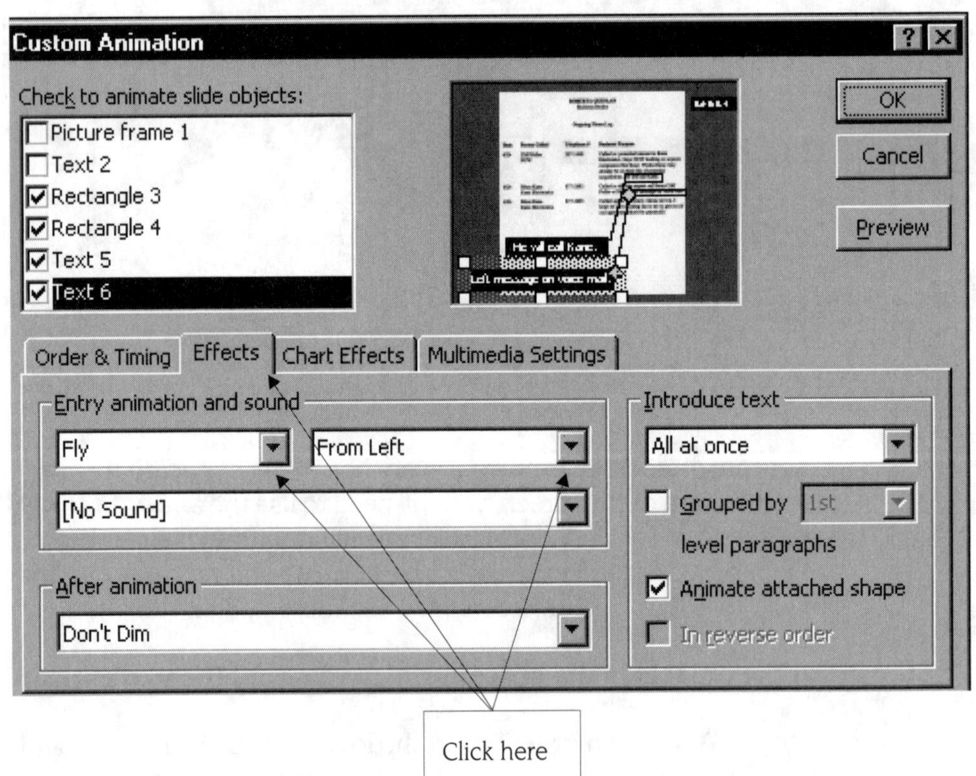

When you switch to the Effects tab while one of the items is highlighted, the Fly From Left option will probably be showing in the Entry animation box as it is in the example above.

B. Put your mouse pointer on the object for animation. Click to highlight it.

C. Use the arrow at the right of the Entry animation box to scroll to the option you want. Click on that.

D. Use the arrow at the right of the direction box to scroll to the direction you want. Click on that.

Anchor boxes within the document: In this example, Rectangle 3 is the box around the anchor item in the text for the first callout, the words "He will call Kane." Rectangle 4 is the box around the anchor item for the second callout, the words "Left message on voice mail." You will want both of these to have the same effect. Select the **Appear** option. The Appear option has no direction, so the direction box to the right will be gray.

Callout boxes: In the example above, Text 5 is the first callout box and Text 6 is the second callout box. Select the **Wipe** option and the **Down** direction.

E. Preview your work by clicking on the Preview button in the upper right.

F. Click on the OK button to preserve your work.

Step 4: Group the anchor box and its callout box so they will be animated together.

With the full view of the slide on the screen—

A. Click on the border of the callout box to activate it. A fuzzy border will appear.

B. Hold down the SHIFT key on your keyboard and click on the anchor box in the text. A fuzzy border will appear on that box as well.

C. Go to the Drawing Toolbar.

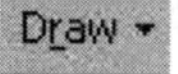

D. Click on the Draw button (1st on the left).

E. A drop-down menu will appear. (Illustration, Exercise 9.4, Step 3.)

F. Click on the Group option. Handles will appear around the group of objects indicating that they will now all move together.

G. Click on the right mouse button (while the handles around the group still appear on the screen). A drop-down menu will appear. (Illustration, Exercise 9.5, Step 1C.)

H. Click on the Custom Animation option. The Custom Animation screen will appear with the name of the group highlighted in blue. The Effects tab will be active.

I. Choose the effect that you want for the whole group.

J. Repeat Steps A-I for the other callout.

Step 5: Do a full-screen preview of your work.

A. Go to the View Bar.

B. Click on the Slide Show button (5th from the left). The slide will appear with the document and the exhibit number.

C. Click your left mouse button to see the effects.

D. Right click when you want to end the show. A drop-down menu will appear. Pick the End Show option.

Step 6: Save your work.

★ The animation should be designed to fit the oral presentation that goes with the slide. If you change your oral presentation, do not forget to check the slide to be sure that the animation you have included still works to make the points in the order you need.

Exercise 9.7: Text—direct callouts

Exercise 7.6 covers direct callouts, which are constructed by copying portions directly from the document text and enlarging them. These callouts are connected to a marked portion of the text of the document usually by two lines, one from either end of the callout. Use the slide that you prepared in Exercise 7.6 for this animation.

Step 1: Designate the objects on the slide that you want to animate.

With the full slide on the screen—

A. Go to the Menu Bar.

B. Click on the Slide Show button. A drop-down menu will appear.

C. Click on the Custom Animation option. The Custom Animation screen will appear.

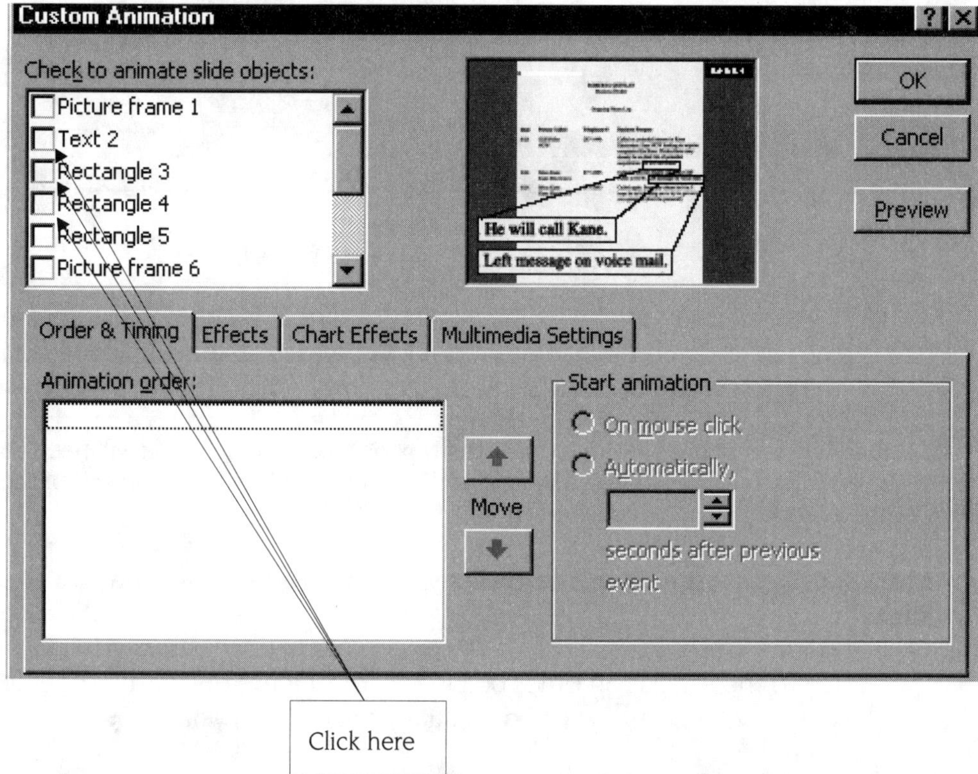

D. Click on the Order & Timing tab if it is not already active.

E. Click on the small check boxes in front of all the objects that will be animated (all but Picture frame 1, the document, and Text 2, the exhibit number). A check mark will appear in the small box and the name of the object will appear in the Animation order box in the lower left. The screen looks like this:

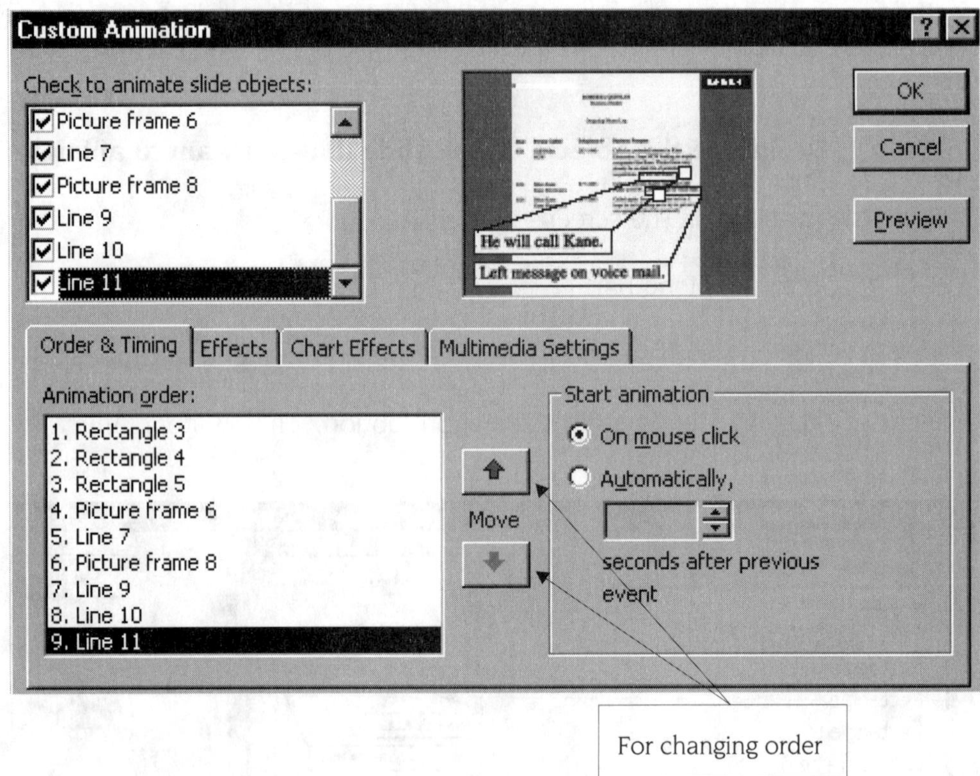

F. If you need to see which object is represented by a particular name in the list, click on the name of the object and it will be highlighted on the thumbnail of your slide in the preview box.

! If there are too many objects to fit in the box on the upper left, you will need to scroll down using the arrow at the right of the box to reach those at the end of the list. Do not leave any out.

Step 2: Get the objects in the order you want them to appear on the slide.

A. Go to the Animation order box in the lower left. Look at the order in which the objects are listed—usually the order in which you created them.

B. If this is not the order you want, click on an object to highlight its name and use the Move arrows at the right of the box to change the relative order of that object.

To animate this kind of callout, you will bring up the document and its identification box first, then the first anchor box in the text followed by the line to its callout box followed by the callout box itself. In a direct callout, the callout box and the line are created separately (and usually not grouped) so each will be listed on the Custom Animation screen.

! In a direct callout slide, the callout box is called a "Picture frame." Because it is a clip from the document, the software treats it as a picture (like the document) rather than a text box.

Step 3: Select the special effect that you want to use for each object.

A. Click on the Effects tab. This will bring a box to the bottom of the screen. It looks like this:

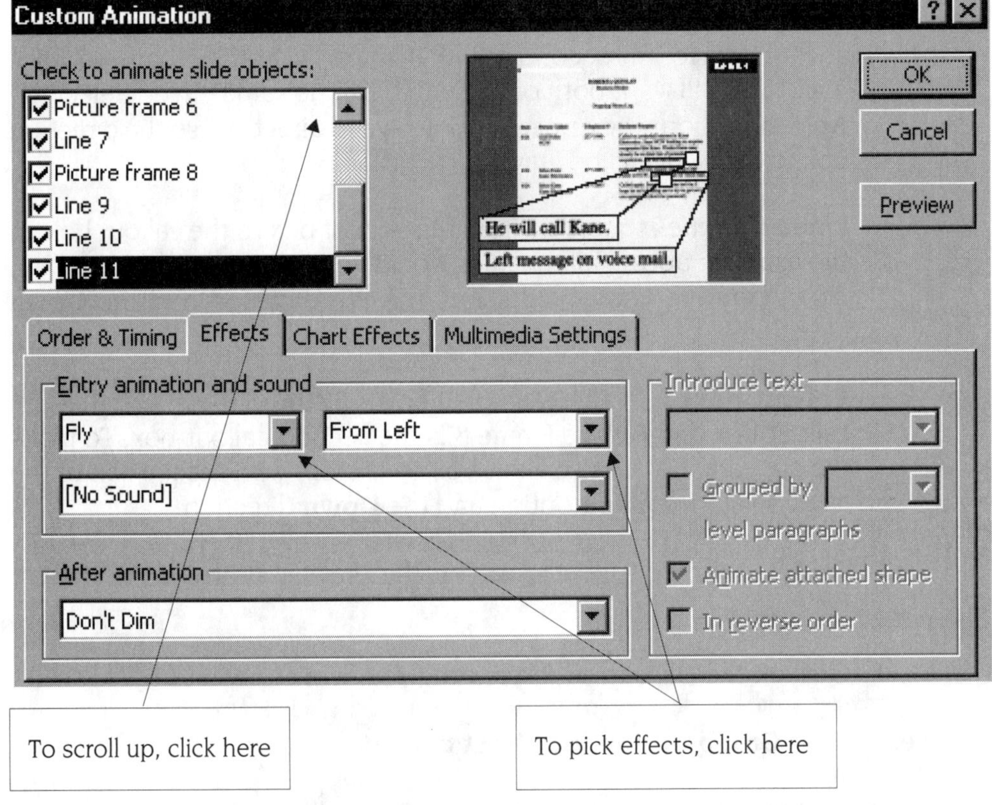

B. Scroll up to the top of your check marked list in the upper left box on the screen. A direct callout often has more objects on the slide than will fit in this box. It is usually easiest to start from the top.

C. When you switch to the Effects tab with one of the object names highlighted, the Fly From Left option will probably be showing in the Entry animation box as it is in the example above.

D. Put your mouse pointer on the object for animation. Click to highlight it.

E. Use the arrow at the right of the Entry animation box to scroll to the option you want. Click on that.

F. Use the arrow at the right of the direction box to scroll to the direction you want. Click on that.

   Anchor boxes within the document: In this example, Rectangle 4 is the anchor box around the item in the text for the first callout, the words "He will call Kane." Rectangle 5 is the anchor box around the anchor item for the second callout, the words "Left message on voice mail." You will want both of these to have the same effect. Select the **Appear** option. The Appear option has no direction, so the direction box to the right will be gray.

   Lines: The lines should go from the anchor box to the callout box. In the example above, all the lines would go down to reach the callout box. Therefore you would select the **Wipe** option and the **Down** direction.

   Callout boxes: In the example above, Picture Frame 4 is the first callout box and Picture Frame 8 is the second callout box. To make the appearance of the callout box consistent with the motion of the lines, select the **Wipe** option and the **Down** direction.

G. Preview your work by clicking on the Preview button in the upper right.

H. Click on the OK button to preserve your work.

Step 4: The Group option for direct callouts.

To group (1) the two callout lines, or (2) the two callout lines and the callout box , or (3) the anchor box, the two callout lines, and the callout box so that the special effect will connect them seamlessly, do this:

With the full view of the slide on the screen—

A. Click on the border of one of the objects to be grouped. This will activate it. A fuzzy border will appear.

B. Hold down the SHIFT key on your keyboard and click on the border of another of the objects to be grouped. A fuzzy border will appear on that box as well. Do this for each of the rest of the objects to be grouped.

C. Go to the Drawing Toolbar.

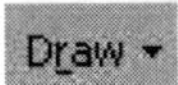

D. Click on the Draw button (1st on the left).

E. A drop-down menu will appear. (Illustration, Exercise 9.4, Step 3.)

F. Click on the Group option. Handles will appear around the group of objects indicating that they will now all move together.

G. Click on the right mouse button (while the handles around the group still appear on the screen). A drop-down menu will appear. (Illustration, Exercise 9.5, Step 1(C).)

H. Click on the Custom Animation option. The Custom Animation screen will appear with the name of the group highlighted in blue. The Effects tab will be active.

I. Choose the effect that you want for the whole group.

J. Repeat Steps A-1 for the second callout.

Step 5: Do a full-screen preview of your work.

A. Go to the View Bar.

B. Click on the Slide Show button (5th from the left). The slide will appear with the document and the exhibit number.

C. Click your left mouse button to see the effects.

D. Right click when you want to end the show. A drop-down menu will appear. Pick the End Show option.

Step 6: Save your work.

★ The animation should be designed to fit the oral presentation that goes with the slide. If you change your oral presentation, do not forget to check the slide to be sure that the animation you included still works to make the points in the order you need.

Exercise 9.8: Annotated diagrams

Exercises 8.1, 8.2, and 8.3 covered the building of an annotated diagram that has labels on key parts of the diagram with dotted lines indicating the route taken between these key points. In this exercise, you will reveal the labels one at a time, cross out some of them to make a point, and add motion to the lines so that they actually crawl across the screen when they are displayed.

Step 1: Designate the objects on the slide that will be animated.

With the full slide on the screen—

A. Go to the Menu Bar.

B. Click on the Slide Show button. A drop-down menu will appear.

C. Click on the Custom Animation option. The Custom Animation screen will appear.

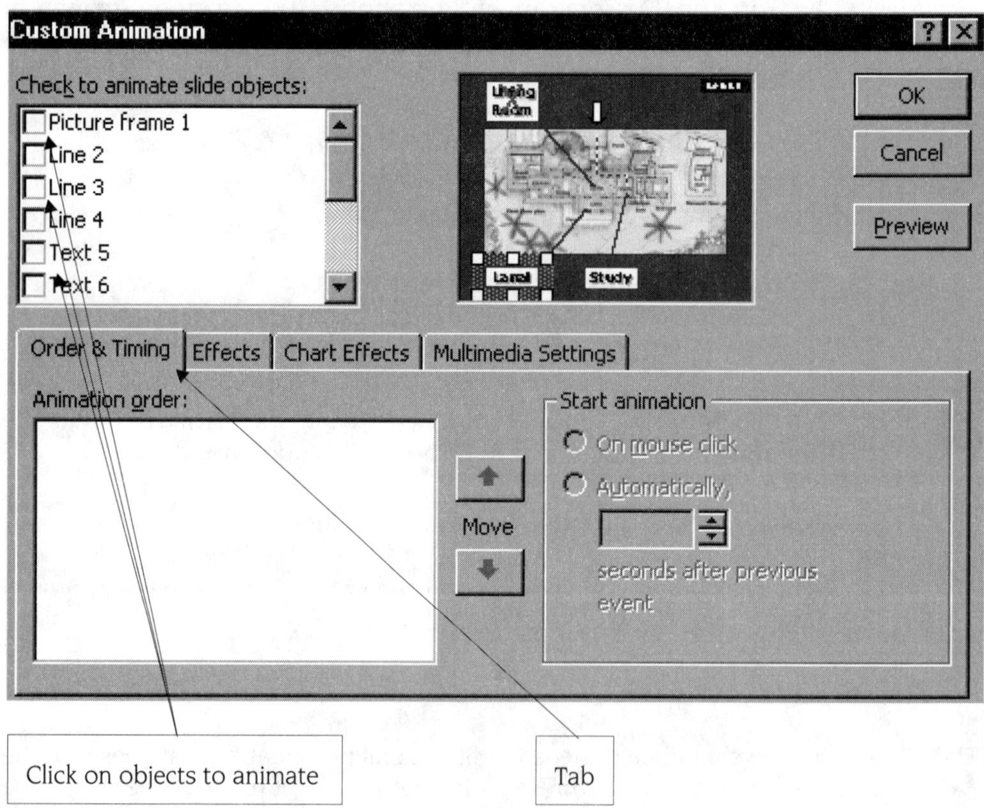

D. Click on the Order & Timing tab in the row of tabs in the middle of the screen if it is not already active. The names that the software has assigned to each of the objects on your slide should be listed there.

E. Click on the small box in front of the name of each of the objects that will be animated. A check mark will appear in the box, and the names of the checked objects will appear in the Animation order box below. In the example above, the diagram (Picture frame 1) and its exhibit number (Text 5) will appear with the slide. These objects will not be animated.

F. If you need to see which object is represented by a particular name in the list, click on the name of the object and it will be highlighted on the thumbnail of your slide in the preview box.

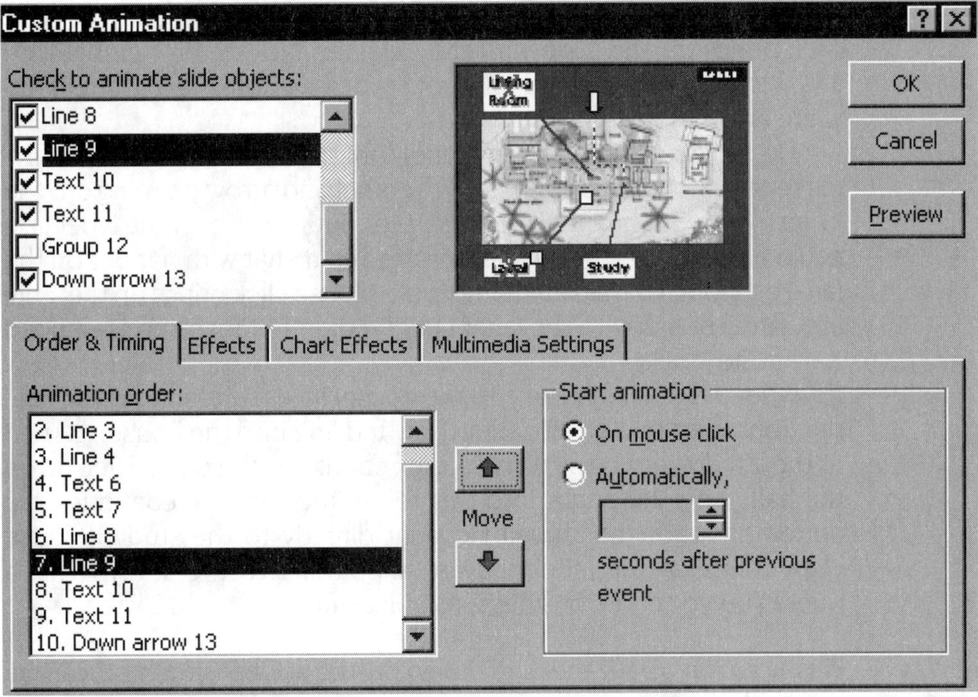

Normally it is a good idea not to animate the underlying diagram unless there is a particular point to be made with the special effect itself. Your viewer will relate better to the exhibit if the diagram and its exhibit number are stable—appearing with the slide—and the motion and effects contribute to the understanding of particular parts of the diagram.

Step 2: Put the objects in the order you want them to appear.

A. Go to the Animation order box in the lower left. Look at the order in which the objects are listed—usually the order in which you created them.

B. If this is not the order you want, click on an object to highlight its name and use the Move arrows at the right of the box to change the relative order of that object.

The order in which the objects appear should reflect your plan for your opening statement, closing argument, or other part of the case in which the slide will be used. In the example used in this section, the lawyer planned to make this argument:

"Let's look at where Mr. Kane chose to have this meeting. (Mouse click brings up the slide with the diagram and exhibit number.) He and Ms. Quinlan entered the house here. (Mouse click brings up white arrow indicating entryway.)

He could have had a nice, friendly, informal talk with her in the living room. (Mouse click brings up the label and arrow pointing out the living room.) But he didn't. (Mouse click puts red X over the label.) He could have enjoyed an iced lemonade and a chat with her out on the lanai overlooking the swimming pool. (Mouse click brings up the label and arrow pointing to the lanai.) But he didn't. (Mouse click puts red X over the label.)

When Ms. Quinlan came to the house, he escorted her in through the front door (mouse click starts dotted line into the house); turned to the left down the hall (mouse click continues the dotted line down the hall); and then right into this room (mouse click continues the dotted line into the study.) He went directly to the study. (Mouse click brings up the label and arrow pointing to the study.) That's where you go to talk business, not pleasure."

This notation about the way the argument will be presented can be kept with the slide. See Chapter 10, Exercise 10.3.

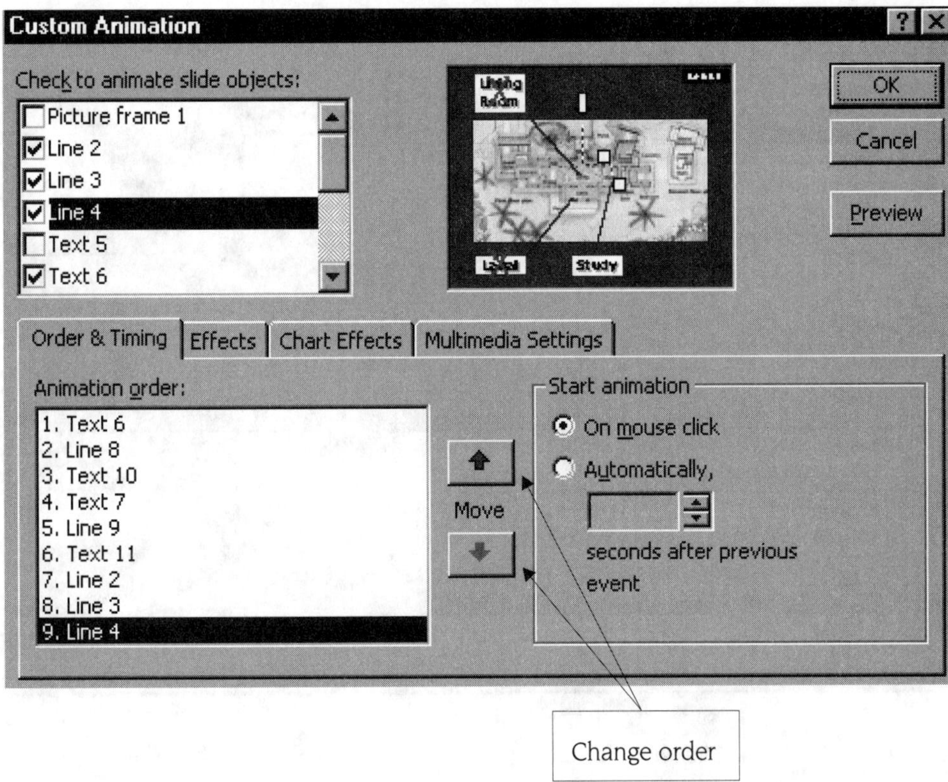

Getting the objects into this order takes quite a bit of shuffling of the order that first appeared in the Animation order box. One alternative is to figure out which object you want to animate first, click on it to activate it, click on the right mouse button to get to the Custom Animation option. This brings up the Custom Animation screen with the name of this object already highlighted. Click on it to put a check mark in the box. Select the effect. Then go back to the slide and repeat this operation with the object that you want to appear second, and so on.

Step 3: Select the effect to be used for each of the objects.

A. Click on the Effects tab. That brings the Entry animation box to the bottom of the screen.

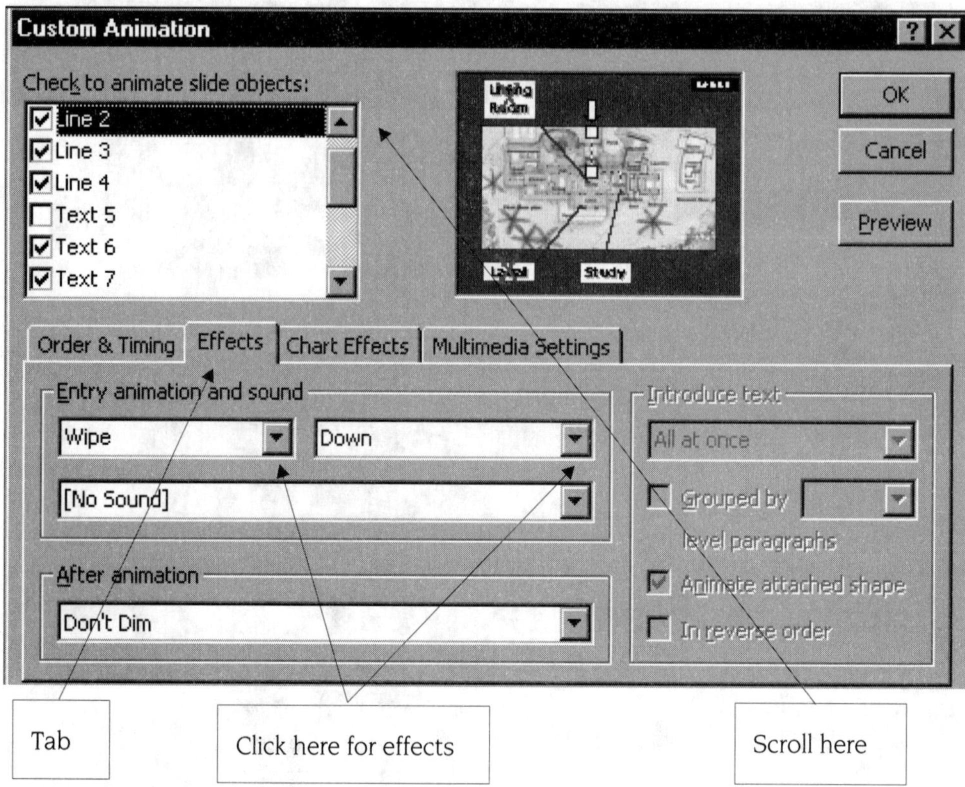

B. Scroll up to get to the top of the list.

C. Put your mouse pointer on the object for animation. Click to highlight it.

D. Use the arrow at the right of the Entry animation box to scroll to the option you want. Click on that.

E. Use the arrow at the right of the direction box to scroll to the direction you want. Click on that.

White arrow: In the example above, the white arrow might be animated with the **Fly** and **Down** option.

Dotted Lines: In the example above, Line 2 is the dotted line that comes through the door of the house. Select **Wipe** for the option and **Down** for the direction. Line 3 is the dotted line that turns left and goes down the hall. Select **Wipe** for the option and **Right** for the direction. Line 3 is the dotted line that turns right and goes into the study. Select **Wipe** for the option and **Down** for the direction. This will make it look like the line is crawling across the screen. Again, your numbering may vary by the order you created your objects and the type of objects.

Labels: For the label for the living room, select **Split** for the option and **Vertical In** for the direction. For the directional arrow pointing out the location, select **Wipe** for the option and **Down** for the direction. For the red X over the label, select **Zoom** for the option and **Out Slightly** for the direction. Use the same effects for the label, directional arrow, and red X which deal with the lanai. For the label and directional arrow which deal with the study use the **Appear** effect (unless you have grouped them, in which case, see below).

F. Preview your work by clicking on the Preview button in the upper right.

G. Click on the OK button to preserve your work.

Step 4: Group the label for the study and its directional arrow.

With the full view of the slide on the screen—

A. Click on the border of one of the objects to be grouped. This will activate it. A fuzzy border will appear.

B. Hold down the SHIFT key on your keyboard and click on the border of the other object to be grouped. A fuzzy border will appear on that box as well.

C. Go to the Drawing Toolbar.

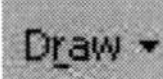

D. Click on the Draw button (1st on the left).

E. A drop-down menu will appear. (Illustration, Exercise 9.4, Step 3.)

F. Click on the Group option. Handles will appear around the group of objects indicating that they will now all move together.

G. Click on the right mouse button (while the handles around the group still appear on the screen). A drop-down menu will appear. (Illustration, Exercise 9.5, Step 1(C).)

H. Click on the Custom Animation option. The Custom Animation screen will appear with the name of the group highlighted in blue. The Effects tab will be active.

I. Choose the effect that you want for the whole group. The special effect that you choose will start at one end of the connected group and go to the other end. Be sure you get the correct direction.

Step 5: Do a full-screen preview of your work.

A. Go to the View Bar.

B. Click on the Slide Show button (5th from the left). The slide will appear with the document and the exhibit number.

C. Click your left mouse button to see the effects.

D. Right click when you want to end the show. A drop-down menu will appear. Pick the End Show option.

Step 6: Save your work.

Chapter 10

Running Your Slide Show

PowerPoint has built-in tools to help you present your slide show competently even if you are a beginner with a computer. This chapter covers the computer operations necessary to making your slides into a completed show.

To prepare your slide show for presentation, you need to do five things:

1. Review and edit your slides
2. Add transitions from one slide to another if useful
3. Add notes about the slides if necessary
4. Make a backup copy
5. Give your slide show a trial run

A slide show is an aid to oral advocacy. The advocacy must drive the slide show, not the other way around. You need to plan out the points you want to make and the order in which it is most persuasive to make them. Putting together a slide show can help in the planning process because it can illuminate weak areas in the logical connections or relationships among facts. But the oral advocacy is still the centerpiece, not the slide show.

The way that you style your slide show for presentation in a courtroom (or elsewhere) is affected by the equipment that you will use to display your slides for the jury. Some basic points about display equipment are presented in Chapter 11.

Exercise 10.1: Review and edit the slides

Slide shows often reveal weaknesses in the logic links necessary to make your points persuasive, and you will want to go back and rework the text and graphics. Some lawyers outline the elements of their case theory in PowerPoint to ensure that the points they want to make are well-articulated and easy to understand.

Step 1: Look over your slides.

A. Go to the View Bar.

B. Click on the Slide Sorter View button. This brings up a Slide Sorter screen that contains thumbnails of each of your slides in the order you created them. (Illustration, Ch. 4, Exercise 4.1.)

C. Check the content and order. To view the full-size display of a slide, just double click on the thumbnail, and the slide will come up on the screen.

Step 2: Use the outline capability, if necessary, to get an overview.

PowerPoint provides an outline that displays the written content of your slide presentation. This allows you to look at the headings and subsidiary points (without any of the decorations you may have put on your slides) and to focus on content rather than style or format.

In PowerPoint 2000, the outline is always on the screen when you are using Full Screen View. To display it (when you have been using the other modes), do this:

A. Go to the View Bar.

B. Click on the Outline button (2nd from the left). An outline will appear on the left side of the screen showing all of the titles and bullet points in your slides. (Illustration, Ch. 1, Section 1.5.)

C. Read over the outline to see if the points are in the right order and the subsidiary points fit correctly into the overall plan for your presentation. A small numbered icon in the left margin will identify the number of the slide where the content is located. Slides with no written content are also represented by small icons in the left margin.

D. Make any necessary changes to the text. You can just delete and add text in the normal fashion, or you can use the Promote and Demote and Move Up and Move Down arrow buttons on the Formatting Toolbar to rearrange bullet points.

E. To get back to your slides, go to the View Toolbar, click on the Full Slide View button (3rd from the left) or the Slide Sorter button (4th from the left).

For PowerPoint 97 users, the Outline view is not displayed on the screen until you call it up. Go to the View Bar. Use the Outline button. When you switch to the outline view, PowerPoint automatically changes the Drawing Toolbar into an Outline Toolbar. The arrow buttons allow you to move headings and subsidiary text up and down in the outline. All of the other buttons are labeled.

The outline is just another view of your slides. Any change that you make when you are looking at the material in the outline will be on the slides when you return to the slide view. Similarly, any change you make in the slides will automatically be reflected on the outline.

Step 3: Delete any unnecessary slides.

With the Slide Sorter View on the screen—

A. Click on the thumbnail of the slide you want to delete to highlight it.

B. Hit the DELETE key on your keyboard. The slide will be deleted, and the remaining slides will be re-ordered and re-numbered.

Step 4: Change the order of the slides where required.

With the Slide Sorter View on the screen—

A. Click on the thumbnail of the slide you want to re-order.

B. Hold down the left mouse button and drag that slide over the slide that it should follow. (If slide #3 should be moved to follow slide #6, drag slide #3 over slide #6.)

C. Release the mouse button. The slide will fall into place and all the slides will be re-numbered.

If you have a large number of slides, there is an alternate (and easier) method for changing the order of the slides which is to cut and paste. These buttons are explained in Chapter 12. An easy method for duplicating a slide from one slide show and inserting it into another is also explained in Chapter 12.

Step 5: Hide slides about which you remain undecided.

In some cases, you may have created a slide that covered a point you are now unsure will be a part of your presentation. If you delete the slide, and then decide you need it, you will have to create it over again. If you move it to another slide collection, you will have to find it and bring it back to the current slide show. PowerPoint offers a "Hide" option that temporarily disconnects an individual slide from a slide show, but leaves it in your collection of thumbnails in the Slide Sorter View so that you can bring it back again quickly if you need it.

A. Hide a slide.

With the Slide Sorter View on the screen—

1. Click on the slide you want to hide.

2. Go to the Menu Bar.

3. Click on the Slide Show button. A drop-down menu will appear.

4. Click on the Hide Slide button. (This button may not be displayed when the menu first appears because it is often in the extension of the menu. To call up the extension, click on the extension button at the bottom of the menu and the additional buttons will appear.) A null sign appears superimposed over the slide number below the slide that you have hidden.

5. When you run your slide show, the software will automatically skip the hidden slide.

B. Display a hidden slide.

With the Slide Sorter View on the screen—

1. Right click on the hidden slide. A drop-down menu will appear.

2. Click on the Hide Slide button, which will toggle off the Hide function. The null sign will disappear from the slide number below the slide that formerly was hidden, and it will now be a part of the slide show.

! You can also call up a hidden slide during a slide show. When you come to the slide that precedes the hidden slide, right click on it. A drop-down menu will appear. Click on the Go option. Click on the Slide Navigator. Then double-click on the slide you want. The slides that are hidden are indicated by numbers in parentheses.

Step 6: Print out your slides, if necessary.

Looking over your slides in hard copy sometimes helps you see inconsistencies in layout, font, and similar attributes that have crept in during the design process. You may need hard copies to share with others, although it is easy to e-mail PowerPoint slides and have them reviewed by your colleagues that way.

A. Go to the Menu Bar.

B. Click on the File button. A drop-down menu will appear.

C. Click on the Print option. A Print screen will appear. It looks like this:

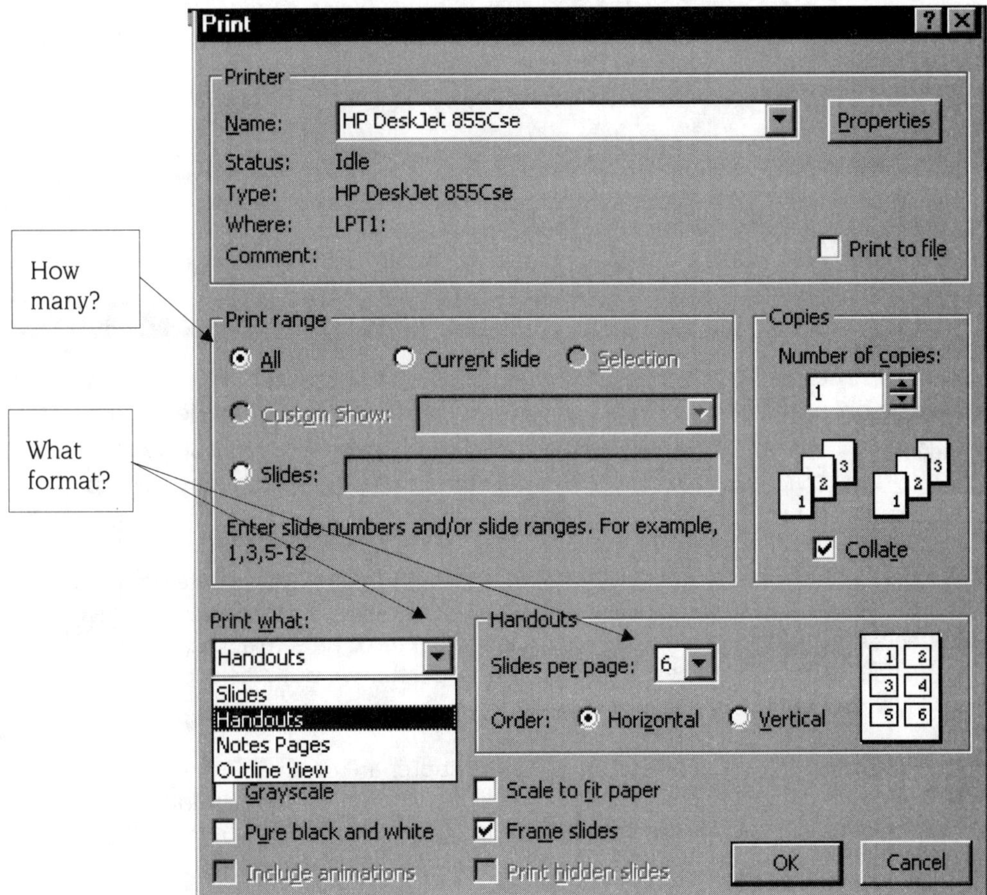

D. In the Print Range box, choose whether to print all, one, or several slides.

E. In the Print What box, choose the whether to print Slides (one slide in 8 x 10 format) or Handouts (up to six slides per page). The Handout format is usually the most helpful at this stage.

F. Click on the OK button.

The PowerPoint 97 Print screen is a little different. See illustration in Exercise 2.4. In the Print What box, choose the Slides (without animations) option.

Some lawyers who do not own digital projectors make color transparencies for testing with an overhead projector to see how the slides will look when enlarged to an eight-foot or ten-foot size. To do this, you need to click on Properties, and select a high resolution. Then put transparency film sheets in the printer. Use the Slides option in the Print What box.

You can create a backup for your in-court digital presentation by printing out high quality color copies on paper to use with an evidence camera. If your computer goes down, you can put the color paper copies on the evidence camera, and keep right on going. To do this, you need photo quality ink jet paper and you need to click on Properties in the Print box to select a high resolution.

Exercise 10.2: Add transitions

PowerPoint has built-in tools that help slides work together. This section deals with motion and special effects when you move from one slide to the next. (Chapter 9 deals with special effects within a single slide.) The software allows you to bring your slides to the screen in a variety of ways which may help to make the point you are urging on the viewer.

Most presentations work well with no transition at all. Concentrate on the potential use of special effects *within* individual slides before turning to whether any special effects are useful in moving from one slide to the next. After reviewing each slide and all of its effects, consider whether any additional persuasive power is added by using yet more special effects in the slide show.

Slides with transitions described in this chapter are on the CD that accompanies this book or can be downloaded from NITA's web site, *www.nitastudent.org*. By examining these models, you can see how transitions change the slides and their impact.

Useful terminology

Transition: A transition is the motion that moves from one slide to the next. PowerPoint's transitions for slide-to-slide motion within the whole presentation include some new options and also some of the same methods as its effects for object-to-object motion within the slide as discussed in Chapter 9.

Black slide: A special kind of transition involves putting a blank (or black) slide on the screen when you are talking about something not covered by a particular slide. By taking the previous slide off the screen, you keep jurors from wondering why you are talking about one thing when the screen is showing something else. With a black slide in place, the jurors are focused solely on you. Black slides also let you know that you have come to the end of your slides on a particular topic.

Transition icon: When you add a transition to bring a slide to the display screen, the software attaches a small icon to the file for that slide. This icon can be viewed in Slide Sorter mode (View Bar, Slide Sorter button—4th from the left). It is located just under the slide on the left side.

Useful General Rules

WHEN TO USE TRANSITIONS: Video designers have developed a lot of rules about when to use various transitions, most of which are quite specialized. In litigation presentations, the question to ask is whether the transition contributes to the flow of your presentation. For example, if you have several documents in a row, a transition that mimics page-turning (like Uncover, left, or Wipe, left) might be appropriate. However, those same transitions would not work well with a single document that was preceded and followed by other kinds of exhibits. A single document usually benefits by Uncover, right, or Wipe, right because that is the orientation of the eye to a single page. The simple motions that move from left to right or top to bottom have the least risk. Complicated forms that move in ways counter to the normal way the eye deals with pages present the most risk of causing more distraction than they are worth.

WHAT TRANSITIONS TO USE: In a courtroom, you want the transitions to be clean and understated. That means in most circumstances transitions will be accomplished with the "No transition" option. Drawing attention to the transition distracts attention from the substance to the special effects and usually does not increase juror appreciation for your points. Motion that affects the entire slide must be chosen even more carefully than motion that affects one object on a slide because the image is larger and the motion is more dominating and potentially nauseating.

Generally Okay	Sometimes Okay	Generally Not Okay
No transition	Box, in/out	Blinds, horizontal/vertical
Split, horizontal-out	Cut through black	Checkerboard, across/down
Split, vertical-out		Cover (all variations)
Wipe, down/right		Fade through black
		Random bars, horiz./vertical
		Random transitions
		Split, horiz.-in, vertical-in
		Strips (all variations)
		Uncover (all variations)
		Wipe, up/left

The transitions in the "generally okay" category are those with the most minimal motion that have the least potential for disruptive effect. Just because a transition is in the "generally okay" category does not mean you should use it on every slide.

The transitions in the "sometimes okay" category work well in specific instances. Boxing in and out works well with slides that have large images and simple designs. Cut through black is a way to introduce a colorful slide that you want to have a substantial impact on introduction.

The transitions in the "generally not okay" category are almost always too disruptive. The transition called "fade through black" is in this category because it does not work on many computers.

As with most rules, there are exceptions. You may find a particular use for a transition in the "generally not okay" category that works well in the context at hand. When constructing slides to mimic or repeat your opponent's arguments so that you can systematically take them apart, the Cover, Uncover, and Checkerboard transitions are sometimes useful. Be conservative. Use transitions only when you have a very good reason.

★ If you are using a projector and ten-foot screen to display your slides, this will magnify the effect of transitions from one slide to the next, and what may be okay on a large fifty-inch monitor may become visually jarring and unacceptable on a large screen.

Here are the steps to take to add transitions.

Step 1: Get the Slide Sorter view on the screen.

A. Go to the View Bar.

B. Click on the Slide Sorter button (4th from the left).

C. The Slide Sorter screen will appear (Illustration, Exercise 4.1) bringing with it the Animation Effects Toolbar which will appear directly under the Standard Toolbar at the top of the screen. It looks like this:

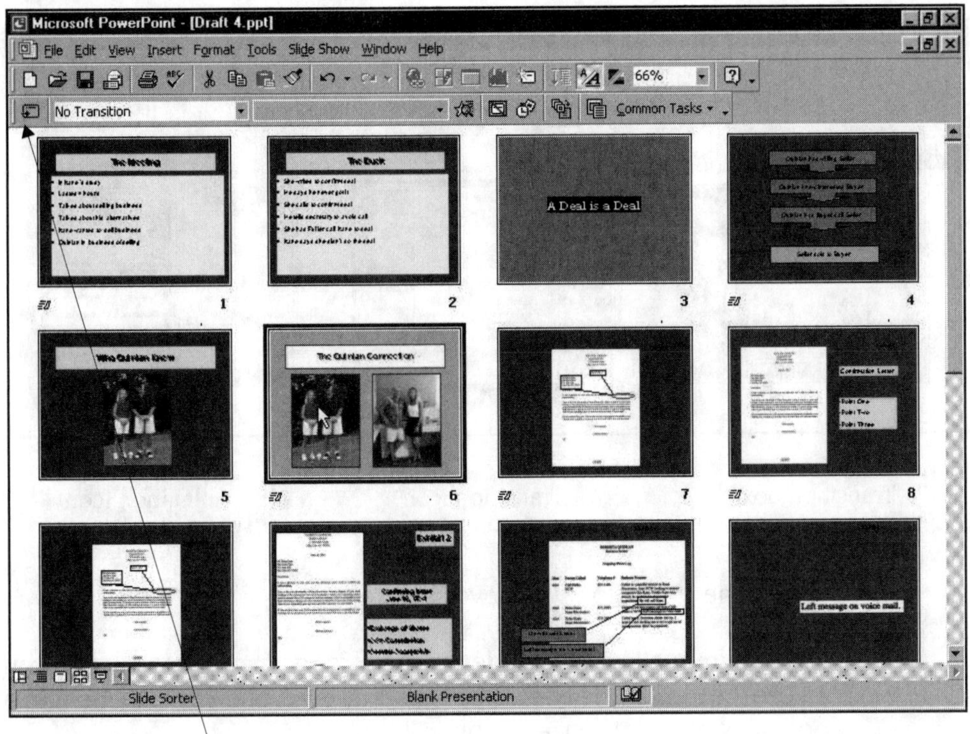

Animation Effects Toolbar

Step 2. Specify the transition you want between each slide and the next slide.

With the Slide Sorter view on the screen—

A. Click on the slide that will appear via a transition.

B. Go to the Slide Show Toolbar.

C. Click on the arrow next to the Transition box displaying the option "No Transition." A drop-down menu will display the options.

D. Choose the option you want. A small icon will appear below the thumbnail of your slide indicating that a transition is in place for this slide.

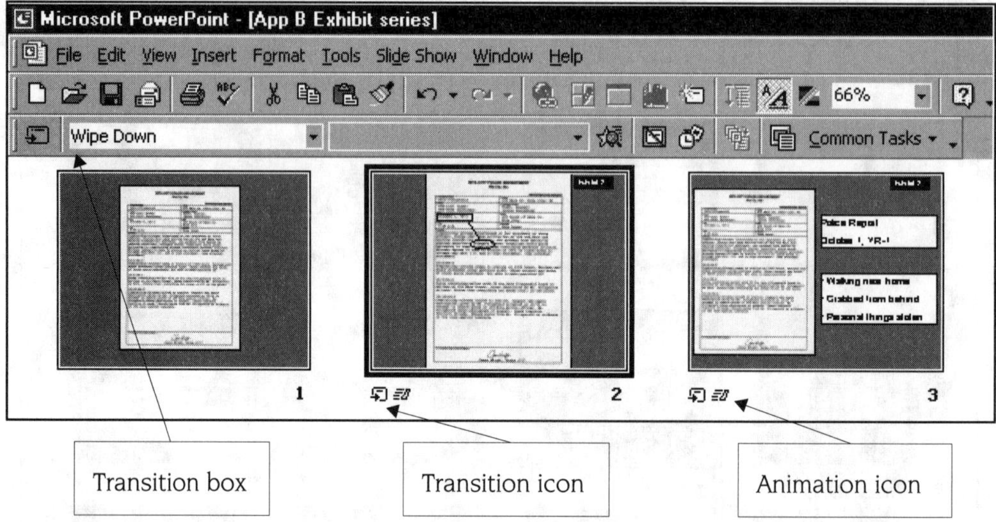

E. Preview the transition you have selected.

1. The thumbnail of your slide will go through that transition so you can see it in action. This is very small, however, and you may not get a good view of how the transition will look.

2. To get a larger view, go to the View Bar.

3. Click on the Slide Show button (5th from the left). Your slide will appear in full size on the screen.

4. Click on your left mouse button. The slide will display the transition you have selected.

5. To get back to the Slide Sorter view, click on the right mouse. A drop-down menu will appear. Click with the left mouse button on the End Show option. Now, go to the View Bar and click on the Slide Sorter button (4th from the left). The Slide Sorter view will reappear.

! If you want all of the slides in your show to have the same transition, go to the Menu bar (while in Slide Sorter view), click on the Edit button, and choose Select All from the drop-down menu. This activates all of your slides. Then choose the transition you want and click outside of the thumbnails.

Step 3: Create a black slide for the end of your presentation.

With the Slide Sorter view on the screen—

A. Create a new slide at the end of your slide presentation.

1. Click on the last slide in your presentation to highlight it.

2. Go to the Standard Toolbar.

3. Click on the New Slide button. The New Slide screen will appear. (Illustration, Exercise 2.1, Step 3.)

4. Click on the blank slide option (bottom row, last on right). A new slide will appear right after the last slide in your presentation.

B. Color the new slide black.

1. Go to the Menu Bar.

2. Click on the Format button. A drop-down menu will appear.

3. Click on the Background option. The Background screen will appear. (Illustration, Ch. 3, Exercise 3.3, Step 1.)

4. Click on the small arrow next to the box underneath the illustration. The color in the box is displaying the current selection. It may be white. A drop-down menu will appear displaying a row of small color boxes. One of them will be black.

5. Click on the black color box. The background of the illustration in the upper part of the Background screen will now be black.

6. Click on the Apply button. The last slide in your slideshow will now be a black one.

Do not use the Apply To All button or the backgrounds of all your slides will turn black.

PowerPoint 2000 provides a Background button on the Formatting Toolbar to eliminate some of the steps in creating the background for slides. To add this button to your toolbar, see instructions in Chapter 12.

Always put a black slide at the end of your slide show. That way, when you have finished, you do not have to leave the last slide on the screen. The black slide will cause the screen to go blank, and then, for example in an opening statement, you can conclude your presentation with the focus exclusively on you. Because your Slide Sorter view will come up if you click beyond the black slide at the end of the show, some lawyers like to put two or three black slides at the end of the show to prevent any nervous clicks from disturbing the flow.

Step 4: Put black slides at the beginning and at other stopping points in your presentation as needed.

With the Slide Sorter view still on the screen—

A. Create three or more duplicate black slides.

1. Click on your black slide at the end of the presentation so that it is active.

2. Hold down the CTRL key on your keyboard, and press the D (for "duplicate") key three times. This will create three more black slides that will appear right after your original black slide. (You will probably want to keep two black slides at the end of your presentation.)

B. Place one of the duplicate black slides at the beginning of the presentation.

1. Click on the first duplicate black slide so that it is active. It will have an extra border around it.

2. With your mouse pointer on the first duplicate black slide, hold down your left mouse button and drag the black slide to the left of the first slide at the beginning of your presentation. You will see a vertical line appear to the left of the first slide.

3. Release the left mouse button. The black slide will now be located right after the first slide.

★ It is useful to have a black slide at the beginning of your presentation. That way, you can leave the slide projector turned on in the courtroom without anything being displayed on the screen. For example, normally you would not use a slide to introduce yourself to the jury. So, at the outset of your opening statement, while you are doing that, a black slide is on the screen.

C. Place another black slide in the middle of your presentation where you need a break point.

1. Click on the second duplicate black slide so that it is active. It will have an extra border around it.

2. With your mouse pointer on the second duplicate black slide, hold down the left mouse button and drag it over the slide that you want the black slide to follow.

3. Release the left mouse button. The black slide will fall into place.

You do not want to have a slide displayed on the screen either before or after you have talked about the point covered by the slide. Using a black slide will keep the screen from competing with you for attention when you are not focused on a particular slide. Black slides are also a good cue for you that it is now time to move on to the next point and that the next slide coming up will be a part of a different series.

The number of black slides you need may depend on the equipment you are using. Because the large screen dominates the attention of jurors so completely, you may need to add more slides that turn the screen black while you are making related but subsidiary points to the display on the slide.

Exercise 10.3: Add notes

You can make notes about your slides and put them in a place that the software makes available to display both the slide and the notes. This is useful if you are creating a slide show while you are working on the best way to present your case, and you are using the slide show to help focus on presentation ideas. When you create a slide, you can jot down your notes so they are readily accessible with the slide. That way, if you are away from this work for awhile and then come back to it, you can click on your notes and review the ideas you had the last time you worked on the presentation. This is also a good way to exchange ideas or publish your annotations to your slides.

The notes are stored separately, so what you do with notes will not affect your slides. You can always hide the notes while working with the slides, and they will not reappear until you decide you need to look at them again.

PowerPoint calls this feature "speaker notes" but they are really only notes about the slide. You cannot have the slide with its accompanying notes on your screen while the judge and jury are looking at a display that contains only the slide. In order to use speaker notes in a courtroom setting, you must set up your notes as a separate slide, then toggle off the display in the courtroom (see Exercise 10.6(D)) and move to the slide containing your notes. In this way, you can refer to your notes without everyone in the courtroom seeing them. This is usually not an effective way to make a presentation.

97 The notes functions for PowerPoint 97 are somewhat different from PowerPoint 2000. Go to Appendix D for an explanation and examples keyed to PowerPoint 97.

A page of notes looks like this:

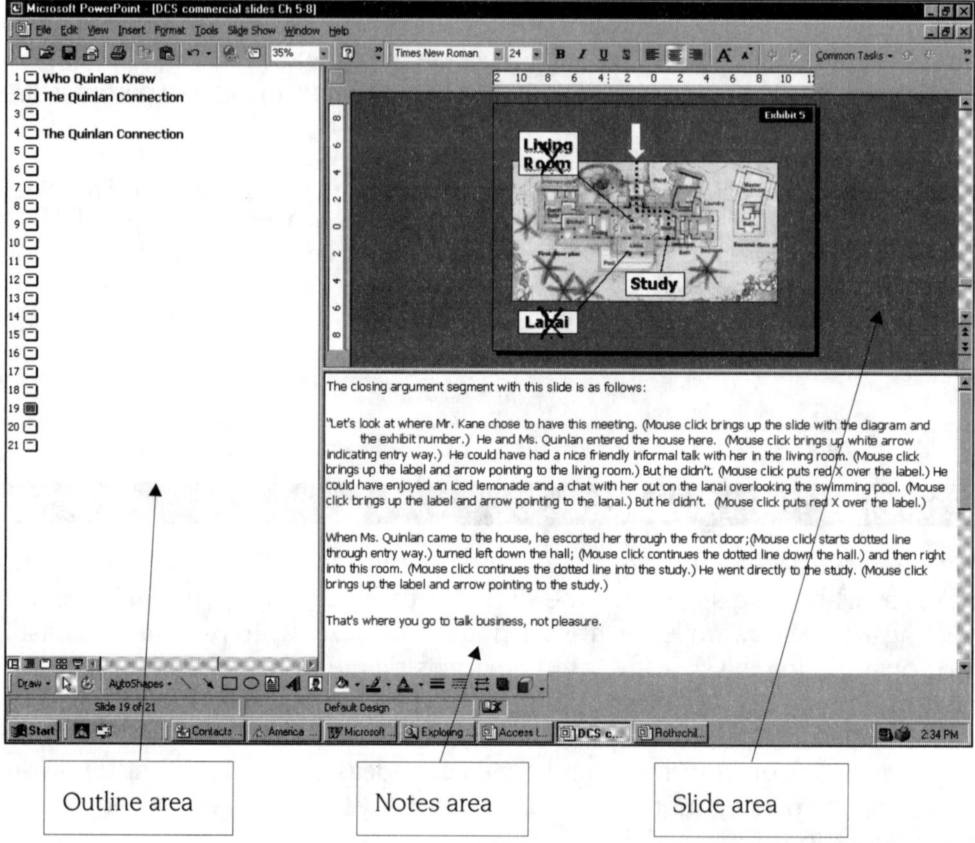

To create notes for a slide, do this:

Step 1: Get the notes area on the screen.

A. Go to the View Bar.

B. Click on the Full Screen View button. This brings up a screen display with the notes area on the bottom under the view of the slide. (The outline area appears to the left of the slide.) The screen will look like this:

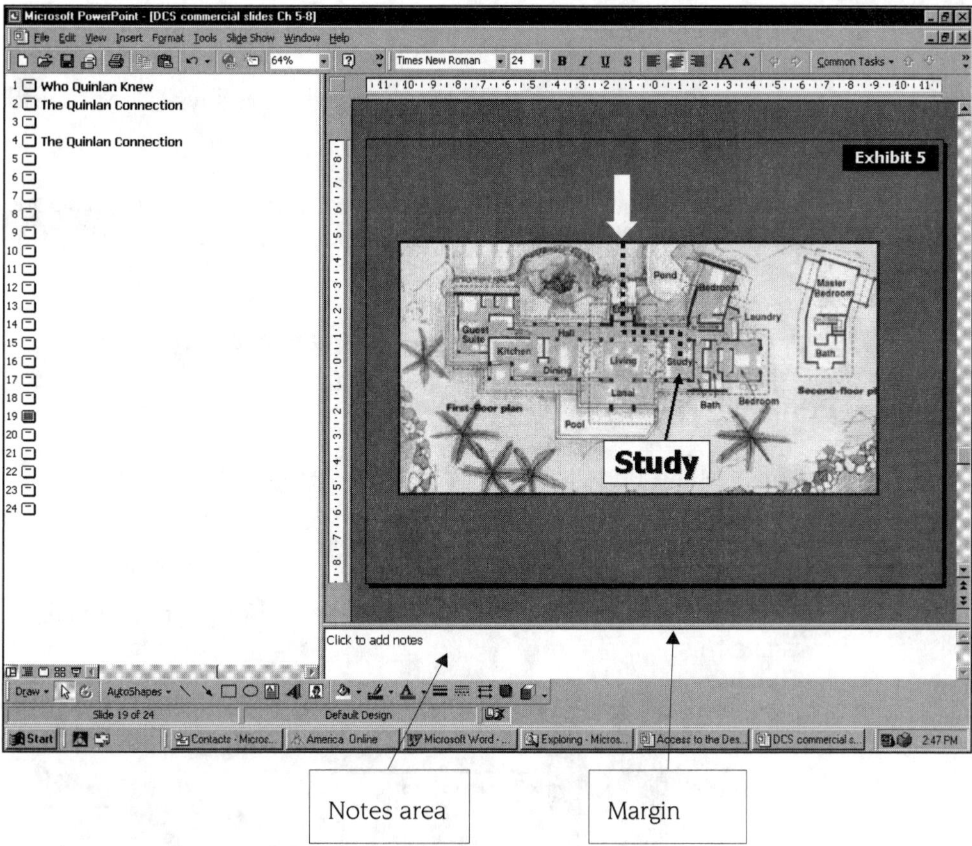

Step 2: Enlarge the notes area.

A. To provide more space for notes as you expand the number of things on the slide, put your mouse pointer anywhere on the margin between the slide area and the notes area as shown above.

B. As you hover over the margin, your one-arrow mouse pointer shape will change. Hold down the left mouse button and drag the margin upward. This will increase the size of the notes area and decrease the size of the slide area.

Step 3: Type in your notes.

A. Put your mouse pointer in the notes area where it says "Click to add notes."

B. As you add labels and annotations to the slide, type in notes about how the slide will be used, other possible alternatives to make the same point, or additions to be considered.

C. If you need more space, enlarge the notes area again.

Step 4: Print your notes if necessary.

A. Go to the Menu Bar.

B. Click on the File button. A drop-down menu will appear.

C. Click on the Print option. The Print screen will appear. The screen looks like this:

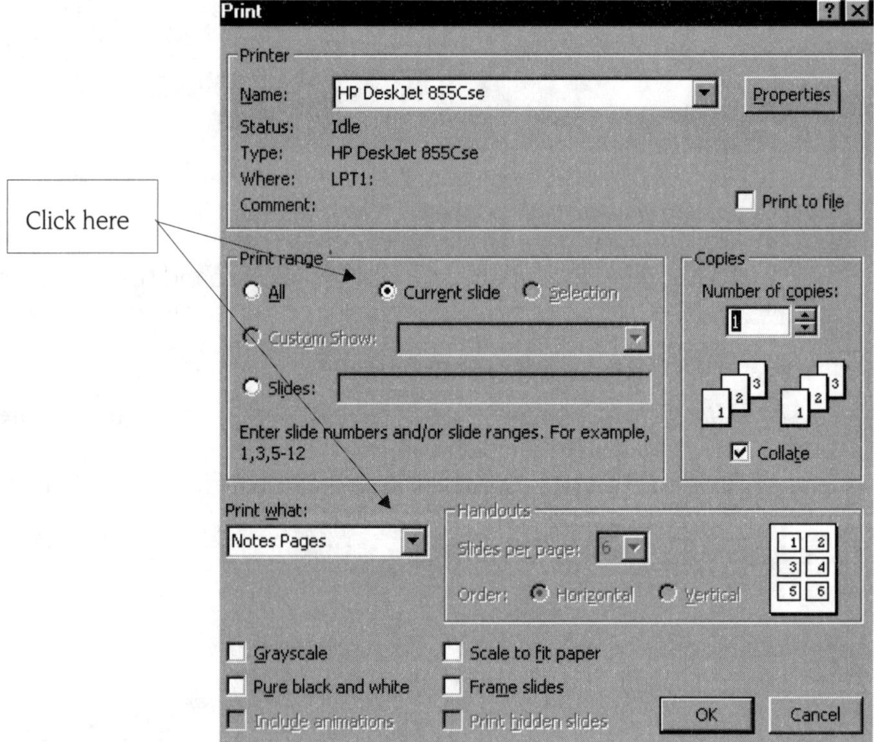

D. Go to the Print Range box in the center of the screen.

E. Click on the Current Slide option, which will print out a single slide at a time.

F. Go to the Print What box at the bottom of the screen.

G. Click on the arrow next to the Print What box to display the option called Notes Pages.

H. Click on OK. This will print a single page with the reduced-size version of he slide at the top and the notes at the bottom.

Step 5: Save your work. The notes will be saved with the slide. You can see them at any time or print them out using the steps set out above.

! To get back to your slide work, go to the View Bar, click on the Full Slide View button or the Slide Sorter button.

Exercise 10.4: Make a backup copy

In working with PowerPoint, it is especially important to make a backup of your work as you go along. The backup can be on floppy disks or on a removable cartridge of an external disk drive or on a CD. With a backup completely separate from your computer, you are saved the disastrous results of computer crashes.

Step 1: Make a backup copy on one floppy disk for small presentations without graphics or photographs.

A. Put a floppy disk in your disk drive. Use a new one. Older ones are more likely to develop flaws that will put your work out of reach.

B. Go to the Menu Bar.

C. Click on the File button. A drop-down menu will appear.

D. Choose the Save As option. This will open a standard Windows dialog box, where you can specify the location where you would like to save this file. The exact content of this box depends on how your computer is configured but, in general, it looks like this:

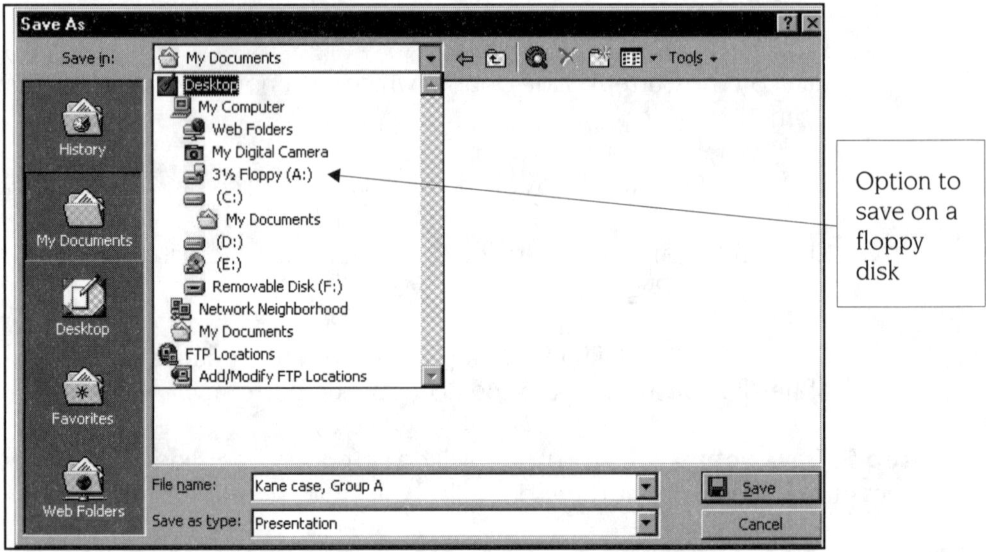

E. Click on the 3½ Floppy option.

F. Go to the File Name box at the bottom of the screen. Give your file a name, and click on the Save button to save the file.

G. Label the floppy with the name of your slide presentation and the date. You may have a number of versions before you are finished, and you will want to know which is your latest work.

97 The PowerPoint 97 screen looks somewhat different, but performs the same functions.

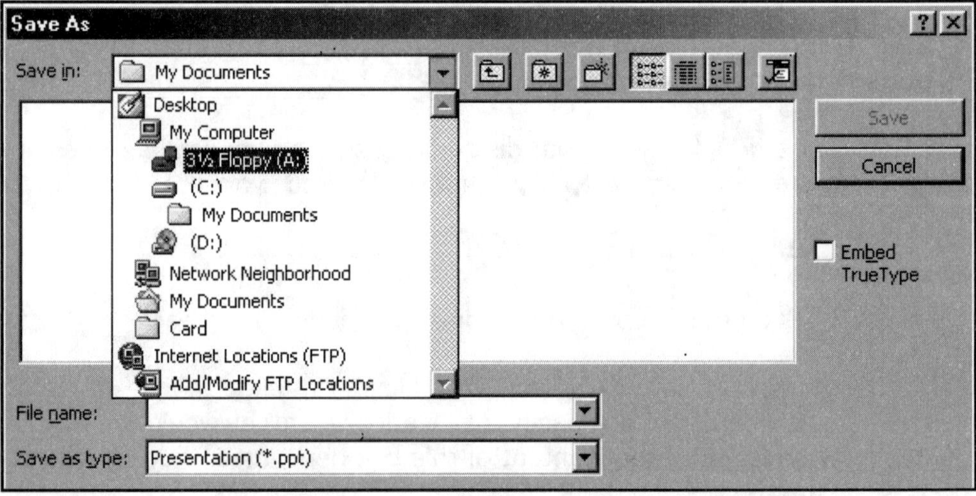

Step 2: Put backup copies on other storage media.

A. Making a backup to an external disk drive proceeds in the same way. External drives that take disks with 100 MB and 250 MB capacity are readily available and inexpensive. These units are easy to take on the road, and they provide a comforting backup if your computer crashes. In that event, all you need is the disk containing your slide show, the external drive, and another computer that is compatible with the external drive, and you can continue your presentation.

B. If you have Internet access, there are options to store your slide show in a commercial storage space provided at an Internet site. This means that your work will be available to you from any computer with an Internet connection, and you can authorize others to enter the storage space and download your work as well.

C. If you have access to a CD writer, you can store your presentations on a CD as another option.

Step 3: Make a backup copy on multiple floppy disks.

A. Put a floppy disk in your disk drive. Use a new disk. Older disks are more likely to have flaws that will put your work out of reach.

B. Go to the Menu Bar.

C. Click on the File button. A drop-down menu will appear.

D. Click on the Pack and Go option. The Pack and Go Wizard screen appears. Floppy disks have relatively limited storage space when your slide presentations contain photos, diagrams, and complicated text treatments. The standard Save function is limited to one disk. The Pack and Go option can store a presentation on successive disks.

   The Pack and Go feature may need the PowerPoint CD in your computer to retrieve the necessary files.

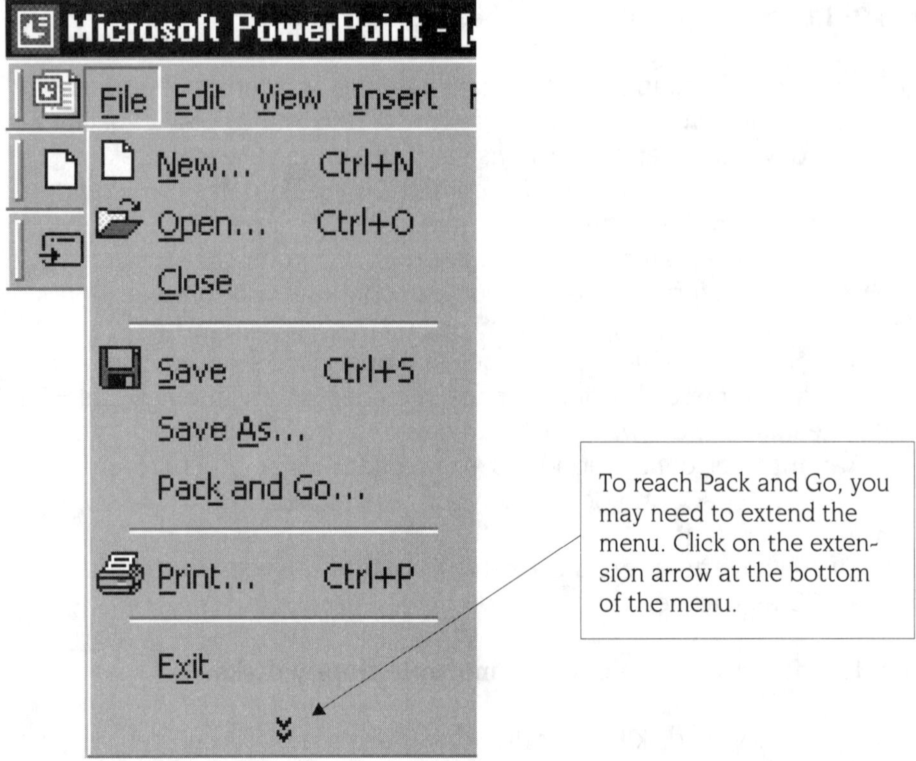

Floppy disks have relatively limited storage space when your slide presentations contain photos, diagrams, and complicated text treatments. The standard Save function is limited to one disk. The Pack and Go option can store a presentation on successive disks.

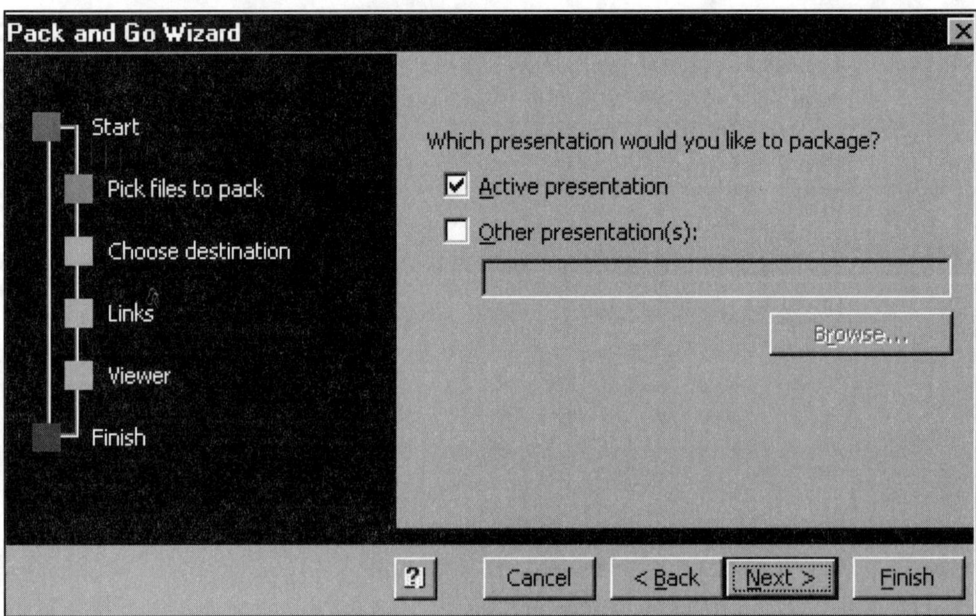

E. Click on the Next button at the bottom of the screen.

F. On the next screen, choose the slide show that you want to pack. If it is not the active file, click on the Browse button to locate it.

G. Click on the Next button at the bottom of the screen.

H. On the next screen, choose the location of the backup file. The screen display will show the A:\ drive (usually your floppy disk drive) as the first alternative.

I. Click on the Next button at the bottom of the screen. On the next screens, you are asked about linked files, embedding True Type fonts, and including a Viewer. You can ignore these.

! Linked files are those from which data for charts typically come. When you update the data file, it automatically updates your PowerPoint presentation. This is not generally useful for lawyers. Embedding the fonts and including a viewer have to do with switching computers. You will normally use your own computer in the courtroom, so these are not necessary either.

J. Click on Finish. If the slide show requires more than one floppy disk, the screen prompt will indicate when you need to insert another one.

K. Label the floppy disks with the name of your slide presentation, the order in which they were created, and the date. You may have a number of versions, and you will want to know which is your latest work.

! The chance of a computer crash some time when you are working on slides approaches 100%. Backup your slides repeatedly!

Exercise 10.5: Give the slide show a trial run

You can run your slide show from your keyboard, with a hardwired mouse or remote control, or using a wireless mouse or remote control. A hardwired control allows you to move anywhere within the length of the cord and does not require that you be in any particular position relative to the computer other than within the length of the cord. A wireless control allows you to move all around the courtroom so long as you stay within the range of the port or ports that receive the signals from the control.

Method 1: The keyboard.

The keyboard option requires no extra equipment. The basic control is the SPACEBAR on your keyboard which is easy to reach and not risky to use. However, this option keeps you tied to your computer which most often is not the optimum positioning. You can operate your slide show only from the place where your computer is located. But it is a reliable method and easy to use.

A. Open the file containing your slide presentation. (Ch. 2, Exercise 2.4, Step 5.)

B. Start the show with the first slide in your presentation.

1. Go to the View Bar.

2. Click on the Slide Show button (5th from the left).

3. The first slide will appear on the screen.

C. Run the slide show in order.

1. Move ahead one step using the SPACEBAR or the ENTER key or the PAGE DOWN key on your keyboard. These keys play each of the "effects" on a slide in order, and they will only move to the next slide when all of the effects on the current slide have been played.

2. Move back one step using the BACKSPACE key or the PAGE UP key. In a slide that has a number of animated objects, this will go back one animation. After it backs up through all of the animations on a slide, it will back up to the previous slide.

D. Display slides randomly (not in order).

1. Activate the slide show with a black slide on the screen.

2. Keep a printed page of the thumbnails of your slides that contains their numbers, keep a list of slide descriptions with their numbers, or put the slide numbers in your notes. When you are in Slide Sorter view, the slide numbers are under the lower right corner of the slide.

3. When you need a particular slide, type its number on the keyboard and press the ENTER key. That slide will come onto the display.

4. When you are finished with the slide, either hit the B key to turn your screen black, or go back to the black slide by typing the number 1 + the ENTER key. The black slide (which is number 1 in your series)

will stay on the screen until you need another slide to accompany your oral presentation.

★ If you are considering using a slide in a direct or cross-examination but are not sure whether you will want or need to do so, you can leave the option open by using the random access method described in Step D above. This is useful in cross-examination where the slide contains a portion of a deposition transcript or a document that is an impeaching exhibit.

Method 2: The hardwired mouse control.

You can operate your slide show with the regular mouse attached to your computer. The mouse option requires that you have an external mouse and (for setting up the show) a surface such as a mousepad where the mouse will operate properly. The left mouse button is the principal control. This option keeps you tied somewhat to your computer (although you can move to another position as far away from the computer as the mouse cord will allow), and is also reliable.

A. Open the file. (See above.)

B. Start the slide show with the first slide in your presentation. (See above.)

C. Run the slide show.

1. Move ahead one step using the left mouse button.

2. Move back one step using the Backspace or Page Up key on your keyboard. The mouse control to go back one step (click on the right mouse button, and then click on the Previous Slide option on the drop-down menu) is not a good choice because it will display the drop-down menu for your viewers to see.

Method 3: The wireless mouse control.

A wireless mouse allows you to have the full range of mouse capabilities without being attached to the computer. The wireless mouse transmits radio signals to a radio frequency receiver, and you need the necessary capability on your portable computer to support it. This unit has a side-to-side range of about ninety degrees and a distance range of up to seventy-five feet. This type of control fits nicely in the palm of the hand and can operate the mouse pointer with a twist of the wrist. Many projectors either come with or have at extra cost a remote unit in both wireless and hardwired form that contains a mouse.

The steps in presenting the slide show are the same as for the hardwired mouse.

Method 4: The hardwired remote control.

A hardwired remote control transmits signals from the remote to the projector through a cord that is plugged into a port on the projector. This allows you to move anywhere on either side of the projector within the length of the cord. This control is often more limited than a mouse. It has buttons for forward (to move one slide ahead) and back (to move one slide back). The tether on the hardwired remote control is about fifteen feet long.

A. Open the file. (See above.)

B. Start the slide show. (See above.)

C. Run the show.

1. Move ahead one step using the Advance key on the remote.

2. Move back one step using the BACKSPACE or PAGE UP keys on the keyboard.

Some projectors have hardwired remote controls with a black screen button which allows you to work on the computer without the computer display being put on the large screen; a freeze button that keeps the current image on the big screen while you work on your laptop (for example to switch to another slide show); and a zoom button that allows you to zoom in on a part of the slide that is on the big screen.

Method 5: The wireless remote control.

A wireless remote control has the same functions as the hardwired remote control. It operates by transmitting infrared signals to an infrared port or ports on your projector. This setup allows you to move around the courtroom, while operating your slide show, so long as you stay within the range of the port. The infrared port can take signals from about 100 degrees around its center point. If there is only one port, it is usually at the front of the projector, which means you have to stay in front of the projector, although you can be ten to fifteen feet away from it. Some newer projectors have infared ports on all four sides.

The uncertainty about being within the range of the infrared port often causes users to worry about whether the signal is getting through and, for that reason, to feel compelled to point the unit at the projector in a fairly obvious way. This detracts from the presentation. For this reason, infrared takes quite a lot of practice before you can work it without a glitch.

The controls on the wireless remote operate in the same fashion as the hardwired remote.

You can use the keyboard method for random access to slides in conjunction with any of the mouse control methods.

One caution: various types of display equipment present colors and fonts differently. The large screen can wash out colors, especially when room light cascades down the screen, so you might elect to use more vibrant tones or adjust the lighting. Any fixture directly above the screen must be disabled for good viewing. The smaller monitors present colors accurately, but have a very limited area so fonts have to be larger. You must be mindful of what can and cannot be seen on these smaller viewing platforms. It is always necessary to test your slides with the actual equipment you will be using at the approximate distances required by the layout of the courtroom to be sure they display your slides in an accurate manner that can be seen easily by your audience. See Chapter 11.

There are PowerPoint slide shows for each case on the CD that accompanies this book (or that can be downloaded from the NITA web site) to try out the methods for running a slide show that are described here.

Exercise 10.6: Other useful slide show features

Four other features included in PowerPoint's long list of options will help with courtroom slide shows.

A. The B key

When you need to make the screen go black at some unexpected moment, you can use the B key on your keyboard. When you are running a slide show, if you hit that key it will make the screen totally black in the same way a black slide does. The screen will stay black until you hit the B key again or click your left mouse button again. This feature allows you to stop at any point and to keep the screen blank while you are pursuing a matter to which the slides are not immediately relevant. Keeping the screen blank focuses attention on you and prevents distraction.

B. The pen feature

CTRL + P (for "pen") changes your mouse pointer into a draw capability so that you can underline or circle things on a slide being displayed on the screen. To try this out, go to the Slide Sorter screen, double click on one of your slides to bring it into full view, go to the View Bar, click on the Slide Show button. This brings the slide to the screen in slide show mode. Hold down the CTRL key and press the P key. The mouse pointer will change to a pen shape. If you hold down the left mouse button and move the mouse button around the screen, it will draw lines on the slide. Hit the E (for "erase") key on your keyboard to take the mouse drawings off the screen while still keeping the pen feature active. CTRL + A changes the mouse pointer back to its normal one-arrow shape and the next mouse click will remove the mouse drawings from the screen.

! The pen feature should be used very sparingly at trial. It is difficult to control a mouse with sufficient consistency to get good marks on the screen. Jurors become more interested in how the scribblings are wandering around the screen than the point that these marks were intended to make.

C. Timing the length of the presentation

To time your presentation while you rehearse it, go to the Menu Bar, click on the Slide Show button. A drop-down menu will appear. Choose the Rehearse Timings option. This starts the slide show. Go through the slide show as you intend to present it, changing slides as you talk. PowerPoint will record the amount of time you spend on each slide and the cumulative amount of time spent on the entire presentation.

! PowerPoint also uses this timing feature to run slide shows automatically. This is not recommended. It rarely works well in the courtroom. Click on "No" when the option arises. You need to be in control of the precise point when each slide or piece of a slide comes up, and thus you want to click for each action on the screen to be synchronized with what you are saying at the time.

D. The "toggle" feature

Most laptops have a toggle feature so that, when connected to projectors, you can work on your laptop (for example switching from one slide show to another) without anything showing on the big screen in the courtroom. Even if you do not use this feature, it is important to understand how it works because it may be active when you bring up your slide show in the courtroom. If that happens, the projector will show a blue screen rather than the slide show that appears on your laptop screen.

A "toggle" is just a shorthand name for a switch. With a two-way toggle, you press the required key for "on," and then press the same key for "off." When toggle is on, your display is showing on both your laptop screen and the big screen. When the toggle is off, your display is showing on your laptop screen and the big screen is blue. With a three-way toggle, you press the required key for option 1, press it again for option 2, and press it again for option 3. When you press it the fourth time, it goes back to option 1.

To toggle, hold down the Fn key on your keyboard and press the F7 key. On some computers, it is the F8 or F5 key. The F key usually will be marked with a small icon showing a blank screen and a screen with a display on it.

! Sometimes when you first hookup a laptop to a projector, either the laptop screen, the projector's screen, or both do not show any image at all. Do not panic! Use the toggle feature, perhaps more than once, to activate the images on both the laptop and projector screens.

Chapter 11

Display Equipment

For lawyers, making digital slide displays is just the first step. Using these illustrative aids in a courtroom to persuade a jury is the ultimate test. This book is not about courtroom technology for displaying exhibits, but this chapter will provide some basic information about equipment.

You have two basic options for displaying digital slides in a courtroom, with many variations on each option. The first option is using a digital projector and eight-foot or ten-foot screen. You connect your laptop computer to the projector, the laptop sends the images to the projector, and the projector puts the images on the screen, magnified many times. There are several sizes and varieties of screens and a number of types of projectors ranging across a wide spectrum of projecting power.

The second option is using one or more monitors in the courtroom. In this layout, you connect your laptop to the monitor (if you are using a single large monitor) or to the junction box (if you are using multiple monitors). The laptop sends images directly to the monitors. There are many types and sizes of monitors. Some courtrooms come already equipped with small flat screen digital monitors for each juror. Others have one large built-in video monitor. Still other courtrooms have no digital equipment or wiring at all, and you will need to rent the monitors you need for the jury, judge, and opposing counsel.

Each option has pluses and minuses. The projector puts a very large and commanding image up on the screen, but this setup takes up quite a bit of space in the courtroom and may not be possible at all in very small courtrooms. The monitors provide clear, crisp images, but glare from the windows may make it impossible for the jurors to see. The table on the following pages answers some of the basic questions.

★ Lighting is a key factor that needs to be assessed in selecting the best option for a particular courtroom. You should not dim the lights in a courtroom. Even if the courtroom has switches that allow sets of lights to be turned on and off individually, dimming the whole courtroom for a slide show is a bad idea. It interrupts your presentation; it makes jurors think about the movies and fiction rather than seeing the slide show as an integral part of your oral advocacy; and, in any case, most judges will not allow it.

Backup is another key factor in selecting your presentation equipment. Every use of technology in the courtroom raises the issue of backup measures. Equipment can and will fail. You need to know what to do if that happens. For example, if you are using a laptop computer and PowerPoint slide shows, you have several options for backup: (1) you can bring along a backup computer; (2) you can use an evidence camera with color prints of your slides; or (3) you can rely on color transparencies and an overhead projector. Similarly, if you are using a projector or an evidence camera, you need spare bulbs in case one goes out in the middle of your presentation. Your plans for backup need to be detailed and complete.

★ Using digital slides alters your personal style as a trial lawyer. The screens compete with you for the jurors' attention. You need to take this into account and make sure you understand the timing and movement differences in working with this type of illustrative aid as compared to hard copies. The National Institute for Trial Advocacy offers several courses on effective advocacy using courtroom technology where you have an opportunity to try various techniques and adjust your style.

Basic Technology for Courtroom Use

DISPLAYS	Best For	Pros	Cons	Cost[1]
Front projection screen	PowerPoint slides, text documents, photos	8'x10' display easily seen; big picture, easy set-up	Requires adequate space for projector in front, adequate viewing angle	$2,000-$299
Rear projection screen	PowerPoint slides, text documents, photos	No shadows; 8'x10' display easily seen; big picture	Requires adequate space for projector in rear, adequate viewing angle	$1,500-$700
Parabolic projection screen	PowerPoint slides, text documents, photos	Increases the amount of reflected light; better clarity	Needs careful adjustments, limited size	$3,000-$2,500
Conventional TV monitor	Conventional video; photos and objects on evidence camera	Readily available, reliable; easiest for evidence camera	40" max. size; not good for text; large box; very heavy. Needs converter to take output from a computer.	$1,500-$900

1. Retail purchase price. The range indicates high and low of equipment or software suitable for courtroom use. Products priced even lower than the range indicated here may be available but do not have the capability or reliability for courtroom use. Rentals are available in most large cities from AV firms. The named products are examples. There are many competing products in each category.

DISPLAYS	Best For	Pros	Cons	Cost
CRT monitor	PowerPoint slides, text, video	Reliable; smoother motion, truer colors; high resolution; various sizes; allows use of touch screen or light pen	42" max. size; large box; very heavy; requires a converter to take output from a document camera or VCR.	$9,500-$4,000
LCD monitor	PowerPoint slides, video	Slim profile; relatively light; easy to transport; high resolution; allows use of touch screen	21" max. xize; limited viewing angle; need special stands for jury box	$3,500-$900
Plasma monitor	Photos; text documents; video; PowerPoint slides	Slim profile; relatively light; high resolution	50" max. size; expensive; compatibility problems with computers and resolutions	$22,000-$9,000
Whiteboard screen	PowerPoint slides, diagrams	Interactive, write directly on screen for emphasis; touch screen controls	Fuzzier resolution, 3'x4' max. size; requires connection to computer and software installation	$4,000-$1,500

PROJECTORS	Best For	Pros	Cons	Cost
DLP projector[2]	Text, PowerPoint slides, photos, video	Images unfiltered & bright; compact size; takes input from evidence camera or VCR	More costly to repair	$16,000-$3,000
LCD projector[3]	Text, PowerPoint slides, photos, video	Sturdy, reliable, compact size, good quality images; takes input from evidence camera or VCR	Less bright images than DLP in lower-end equipment; larger size; less quality on video	$16,000-$3,000

2. Digital light processing; uses a chip dotted with thousands of mirrors to switch light pixels at high speed.

3. Liquid crystal display; filters light through an LCD panel to produce images. LCD projectors are different from LCD panels which sit on top of conventional overhead projectors.

CONTROLS	Best For	Pros	Cons	Cost
Wireless mouse	Courtroom where lawyers are allowed to move around	Small, fits in the hand, provides all of the mouse contols, good range	Very difficult to operate smoothly without extensive practice	$70
Hardwired remote control	Courtroom where lawyers are in a relatively fixed position	Easier and less obtrusive than the regular mouse; reliable	Range limited to length of cord that provides connection, limited controls	Included with the projector
Wireless remote control	Slide shows with numerous slides used intermittently	Small, unobtrusive, good range	Needs some practice to operate smoothly	$150-$50

OTHER HARDWARE	Best For	Pros	Cons	Cost
Digital camera	Photos to be displayed with computer equipment	Rapid transfer of photos to computer	Long-range and technical shots lower quality than SLR cameras	$1,000-$300
Scanner	Last minute exhibits from documents and photos	Portable, easy to use, capability to deal with sizing, cropping	Image quality not quite as high as commercial models that use high-end software	$1,200-$400
Color printer	Create backup color transparancies	Portable, easy to use	Image quallity not quite as high as commercial models	$1,150-$400
Speakers & amplifier for courtroom audio playback	Videotapes with audio portions	Makes sound clearer and more realistic than computer speakers	May increase the impression of a sound and light show	$1,500-$50

SOFTWARE	Best For	Pros	Cons	Cost
Slide presentation software	Bullet point lists; presenting text documents; photos	Easy, helps focus openings & closings	Once slide show is composed, lacks flexibility; no changes on the fly	\$356-\$95 for Microsoft PowerPoint
Illustration & design software	Diagrams, complicated organization charts, maps, drawings	Easy, helps focus witness testimony	Output is put into PowerPoint slide show or evidence display presentation	\$1,600-\$115 for Adobe Illustrator 8.0; \$500 for Visio
Evidence display software	Call-outs, labeling, inserting video and photos, comparison of multiple documents	Adds motion and flexibility; makes changes on the fly; helps focus witness testimony	Somewhat more complicated; requires PowerPoint as a first step	\$139 for ANIX, a PowerPoint plug-in
Photo edit software	Digital alteration of photos	Eliminates unnecessary details	May invite objections	\$625-\$175 for Adobe Photoshop 5.0
Video edit software	Clips from long videotapes	Eliminates unnecessary portions	May lead to Rule 106 objections	\$50 for ViEdit[4]
Feature animation software	Full motion animations to represent physical facts over time	Very powerful in teaching concepts and relating ideas	Relatively expensive; difficult to use; high-end equipment required	\$5,000 for StudioMax[5]

4. Video editing is generally done by professionals for approximately \$150/hr.
5. Animations are generally done by professionals for \$5,000 and up for completed animation.

Chapter 12

Learning the Next Level

Chapters 1 through 10 are designed to provide the lawyers with sufficient basic tools to do their work efficiently. For the reasons pointed out in the preface, every trial lawyer can benefit from learning these tools, no matter what overall approach is taken to incorporating computer technology in other areas of the practice. At some point, depending on the type of practice you have or your personal inclination to learn new software, you may decide to leave further work in this area to your support personnel or outside consultants. This chapter may tempt you to consider learning a few of the more useful methods beyond the basic level.

Sixteen additional features or operations are often useful to lawyers.

1. Use alternative control commands
2. Try shortcuts and easy enhancements
3. Change the PowerPoint screen display
4. Duplicate slides from another show
5. Highlight with the semitransparent effect
6. Use a cover to highlight text
7. Put organization charts on slides
8. Add video clips to slides
9. Create statistical charts for slides
10. Enhance time lines with illustrations
11. Import and use clip art
12. Put PowerPoint displays into briefs
13. De-construct someone else's slides
14. Scan material for use in slides

15. Use slides for document control

16. Add ANIX software for more capability

Most of these are easy to master on your own. The summary description in this chapter is enough to get you started. More detailed instructions can be found in the on-screen help provided by the software and in general manuals on PowerPoint.

Those who want to move to the next level should also consult the works of Edward Rolf Tufte, the ultimate guru of information design. Tufte is a professor at Yale, where he teaches courses in statistical evidence and information design. See *Visual Explanations* (Graphics Press 1997), *The Visual Display of Quantitative Information* (Graphics Press 1983), and *Envisioning Information* (Graphics Press 1990).

Exercise 12.1: Use alternative control commands

This section describes some of the alternate ways of doing things using PowerPoint. For example, if you want to save your work, one option is to go to the Standard Toolbar and click on the Save button; another option is to go to the Menu Bar, click on the File button, and pick the Save option; and a third option is to go to the keyboard and press the CTRL key and the S key at the same time. All three methods produce exactly the same result. In chapters 2 through 10, only one way of doing each PowerPoint operation is described in order to keep the text simple and easy to understand. As you work with PowerPoint, you may decide that you prefer keyboard options for most operations or you may find that the Menu Bar (with its word descriptions for buttons) is easier for you than the various icons on the buttons on other Toolbars.

Keyboard commands

Many of the commands performed with menus and buttons can also be performed with the keys on your computer keyboard. When you are using the keyboard for typing, as is often the case in creating PowerPoint slides, sometimes it is more efficient to use the keyboard for commands as well.

Control key commands

CTRL + A	Select All	Highlights everything in the object where your cursor is currently located. Turn off by clicking on the left mouse button.
CTRL + B	Bold face	Bold faces everything you type after you turn this command on or everything you have highlighted when you turn it on. Turn off by CTRL + B again.

CTRL + C	Copy	Copies to the clipboard everything that is highlighed when you turn this command on. (CTRL + V is the paste command to insert what you copied.)
CTRL + E	Center Align	Aligns to the center the text you are about to type or have highlighted. Same function as Formatting Toolbar, Center Align button. Turn off by selecting another alignment.
CTRL + F	Find	Search for specific text in your presentation.
CTRL + H	Replace	Search for and replace specific text in your presentation.
CTRL + I	Italic	Italicizes everything you type after you turn this command on or everything you have highlighted when you turn it on. Turn off by CTRL + I again.
CTRL + J	Justify	Justifies text you are about to type or have highlighted to both the left and right margins. Turn off by selecting another alignment. May not work on your computer.
CTRL + K	Hyperlink	Connects one slide or object on a slide to another.
CTRL + L	Left Align	Aligns to the left margin text you are about to type or have highlighted. Same function as Formatting Toolbar, Left Align button. Turn off by selecting another alignment.
CTRL + M	New Slide	Brings up New Slide Screen. Same function as Standard Toolbar, New Slide button.
CTRL + N	New	Open up a new presentation. Same function as Menu Bar, File⇒New.
CTRL + O	Open	Open a file. Same function as Menu Bar, File⇒Open.
CTRL + P	Print	Print a file. Same function as Menu Bar, File⇒Print.
CTRL + R	Right Align	Aligns to the right margin text you are about to type or have highlighted. Same function as Formatting Toolbar, Right Align button. Turn off by selecting another alignment.
CTRL + S	Save	Saves the file you are working on. Same function as Menu Bar, File⇒Save or Save As.

CTRL + U	Underline	Underlines the text you are about to type or have highlighted. Same function as Formatting Toolbar, Underline button. Turn off by CTRL + U again.
CTRL + V	Paste	Pastes material copied to the clipboard. Same function as Standard Toolbar, Paste button.
CTRL + X	Cut	Cuts material that you have highlighted from the text. Same function as Standard Toolbar, Cut button.
CTRL + Y	Repeat New Slide	Brings up New Slide screen with same layout selected as slide on the screen.
CTRL + Z	Undo	Undoes the last thing you did. Same function as Standard Toolbar, Undo button.

Function key commands

F1	Help	Access PowerPoint's on-screen help functions
F5	Slide Show	Go to the slide show view
F6	Next Pane	Change from the slide area to the notes area to the outline area of the full screen view
F7	Spell Check	Show possible misspelling of the text in slides

Shift key commands

CTRL + SHIFT + >	Increase font size	Increases the current font by one size with each click
CTRL + SHIFT + <	Decrease font size	Decreases the current font by one size with each click
ALT + SHIFT + ←	Promote	Moves bullet point from current level to next level up
ALT + SHIFT + →	Demote	Moves bullet point from current level to next level down
ALT + SHIFT + ↑	Move up	Moves bullet point up one place on the slide
ALT + SHIFT + ↓	Move down	Moves bullet point down one place on the slide

Menu bar commands

Some of the commands controlled by buttons on the other toolbars can also be given using the Menu Bar buttons and drop down menus.

Edit button	Cut Copy Paste Select all Duplicate Delete Find Replace
View button	Normal Slide Sorter Notes Page Slide show
Insert button	New Slide Duplicate Slide Picture (From File) Movies and Sounds (video) (Movie from File)
Format button	Font (typeface and type size) Bullets and Numbering Alignment (left, center, right) Background

Exercise 12.2: Try shortcuts and easy enhancements

This book describes the minimum number of PowerPoint features necessary to create effective visual aids for trial, mediation, arbitration, and appeal. Here are some additional features you may want to explore on your own, either with the aid of the help screens built into PowerPoint (click on the Help button on the Menu Bar) or with a general purpose PowerPoint manual.

Nudge: The Draw button menu provides a Nudge option that is very useful in making more precise adjustments when you are trying to move one object into close proximity to another. The Nudge moves the object the minimum amount available in the direction you choose—up, down, left, or right. To use the Nudge, activate the object that you want to move, go to the Drawing Toolbar, click on the Draw button (1st on the left), highlight the Nudge option, and pick the direction from the side menu that comes up.

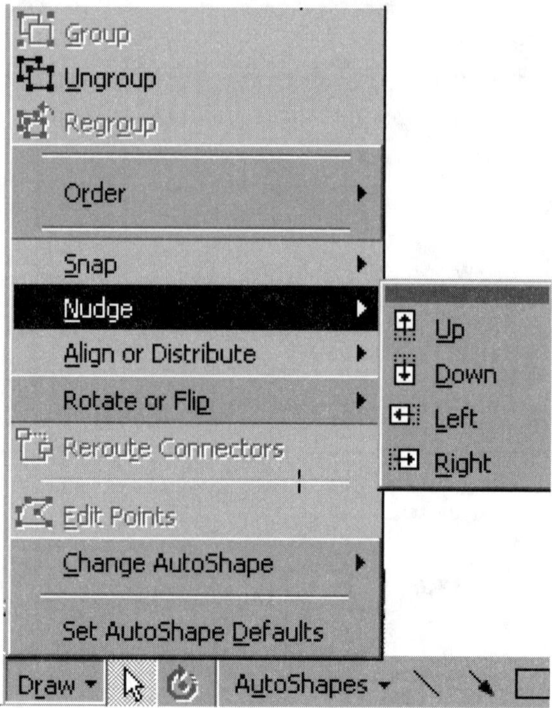

Align: The Draw button menu provides an Align feature that helps put groups of objects into better order. If you have four boxes on your slide, for example, you can align them across their tops, along their bottoms, by their left or right margins, and also by their centers. Click on the first object to activate it. Hold down the SHIFT key, and click on each of the rest of the objects to be lined up. Then go to the Drawing Toolbar, click on the Draw button (1st on the left), highlight the Align and Distribute option, and pick the direction from the side menu that comes up.

For example, the Align By Top option lined up these different sized boxes evenly at their tops.

Distribute: If you want a group of objects evenly spaced across a given distance, use the Distribute function. Put one object at one end of the range, and another object at the other end of the range. Activate the first object by clicking on it. Hold down the SHIFT key and click on each of the rest of the objects. Then go to the Drawing Toolbar, click on the Draw button (1st on the left), highlight the Align and Distribute option, and pick the direction (horizontally or vertically) in which you want the objects arranged.

For example, the Distribute Horizontally puts an equal amount of distance between the boxes.

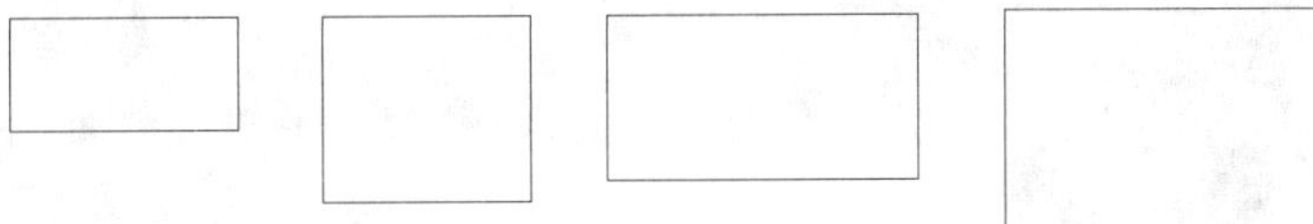

Order: When you have several objects to put on a slide and you want them to overlap, so that one object is in the front and another is in the back, use the Order function. Highlight the object to move to the front or to the back. Go to the Drawing Toolbar, click on the Draw button (1st on the left), highlight the Order option, and pick the direction (front to back) in which you want the objects arranged.

The Order function allows you to move any of the boxes to the foreground or background.

Copy-and-paste: To duplicate an object (a document, photo, diagram, logo) on several slides: Select the object, use the CTRL + C command to copy to the clipboard, move the mouse pointer to the slide where the object is to go; click there; then use CTRL + V command to paste the object in each new slide.

Exercise 12.3: Change the PowerPoint screen display

The Standard Toolbar hides some of its buttons. To display the missing buttons, click on the extension arrow at the end of the toolbar. An Add or Remove Buttons option appears. Click on that to display a full list of all of the Standard Toolbar buttons.

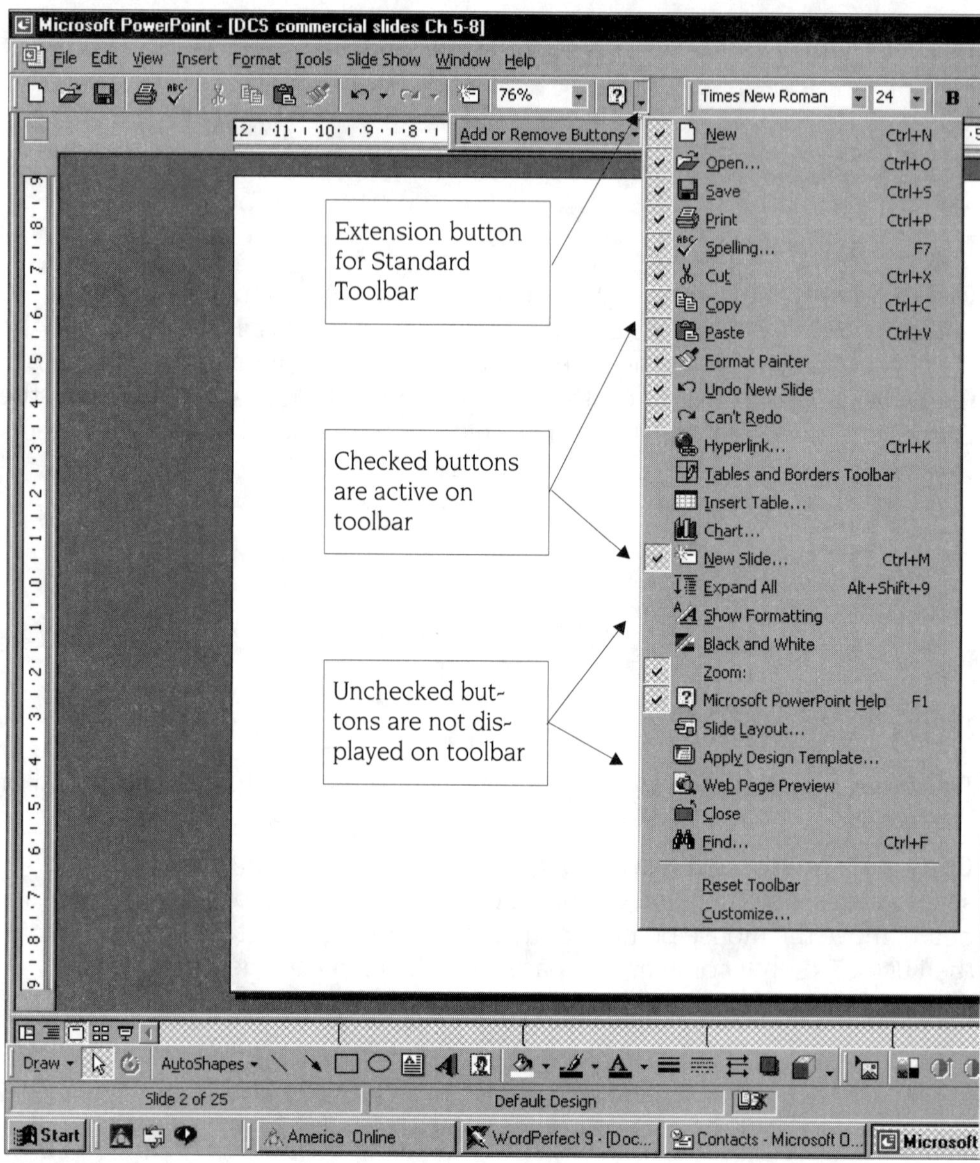

For example, the Hyperlink, Tables and Borders, Insert Table, Chart, Expand All, Show Formatting, and Black and White Mode buttons are not particularly useful for building litigation slides. You might consider removing them from the toolbar. To remove a button, click on it and the check mark disappears.

The Formatting Toolbar also hides some if its buttons when it is located on the same level as the Standard Toolbar. To display the missing buttons, click on the extension arrow at the end of the toolbar. A drop-down menu will appear containing all of the missing buttons. In addition, that menu has a button to add or remove buttons. Click on that button to display a full list of all of the Formatting Toolbar buttons.

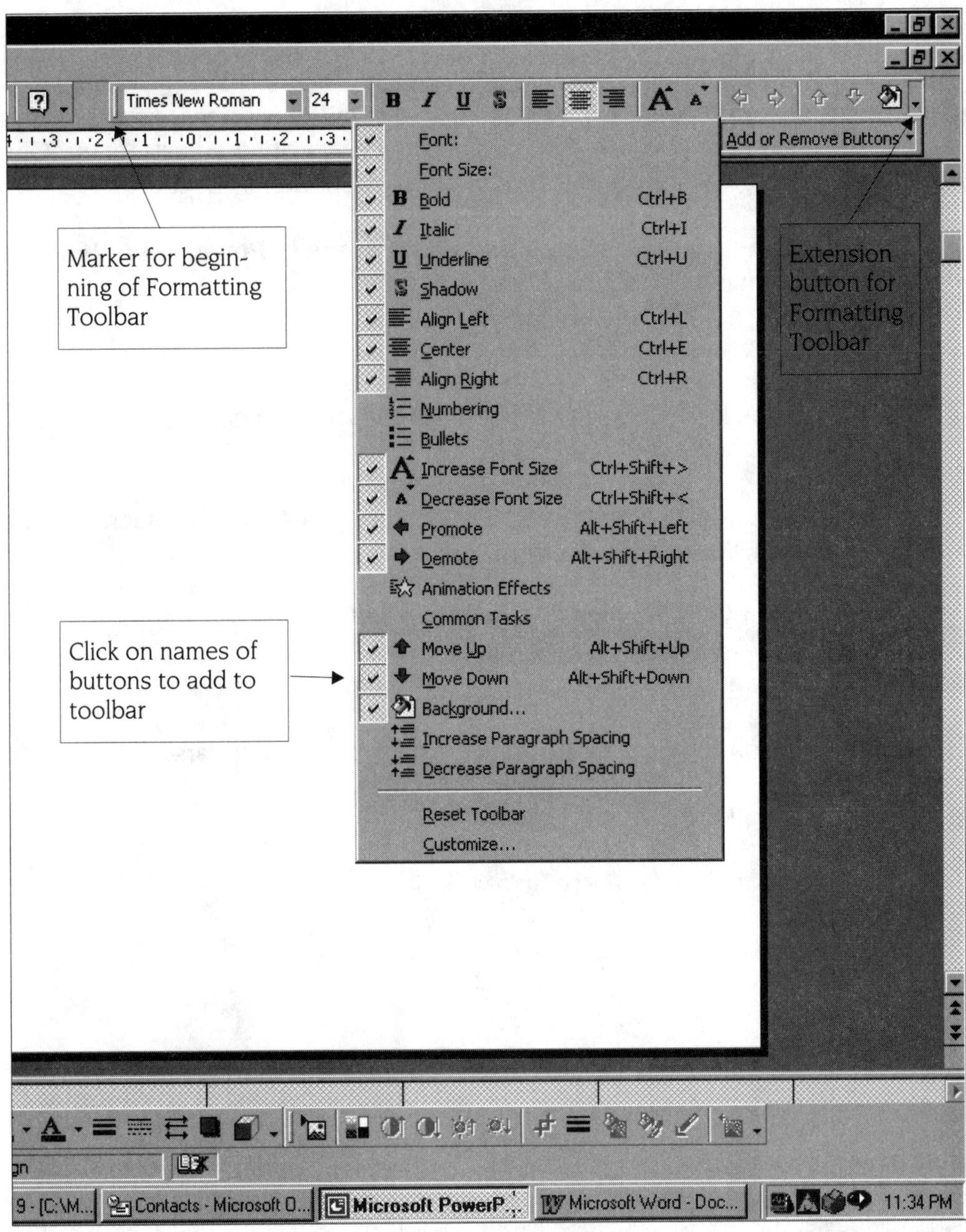

The Move Up, Move Down, and Background buttons are useful for building litigation slides, and you might consider adding them to your toolbar. The Increase Paragraph Spacing and Decrease Paragraph Spacing are also sometimes useful for bullet point slides.

To remove a button from a toolbar, click on the checkbox next to its name. The check mark will disappear. This takes the button off the toolbar.

To add a button to a toolbar, click on the name. A box and check mark will appear. This adds the button to the toolbar. If there is not space on the toolbar for all the buttons you have activated, they will be displayed in an extension box with the button for Add or Remove buttons.

Customizing your screen: You can make the PowerPoint screen display always produce the features you like to use (and avoid repetitive adjustments). One such customization is shown in the illustration in Chapter 1, Section 1.5.

Step 1: Eliminate the outlines and notes areas in PowerPoint 2000 (as these are primarily for business and sales uses).

A. Open a new presentation.

B. Set the layout you most often use for your slides. (Blank screen is a good choice.)

C. Set the options you want for each new presentation, such as slide size, text styles.

D. Go to the Menu Bar.

E. Click on the File button. A drop-down menu appears.

F. Click on the Save As option. The Save screen appears.

G. Click on the Save As Type option.

H. Click on the Design Template option.

I. Name the file "Blank presentation.pot."

J. Click on the Save button.

This file will now be used as the basis for all new presentations. When you call up old presentations, they will still be in the old format. Anything new will start with all of the options with which you normally work, thus saving time in repeatedly changing settings.

! If you set the new presentation for "blank screen" as recommended above, then each time you open a new presentation the first slide will be a blank one. This can later be made a black slide (see discussion in Chapter 10, Exercise 10.2, Step 3) which is useful for the start of any presentation. When you want something other than a blank slide, click on the New Slide button which will present all of the available layouts.

Step 2: Modify the PowerPoint 2000 display to put the Formatting Toolbar under the Standard Toolbar so all the buttons can be displayed at once.

A. Go to the move handle at the front of the Formatting Toolbar.

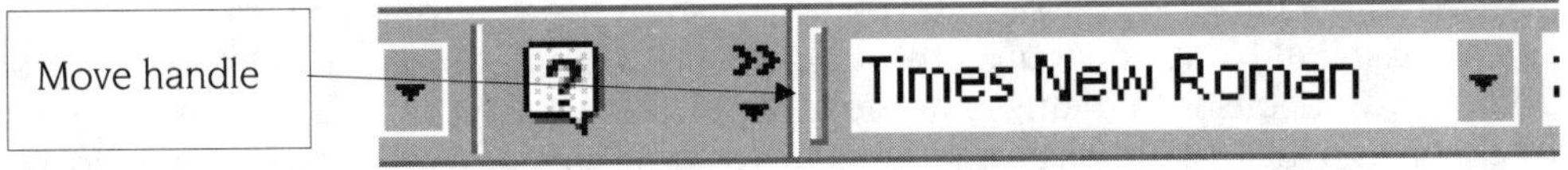

B. The mouse pointer will change to a four-arrow shape.

C. Hold down the left mouse button. Drag the toolbar to the left and place it under the Standard Toolbar. PowerPoint will dock the Formatting Toolbar in a way that will not cover up any of your work. The toolbar will stay in that location until you move it.

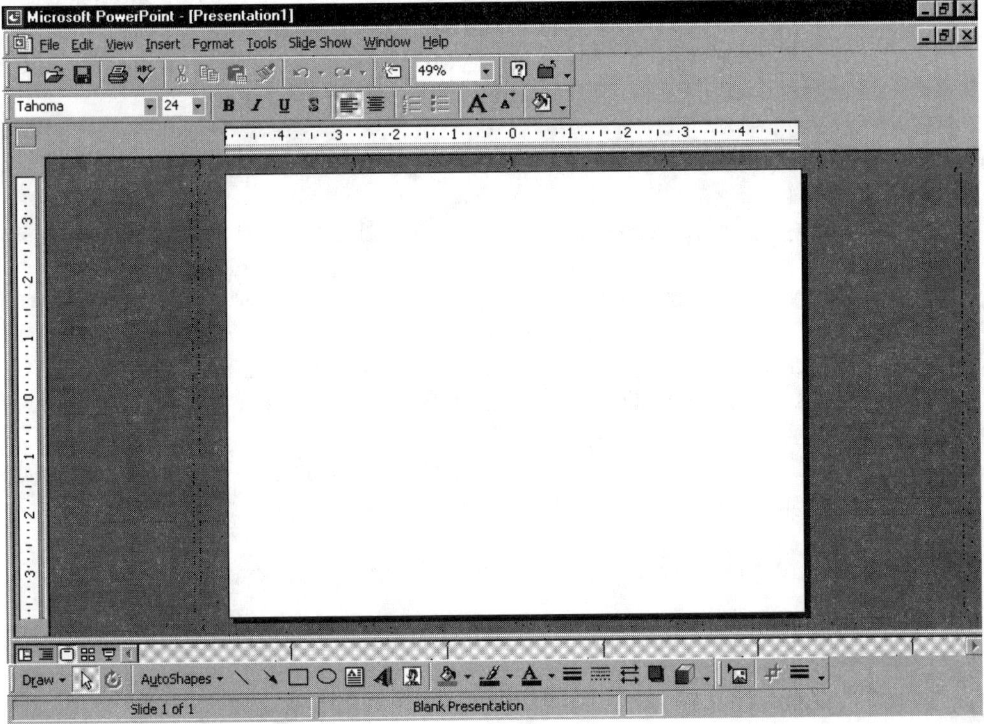

This is how the screen display would look after the toolbars have been moved and all the useful buttons displayed.

! There is an alternative way to rearrange the toolbars. Go to the Standard Toolbar. Click on the Expansion button at the very end. Click on the Add or Remove Buttons button. Go to the bottom of the drop-down menu and select the Customize button. A box will come up. In the Options tab, remove the check marks under "Standard and Formatting Toolbars share one row" and "Menus show recently used commands first." Click on Close. Follow the same procedure for the Formatting Toolbar.

97 For PowerPoint 97, go to the Menu Bar. Click on the View button. Select Toolbars, then Customize. A dialog box appears. Click on the middle tab labeled Commands. There you see on the left a list of the Menu Bar categories: File, Edit, View, etc. By clicking on the category on the left, you get a list on the right of the functions that are listed under that Menu Bar item on the drop-down list. Some are already on the toolbars. Some have buttons with them; some are text. Anything listed can be added to a toolbar by clicking on the item. It will be added to the toolbar that corresponds to the function.

Exercise 12.4: Duplicate slides from another show

As you accumulate more slide shows, you will have stock slides or slide designs that you want to use in the new slide shows that you are putting together. At times there are a number of slides that you want to duplicate from one slide show and insert into another. To do this:

Step 1: Get both slide shows on the screen.

A. Open the first slide show. Then open the second one.

B. Go to the Menu Bar.

C. Click on the Windows button. A drop-down menu will appear. The names of both slide presentations will be listed.

D. Click on the Arrange All option. This will bring up two windows, side by side, each of which has one of the slide presentations in it.

E. Go to the View Bar at the bottom of each window.

F. Double click on the Slide Sorter button (3rd from the left) at the bottom of each window. All of the slides in both slide shows will now be on the screen (or available by scrolling down) in thumbnail form.

Step 2: Copy the slide from one show.

A. Go to the slide presentation from which you want to take a copy. Click on the slide that you want to copy. The software will highlight it.

B. Go to the Standard Toolbar. Click on the Copy button.

Step 3: Paste the slide into the other show.

A. Go to the slide presentation where you want the duplicate slide to go. Click on the slide you want the copy to follow. A vertical line will appear after that slide indicating where the copy will go.

B. Go to the Standard Toolbar. Click on the Paste button. The software will put the copy right after that slide.

Step 4: Save your work.

There are three PowerPoint slide shows on the CD accompanying this book that can be used to try out the method described here.

Exercise 12.5: Highlight with the semitransparent effect

Unfortunately, PowerPoint does not have a highlighter for documents. The ANIX software described in Exercise 12.16 does have this capability. If you put a box around text in a document and use a yellow fill, for example, it will cover the text. PowerPoint has a semitransparent effect which allows you to color a box or a circle that you put over text in a document but to have the text show through. The principal limitation is that you must use a light color in order to be able to see the text underneath. The text will not be as clear and readable through the semitransparent color as it was in the original.

Step 1: Put a box over the text to be highlighted. (Exercise 7.1.)

Step 2: Put a light fill color in the box.

A. Select (activate) the box by clicking on it. The fuzzy border with handles should appear.

B. Go to the Drawing Toolbar.

C. Click on the arrow to the right of the Fill Color button. A drop-down menu will appear.

D. Click on the More Fill Colors option. The Colors dialog box will appear. It looks like this:

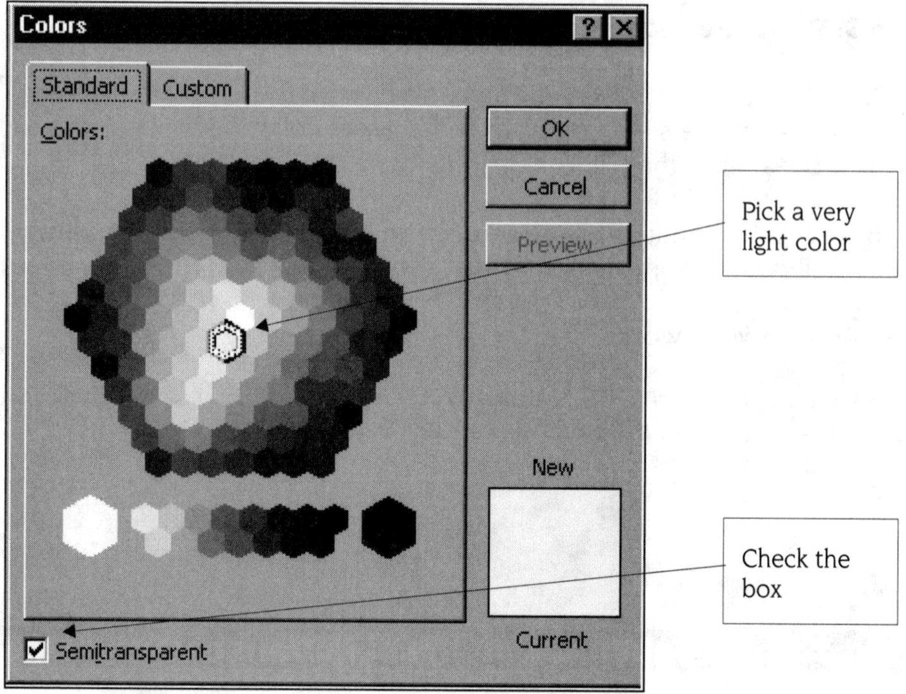

E. Pick a light color by clicking on it.

Step 3: Make the fill color semitransparent so the text will show through.

A. Click on the Semitransparent box in the lower left corner.

B. Click on OK. Your slide will be back on the screen with the box highlighted in the color you chose. If the color is not light enough for the text to show through clearly, go back and pick another.

Step 4: Save your work.

! The semitransparent highlighter is used only for a box or circle on an existing document that you have scanned into digital format to use with your slides. If you are creating new text by typing into text boxes or shapes on your slides, the fill color allows anything that you have typed to show through clearly.

Exercise 12.6: Use a cover to highlight text

Sometimes you can best emphasize what a document says by pointing out all of the parts of it that are not important. By covering up what is not important, you can isolate the sections on which you want the viewer to focus.

To create a cover, do this:

Step 1: Get the document on the slide in the size and shape in which you plan to use it.

Step 2: Create a rectangle with a white fill that is approximately the size of the area on the document that you need to cover.

A. Go to the Drawing Toolbar. Click on the Rectangle button.

B. Move your mouse pointer to the area on the document that you want to cover. Click there to bring the rectangle to the screen.

C. Go to the Drawing Toolbar. Click on the arrow next to the Fill Color button. Choose white as the fill color.

D. Position the white rectangle over the area of the document that you want to cover. The text or other markings will disappear under the white fill of the rectangle. Resize as necessary.

! It may take several rectangles to cover odd-shaped areas.

Step 3: Remove the line around the rectangle.

A. Go to the Drawing Toolbar. Click on the arrow next to the Line Color button. A drop-down menu will appear.

B. Choose the No Line option at the top. The line around the rectangle will disappear.

Step 4: Group the rectangle (or rectangles) with the document so that they will always move with the document.

A. Highlight one of the rectangles.

B. Hold down the SHIFT key and highlight each of the remaining rectangles and the document itself, so that handles are showing around each of the objects at once.

C. Go to the Drawing Toolbar. Click on the Draw button. A drop-down menu will appear. Click on the Group option. Handles will now appear around the entire set of objects and they will all move together as a group.

! To remove the rectangles and expose the text underneath, you will need to Ungroup the objects. Click within the grouped objects to highlight the group. Go to the Drawing Toolbar. Click on the Draw button. A drop-down menu will appear. Click on the Ungroup option. The handles around the group will disappear. Click on each white rectangle to activate it. Use the DELETE key on your keyboard.

The process looks like this:

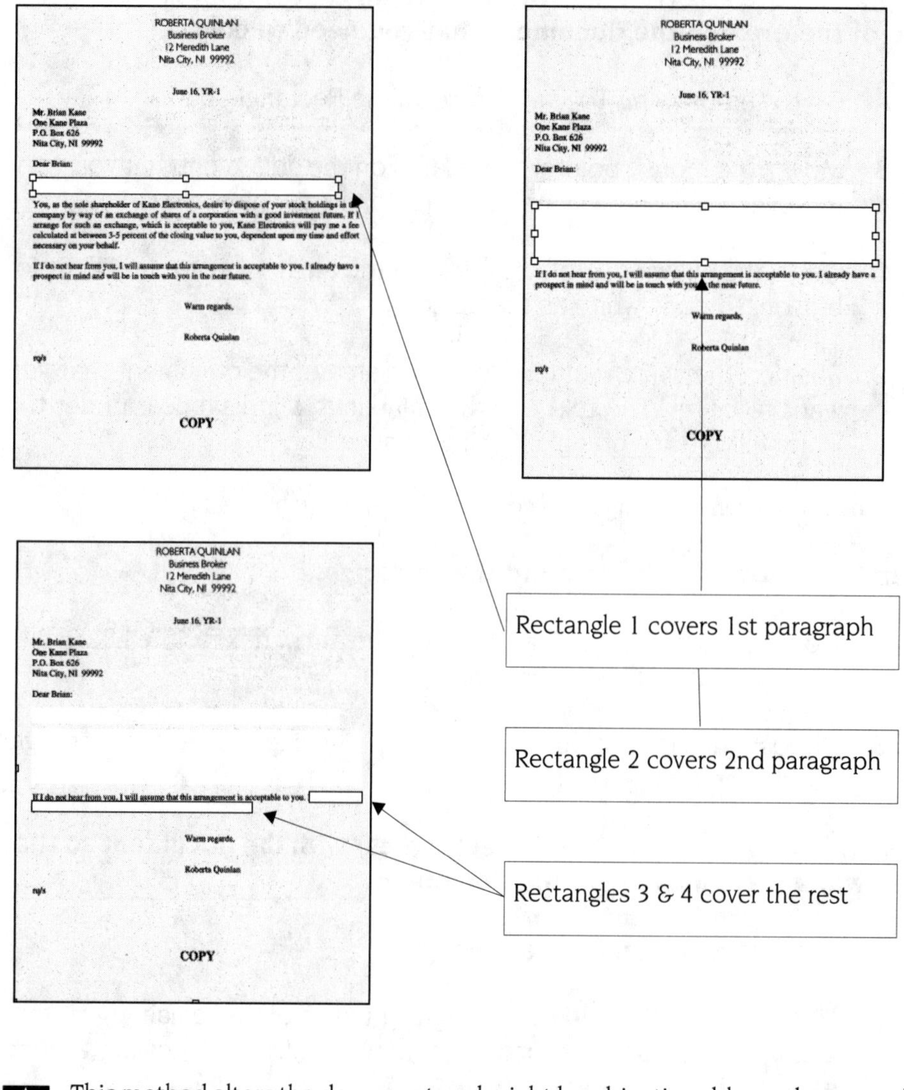

ROBERTA QUINLAN
Business Broker
12 Meredith Lane
Nita City, NI 99992

June 16, YR-1

Mr. Brian Kane
One Kane Plaza
P.O. Box 626
Nita City, NI 99992

Dear Brian:

You, as the sole shareholder of Kane Electronics, desire to dispose of your stock holdings in the company by way of an exchange of shares of a corporation with a good investment future. If I arrange for such an exchange, which is acceptable to you, Kane Electronics will pay me a fee calculated at between 3-5 percent of the closing value to you, dependent upon my time and effort necessary on your behalf.

If I do not hear from you, I will assume that this arrangement is acceptable to you. I already have a prospect in mind and will be in touch with you in the near future.

Warm regards,

Roberta Quinlan

rq/s

COPY

ROBERTA QUINLAN
Business Broker
12 Meredith Lane
Nita City, NI 99992

June 16, YR-1

Mr. Brian Kane
One Kane Plaza
P.O. Box 626
Nita City, NI 99992

Dear Brian:

If I do not hear from you, I will assume that this arrangement is acceptable to you. I already have a prospect in mind and will be in touch with you in the near future.

Warm regards,

Roberta Quinlan

rq/s

COPY

ROBERTA QUINLAN
Business Broker
12 Meredith Lane
Nita City, NI 99992

June 16, YR-1

Mr. Brian Kane
One Kane Plaza
P.O. Box 626
Nita City, NI 99992

Dear Brian:

If I do not hear from you, I will assume that this arrangement is acceptable to you.

Warm regards,

Roberta Quinlan

rq/s

COPY

Rectangle 1 covers 1st paragraph

Rectangle 2 covers 2nd paragraph

Rectangles 3 & 4 cover the rest

This method alters the document and might be objectionable on the ground that it takes things out of contect. A re-keyed callout or direct callout might be better.

Step 5: Save your work.

! You can also use the cover technique on any object that has a white background. Colored backgrounds are more difficult to match exactly.

Exercise 12.7: Put organization charts on slides

PowerPoint provides a template for organization charts that is easy to use and accommodates many of the points about organizational structure you might want to make with an illustrative aid at trial.

Step 1: Bring up the slide layout for organization charts.

A. Go to the Standard Toolbar.

B. Click on the New Slide button. The New Slide screen will appear. (Illustration, Ch. 2, Exercise 2.1.)

C. Double click on the Organization Chart layout (2nd row, 3rd from the left). You may be asked to insert your CD containing the PowerPoint software. This will bring a basic organization chart layout to the screen. It looks like this:

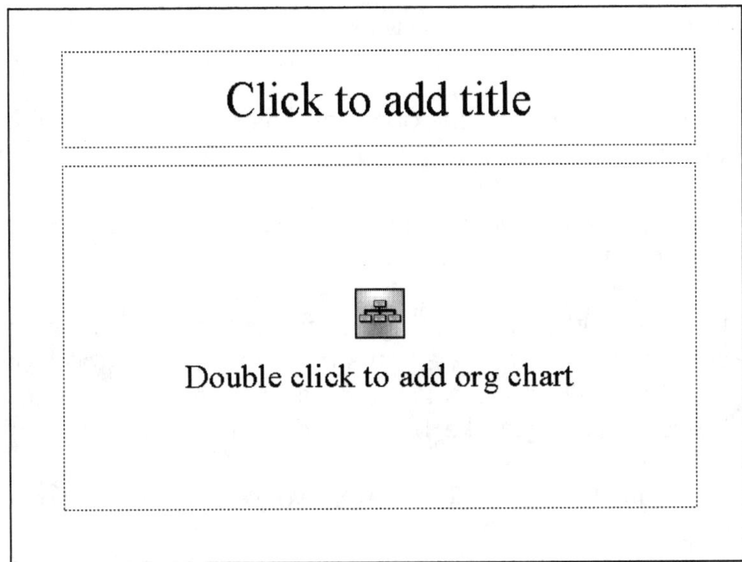

Step 2: Add the titles and other details to the organization chart.

A. Double click on the icon in the center of the screen. The software will open a special window that contains a basic organization chart structure. Not all of the window will be showing. The screen looks like this:

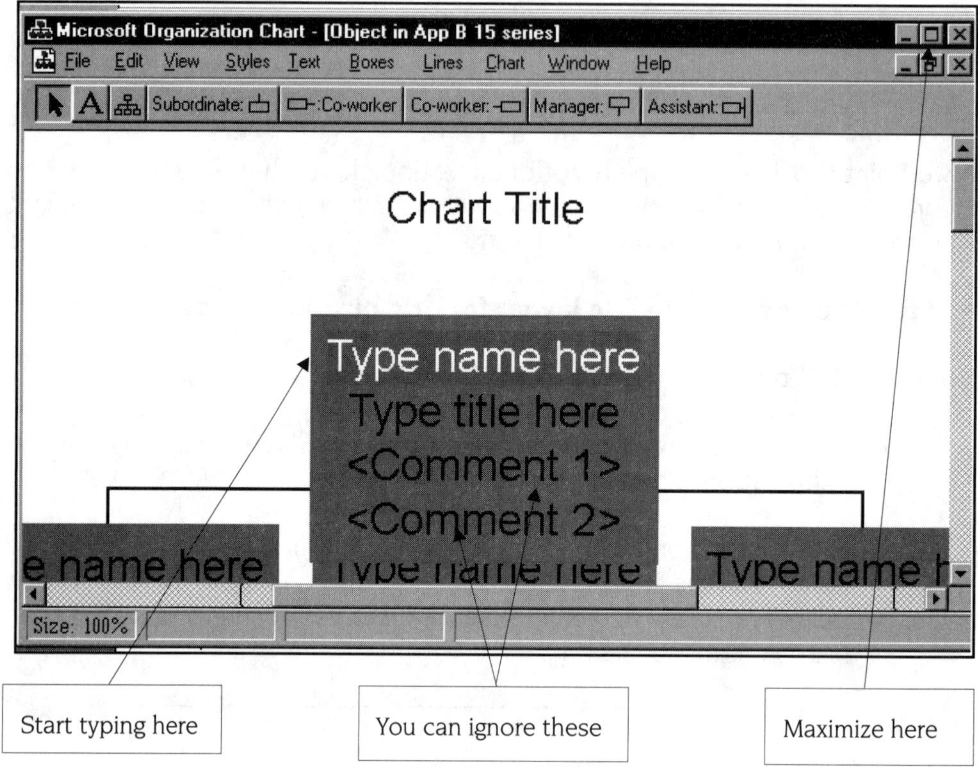

B. Maximize the size of the organization chart box to make it easier to work with.

C. Start typing in the colored box that says "Type Name Here." You do not need to click on the box.

D. Fill in any other information needed in the first box. If you are not going to use the text elements the form suggests, click outside the box. They will disappear. If they do not, highlight them, press the DELETE key on your keyboard, and then click outside the box.

E. If the sample organization chart fits your needs, fill in the other boxes.

F. If you need a different organization chart, create additional elements of the organization chart using the toolbars at the top of the special window. Click on the toolbar button, then click on the element of the organization chart to which you are going to add that element.

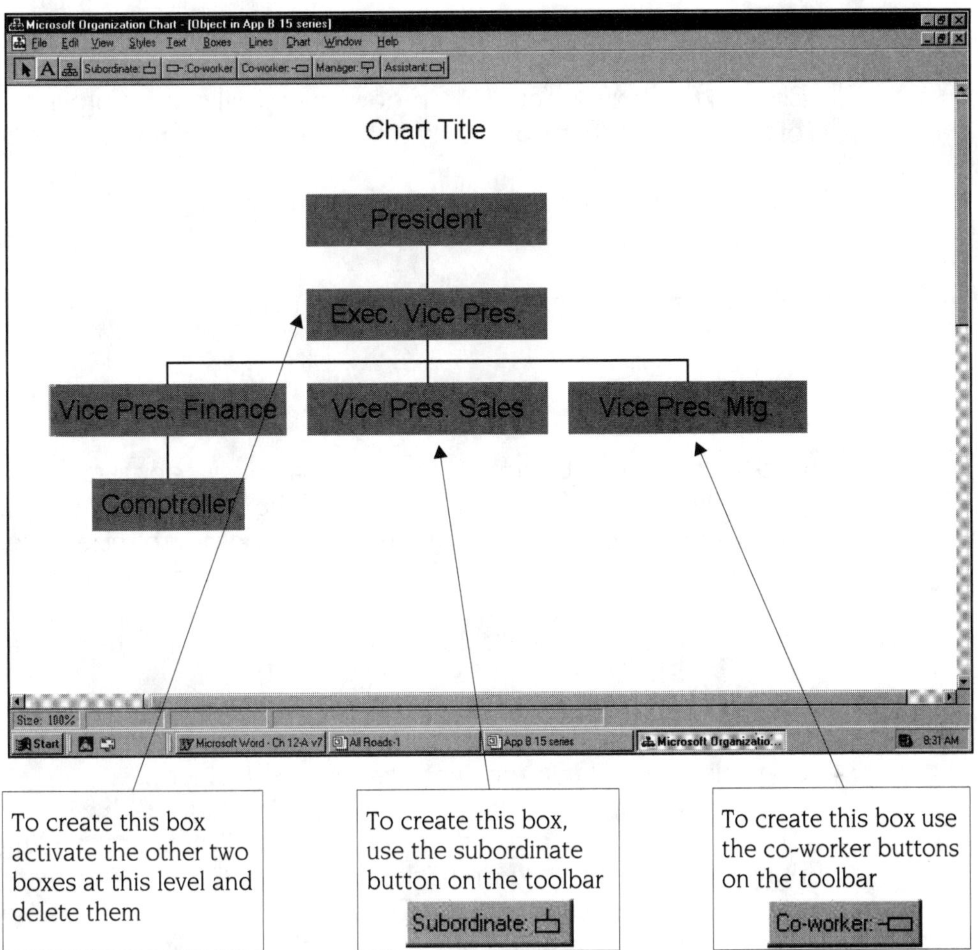

For additional organization chart shapes, go to the Menu Bar in the Organization Chart window, and click on the Styles button. A drop-down menu shows available options.

Step 3: Dress up your chart.

When you work on an organization chart, you need to do the stylistic work primarily in the Organization Chart window. All the tools that you need are there. Once the organization chart that you have designed is returned to your slide, you have very limited options to make it look better.

A. Set the typeface, size, color, and alignment for the text in your organization chart.

1. Click on the box within the organization chart that you want to work on.

2. Go to the Menu Bar in the Organization Chart window.

3. Click on the Text button. A drop-down menu will appear providing all of the options with respect to typeface, size, color, and alignment.

B. Set the fill color and shading for the box and the border size, style, and color.

1. Click on the box within the organization chart that you want to work on.

2. Go to the Menu Bar in the Organization Chart window.

3. Click on the Boxes button. A drop-down menu will appear providing all of the options for coloring the fill of the box and providing a shadow around the outside of the box. The options for the size, style, and color of the line around the border of the box are also here.

C. Set the thickness, style, and color for the lines connecting the boxes.

1. Click on the line that you want to activate.

2. Go to the Menu Bar in the Organization Chart window.

3. Click on the Lines button. A drop-down menu will appear providing options for thickness, style, and color of the lines. Each line segment between two boxes can be treated separately with dotted lines, no lines at all, or specially colored lines to emphasize a point about the organization.

D. Color the fill background of the organization chart.

1. Go to the Menu Bar in the Organization Chart window.

2. Click on the Chart button. Select the menu called Background Color. A color chart appears from which you can select the background color. This selection applies only to the area behind the organization chart, not the entire background of the slide. That background is selected when you are back working on the slide itself.

Step 4: Return to the slide.

After you are finished with the design of the organization chart, return to the slide by doing this:

A. Go to the Menu Bar in the Organization Chart window.

B. Click on the File button. A drop-down menu will appear.

C. Choose the Update option. (PowerPoint may add the name of your slideshow if you have already given the file a name, so the option will read Update [file name].) This updates your slide to add the organization chart (or changes to the organization chart) that you have made.

D. Go back to the File button.

E. This time choose the Close and Return option. This closes the Organization Chart window and returns you to your slide.

Step 5: Edit your organization chart once it is on your slide.

A. Click on the organization chart. Its border and handles will appear.

B. Right click with your mouse. A drop-down menu will appear.

C. Choose the MS Org Chart option. Choose Edit. This will take you back to the Organization Chart window where you can make your changes.

Step 6: Add the title to the title box on your slide. (The organization chart has a place for a title. Ignore this when the organization chart is the main feature of the slide. This is useful when the organization chart is one of the objects on a slide and needs its own title.)

Step 7: Save your work.

! To add an organization chart to a slide as one of several objects on a slide, go to the Menu Bar, click on the Insert button. Click on the Picture option. Click on the Organization Chart option. This creates an object on your slide, and brings up the Organization Chart window that you can use to fill this object.

Exercise 12.8: Add video clips to slides

The file that contains the video clips is on the CD that came with this book or can be downloaded from the NITA web site. Be sure that the CD is in the CD drive on your computer. You are going to locate a clip on the CD and import it into your slide. The name of this clip is Video-1.

Step 1: Set up the slide.

A. Go to the Standard Toolbar.

B. Click on the New Slide button (10th from left). This brings up the New Slide screen that shows the 12 basic slide formats.

C. Choose either the Title Only format (bottom row, 2nd from right), if you want to label this video clip something like "Quinlan depo p. 13," or the Blank Slide button (bottom row, last on right) if all you want to show is the video.

Step 2: Insert the video clip.

A. On the Menu Bar select Insert. From the drop-down menu, select Movies and Sounds. Then choose Movie from File.

B. The Insert Movie dialog box will appear. The My Documents directory is displayed in the Look In white box at the top. The larger central white box will display whatever folders you have in your My Document directory. It looks generally like this:

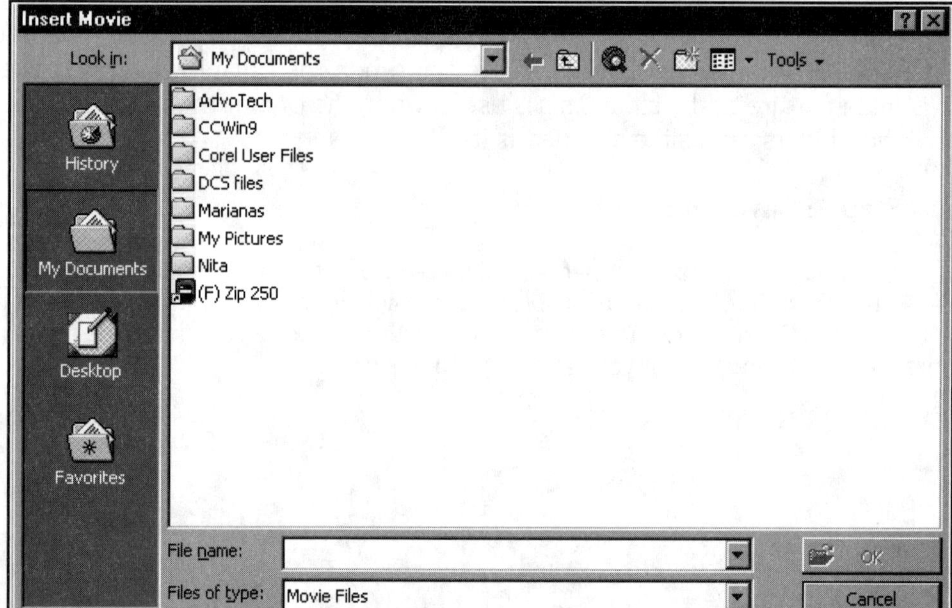

 The PowerPoint 97 screen is slightly different but performs the same function.

C. Click on the down arrow next to the Look In box and select your CD-ROM drive and then the directory where the video is located. Either click on the selection and hit OK or double click the selection.

D. A picture of the first frame of the video will now appear with handles on the screen. You can resize to the desired width and height using the corner handles. If you want to keep the object located in the same spot, hold down the CTRL key as you pull the corner handles. If you want to locate the video elsewhere on the slide, simply drag it using the four-arrow pointer while holding down the left mouse button.

Step 3: Dress up the slide.

A. Color the background of the slide by selecting Format from the Menu Bar, then click Background from the drop-down menu. From the Background screen click on the small arrow next to the color box. From the Color Options screen, click More Colors and select an appropriate color (a dark gray often works best).

B. Put a line around the video box by selecting the image, then click on the Line Styles button (15th from the left) on the Drawing Toolbar, and select a size (no more than 3 point). Then select a color from the Line Color icon (13th from the left). Black or white usually work best for this task.

Step 4: Preview the video by double clicking inside the object.

Step 5: Save your work.

! To play the video as a part of your slide show, go to the View Bar and click on the Slide Show button. You will see that the pointer turns into a little hand. Click once to play the video. You can again stop and start the video by clicking once inside the object.

! If you would rather have the video play automatically once the slide comes up, get the full slide on the screen (View Bar, Full Slide View button, select the object, then right click and select Custom Animation). The Custom Animation dialog box appears. Select the Timing tab, click Animate and Automatically, then choose how many seconds you want to wait before the video begins to play. The default is for zero seconds, which may appear jerky. It is better to select one or two seconds. Click OK.

Exercise 12.9: Create statistical charts for slides

PowerPoint gives you the basic tools to create the types of statistical charts most often used in litigation. Even if you decide to have a professional do the final product, you may want to look over the alternatives to see which method is most effective, and try out several different ways to present the data you have.

Step 1: Create a slide with an object for a chart on it.

A. Go to the Standard Toolbar.

B. Click on the New Slide button (6th from the right). The New Slide screen will appear.

C. Double click on the Chart-Plus-Title option, which is in the second row, the last option to the right. You now have a title box at the top and a chart box underneath. The screen display will look like this:

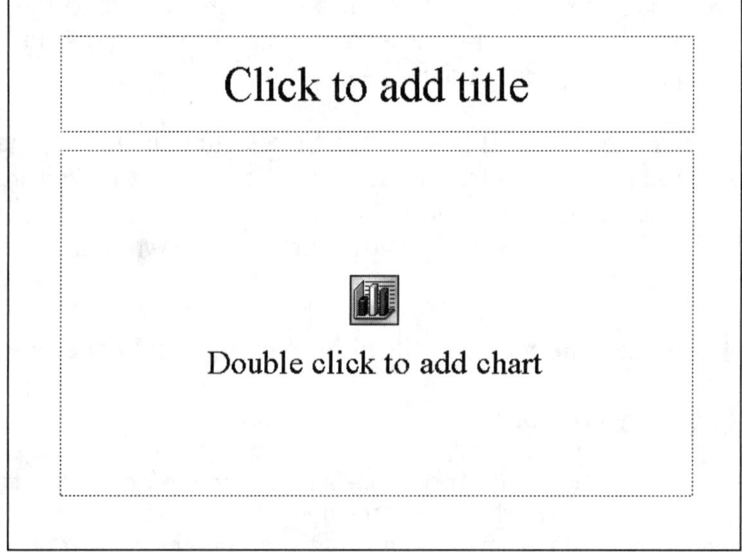

D. Put your mouse pointer on the icon in the center of the chart box on the chart icon. Double click there. This brings up the Chart Preparation screen. It looks like this:

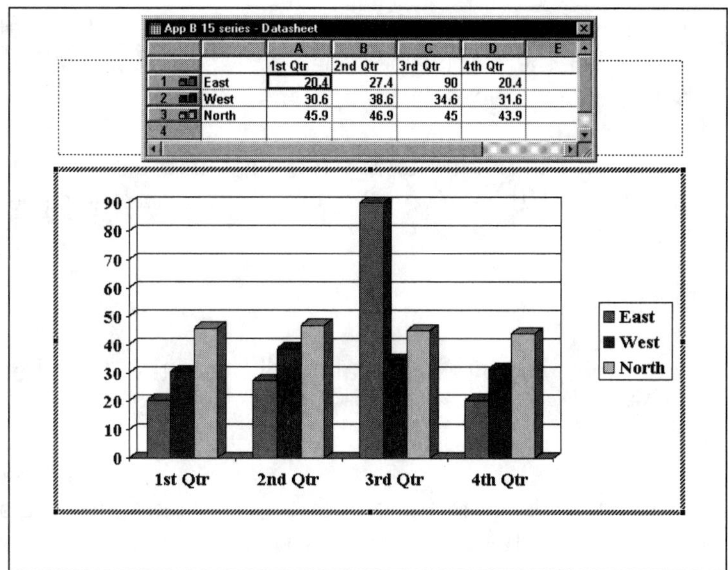

E. This is a template. The data sheet at the top of the screen shows you where to put your data. That will disappear when you are finished with your work, leaving just a chart that will fill the object underneath the title. The idea is that you put your own data into the data sheet in place of the "mock" data now there.

Step 2: Enter the data that you want the chart to reflect.

A. Assume you had a set of numbers comparing three loans that you want to make into a chart. The table containing just the relevant numbers looks like this:

Transaction	Principal	Interest	Total
Loan A	500	65	565
Loan B	475	90	565
Loan C	610	50	660

B. You need to substitute this data for the "mock" data in the data sheet that is displayed on your screen.

C. Put your mouse pointer on the rectangle in the data sheet on your screen that says "East." The mouse pointer will have a fat cross shape. Click there. The rectangle will be highlighted. Type "Loan A." The word "East" will disappear.

D. Put your mouse pointer on the rectangle on the data sheet that says "West." Click there and type "Loan B." Move down one row and type "Loan C" where "North" now appears.

E. Put your mouse pointer on the rectangle in the data sheet that says "1st Qtr." Click there. Type "Principal" there. Do the same for "Interest" and "Total."

F. Fill in the amounts in the same way.

G. To add rows, go to the vertical scroll bar in the data sheet box and click on the one-arrow button pointing down. Click once on that button for each new row that you need.

H. To add columns, go to the one-arrow button on the horizontal scroll bar in the data sheet box and click on the one-arrow button pointing to the right. Click once for each new column that you want to add.

Step 3: Eliminate any rows or columns on the "mock" data sheet that you do not need. In this case, the column captioned "4th Qtr." is not needed. Highlight it and press the DELETE key on your keyboard. The screen should now look like this:

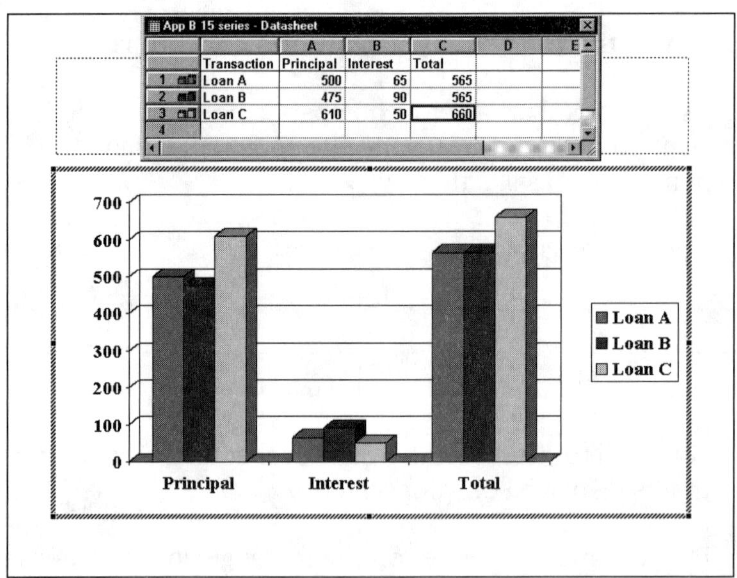

The bars on the chart now reflect your data that you entered on the data sheet.

! This works like an Excel spreadsheet. By deleting just the text, your chart still accommodates for missing data, anticipating new. However, by clicking on the gray column letter (here it is "D"), the entire column is selected, and by hitting the DELETE key, the chart adjusts to tighten up the space for only three sets of data.

Step 4: Choose the type of chart that is appropriate for this data.

Assume you decided that a horizontal bar chart would be best for this data, do this:

A. Go to the Menu Bar.

B. Click on the Chart button. (This button is added to the Menu Bar when you choose one of the chart formats.) A drop-down menu appears.

C. Click on the Chart Type option. A dialog box appears that looks like this:

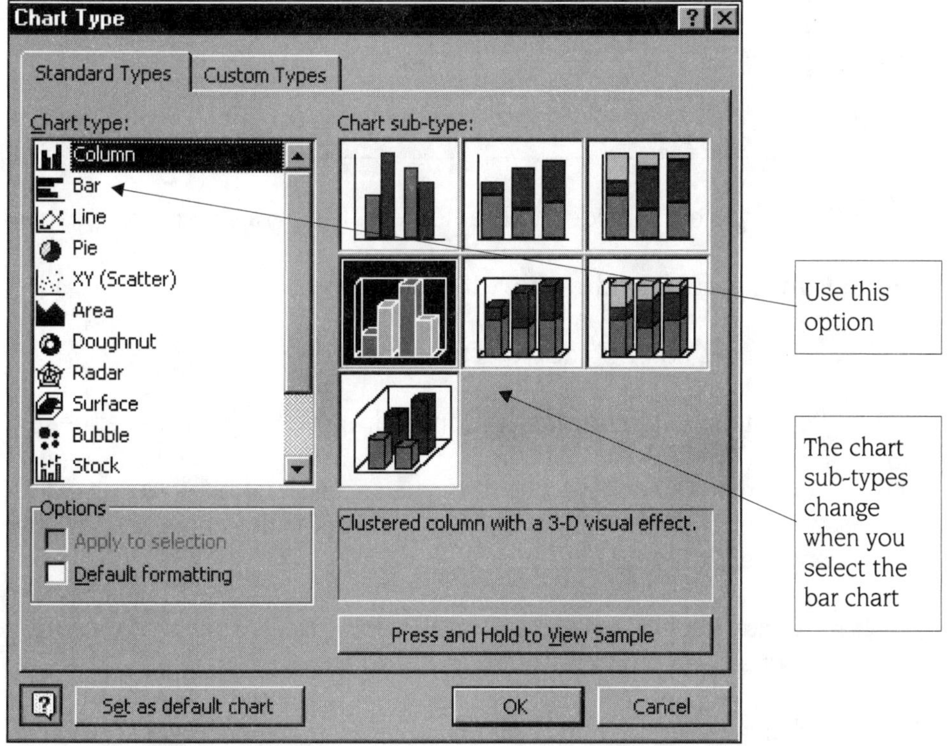

D. This shows the current choice (which is called "Columns" and which is highlighted).

E. In the Chart Type box, click on the Bar option. The Chart sub-type box on the right now shows you the six kinds of bar chart formats available. Click on the one in the upper left corner.

F. Click on the OK button. The vertical bar chart is now changed to a horizontal bar chart that looks like this:

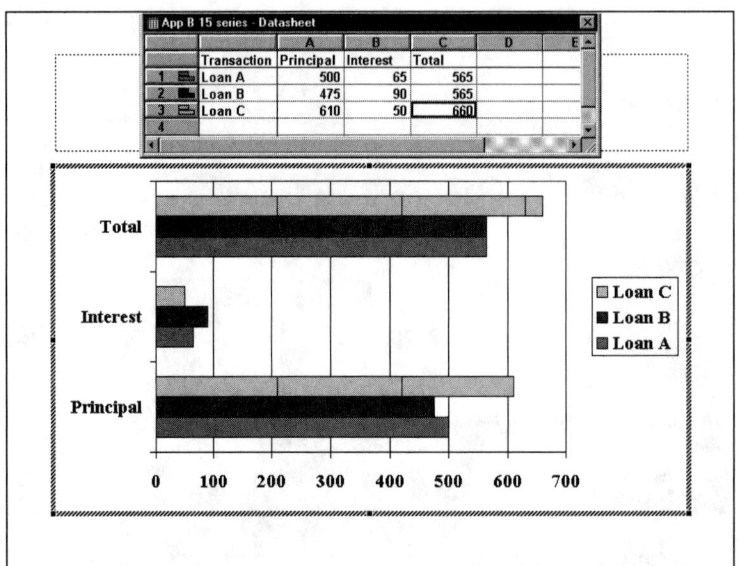

G. Click anywhere outside the chart object. The data sheet disappears.

Step 5: Edit the data in the chart if necessary.

A. Click on the chart object to activate it.

B. Click with the right mouse button. A drop-down menu will appear.

C. Click on the Chart Object option. Then select Edit. (You can also activate your chart by simply double-clicking on the chart object.) The data sheet will reappear.

D. Make any necessary changes on the data sheet. They will appear on your chart as you enter them.

E. Click anywhere outside the chart object to view your work.

97 PowerPoint 97 is a little different. When the drop-down menu appears, click on the Edit Chart option. The data sheet will reappear.

Step 6: Dress up your chart.

A. Change the representations of the data if necessary.

1. Double click on the chart object to activate the Chart Preparation screen. Put your mouse pointer on one of the data elements shown on the chart (for example, the bar showing the principal amount for Loan A). Click once. This will activate all of the Loan A bars. Colored squares will appear in each bar. Any changes you make will affect all of these bars.

2. With your cursor in one of the Loan A bars, double click. The Format Data Series dialog box will appear. It looks like this:

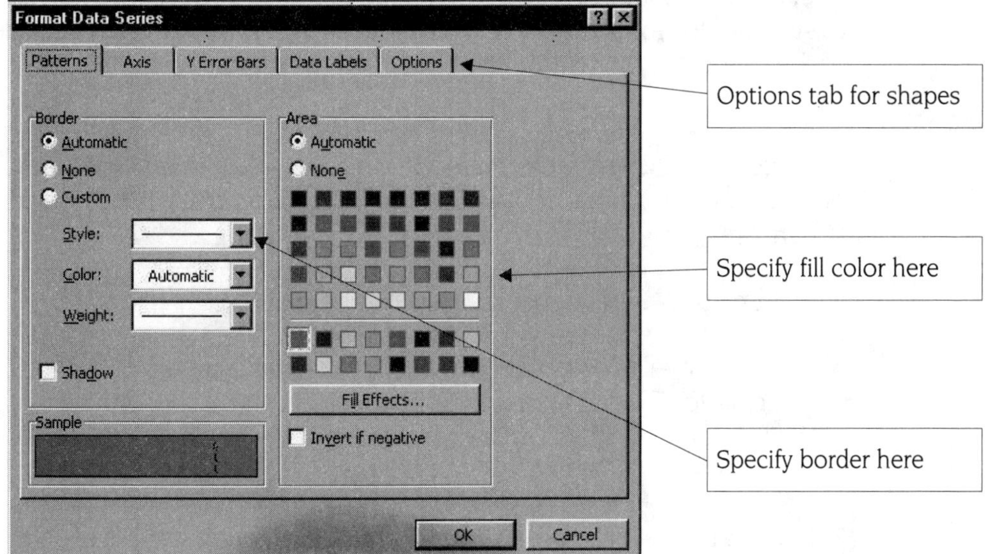

The Patterns tab allows you to change the border and fill of each of the bars. The Options tab lets you change the shape of the chart to give it more depth or to increase or decrease the space between the sets of bars on the chart.

B. Change the grid behind the data if necessary.

1. Put your mouse pointer on one of the grid lines behind the data.

2. Right click. A menu with two choices appears. The Format Gridlines choice brings up a dialog box that allows you to alter the way the grid appears—choosing dashes instead of solid lines, substituting thinner or thicker lines, and adding color to the grid lines. The Clear choice will take out any grid background.

C. Color the background behind the chart.

There are three distinct areas that can be colored as part of a data chart. The Plot area can be found inside the walls or border of the grid. The Chart area is outside of the grid area and to the edge of the chart. The Legend area is inside the legend box. The method for changing the background color and line styles, colors, and weights is the same for each.

1. To color the Plot area, put your mouse pointer inside the grid on an open area (a box labeled "Plot Area" will appear).

2. Right click. A drop-down menu will appear.

3. Click on Format Plot Area. The dialog box that appears allows you to select color for this area as well as the line color, style, and weight of the border around this area of the chart. Make your selections and click OK.

4. To color the Chart area, put your mouse pointer in an open spot outside the Plot Area and within the fuzzy border. A box labeled "Chart Area" will appear.

5. Right click. A drop-down menu will appear.

6. Select Format Chart Area. The dialog box that appears allows you to select color for this area as well as the line color, style, and weight of the border around this area of the chart. Make your selections and click OK.

7. To color the Legend area, put your mouse pointer inside the legend.

8. Right click and select Format Legend.

9. Make your selections as above and click OK.

10. Click anywhere outside the chart object to view your work.

! Any item can be changed by using the same procedure.

Step 7: Add the title.

A. Click anywhere in the lettering within the title box to activate it.

B. Type in your title.

C. Adjust the font if necessary. (Ch. 3, Exercise 3.1.)

Step 8: Animate the chart if necessary.

A. Put your mouse pointer on the chart and click once to activate the chart object. The handles should appear. (The data sheet should not appear. If you get the data sheet, click anywhere outside the chart and start over.)

B. Click on the right mouse button. A drop-down menu will appear.

C. Click on the Custom Animation option. The Custom Animation screen will appear.

D. Click on the Chart Effects tab in the middle of the screen. The screen will look like this:

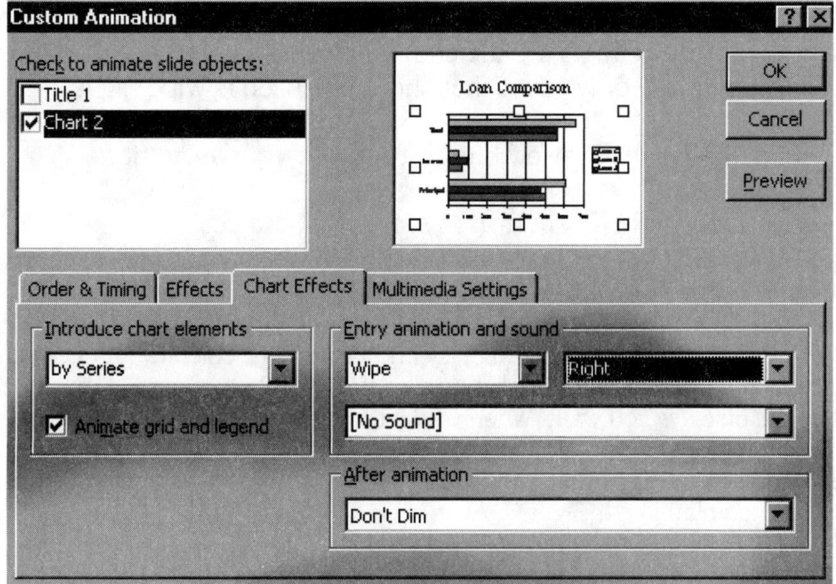

E. Pick the animation features.

1. Decide how the bars on the chart should make their appearance on the slide. The Introduce Chart Elements box on the left provides options that are reached by clicking on the arrow to the right of the box.

The By Series option displays the elements in each row together. In the example used in this exercise, all of the elements (principal, interest, and total) for the row containing Loan A would appear together.

The By Category option displays the elements in each column together. In the example used in this exercise, all the elements (Loan A, Loan B, and Loan C) for the column containing principal would appear together.

The By Element in Series option displays each element in each row seriatim.

2. Specify whether the grid should be included in the animation. There is a small white box under the Introduce Chart Elements box. It says: "Animate Grid and Legend." If you click on the white box, a check mark appears. The software will animate the background of the chart as well as the bars on the chart. This is almost never a good idea. This box should remain blank.

3. Pick an effect. The Entry Animation and Sound box on the right provides effects available for displaying a chart. For a horizontal bar chart, the only effect that should be used is Wipe Right.

F. Click on the Preview button to review your animation.

G. Click on the OK button to store your choices.

Step 9: Save your work.

The PowerPoint template is an easy and fast way to convert data from a table or list of numbers to a graph. Use it to consider the options and to produce rough drafts of the displays you want. When you get to production of the final version of the slide, you may want to work in Excel or have someone do that work for you. Excel is a full-featured spreadsheet that can produce several important modifications to the PowerPoint template.

Charts normally should not have the legend separate from the graph. This requires jurors to take two steps to evaluate the chart. They have to look at the chart, then look at the legend, then look back at the chart. It is better to put the information from the legend directly on the chart. For example, the bars themselves would be labeled Loan A, Loan B, and Loan C rather than having a separate box to the right of the graph showing the color legend for each loan. In this case, only the bottom set of bars would be labeled because the pattern is the same for each set of bars.

Bar charts usually should have the actual data at the end of each bar so that the reader does not have to consult a separate table or guess from the position of the bar what the actual number is. In this case, for example, the actual numbers for principal are 500 (Loan A), 475 (Loan B), and 610 (Loan C). Those numbers would appear at the right end of each bar.

Exercise 12.10: Enhance time lines with illustrations

An advanced time line uses pictures of exhibits in the case or other illustrations to connect events and to explain the underlying theory. Thumbnails of the exhibits displayed in a time line remind the viewer how all the evidence ties together.

In the commercial case, for example, timing is important to support the plaintiff's contention that she had an agreement with the defendant to sell his business. Kane told Quinlan of his decision to sell his business during a round of golf on June 15. Kane invited Quinlan over to his house the next day to talk about the sale of his business. Several phone calls and a letter followed. Then on June 26, Kane was contacted by Fuller who was a prospective buyer found by Quinlan. Shortly thereafter, on August 4, the business was sold.

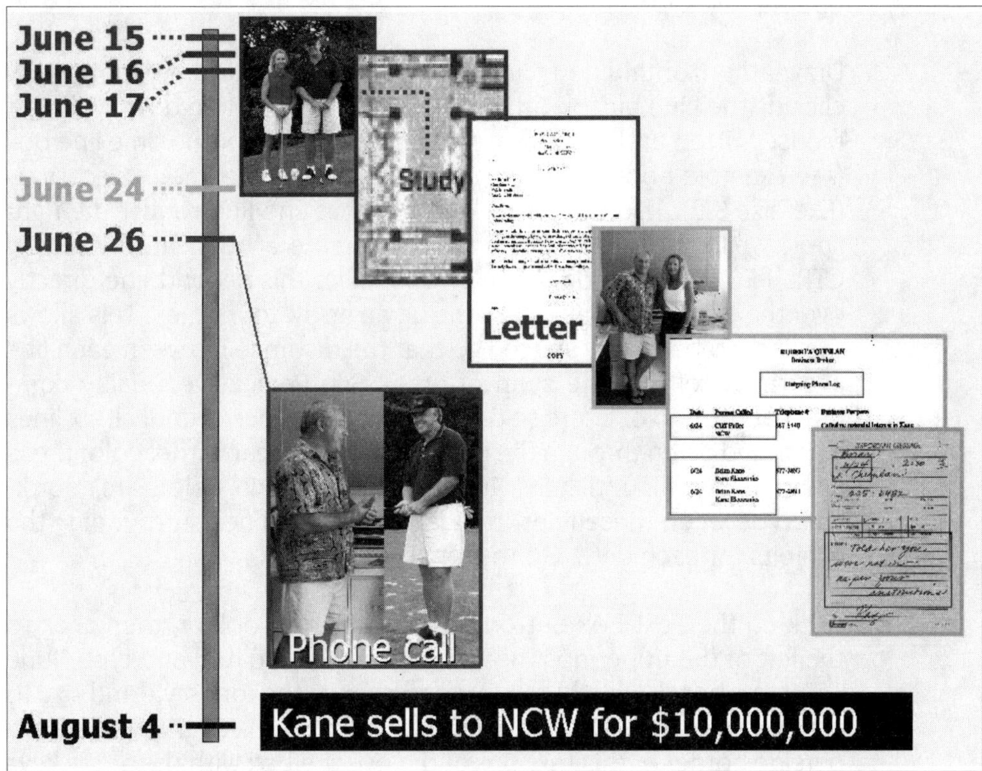

This time line shows all the key dates and all the key exhibits. The layout for an advanced time line can be either vertical, as in this example, or horizontal.

Go to the CD to see this time line and one with a horizontal layout in full color and with animations. Comparable illustrated time lines are in each slide show on the CD.

To create this time line, do this:

Step 1: Create a box with date references for annotation.

A. Click on the New Slide button. The New Slide Screen will appear. Double click on the Blank Slide option (bottom row, last on right). You now have a blank slide to work on.

B. Click on the rectangle button on the Drawing Toolbar and hold down the left mouse button. Dragging your mouse, use it to draw a tall, thin, box roughly the same size as the one shown on the above example. Click on the down arrow next to the Fill Color button and select either "No fill" or a color you think you might want to use (for a change of pace, consider clicking the "semitransparent" color option). Click OK.

C. Draw a horizontal line to indicate one day on the time line box by clicking the Line button on the Drawing Toolbar. Hold down your left mouse button and draw a short line near the top of the time line box (see example above). Adjust the point size of the line, if necessary (Exercise 3.2). Use the arrow keys to move the line to just the right spot. While the line is still activated, create a duplicate by hitting CTRL+D. Using the direction arrows, align this second line directly over the original line and click the down arrow four times. This allows the lines to be evenly spaced so that the distance between each line accurately reflects the span of time. (See Persuasive Quality comment at the end of Exercise 6.3). Repeat this process until all six lines are placed down through the time line box. You can either color these lines now or wait until later. (In the example above, colors are coordinated between these lines, the dates, and the lines surrounding the exhibits for each date. Go to the CD to see this.)

D. Click on the Text Box button on the Drawing Toolbar, then click to the left of the uppermost horizontal line just created and type "June 15" in the box. Highlight the text and change the font style and size to your liking (Tahoma 24 Bold in the slide above). Click on the fuzzy outside border of this text box and move the box with the arrow keys to just the spot to the left of the top line (the vertical alignment is easily done with use of the Ruler). With the Text Box saying "June 15" still activated, hit CTRL+D to make a duplicate. Using the direction arrows, align this box directly over the original box and click the down arrow 4 times. Now click inside this second text box and change the date to June 16. Repeat this process until all of your dates are placed alongside the date lines.

E. Because the first three dates are so close together, you need to draw dotted lines from the dates to the corresponding lines as they cannot line up horizontally. Click the Line button and use the mouse to draw the necessary lines. Click on the Dash Style button and select "Square Dot," then go to the Line Style button directly to the left of the Dash Style button and select a larger line size (3 pt). Make the line the exact length and to the exact spot you want by using the handles on either side of the line. Group each date and corresponding line so they can be animated together. (Exercise 9.6, Step 4.)

Step 2: Import and line up exhibits.

A. For each exhibit, click the "Import Picture from File" button on the Picture Toolbar (1st on left) and browse the directory to find the photos, diagram, and documents pictured above. After inserting each, size them down and move them around so they all fit on the screen. (Exercise 5.2.)

B. Start with the photo of Quinlan and Kane on the golf course and size it so that it can be seen but also allows enough room for the other objects to follow. Place a line around the photo by clicking the Line Color button on the Drawing Toolbar and then click the Line Style button to make the line a bit wider. You can color coordinate this either now or wait to color the lines in the entire slide later. Size the photo of Quinlan and Fuller exactly the same as this first photo by moving it directly over the first photo by use of the direction arrows, and then using the handlebars to make it bigger or smaller for an exact fit. Move this second photo out of the way for later use.

C. Next crop the diagram of Kane's house so that you have only the study showing. It is easier to crop accurately if you first enlarge the diagram before initiating the Crop button on the Picture Toolbar (7th from left). When the cropping is done, click the crop button to de-activate it and then use the corner handles to size the image to the same size as the photos. You can add dotted lines to show the path taken into the study as already done in Chapter 8. Group the dotted lines and the cropped diagram so they will all animate together.

D. Move the grouping of this cropped diagram with lines to partially overlap the first photo by selecting the group and using the arrow keys. If the portion of the diagram that is overlapped is hidden behind the photo, click on the Draw button (1st on left) and select "Order" from the menu and then click on "Bring to Front." You will need to use this feature for the rest of the objects you overlap to create the effect shown above. (Exercise 6.3, Step 5.)

E. Size the confirmation letter just a bit bigger than the photos and move it to where it overlaps the cropped diagram but does not cover up the all-important word "Study." You can utilize a Text Box to put the word "Letter" on the letter for emphasis. Place this box on the left bottom of the document so that it is not hidden by the overlapping photo that comes next. If you do put in this text box, Group the letter and text box saying "Letter" so they will all animate together.

F. Place the photo of Quinlan and Fuller next, making sure not to cover up the "Letter" text box.

G. Crop the "Outgoing Phone Log" as shown above and size to fit, move it to where it overlaps the photo above, then place rectangles around the identification of the document and the dates and who Quinlan called. (Exercise 7.1.) These rectangles have purposefully not been grouped with the document so that instead they can be animated separately to identify and give emphasis to the document after it is brought up.

H. Size the pink phone slip, place it to overlap the log, and place rectangles around the date and handwritten message from Kane's secretary. Again, these rectangles have purposefully not been grouped with the document for emphasis during the presentation.

I. Crop each of the other two photos of Quinlan with Kane and Fuller to eliminate Quinlan from the photo. Size the photo of Fuller so as to fit in the remaining space with plenty of room to spare, then move the photo of Kane next to the one of Fuller and using the handles bring it up or down to the same size. Once they are properly sized and directly next to each other, create a border around the combined photos by placing a rectangle with no fill around them. Now, group these three so they can be animated together. Another line needs to be added from the date these two first talked, June 26, to the photo itself. This line should also be grouped with the already grouped photo of Kane and Fuller for animation purposes. Adding a text box with the words "phone call" is optional, but if done must be grouped as well.

J. Create the final text box saying "Kane sells to NCW for $10,000,000." Click on the Text Box button, click to the right of the August 4 date line, and type the words. Then select font style and size (Tahoma 28 in our example), color the box and font as you wish, and align the text in the box to the left (to have the words closer to and aligned with the date). Then move the entire box to where it is vertically aligned with the date and date line.

Step 3: Animate the slide.

A. Click on the "June 15" date, then right click, select the Custom Animation option. The Custom Animation screen appears. You grouped this text box with the dotted line to its right, so Group 3 should be highlighted in dark blue in the "Check to animate slide objects" window. Choose a category and direction effect (Appear or Wipe Right are obvious choices). You may need to use the up and down scroll arrows to view all the objects.

B. Find the Picture Frame that corresponds with the first photo showing Quinlan with Kane in the "Check to animate slide objects" window. Choose a category and direct effect (try Wipe Down or Strips Right-Down).

C. Click on the Order & Timing tab to make sure the first item listed is Group 3 and the second is the Picture Frame you just animated. You can always click the Preview button to watch your animation in the thumbnail version and move objects to a different order with the up or down arrows where it says "Move."

D. Continue to animate the grouped dates and lines and exhibit objects as discussed above. When you get to the "Outgoing Phone Log" and pink slip, you will also need to animate the rectangles and order them to come up after the document itself. Continue to adjust the animation order as necessary in the Order & Timing tab window with the up and down arrows.

E. If you have not already, add color to the text boxes, lines, and slide background.

Step 4: Save your work.

Exercise 12.11: Import and use clip art

Clip art consists of icons, stylized pictures, cartoons, symbols, signs, and other art material available in pre-packaged form. Office 97 has a large collection of some 5,000 clip art images. If you have access to the Web, you can go to Microsoft's website and download additional images. Commercial publishers also provide thousands of clip art images on CDs.

Most clip art is not suitable for litigation purposes.

However a few symbols, like a phone denoting a phone call on a particular date, work well to make your presentations less cluttered and more efficient. Here's how to import clip art.

Step 1: Import clip art from the basic collection provided by Microsoft.

With the slide into which the clip art will go on the screen—

A. Open the clip art gallery.

1. Go to the Menu Bar.

2. Click on the Insert button. A drop-down menu will appear.

3. Click on the Picture option. Another drop-down menu will appear.

4. Click on the Clip Art option. The Clip Art Gallery screen will appear.

B. Pick the clip art that you want.

1. Click on the Pictures tab at the top of the screen (1st on the left.).

2. Click on the category that contains the image you want. The images in that category will appear in thumbnail form.

3. Click on one of the image to select it.

C. Insert the clip art on the slide.

1. When the clip art image is activated (highlighted), a small toolbar appears beside it. Click on the top icon to insert the clip art.

2. The clip art image will appear in the middle of your slide. Close the Clip Art window.

3. Use the mouse to drag the clip art into place.

D. Fix up the clip art, if necessary.

1. Resize the image. (Ch. 2, Exercise 2.3.)

2. Box the image. (Ch. 3, Exercise 3.2.)

3. Edit the clip art using the Ungroup option (Drawing Toolbar, Draw button, Ungroup). Right click on the clip art image, and select Ungroup from the drop-down menu. Use the handles to edit the individual parts of the clip art image.

E. Save your work.

Step 2: Import clip art from a commercial CD.

A. Go to the Menu Bar.

B. Click on the Insert button. A drop-down menu will appear.

C. Click on the Picture option. Another drop-down menu will appear.

D. Click on the From File option. The Insert Picture dialog box will appear.

E. Identify the drive where the CD is located. The available clip art will appear on your screen. Follow the instructions to insert it onto your slide.

F. Save your work.

Exercise 12.12: Put PowerPoint displays into briefs

PowerPoint provides an easy way to put illustrations into memoranda and briefs. After you compose your slide, do this:

Step 1: Get the slide into Windows Metafile format.

With the slide that you want to put into your memo on the screen—

A. Go to the Menu Bar.

B. Click on the File button. A drop-down menu will appear.

C. Click on the Save As option. The Save dialog box will appear. It looks like this:

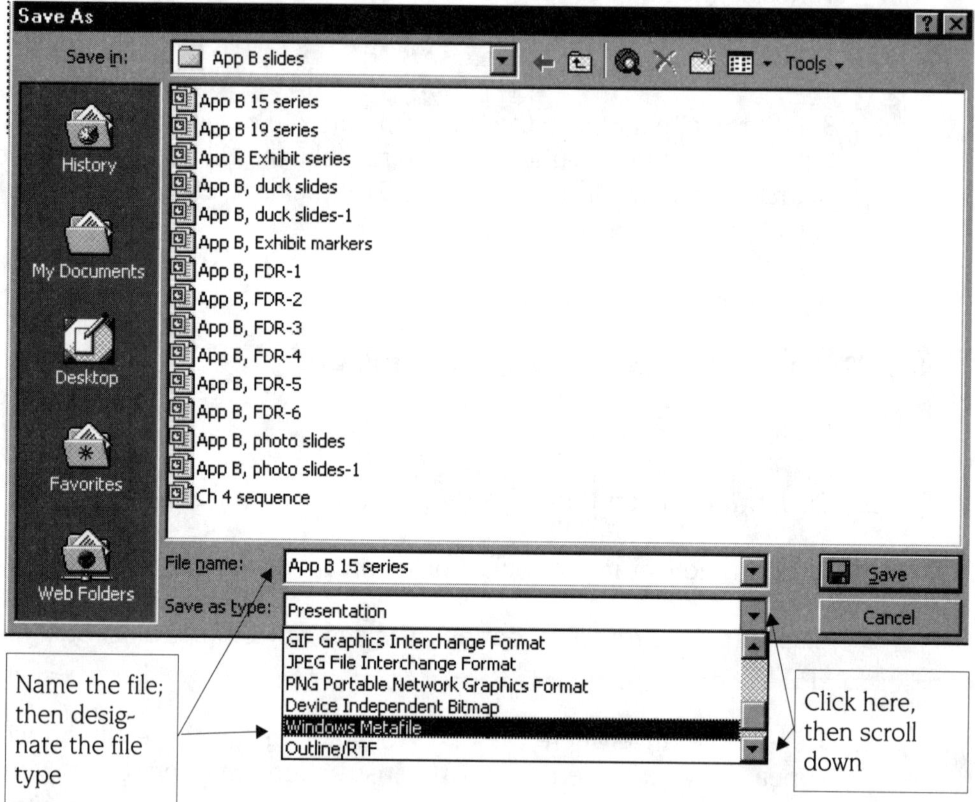

D. Put the name of the slide in the File Name box at the bottom.

E. Click on the arrow to the right of the Save As Type box and select the Windows Metafile option. This is a format that allows you to put graphics into a word processing document.

F. Go to the Save In box at the top. Click on the arrow next to the box to display the directories and folders available on your computer and decide where you want to put the file containing the slide. Click on that option.

G. Click on the Save button in the upper right corner. A dialog box will appear inquiring whether you want to import every slide in the show. Click on the No option. This will import just the slide on which you are currently working.

Step 2: Bring the slide into your word processing document. These instructions are for working with Microsoft Word®. The instructions for other word processing programs are similar.

A. Go back to your word processing document. (There should be a button on the bottom bar on your screen for your word processing program. Click on that. If not, launch your word processing program from the Start button and go to your document.)

B. Put your cursor on the page and at the position where you want the illustration to go.

C. Go to the Menu Bar.

D. Click on the Insert button. A drop-down menu will appear.

E. Click on the Picture option. Another drop-down menu will appear.

F. Click on the From File option. The Insert Picture dialog box will appear. If you are using Microsoft Word, it looks like this:

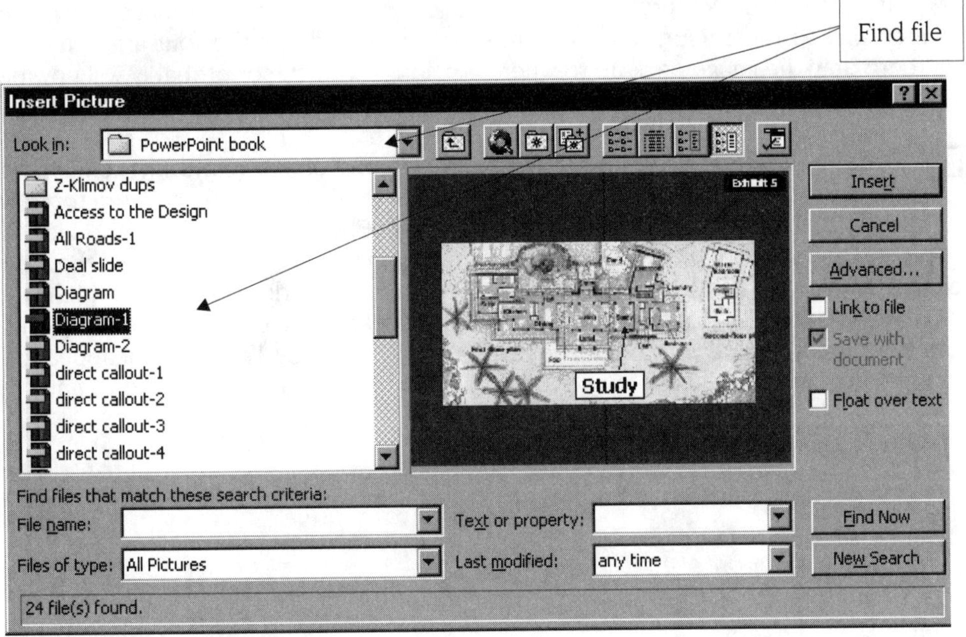

G. Go to the Look In box at the top.

H. Find the place where you stored the slide in Metafile format.

I. When you find the folder where you stored the slide, the display below the Look In box will show all of the slides in that folder. Click once on the one you need for the word processing document. Its name will be highlighted and a thumbnail of the slide will appear in the box on the right.

J. Click on the Insert button at the top right. The slide will pop up on your word processing page. It often appears at a location other than the one where your mouse pointer indicated it should go.

K. Re-position the image. Click on the image to activate it. With the four-arrow mouse pointer active, drag the image to the place where you want it to go. If it is too large to fit on the remaining space on the page, it will skip over and locate itself on the next page.

L. Crop the image to a smaller size if necessary. Use the crop tool on your word processor.

Step 3: Save your work.

! You may have to juggle a bit to get the cursor below the image so that you can go on typing. When you press the ENTER key on your keyboard, the image may move down as well as the cursor. If so, activate the image and use the four-arrow mouse pointer to drag the image back up to where it belongs. The cursor probably will now be below the image and you can continue with your text. If not, repeat this operation.

! There is an alternative method for putting PowerPoint displays into briefs and memoranda for keyboards that provide a Print Screen key (usually in the top row on the right). Go to the View Bar and click on the Slide Show button to bring the slide to the screen in show mode when nothing else appears on the screen with it. Press the Print Screen button. Go to your word processing program and the document into which you want to insert the slide. Go to the Standard Toolbar and click on the Paste button. (Some word processors require you to use the SHIFT + INSERT keys.) The slide will appear on the page and can be sized and cropped and moved to the exact position you want.

Exercise 12.13: De-construct someone else's slides

De-constructing slides can give you good ideas for constructing your own slides. All of the slides on the CD that comes with this book can be de-constructed so you can learn exactly how everything was done, and then do it yourself. Also, in case preparation, if you are able to persuade a judge to require your opponent to turn over PowerPoint slides, be sure to ask for the digital files so that you can de-construct them to see what has been done. This allows you to object and require changes to or the elimination of slides that are inaccurate, distorted, unnecessarily argumentative, or otherwise unfair. In the alternative, you can prepare counter slides that turn your opponent's points or expose the manipulation used in their presentation.

Step 1: Open the file containing the PowerPoint slides. (Exercise 2.4.)

Step 2: Make an off-line backup copy. (Exercise 10.4.)

Step 3: Get an overview with the Slide Sorter.

A. Go to the View Bar. Click on the Slide Sorter button (5th from the left).

B. Print out the slides (in a Handout format) for a handy guide.

Step 4: Run the slide show to see how it looks and how the slides relate to one another. (Exercise 10.5.)

Step 5: Analyze each slide.

With the slide in full size view—

A. Click each object and its effects.

1. Go to the Custom Animation screen. (Standard Toolbar, Slide Show Button, Custom Animation option.) Make a note of the number of objects. All of them will be listed in the box in the upper left corner.

2. Click on each numbered item to locate the item in the thumbnail preview. (There may be hidden objects that can only be seen this way.) You can also look at the effects in the effects box at bottom of the screen.

3. Check which objects are Grouped.

4. Click on the Order & Timing tab. This will show you the order in which the objects are scheduled to appear.

B. Check out the color scheme.

1. Click on each object in turn.

2. Go to the Drawing Toolbar. Check out the color palette behind the Fill Color, Font Color, and Line Color buttons.

3. Go to the Formatting Toolbar. Click on the Background option. Check out the color used for the background of the slide.

C. Check out the fonts used for the titles, labels, and bullet points.

1. Click within the text of each object.

2. Go to the Formatting Toolbar. Look at the Font name and Font size boxes. They will tell you what typeface and type size are being used.

3. Look at the Bold, Italic, and Shadowing buttons. If they are in use, they will appear somewhat highlighted.

Step 6: Look at the transitions between slides.

A. Go to the Slide Sorter view (View Toolbar, 4th from left).

B. Click on the thumbnail of any slide that has a transition icon below it. The slide will be highlighted. Look at the Transitions Toolbar that appears just under the Standard Toolbar at the top of the screen whenever you go into the Slide Sorter view. The name of the transition will be displayed in the box.

The CD accompanying this book contains three slide shows that can be used to try out the methods explained here.

Step 7: Compare photos, documents, and diagrams to originals. Check carefully to see if they have been altered and what changes were made.

Step 8: Check quotes for possible errors or unfair excerpting.

Step 9: Use the notes area to keep track of your findings. (Exercise 10.3.)

Exercise 12.14: Scan material for use in slides

Scanning is the process of turning paper copies into digital files. The digital files are often called "images" and the process is sometimes called "imaging." You can take your paper files (photos, documents, diagrams, charts, and graphs) to any national (and many local) copying chain and they will do the scanning for you. You can also use a small office scanner, which will be quite adequate for most kinds of things that are used in PowerPoint slides. A checklist of ten steps will help ensure that the scanned material works well for PowerPoint slides.

Step 1: File size.

Your objective is to obtain the smallest file size that will do the job. Small file size is particularly important with PowerPoint uses. It will take longer to display large files, so if you use file formats that produce large size files, your viewers will sit and wait while the computer brings the file to the screen. It takes much more storage space to handle large files, so your slides will require more floppy disks, more hard disk space, and more external disk cartridges. And large files are harder to handle when you are constructing slides. File size is primarily a function of file format, resolution, and color.

Step 2: File format.

There are a lot of file formats for graphics materials stored in digital form. Each file format is optimized for a particular kind of task. After a paper copy is scanned, it can be saved in any one of these many formats. This is like a word processing file that can be saved in Word, or WordPerfect, or HTML (for web uses), or RTF (for Macintosh), or other formats. This save function is handled by the software that manages the scanning process such as Adobe PhotoDeluxe.

PowerPoint can handle all of the common formats. The best one for most photographs for PowerPoint purposes is known as JPEG (pronounced jay-peg) which stands for Joint Photographic Experts Group. This format produces reasonably high quality with relatively small files. The best format for most documents is called TIFF (Tag Image File Format). Other common file formats are GIF (Graphics Interchange Format) and PDF (Portable Document Format). Using the right file format is important. For example, a typical photo that might be used on a PowerPoint slide might be one-tenth the size in a JPEG format compared to a TIFF file with no noticeable difference in quality when projected on a large screen.

Step 3: Resolution.

Most scanners can produce output in a range of resolutions. Resolution is measured in dots per inch (dpi). The same photo can be scanned at 300 dpi, 200 dpi, or 150 dpi on most scanners. Many scanners offer resolutions of 600 dpi and higher. It is important to get digital files with enough resolution so that they display clearly, but not any more than that. Higher resolution makes the file size bigger, often very much bigger. For screen displays, a file size of 150 dpi for photos can be perfectly adequate. For printouts, you will normally want 200 dpi. For documents, you may need 300 dpi to get an image that will enlarge well.

Step 4: Colors.

Color capabilities come in the hundreds, thousands, and millions. For PowerPoint purposes, 256 colors is sufficient. Images for trial purposes do not use subtle gradations of color because the monitors and screens used to display them in a courtroom cannot project accurately enough to distinguish them.

Step 5: Compression.

Compression software can help reduce the file size of images while maintaining quality. For example, in scanning documents, you normally would want to use 300 dpi which produces a good quality image on a monitor or screen both at full size and if cropped and blown up. The file size at 300 dpi is quite large. If you drop down to 150 dpi to get a smaller file size, the image may be adequate at full size, but may be barely passable after enlargement. Using compression software on the file containing the image at 300 dpi will produce a very substantial drop in file size with no drop in quality.

Step 6: Conversion.

A file that has been scanned in one format can be converted to another format. The scanning software or image editor software can be used to do this. There is a Save As function where you can specify the format you want. For example, if you have a photo in TIFF format and you want to put it into JPEG format, you can call up the TIFF image and save it in a JPEG format. This gives you the advantages of the JPEG format in making PowerPoint slides with no loss in quality. You can work with the image in any format and then convert and save it to another format. However, because working with a large file takes a long time for each operation (such as rotating a photo), it is more efficient to convert it to a format that will give you a smaller file first and then work with the smaller file.

Step 7: File names.

When you are working with scanned images, it is important to have a labeling or file naming system so that you know what each image is just by the name or designation. Otherwise, you have to spend a lot of time pulling up thumbnails or entire files trying to figure out which is the one you are looking for.

Step 8: Document touch-up.

Scanning processes include a number of touch-up capabilities that help produce a clean image even if the original document is not in very good condition. These include de-skewing (straightening up the document if the paper version is a copy that is a little crooked on the page) and de-specking (taking off the specks that sometimes occur when the paper version is a copy made on a copier with dust on it). You need to be careful about how much document touch-up you authorize if you are planning to represent the image you are using as a "duplicate" of the original.

Step 9: Photo alteration.

Digital photo files are easy to alter. People can be taken out of the photo or put in, objects can be moved, and colors can be changed. Altering a photo does not necessarily make it inadmissible in evidence, but you need to be cautious about any alterations because even if the photo is admitted (for example, on a witness's testimony that it is a fair representation of what he or she saw), the judge and jurors may regard it as less persuasive.

Step 10: Storage media.

Your image files can be stored on a cartridge for an external hard disk, a CD, a file server (computer equipment with large hard disk storage capacity), or an internet service. A CD will hold about 650 megabytes; common size cartridges for external hard disk drives hold 100 or 250 megabytes. The file server and internet service alternatives vary widely in capacity. You could also load all your images onto your laptop, but this would eat up a lot of your available storage.

Exercise 12.15: Use slides for document control

PowerPoint slides are a convenient way to implement a document control system for a small case. You can have all of your documents in one place in a format where you can display them readily in the courtroom, print them out if necessary for hard copy exhibits, or enlarge portions to use in direct or cross-examination.

Step 1: Scan each potential exhibit into digital format. (Exercise 12.14.)

Step 2: Create a numbered index on paper.

A. Organize the potential exhibits in a way that makes an index easy to use.

B. Assign each exhibit a number on the index. Save the number 1 on your index for a black slide.

C. Name the exhibits on the index in a way that will allow for quick identification of each one.

Step 3: Create a black slide as the Number 1 slide in your exhibit series. (Ch. 10, Exercise 10.2, Step 3.)

Step 4: Import each image onto a PowerPoint slide in the order of your index.

A. Go to the Standard Toolbar.

B. Click on the New Slide button (10th from the right). (If the New Slide button is not active, click on the New button at the far left of the Standard Toolbar.) The New Slide screen will appear. (Illustration, Ch. 2, Exercise 2.1.)

C. Double click on the Blank slide option (bottom row, 1st on right). A blank slide will appear on the screen.

D. Go to the Picture Toolbar.

E. Click on the Insert Picture button. The Insert Picture screen will appear.

F. Open the folder where you stored the images of your potential exhibits.

G. Click on the first one to be put on a slide. A thumbnail of the exhibit will appear in the box to the right of the list of file names.

H. Click on the Insert button at the top right. The image will now be on your slide.

I. Size the image on the slide so that it is large enough to be seen. (Do not size down when working with a document control system.)

J. Repeat this operation until you have all the exhibits on slides in the order of your index. You will need a separate slide for each page of a multi-page document.

K. Decide whether you want a background color other than white. If so, go to the Formatting Toolbar, click on the Background icon, select a color, and click on the option "Apply to All."

L. Make sure the slide numbers match your index.

1. Go to the View Bar.

2. Click on the Slide Sorter button (4th from the left). This will show you thumbnails of all the slides in your file. Each slide has an identifying number just under the lower right corner. The black slide should be Slide #1. If you created the slides in the same order as you arranged your index, the numbers on the slides should now match your hard copy index. If not, adjust the index, or rearrange the slides. (Exercise 10.1, Step 4.)

M. Save your work. Be sure that the file name you assign to the slide show allows quick identification of what it contains.

For PowerPoint 97 users, there is no Background button, so go to the Menu Bar, click on the Format button, and pick the Background option.

Step 5: Recall an exhibit when you need it.

A. Open the slide show containing the exhibits. (Exercise 2.4, Step 5.)

B. Go to Slide Show mode.

1. Go to the View Bar.

2. Click on the Slide Show button (1st on the right). This brings up the black slide, so the screen will be blank.

C. Select the exhibit you want to display.

1. Consult your paper index for the slide number of the exhibit you want.

2. Type in the slide number (such as 14) and press the ENTER key on your keyboard.

3. Slide #14 should appear.

D. Use the B key to blank the screen when you are finished. (Press the B key on your keyboard. The screen should go black.)

E. Go to the next exhibit that you want to display.

1. Consult your paper index for the slide number.

2. Type in the slide number and press the ENTER key on your keyboard.

3. The slide you selected should appear.

★ Once you have all of your potential exhibits on PowerPoint slides, you can examine them for potential excerpts you might want to use in direct and cross-examination. This would include portions of a deposition, preliminary hearing, or grand jury transcript you have scanned for purposes of impeachment should a witness change critical testimony at trial. Put each of the excerpts onto a separate slide (Ch. 7, Exercise 7.6). Create an index so that you know where each of the excerpts are. Then, if you need them, you can bring them to the screen right away.

Exercise 12.16: Add ANIX for more capability

When lawyers use PowerPoint, they run into some limitations that affect the range of potential uses in a courtroom. The software was designed principally for business and sales presentations in a context where adversaries are not flinging formal objections and responses at each other. This chapter introduces ANIX, a software product that enhances PowerPoint with features designed specifically for lawyers and courtroom presentations. ANIX is a plug-in to PowerPoint, which means that it runs at the same time as PowerPoint. It also adds evidence display capabilities which means that it can act as your "command central" in the courtroom.

ANIX versions are available for both PowerPoint 97 and PowerPoint 2000. To obtain a demonstration copy of ANIX, download the fully functional demo version from the web at *www.doar.com/anix.htm*, or call DOAR Communications, Inc. at (800) 875-8705 for a CD copy.

Access to all exhibits. You can call up to the courtroom screen or monitors almost instantly any document among the thousands you might have in a large case, any photo or video, and any other exhibit such as a drawing, map, chart, graph, table, time line, printout, or PowerPoint slide. Anything that has been scanned into digital format or that was created using a computer and is already in digital format (like PowerPoint slides) can be brought to the courtroom on a computer storage medium such as a hard disk drive, a CD-ROM, or an external storage drive. From that storage, the evidence display software can locate what you need and get it onto the screen or monitor very quickly.

More presentation alternatives. You can create displays that are either beyond PowerPoint's capabilities or that would be relatively difficult and time consuming using PowerPoint. These tasks include:

1. Highlighting directly on the document
2. Dimming irrelevant portions of the document
3. Creating direct callouts quickly, on-the-fly
4. Stamping displays with pre-defined icons
5. Changing shapes
6. Using multi-page TIFF images
7. Adding 3-D to objects with animation

There are several evidence display software packages on the market. ANIX[tm] is used by the National Institute for Trial Advocacy for teaching courtroom technology because it is inexpensive and operates as a plug-in to PowerPoint. This means that lawyers familiar with PowerPoint do not have to learn a whole new software package to use advanced capabilities.

Automation of multi-step PowerPoint functions. ANIX was designed specifically for lawyers. It automates some of the tasks that take many individual steps in PowerPoint.

1. Resizing photos and documents: ANIX makes them fit into your designated box automatically
2. Re-positioning images: ANIX has a special Position button that puts images in place with one click

3. Making direct callouts: ANIX allows you to mark the section of text you want and it creates the callout automatically

Extended presentation capability. ANIX extends the slide show presentation capability of PowerPoint by making it interactive. The user can copy and create new slides and add annotations and objects in real time. This allows changes to be made on the spot in the event the court sustains an objection to part of a visual aid, but will allow use of the exhibit with the objectionable parts removed.

The CD accompanying this book contains examples of ANIX slides. The ANIX software must first be loaded in order to view and appreciate the extra capabilities of this slide show (go to ANIX.exe on the CD to start the software). These slides can also be downloaded from the NITA web site, *www.nitastudent.org*.

In Conclusion

Courtroom visuals help the judge and jurors grasp the overall theme, absorb the details, and learn the relationships among facts much more readily than can be accomplished by speech alone. When people listen to you explain something new, they try to picture it in their minds. Using a visual aid ensures that your listeners will have a good opportunity to form the same mental picture of the facts as you have. Visuals motivate people to pay more attention, and they make understanding easier. For a well-prepared lawyer, the advantage gained by adding visual displays is almost always substantial, no matter what kind of case is being litigated. If your opponent uses visuals effectively, that is an advantage you cannot afford to give away.

The National Institute for Trial Advocacy
March 2000

Appendix A

Business Contract Case

Quinlan v. Kane Electronics

Roberta Quinlan is a business broker who specializes in the buying and selling of electronics manufacturing and sales firms. Business brokers are agents for buyers or sellers of businesses, and generally work on a commission basis. Quinlan has been a broker in the electronics industry for ten years. Kane Electronics was a family-owned chain of retail electronics outlets located throughout the State of Nita in 26 locations. Its president, founder, and sole shareholder was Brian Kane.

On August 4, YR-1[1], Kane Electronics was sold to Nita Computer World (NCW), a national retailer of computers and other electronic business equipment, for $10,000,000 of NCW stock. Roberta Quinlan claims that she served as the broker for this transaction and that she had an agreement with Brian Kane to do so. She claims that the agreement was set forth during a business meeting held at Kane's house on June 16, YR-1 and in a confirming letter that she mailed to Kane the next day, June 17. She has sued Kane for $300,000.

Kane and Quinlan have known each other for about ten years, mainly as golf partners. Kane admits that he decided to sell his business in early June and that he told Quinlan of his decision during a round of golf on June 15. Kane admits to inviting Quinlan over to his house the next day to talk about the sale of his business. Kane also admits he had several conversations with Quinlan about the possible sale of his company over the years, but he says they were all preliminary and brainstorming in nature. Kane regarded Quinlan as a friend who was giving him advice on a voluntary basis. He denies there was an agreement between him and Quinlan for her to act as his agent. He also denies ever receiving a confirming letter of agreement from Quinlan. He admits that when he was first contacted by phone by Cliff Fuller of NCW on June 26, YR-1, that Fuller said he had been referred by Roberta Quinlan. He also admits that he did not know Fuller or of NCW's interest in his company, before the Fuller phone call. Kane maintains he negotiated his own deal with NCW and does not owe Quinlan a commission.

Both sides have ten exhibits in the file, and both sides have a copy of the CD containing the digital files of these exhibits. The exhibits in this Appendix would

1. NITA uses a convention for dates as follows: YR-0 (this year), YR-1 (last year), YR-2 (two years ago), and so on.

be used by both sides to create illustrative aids for trial. Printed copies of each of these exhibits, except the video deposition, are in this Appendix.

(1) Telephone message slip from Kane's secretary showing a call from Quinlan (Kane Phone Slip).

(2) Copy of a letter that Quinlan says she sent Kane confirming the commission deal (Quinlan Letter).

(3) Page from Quinlan's phone log showing a call from Kane (Quinlan Phone Log).

(4) Photo of Quinlan and Kane at the tee (Photo-1).

(5) Second photo of Quinlan and Kane at the tee (Photo-2).

(6) Photo of Quinlan and Fuller at an office party (Photo-3).

(7) Second photo of Quinlan and Fuller at an office party (Photo-4)

(8) Diagram of Kane's house where the key meeting took place (Diagram–Kane Floor plan).

(9) Page 35 of the transcript of the Quinlan deposition (Transcript Quinlan depo 35).

(10) Page 36 of the transcript of the Quinlan deposition (Transcript Quinlan depo 36).

(11) Video clip of a portion of the Quinlan deposition (Quinlan depo 35-36).

The CD also contains a PowerPoint slide show for this case containing the slides shown in each chapter so that you can see them in full color and with full motion.

The digital files on the CD-ROM can also be downloaded from the NITA web site, *www.nitastudent.org*. When you use exhibits from your file to create PowerPoint slides, you will take them from this CD or from the files you downloaded. When you open the CD, the Business Contract Case folder looks like this:

The illustrative aids used as examples in this Appendix assume that you represent Roberta Quinlan, the plaintiff. Assume further that your approach to the case is that Ms. Quinlan had a lengthy business meeting with Mr. Kane at which time he agreed to have her broker the sale of his electronics business. You want to show that this was not just a casual conversation, as were many conversations that they had in the past, but instead was a serious, case-specific meeting focusing on the sale of this business.

IMPORTANT MESSAGE

For Brian

Day 6/24 Time 2:30 A.M. P.M.

Ms. Quinlan

Of

Phone 225 · 6482
FAX Area Code Number Extension
MOBILE
Area Code Number Extension

Telephoned		Returned your call	✓	RUSH	
Came to see you		Please call		Special attention	
Wants to see you		Will call again		Caller on hold	

Message Told her you were not in— as per your instructions

Signed Peg

Universal 48023 LITHO IN U.S.A.

ROBERTA QUINLAN
Business Broker
12 Meredith Lane
Nita City, NI 99992

June 16, YR-1

Mr. Brian Kane
One Kane Plaza
P.O. Box 626
Nita City, NI 99992

Dear Brian:

It was a pleasure to visit with you this afternoon, and I write to confirm our understanding.

You, as the sole shareholder of Kane Electronics, desire to dispose of your stock holdings in the company by way of an exchange of shares of a corporation with a good investment future. If I arrange for such an exchange, which is acceptable to you, Kane Electronics will pay me a fee calculated at between 3-5 percent of the closing value to you, dependent upon my time and effort necessary on your behalf.

If I do not hear from you, I will assume that this arrangement is acceptable to you. I already have a prospect in mind and will be in touch with you in the near future.

Warm regards,

Roberta Quinlan

rq/s

COPY

ROBERTA QUINLAN
Business Broker

Outgoing Phone Log

Date	Person Called	Telephone #	Business Purpose
6/24	Cliff Fuller NCW	287-1440	Called re: potential interest in Kane Electronics. Says NCW looking to acquire companies like Kane. Thinks Kane may already be on their list of potential acquisitions. He will call Kane.
6/24	Brian Kane Kane Electronics	877-2893	Called to tell him expect call from Cliff Fuller at NCW. Left message on voice mail.
6/24	Brian Kane Kane Electronics	877-2893	Called again. Secretary claims isn't in. I hope he isn't ducking me to try to get out of our agreement (don't be paranoid)

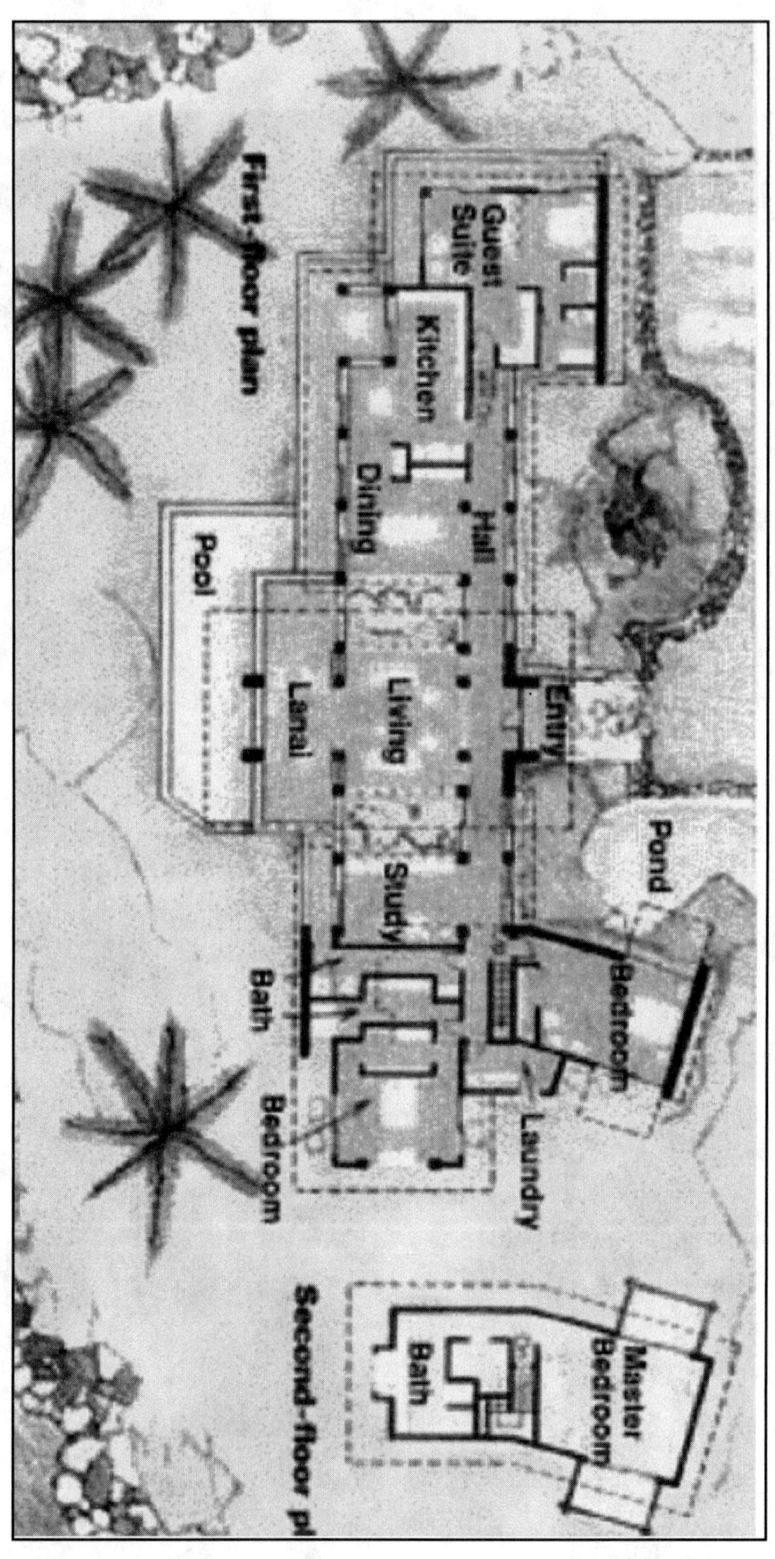
First-floor plan
Guest Suite
Kitchen
Dining
Hall
Pool
Lanai
Living
Entry
Pond
Study
Bath
Bedroom
Bedroom
Laundry
Master Bedroom
Bath
Second-floor pl

DEPOSITION OF ROBERTA QUINLAN

Q: As I understand it, you talked with Mr. Kane at his house in June of last year?
A: Yes.
Q: The two of you discussed various options of how he might sell his business?
A: Among other things, yes.
Q: Thank you, and among those other things was you telling him your fees in brokering deals?
A: Yes, and he seemed pleased by my assurance I would keep those fees as low as possible.
Q: But all you discussed was a range of fees, being three to five percent, isn't that correct?
A: Yes.
Q: Nothing more concrete than that?
A: That's customary.
Q: Well, whether that's customary or not, it was no more concrete than a range of three to five percent, right?
A: Yes, that's right.
Q: You told him you had contacts in the industry?
A: Yes I did.

Q: Mr. Kane knew that anyhow, didn't he?

A: Yes he did.

Q: You even had someone in mind to buy his business, didn't you?

A: Yes, Nita Computer World.

Q: When at his house, you did not tell Mr. Kane that you had someone in mind who might be interested, did you?

A: No.

Q: At the end of the talk, you told him you would do some checking and would get back to him?

A: Yes.

Q: Mr. Kane did not ask you to check on this, did he?

A: He didn't say not to.

Q: And he didn't say that you should do some checking either, did he?

A: Not in so many words, no.

Q: Speaking of words, the word "Hire" was never said by Mr. Kane was it?

A: I'm not sure what you mean.

Q: As in "You're hired" or "I want to hire you to help sell my business."

A: No, not that specific word.

Q: What specific word do you say he used to hire you?

A: Brian never said we had a deal explicitly, but he also didn't tell me not to go forward on his behalf, either.

Appendix B

Criminal Case

State v. Lawrence

The defendant, James Lawrence, has been charged with larceny and assault as the result of a purse-snatching incident that occurred on October 1, YR-1[1]. The victim of the purse snatching was Gale Fitzgerald. At approximately 9:45 p.m. Ms. Fitzgerald was walking home on the sidewalk along Main Street after a long day at work. A person came up from behind and pulled at her purse. After struggling for the purse, her attacker threw her to the ground, took the purse, and ran off towards 5th Street. As soon as she got to her apartment at 410 Main Street, Ms. Fitzgerald called the police. Officer James Wright responded and took a statement from her that night. Ms. Fitzgerald was called to the police station on October 3rd to look through mug books to see if she could pick out her attacker. She was unable to make an identification. A photograph of defendant was among those contained in the mug books shown Ms. Fitzgerald. Ms. Fitzgerald was also shown a purse that had been found in a mailbox near her house, which she identified as hers. She reviewed and signed her original statement given on October 1st, and also signed a supplemental statement that day indicating the events that took place on that date. Ms. Fitzgerald was again called to the police station on October 16th after police had arrested Mr. Lawrence for attempting to snatch a purse from an off-duty police officer. Officer Wright showed her one photograph, and she positively identified the person in the photograph as her attacker. The photo was of James Lawrence. She gave another signed supplemental statement at that time. As per police procedures, videos were made of both the October 3rd and October 16th identification sessions and a transcript was prepared of each.

Both sides have eleven exhibits in the file, and both sides have a copy of a CD containing the digital files of these exhibits. The exhibits would be used by both sides to create illustrative aids for the trial. Printed copies of each of these items, except the video clips, are in this Appendix.

(1) Statement of Gale Fitzgerald, October 1, YR-1

(2) Supplemental Statement of Gale Fitzgerald, October 3, YR-1

1. NITA uses a convention for dates as follows: YR-0 (this year), YR-1 (last year), YR-2 (two years ago), and so on.

(3) Supplemental Statement of Gale Fitzgerald, October 16, YR-1

(4) Police Report by Officer James Wright, October 1-16, YR-1

(5) Diagram of the location prepared by Officer Wright, YR-0

(6) Photograph of the approximate scene of the mugging, YR-0

(7) Photograph of the street at scene of the mugging, YR-0

(8) Transcript, identification procedure October 3, YR-1

(9) Transcript, identification procedure October 16, YR-1

(10) Video clip-1, identification procedure October 3, YR-1

(11) Video clip-2, identification procedure October 16, YR-1

The CD also contains a PowerPoint slide show for this case containing the slides shown in this appendix so that you can see them in full color and with full motion.

The digital files on the CD-ROM supplied by NITA can also be downloaded from the NITA web site, *www.nitastudent.org*. When you use material from the file to create exhibits, you will take it from this CD or from the files you downloaded. When you open the CD, the Criminal Case folder looks like this:

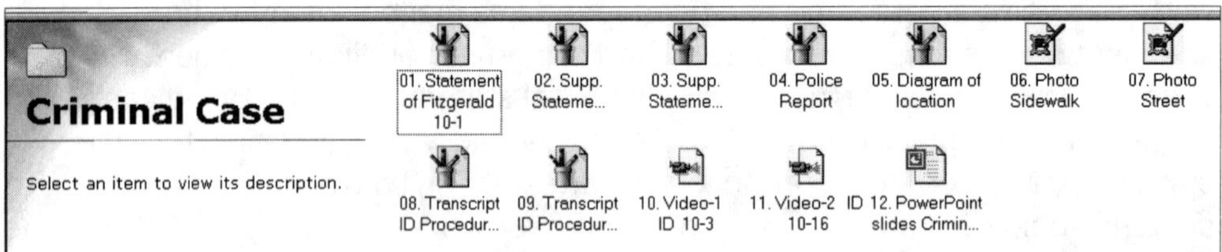

The illustrative aids in this Appendix assume that you represent James Lawrence, the defendant. Assume that you have decided to defend the case on the basis of suggestive circumstances in showing Ms. Fitzgerald the photo from which she identified Mr. Lawrence. Lawrence also claims mistaken identification under poor lighting conditions at night on a street where the trees shaded the available illumination from the streetlights. The defense might also assert that Ms. Fitzgerald was frightened during the incident and her fright decreased her ability to record an accurate mental impression from which to make a good identification.

STATEMENT OF GALE FITZGERALD
OCTOBER 1, YR-1

My name is Gale Fitzgerald. I am twenty-eight years old. I am single and live in an apartment at 410 Main Street in Nita City. I work for Harry Loomis, a personal injury lawyer, as a secretary and paralegal. His offices are in the Public Ledger Building in downtown Nita City.

On October 1, YR-1, I worked late. Harry was in the middle of a trial and we had been at the office until at least 9:00 p.m. every night for the week before October 1st. I left the office at 9:15 p.m. and got lucky and caught a bus right away outside the building. The bus, which travels up 5th Street, let me off at the bus stop at the corner of 5th and Main Streets. I got off the bus and started to walk on the sidewalk toward my apartment. There are streetlights on the corners of the intersection and some small lights on the houses on that block. I would say that the visibility was fairly good given that it was nighttime.

As I walked towards my apartment, I got to about the middle of the block when I heard fast footsteps behind me. Before I could turn around I felt a sharp pull on my purse, which I was carrying on my right shoulder. The tug on the purse turned me around and I was facing my attacker. I know it was stupid, but I struggled with him. I had taken $200 out of the ATM in our building just before I left for the night and didn't want to lose it. I also had in my purse a letter I received at the office from a good friend that I hadn't yet had a chance to read.

We struggled over the purse for what seemed like a long time, but I guess was less than 30 seconds, until he threw me to the ground. Somehow the strap broke on my purse and my attacker ran off with my purse across the street and in the direction that he came from, towards 5th Street. My attacker was a white man, approximately 5'8" to 5'10" in height, 160-175 pounds, with longish dark hair (dark brown or black), wearing dark pants, running shoes, and a tan windbreaker jacket.

As soon as I got into my apartment I called the police. Officer Wright came to my apartment soon afterwards, where I am now giving this statement. That's all I can remember. I am very upset by this. I've never been attacked before.

Signed: Gale Fitzgerald
Gale Fitzgerald
October 3, YR-1

SUPPLEMENTAL STATEMENT OF GALE FITZGERALD
OCTOBER 3, YR-1

I have come to the police station today at the request of Officer Jim Wright. Officer Wright returned my purse to me, which he told me was recovered from a mailbox in the 800 block of Main Street.

The purse has a torn shoulder strap. All of my personal belongings and my wallet with all my identification are still in it. All of my money, including the money I took out of the ATM before going home on the day of the mugging, is gone.

I have been shown several books of mug shot photographs and have not been able to identify my attacker among them.

Signed: Gale Fitzgerald
Gale Fitzgerald
October 3, YR-1

SUPPLEMENTAL STATEMENT OF GALE FITZGERALD
OCTOBER 16, YR-1

I have come to the Nita City police station today at the request of Officer Jim Wright for the purpose of participating further in the investigation of the attack on me on October 1, YR-1.

I have been shown a photograph of an individual who I can positively identify as my attacker. I had never seen this man before October 1st when he attacked me. I am informed that the name of my attacker if James Lawrence.

At Officer Wright's request, I am returning my purse, which I haven't yet had the time to repair, to be kept as evidence in the case.

Signed: ____________________
Gale Fitzgerald
October 16, YR-1

NITA CITY POLICE DEPARTMENT

Nita City, Nita

INVESTIGATIVE REPORT

1. Complaining Witness Gale Fitzgerald	2. Address 410 Main St., Nita City, NI
2. Phone 449-5327 (home) 889-9000 (work)	4. Complained of Offense Theft, Assault (purse snatching)
5. Date October 1, YR-1	6. Place 400 block of Main St. Nita City

7. Narrative

Complaining witness interviewed at her apartment at above address. States that upon exiting bus at 4th and Main and walking towards her apartment, was grabbed from behind by unknown assailant. Struggle ensues. Assailant stole purse belonging to complaining witness containing personal articles. Witness agrees to come to station on 10/3 on lunch break to attempt mug shot ID and to sign statement (See attached statement).

10/3/YR-1

Complaining witness comes to station at 1300 hours. Reviews and signs statement given two nights previous. Shown several mug books of known purse snatchers. Not able to make positive ID. Purse containing wallet with ID for Gale Fitzgerald found in mailbox at 814 Main Street. Purse identified by Ms. Fitzgerald as hers. States that everything but money still in the purse. Reviews and signs supplemental statement (See attached supplemental statement).

10/16/YR-1

Complaining witness called to station. Suspect who meets description given by Ms. Fitzgerald arrested on 10/15 in attempt to snatch purse of off-duty police officer. Ms. Fitzgerald shown photograph of suspect, James Lawrence. Positive ID made. Obtain purse from Ms. Fitzgerald as evidence in the case against Lawrence. This officer notes that photograph of suspect was among those included in mug books complaining witness viewed on 10/2/YR-1.

10. Investigating Officer – Name and Signature

James Wright

James Wright, Badge #007

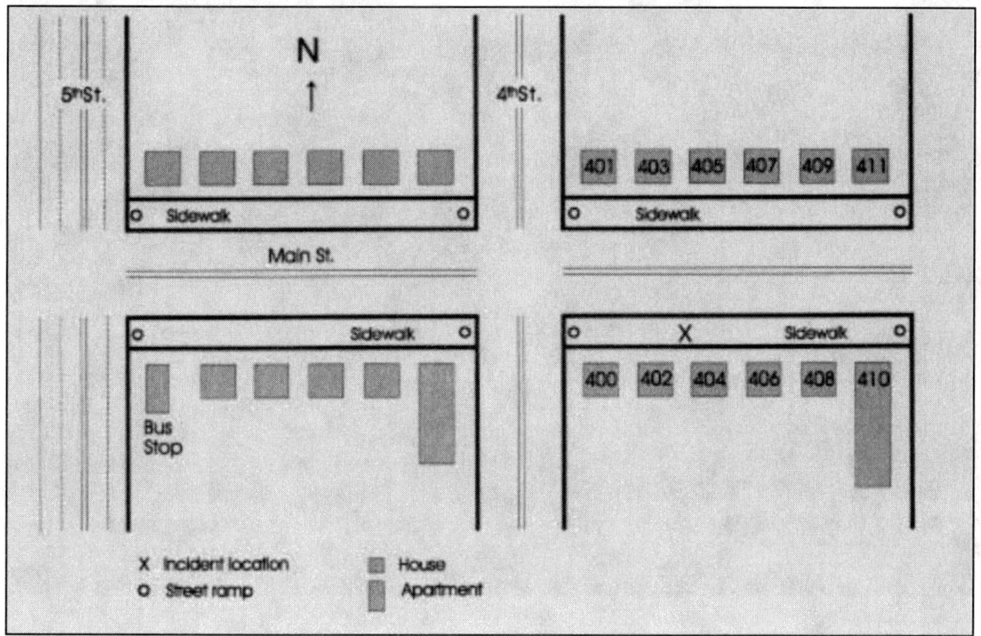
N
5th St.
4th St.
401
403
405
407
409
411
Sidewalk
Sidewalk
Main St.
Sidewalk
X
Sidewalk
400
402
404
406
408
410
Bus
Stop
X Incident location
o Street ramp
House
Apartment

Transcript—Gale Fitzgerald—10/3/YR-1

Officer Wright: The time is 10:37 a.m., the date October third, and we are in the Nita City Police Department conference room with Ms. Gale Fitzgerald. Ms. Fitzgerald, I have already told you this session will be videotaped and you have given your approval to the taping, but I want it on the record that you in fact agree to this videotaping.

Ms. Fitzgerald: Yes, I know and I approve.

Officer Wright: I have placed in front of you several books filled with photographs of various males that our department has collected. I want you to look through these books, please take your time. We would like you to tell us if anyone pictured in these books looks like the man who attacked you two nights ago and took your purse. If someone could be that person but you are not sure, we would still like for you to tell us. If nobody looks like the person you saw, then tell us that as well. Obviously, if someone appears to you to be that person, we want to know that too. We've given you little yellow stickies to mark any photos you want to flag for later review or discussion. We would like you to withhold saying anything until you have looked at all of the photographs. I will turn tape off now until you have completed looking through all of the books. (Turned off tape.)

Officer Wright: (Turning tape back on.) The time is 11:10 and Ms. Fitzgerald has finished looking through the books. What can you tell us about the photographs you have just seen?

Ms. Fitzgerald: There were so many faces, it was so confusing trying to look at all of them at once and pick somebody out. It all happened so fast, and it was night time, you know.

Officer Wright: Yes, I know and understand Ms. Fitzgerald. Have you picked anybody out either as the person, or possibly the person?

Ms. Fitzgerald: No, it was just too hard. I don't know if he's in there or not.

Officer Wright: Thank you, Ms. Fitzgerald. We will go off record.

Transcript—Gale Fitzgerald—10/16/YR-1

Officer Wright:	The time is 5:18 p.m., the date October sixteenth, and we are in the Nita City Police Department conference room with Ms. Gale Fitzgerald. Ms. Fitzgerald, we are again taping this session with your knowledge and permission, is that correct?
Ms. Fitzgerald:	Yes, that's true.
Officer Wright:	We have again asked you to come to the station to help us in our investigation of the mugging that took place on October first in which you were the victim. We really appreciate your coming down after work to help us out. We have a photograph we'd like to show you. Please tell us if this is the man who attacked you and took your purse.
Ms. Fitzgerald:	Why yes, that's him. Oh yes, how did you know? What's his name? Has he done this before...to others?
Officer Wright:	I can't tell you ma'am any details about our investigation. Are you certain this is the man who attacked you on October first?
Ms. Fitzgerald:	Well, I wouldn't put my life on it, it was dark you know, but there was enough light for me to see his face for just a second, and yes this looks just like the man. I mean his clothes and hair were different, and.... No, I'm sure this is the guy.
Officer Wright:	Thank you very much, Ms. Fitzgerald. We will be letting you know when you are needed for trial. Off record.

Exercise 2.1: Construct a basic bullet point list

Defense counsel's plan for the opening statement might be to urge that this is a case of mistaken identity. Ms. Fitzgerald, while well-meaning and a nice person, was frightened by the attack and glimpsed her attacker only momentarily before he ran off. She gave an extremely general description that fits half of the male population of Nita City, failed to identify anyone when she looked at mug books, and identified Lawrence only when shown a single photo under suggestive circumstances. The examples in this Appendix might be constructed for a part of this opening statement.

Defense counsel might want to start with a slide that sets the scene for the mistaken identity. The title for this slide could be "The Scene."

First, assess what facts are available that help support the conclusion that under the circumstances it was highly unlikely that Ms. Fitzgerald got a look at her attacker good enough to support a positive identification. The bullet points under this title need to use these facts in a persuasive way. The initial list of points might be:

The Scene

- October 1, YR-1, 9:15 at night
- It was cloudy, no moon
- Street lights located at intersections
- Porch lights on houses are very small
- Leafy trees make the street very dark

Exercise 2.2: Edit the text

When you look over the wording of this slide, you might decide to get rid of some of the words to simplify and shorten the points. This will make your points more effective and easier to enlarge, keeping each one on one line.

One way to shorten the title and the bullet points without losing anything would be to do this:

Scene

- Night of October 1
- Cloudy, no moon
- Street lights only at intersections
- House porch lights small
- Leafy trees up and down block
- Happened on sidewalk, mid-block

You will usually want to avoid using "the," an," and similar words if they do not add meaning. The "YR-1" can be dropped from the first bullet point because all of the events relevant to this case took place in the same year. Short non-action verbs like "was" and "are" normally do not add much.

The fifth bullet point might raise an objection as argumentative. It could be changed to "Leafy trees up and down block," which is more factual.

You might decide that the slide needs another point to help bring home the point of the previous bullets. You could add: "Happened on sidewalk, mid-block."

You can make room for this new bullet point by consolidating the first two bullet points.

Now the slide looks like this:

Scene

- October 1, cloudy night, no moon
- Street lights only at intersections
- House porch lights small
- Leafy trees up and down block
- Happened on sidewalk, mid-block

Exercise 3.1: Set the typeface, size, and alignment

Change the typeface to Arial or Tahoma.

Change the type size to 48-point for the title and 36-point for the bullet list text.

Put the title in bold face.

Add shadowing to the title.

Now your slide looks like this:

Scene

- October 1, cloudy night, no moon
- Street lights only at intersections
- House porch lights small
- Leafy trees up and down block
- Happened on sidewalk, mid-block

Exercise 3.2: Put boxes around the title and text

The boxes around the title and text will give your visual aid a more polished look. This example uses a 1½ point line style for each box. The slide that you have been working on will look like this:

Scene

- October 1, cloudy night, no moon
- Street lights only at intersections
- House porch lights small
- Leafy trees up and down block
- Happened on sidewalk, mid-block

If you try out a shadow around the title box, it should look like this:

Scene

- October 1, cloudy night, no moon
- Street lights only at intersections
- House porch lights small
- Leafy trees up and down block
- Happened on sidewalk, mid-block

Exercise 3.3: Add color to the components of the slide

Because this book is printed in black and white, the background of the slide has been changed to gray to illustrate how the slide looks after color is added.

The slide now looks like this:

Scene

- October 1, cloudy night, no moon
- Street lights only at intersections
- House porch lights small
- Leafy trees up and down block
- Happened on sidewalk, mid-block

When you add color to the title box, the slide looks like this:

Scene

- October 1, cloudy night, no moon
- Street lights only at intersections
- House porch lights small
- Leafy trees up and down block
- Happened on sidewalk, mid-block

To see this slide in color, go to your CD. The CD also shows this slide with color in the box containing the bullet points; color added to the lines around the boxes; and color added to the bullet points.

Exercise 3.4: Change bullet shape, size, and spacing

This slide uses the square bullet option provided by PowerPoint 2000. For PowerPoint 97, the same shape is found in the Monotype Sorts.

Scene

- October 1, cloudy night, no moon
- Street lights only at intersections
- House porch lights small
- Leafy trees up and down block
- Happened on sidewalk, mid-block

The CD shows slides with different bullet sizes and spacing.

Exercise 3.5: Create subordinate points

An alternative way to make the first point would be to create subordinate points under the first bullet.

Scene
Night of October 1
cloudy
no moon
Street lights only at intersections
House porch lights small
Leafy trees up and down block
Happened on sidewalk, mid-block

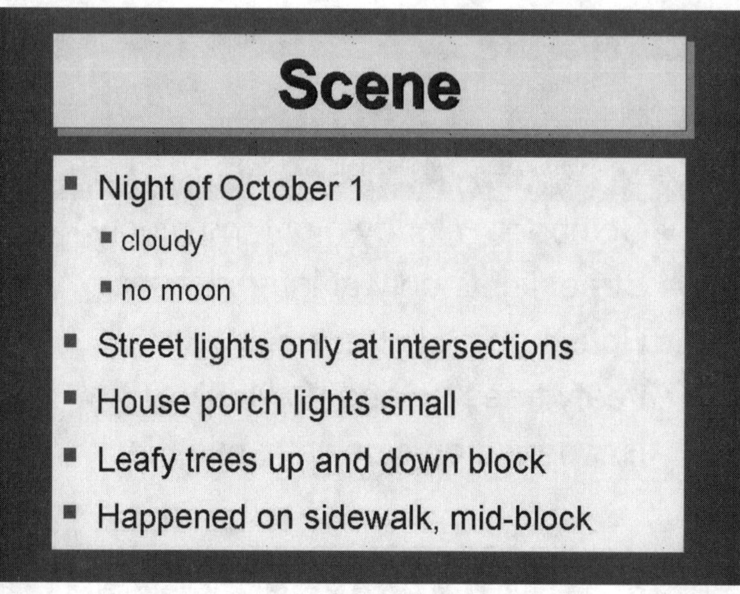

Alternatively, you could emphasize the visibility factors by grouping them all together under one point like this:

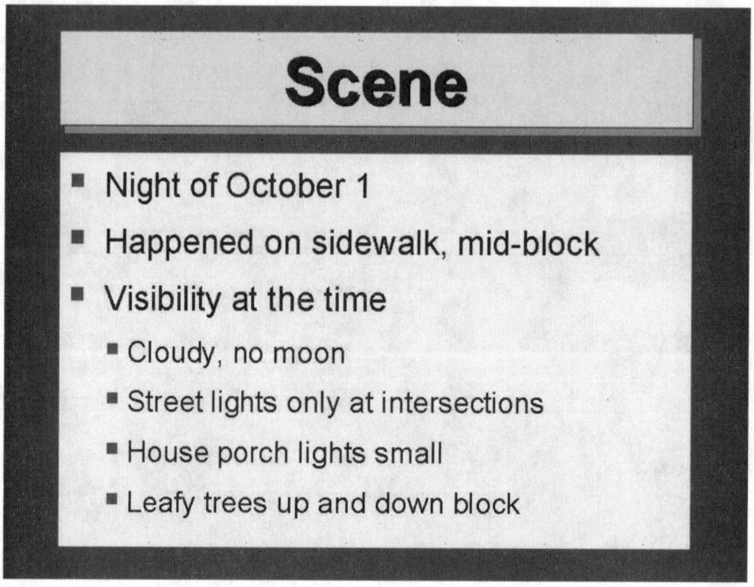

Scene
Night of October 1
Happened on sidewalk, mid-block
Visibility at the time
Cloudy, no moon
Street lights only at intersections
House porch lights small
Leafy trees up and down block

Exercise 4.1: Make a companion slide

After the opening statement in the Lawrence case covered the "Scene" with the first slide, defense counsel might want to cover the "Identification" with the next slide. This slide might include all the facts supporting the argument about mistaken identification, including:

- the portion of the first statement in which Ms. Fitzgerald says the incident occurred in "less than 30 seconds"
- the very general description Ms. Fitzgerald gave in her original report
- the failure to pick out Mr. Lawrence from the mug shots
- the identification of the single photo when given to her by an officer

You can make this slide look just like the first one by creating a duplicate of the first slide and then changing the title and the text.

This slide would look like this:

Identification

- Happened in less than 30 seconds
- 5' 8" – 5' 10" 160 – 175 pounds
- Longish hair, dark pants
- 10/3 – Shown mug books, no ID
- 10/16 – Shown only 1 photo, ID

Exercise 4.2: Construct a no-title slide

From the defense perspective, the "beyond a reasonable doubt" standard is one opportunity for a no-title slide. It would look like this:

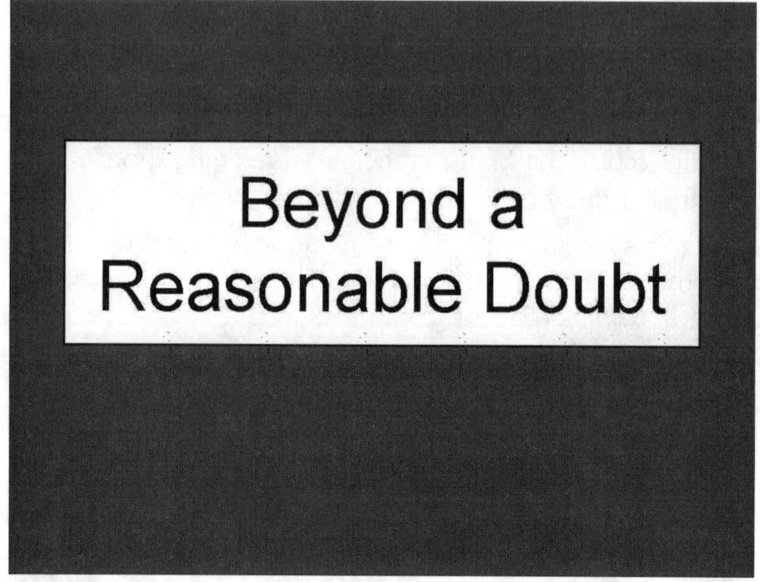

Exercises 5.1, 5.2, 5.3, and 5.4: Create a labeled photo

One photo in the file shows the sidewalk where the mugging occurred. It can be used to illustrate the fact that the trees shaded light sources from the porch lights on the houses and the relatively distant street lamps. The title needs to identify the photo and convey the point to be made.

This photo was taken during the daytime, and does not purport to represent fairly and accurately the lighting conditions on the night of the mugging, so you need to take account of that. "Lighting on Main St." is an objectionable title under these circumstances. The words "Main Street" or "Main St." will identify the photo sufficiently, but "Tree Cover on Main Street" will help get across the point you want to make. "Tree Cover on Main St." is not objectionable. The trees are the same whether conditions are night or day.

In conveying the point about the capability of the witness to see her attacker clearly, you need to be careful to avoid argument. Adjectives and adverbs generally are argument material, so avoid "*poor* lighting" or "*dark* conditions."

Your slide will look like this:

Exercise 6.1: Zap-Zap-I-Win relationship chart

In this case, the defense counsel has four useful facts that could be used for a relationship chart:

- the witness was shown mug books;
- she could not identify anyone;
- the witness was shown a single photo by a police officer;
- only then could she make a positive identification.

A chart could highlight the relationship between the number of photos that Ms. Fitzgerald was shown and the identification she was able to make.

An easy relationship chart to illustrate this point would look like this:

The animation for this relationship chart is shown on the CD.

Exercise 6.2: All-Roads-Lead-to-Rome relationship chart

This model of relationship chart uses the familiar metaphor to suggest that particular facts in this case point to the same central theme that the identification is suspect and the victim really does not know who took her purse. This slide could be used as a visual outline for the entire closing argument.

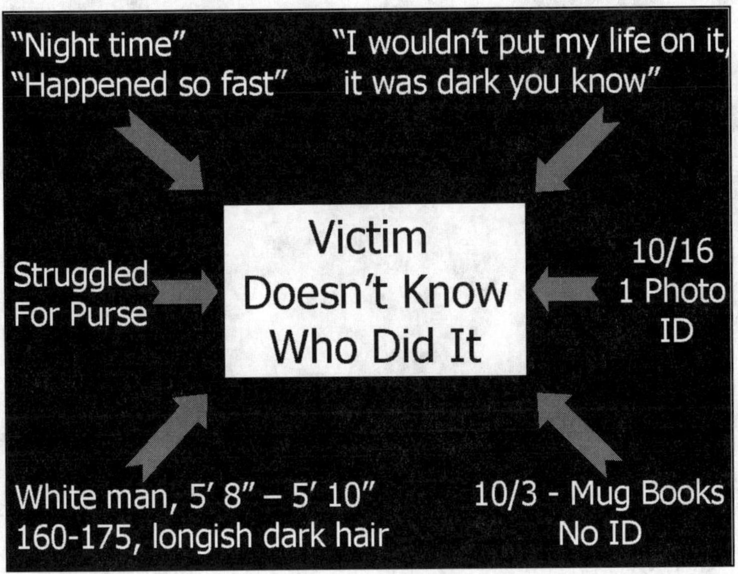

The animation for this relationship chart is shown on the CD.

Exercise 6.3: The basic time line

A simple time line designed to show the fuzzy nature of the victim's initial description and later identification procedures could look like this:

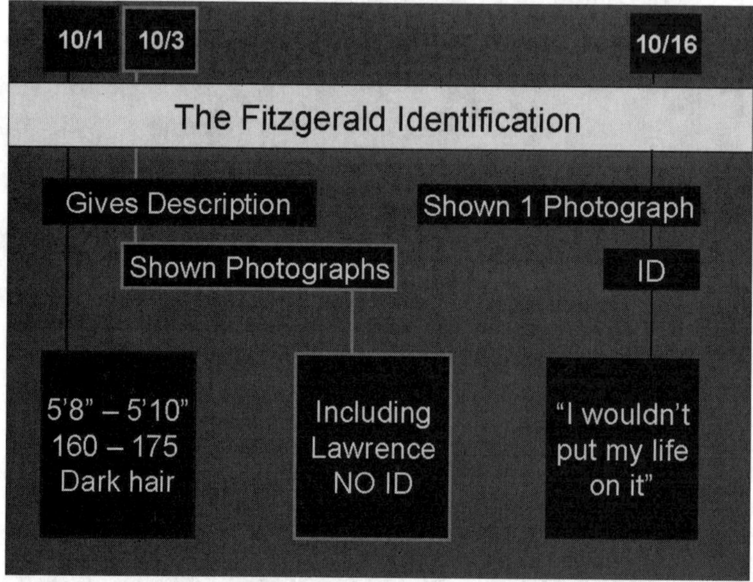

This format allows you to emphasize the time interval between the purse snatching and the first attempt at an identification, and the much longer time interval before the next attempt at an identification.

This slide design can use color to tie together the dates and key points. This is shown on the CD.

Exercise 7.1: Use a box for focus

Defense counsel might want to cross-examine Ms. Fitzgerald about the facts in the police report, made on October 3, YR-1, shortly after the crime took place.

That examination could start by establishing the date on which the police report was made. To help the jury follow questions of Ms. Fitzgerald, the date that appears on the face of the report can be highlighted by putting a box around it.

Import the document to the slide, create an identification box for the exhibit number, and color the background of the slide.

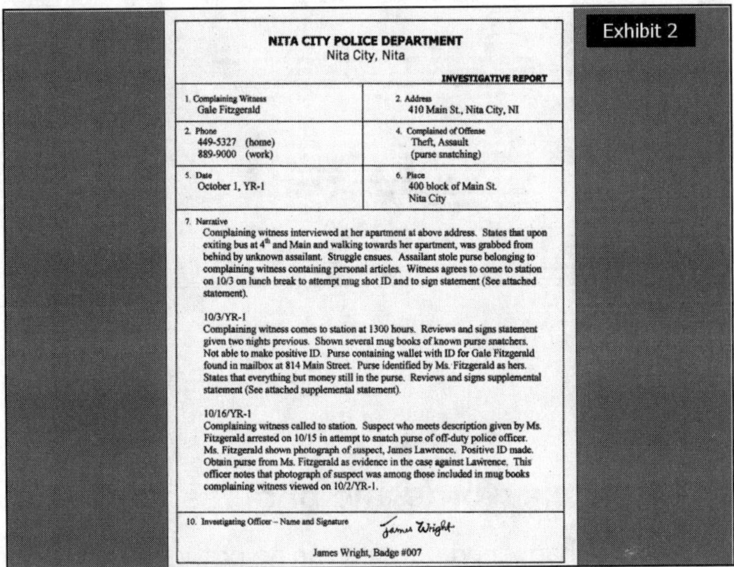

Exhibit 2

NITA CITY POLICE DEPARTMENT
Nita City, Nita

INVESTIGATIVE REPORT

1. Complaining Witness Gale Fitzgerald	2. Address 410 Main St., Nita City, NI
2. Phone 449-5327 (home) 889-9000 (work)	4. Complained of Offense Theft, Assault (purse snatching)
5. Date October 1, YR-1	6. Place 400 block of Main St. Nita City

7. Narrative

Complaining witness interviewed at her apartment at above address. States that upon exiting bus at 4th and Main and walking towards her apartment, was grabbed from behind by unknown assailant. Struggle ensues. Assailant stole purse belonging to complaining witness containing personal articles. Witness agrees to come to station on 10/3 on lunch break to attempt mug shot ID and to sign statement (See attached statement).

10/3/YR-1
Complaining witness comes to station at 1300 hours. Reviews and signs statement given two nights previous. Shown several mug books of known purse snatchers. Not able to make positive ID. Purse containing wallet with ID for Gale Fitzgerald found in mailbox at 814 Main Street. Purse identified by Ms. Fitzgerald as hers. States that everything but money still in the purse. Reviews and signs supplemental statement (See attached supplemental statement).

10/16/YR-1
Complaining witness called to station. Suspect who meets description given by Ms. Fitzgerald arrested on 10/15 in attempt to snatch purse of off-duty police officer. Ms. Fitzgerald shown photograph of suspect, James Lawrence. Positive ID made. Obtain purse from Ms. Fitzgerald as evidence in the case against Lawrence. This officer notes that photograph of suspect was among those included in mug books complaining witness viewed on 10/2/YR-1.

10. Investigating Officer – Name and Signature   James Wright

James Wright, Badge #007

Then put a rectangle on the date of the report. Try to shape your rectangle so that it fits directly over and highlights the whole of the box on the report. Use a 3-point line size to set the box off from the rest of the document.

The slide looks like this:

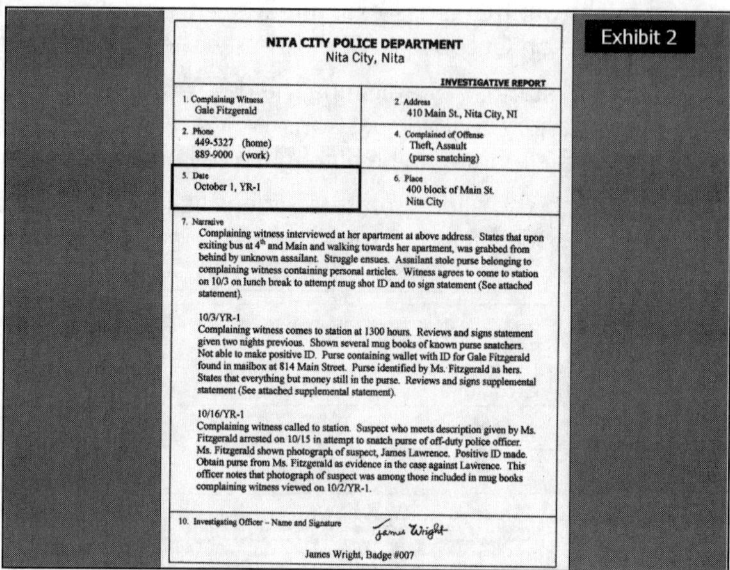

NITA CITY POLICE DEPARTMENT
Nita City, Nita

INVESTIGATIVE REPORT

1. Complaining Witness Gale Fitzgerald	2. Address 410 Main St., Nita City, NI
2. Phone 449-5327 (home) 889-9000 (work)	4. Complained of Offense Theft, Assault (purse snatching)
5. Date October 1, YR-1	6. Place 400 block of Main St. Nita City

7. Narrative

Complaining witness interviewed at her apartment at above address. States that upon exiting bus at 4th and Main and walking towards her apartment, was grabbed from behind by unknown assailant. Struggle ensues. Assailant stole purse belonging to complaining witness containing personal articles. Witness agrees to come to station on 10/3 on lunch break to attempt mug shot ID and to sign statement (See attached statement).

10/3/YR-1
Complaining witness comes to station at 1300 hours. Reviews and signs statement given two nights previous. Shown several mug books of known purse snatchers. Not able to make positive ID. Purse containing wallet with ID for Gale Fitzgerald found in mailbox at 814 Main Street. Purse identified by Ms. Fitzgerald as hers. States that everything but money still in the purse. Reviews and signs supplemental statement (See attached supplemental statement).

10/16/YR-1
Complaining witness called to station. Suspect who meets description given by Ms. Fitzgerald arrested on 10/15 in attempt to snatch purse of off-duty police officer. Ms. Fitzgerald shown photograph of suspect, James Lawrence. Positive ID made. Obtain purse from Ms. Fitzgerald as evidence in the case against Lawrence. This officer notes that photograph of suspect was among those included in mug books complaining witness viewed on 10/2/YR-1.

10. Investigating Officer – Name and Signature

James Wright

James Wright, Badge #007

Exercise 7.2: Circle words and phrases for emphasis

One of the things that happened on the evening of the mugging, about which defense counsel will want to question Ms. Fitzgerald, is her opportunity to get a clear view of the purse snatcher. She reported a struggle. It would be useful to emphasize her fright at that time in order to argue later that she had a diminished capacity to observe.

Circle the word "struggle" on the police report. This helps emphasize that the "less than 30 seconds" Ms. Fitzgerald spent with the purse snatcher involved fighting for control of the purse and not looking carefully at his face.

Your slide will look like this:

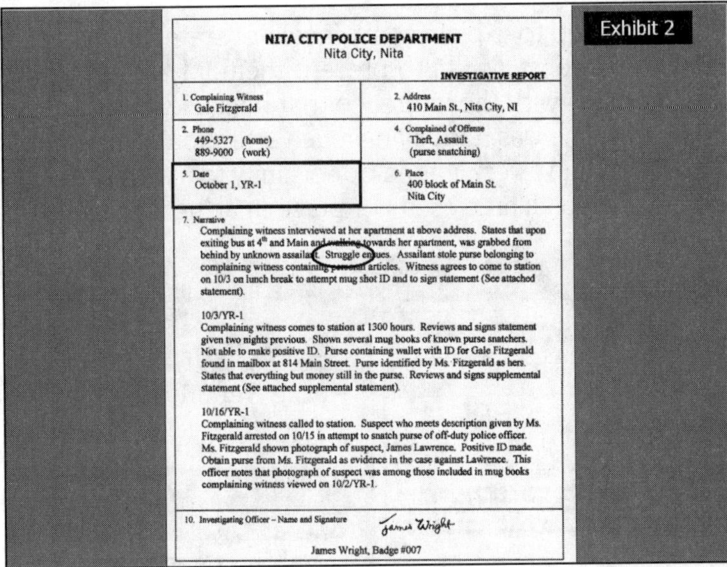

Exhibit 2

NITA CITY POLICE DEPARTMENT
Nita City, Nita

INVESTIGATIVE REPORT

1. Complaining Witness Gale Fitzgerald	2. Address 410 Main St., Nita City, NI
2. Phone 449-5327 (home) 889-9000 (work)	4. Complained of Offense Theft, Assault (purse snatching)
5. Date October 1, YR-1	6. Place 400 block of Main St. Nita City

7. Narrative

Complaining witness interviewed at her apartment at above address. States that upon exiting bus at 4th and Main and walking towards her apartment, was grabbed from behind by unknown assailant. Struggle ensues. Assailant stole purse belonging to complaining witness containing personal articles. Witness agrees to come to station on 10/3 on lunch break to attempt mug shot ID and to sign statement (See attached statement).

10/3/YR-1
Complaining witness comes to station at 1300 hours. Reviews and signs statement given two nights previous. Shown several mug books of known purse snatchers. Not able to make positive ID. Purse containing wallet with ID for Gale Fitzgerald found in mailbox at 814 Main Street. Purse identified by Ms. Fitzgerald as hers. States that everything but money still in the purse. Reviews and signs supplemental statement (See attached supplemental statement).

10/16/YR-1
Complaining witness called to station. Suspect who meets description given by Ms. Fitzgerald arrested on 10/15 in attempt to snatch purse of off-duty police officer. Ms. Fitzgerald shown photograph of suspect, James Lawrence. Positive ID made. Obtain purse from Ms. Fitzgerald as evidence in the case against Lawrence. This officer notes that photograph of suspect was among those included in mug books complaining witness viewed on 10/2/YR-1.

10. Investigating Officer – Name and Signature James Wright

James Wright, Badge #007

The size of the line in the circle should be the same as the size of the line in the box.

Exercise 7.3: Link key terms with a line

Now you can link the date on which the mugging occurred, which was when Ms. Fitzgerald saw the mugger for "less than 30 seconds" while she was struggling to retain possession of her purse.

Your slide will look like this:

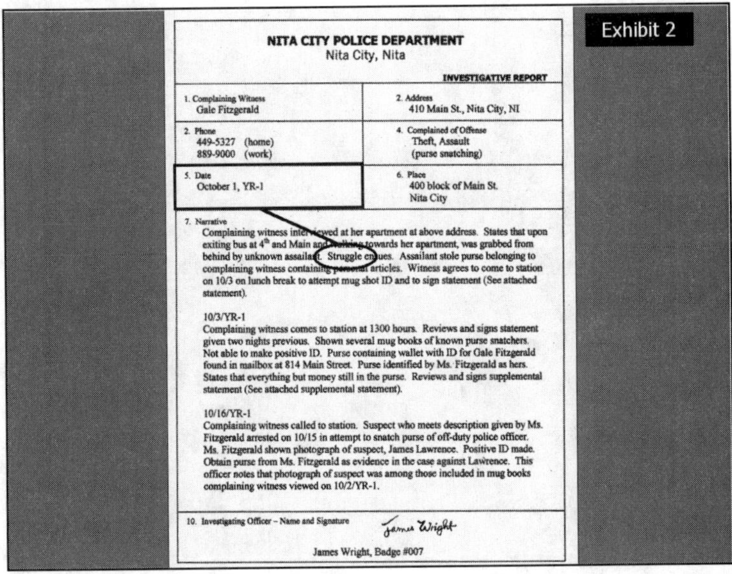

Exhibit 2

NITA CITY POLICE DEPARTMENT
Nita City, Nita

INVESTIGATIVE REPORT

1. Complaining Witness Gale Fitzgerald	2. Address 410 Main St., Nita City, NI
2. Phone 449-5327 (home) 889-9000 (work)	4. Complained of Offense Theft, Assault (purse snatching)
5. Date October 1, YR-1	6. Place 400 block of Main St. Nita City

7. Narrative

Complaining witness interviewed at her apartment at above address. States that upon exiting bus at 4th and Main and walking towards her apartment, was grabbed from behind by unknown assailant. Struggle ensues. Assailant stole purse belonging to complaining witness containing personal articles. Witness agrees to come to station on 10/3 on lunch break to attempt mug shot ID and to sign statement (See attached statement).

10/3/YR-1
Complaining witness comes to station at 1300 hours. Reviews and signs statement given two nights previous. Shown several mug books of known purse snatchers. Not able to make positive ID. Purse containing wallet with ID for Gale Fitzgerald found in mailbox at 814 Main Street. Purse identified by Ms. Fitzgerald as hers. States that everything but money still in the purse. Reviews and signs supplemental statement (See attached supplemental statement).

10/16/YR-1
Complaining witness called to station. Suspect who meets description given by Ms. Fitzgerald arrested on 10/15 in attempt to snatch purse of off-duty police officer. Ms. Fitzgerald shown photograph of suspect, James Lawrence. Positive ID made. Obtain purse from Ms. Fitzgerald as evidence in the case against Lawrence. This officer notes that photograph of suspect was among those included in mug books complaining witness viewed on 10/2/YR-1.

10. Investigating Officer – Name and Signature James Wright

James Wright, Badge #007

Exercise 7.4: Explain with a split screen and bullets

Bullet points can be used to explain some facts not stated in the police report in the precise way the defense wants to present them. Ms. Fitzgerald was walking near her home (perhaps with the inference that because it was late and she was in a very familiar area, she was not paying much attention); she was grabbed from behind (and therefore had a very limited opportunity to see her attacker); and that she had important personal articles in her purse (making it worth fighting over).

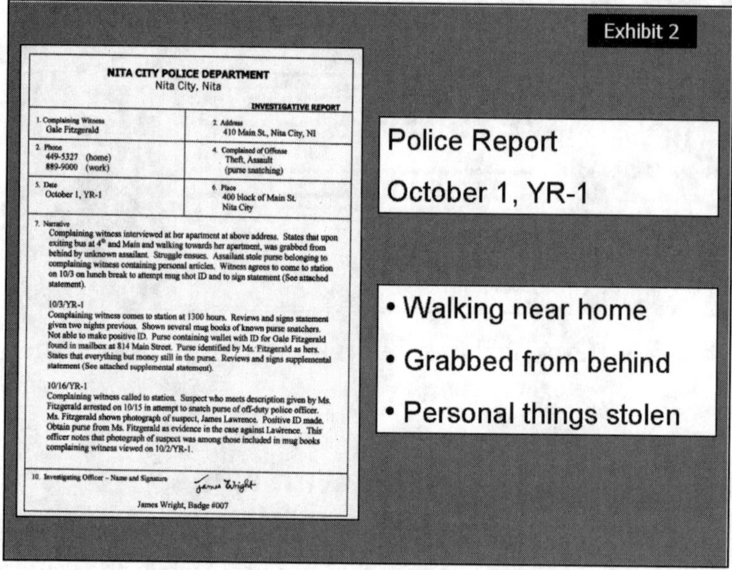

When using a slide for cross-examination, be careful about "color" words. If you stick with the words in the document or a sensible summary, the witness does not have an opportunity to quibble with your choice of words.

Exercise 7.5: Construct re-keyed callouts

Defense counsel might decide to use the initial statement that Fitzgerald gave to the police officer on October 1, the date of the mugging. There are two very useful statements that Fitzgerald made in this statement from the defense viewpoint.

The first is "less than 30 seconds" which describes the amount of time she had in which to look at her attacker face first.

The second is "very upset by this" which describes her emotional state at the time of the purse snatching and possible limitation on a capacity to make a good identification.

When you use callouts, you need to point to the exact place in the document from which the callout was taken, therefore be sure that your lines go to the right place. The typeface and size that you use in the callout can be different from the original.

When you are finished, your screen will look like this:

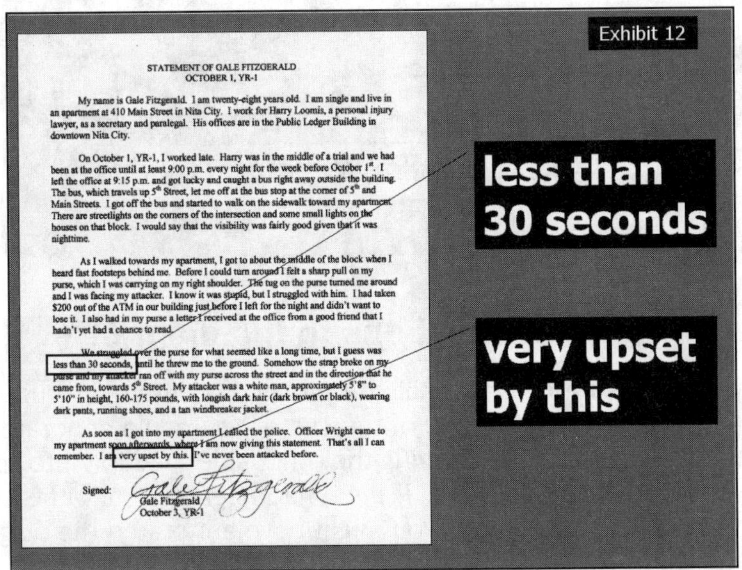

STATEMENT OF GALE FITZGERALD
OCTOBER 1, YR-1

My name is Gale Fitzgerald. I am twenty-eight years old. I am single and live in an apartment at 410 Main Street in Nita City. I work for Harry Loomis, a personal injury lawyer, as a secretary and paralegal. His offices are in the Public Ledger Building in downtown Nita City.

On October 1, YR-1, I worked late. Harry was in the middle of a trial and we had been at the office until at least 9:00 p.m. every night for the week before October 1st. I left the office at 9:15 p.m. and got lucky and caught a bus right away outside the building. The bus, which travels up 5th Street, let me off at the bus stop at the corner of 5th and Main Streets. I got off the bus and started to walk on the sidewalk toward my apartment. There are streetlights on the corners of the intersection and some small lights on the houses on that block. I would say that the visibility was fairly good given that it was nighttime.

As I walked towards my apartment, I got to about the middle of the block when I heard fast footsteps behind me. Before I could turn around I felt a sharp pull on my purse, which I was carrying on my right shoulder. The tug on the purse turned me around and I was facing my attacker. I know it was stupid, but I struggled with him. I had taken $200 out of the ATM in our building just before I left for the night and didn't want to lose it. I also had in my purse a letter I received at the office from a good friend that I hadn't yet had a chance to read.

We struggled over the purse for what seemed like a long time, but I guess was less than 30 seconds, until he threw me to the ground. Somehow the strap broke on my purse and my attacker ran off with my purse across the street and in the direction that he came from, towards 5th Street. My attacker was a white man, approximately 5'8" to 5'10" in height, 160-175 pounds, with longish dark hair (dark brown or black), wearing dark pants, running shoes, and a tan windbreaker jacket.

As soon as I got into my apartment I called the police. Officer Wright came to my apartment soon afterwards, where I am now giving this statement. That's all I can remember. I am very upset by this. I've never been attacked before.

Signed: Gale Fitzgerald
Gale Fitzgerald
October 3, YR-1

Exercise 7.6: Extract direct callouts

Pull the key phrases out of the text of the document using direct callouts.

In this case, the typeface will be the same as the original. To make your callout easy to read, you will need to enlarge the size quite a bit. This limits your choices as to where you will place the callouts. In this case you will need to shrink the document a bit to make room.

Your slide will look like this:

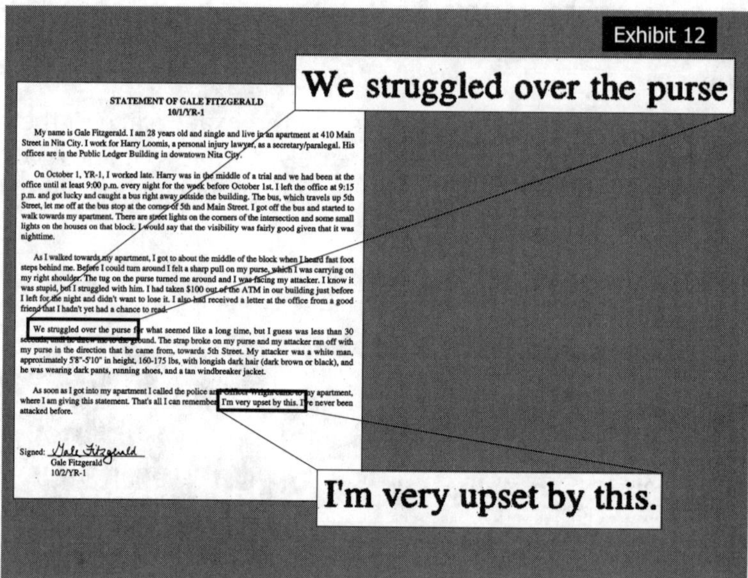

Exercise 8.1: Add annotations to the diagram

In this case, you have a diagram that the prosecutor intends to use with the police witness to identify the scene of the crime. You could annotate this diagram to help make your points. Turning the other side's exhibit into something useful for your case is a good move. If there had been several witnesses to the mugging in this case, for example, you might have annotated the diagram with locations and labels for each of them.

Your superimposed Label #1 on the diagram would be the spot that Ms. Fitzgerald got off the bus.

Assume that defense counsel contests the prosecutor's "X" marking the spot where the mugging occurred and contends that it was actually a little farther down the street and not between 402 and 404 as marked. Your superimposed Label #2 can show that.

Add a title to identify the diagram and make it appear different from the one the prosecutor will use.

Your slide would look like this:

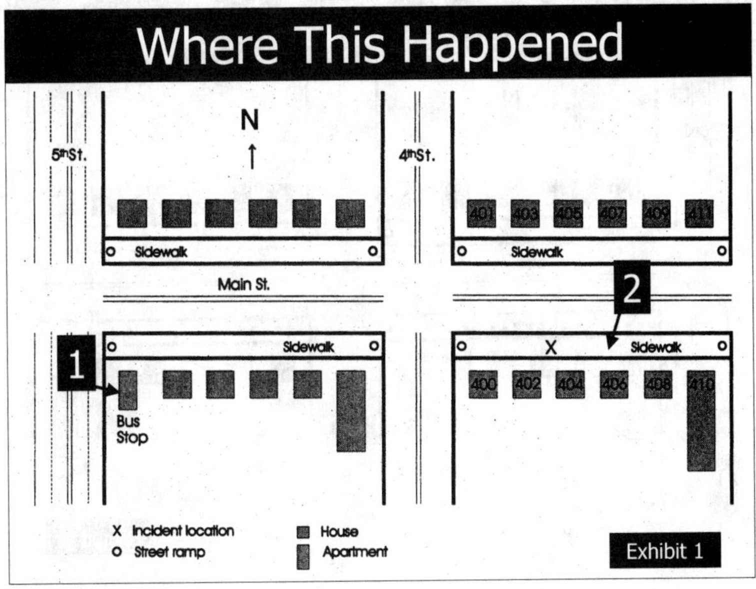

Exercise 8.2: Use dotted lines to show action

Dotted lines added to the diagram can show the route the witness took and the route that the mugger took to amplify the defense's points that Ms. Fitzgerald had a very limited opportunity to observe.

Line #1 (Ms. Fitzgerald) goes from the corner of 5th Street and Main Street along the sidewalk to the point of the mugging.

Line #2 (the mugger) comes up behind Ms. Fitzgerald. This line starts where it is assumed the mugger came from.

Line #3 (the mugger running off after the attack) goes from the point of the mugging across Main Street to the sidewalk on the other side, where Ms. Fitzgerald lost sight of him.

Your slide will look like this:

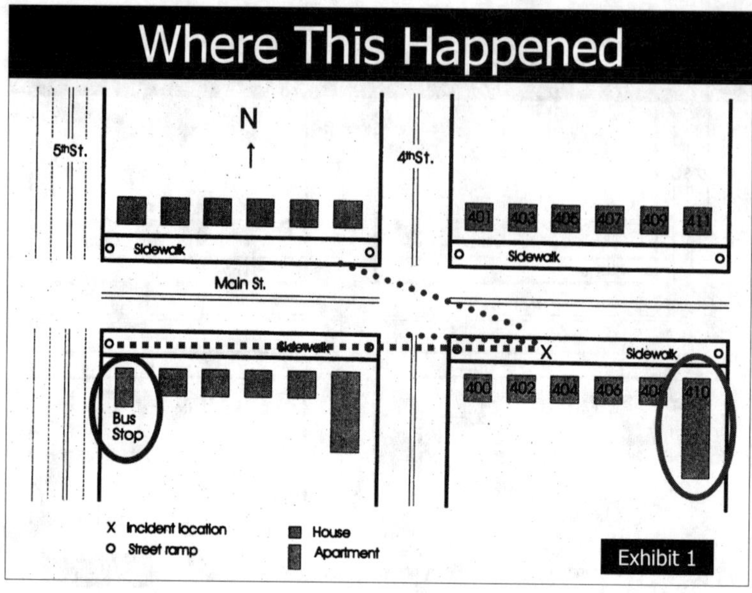

Go to the CD to see the color version of this slide with the lines in motion.

Exercise 8.3: Layered annotations

Annotations can sometimes be made more expressive by putting one layer over another.

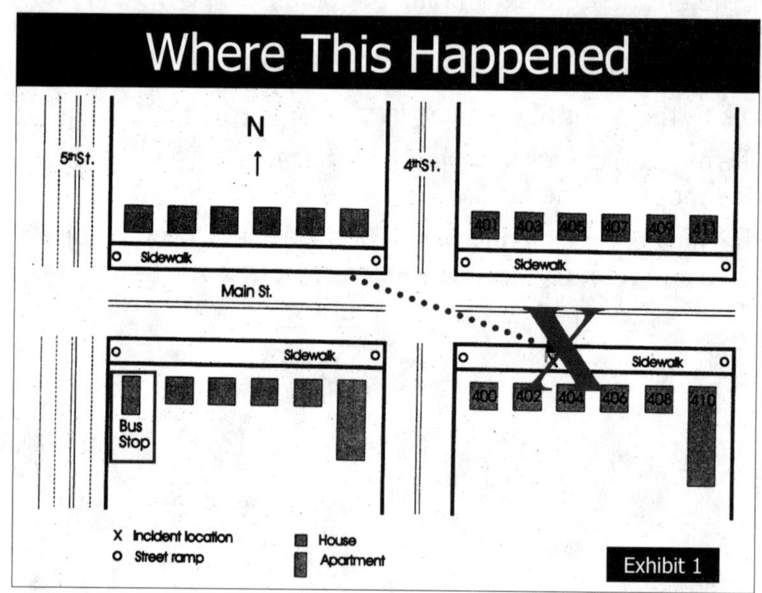

Exercises 9.1-9.8: Motion and special effects

Many of the slides for this case file have been animated as described Chapter 9 and are included in animated form on the CD that comes with this book. This slide show can also be downloaded from NITA's web site, *www.nitastudent.org*. To learn how these animations were done, deconstruct the slides as described in Chapter 12.13.

Exercises 10.1-10.5: Running your slide show

The slide show for this case on the CD includes the slides with transitions. They can be viewed in slide sorter mode to see what transitions were added and in slide show mode to see the transition in action.

Appendix C

Personal Injury Case

Brown v. Byrd

Kenneth Brown brought suit against Robert Byrd for damages arising out of a collision between their cars on April 20, YR-1[1] near the intersection of 12th Avenue and East Main Street in Nita City. Brown alleges that Byrd was following him too closely and failed to keep a proper lookout. Brown is seeking to recover damages in excess of $50,000 for his neck and back injury, which he claims were caused by Byrd's negligence. Byrd denies liability and asserts that the impact, even if it was his fault, was not sufficient to cause and did not cause any physical injury to Brown.

The accident was investigated at the scene by Officer David Pierce of the Nita City Police Department. He filed a report on the accident, which is part of this file. In a brief deposition, Officer Pierce testified that he was called to the scene of this accident by radio dispatch at 3:40 p.m. and that he conducted the investigation as reflected in his report. He obtained the information contained in the report by interviewing the two drivers involved in the accident. The accident was, in his opinion, unavoidable. That, coupled with the fact that there were no injuries either visible or complained of by either party, caused him to issue no citations for this accident.

Brown alleged that as a result of being rear-ended by Byrd's car he suffered a permanent back injury. He further claims that the injury precludes him from engaging in any strenuous exercise or activity, and that the muscle relaxant prescription drugs he is required to take prevent him from drinking any alcoholic beverages, even beer. Brown asserts that his permanent back injury, the pain and suffering, and the deprivation of his activities warrant substantial compensation.

Byrd's insurance carrier asked one of its investigators, David Randolf, to review and verify Brown's alleged injuries. After an investigation, Randolf filed a report with the insurance carrier disputing the extent of the injuries claimed by Brown. Randolf began his investigation by identifying Brown using a picture provided by the insurance company and by setting up a surveillance of Brown's home on June 24, YR-1. He noted no unusual activity on the first day of

1. NITA uses a convention for dates as follows: YR-0 (this year), YR-1 (last year), YR-2 (two years ago), and so on.

the surveillance. On June 25th, Randolf followed the Brown to the Nita Country Club. This was just over two months after the Brown's alleged injury. At that time, Randolf observed Brown play two sets of tennis and then consume four or five beers, both at the tennis court and at the nearby outdoor patio bar. Randolf took several photographs of Brown playing tennis and drinking afterwards.

Both sides have seventeen exhibits in the file, and both sides have a copy of the CD containing the digital files of these exhibits. The exhibits in this Appendix would be used by both sides to create illustrative aids for trial. Printed copies of each of these exhibits except the video deposition are in the Appendix.

(1) Police report of Officer Pierce (Police Report)

(2) Plaintiff's Complaint (Complaint, p. 3)

(3) Photo of Brown playing tennis (Photo-1)

(4) Photo of Brown playing tennis (Photo-2)

(5) Photo of Brown playing tennis (Photo-3)

(6) Photo of Brown playing tennis (Photo-4)

(7) Photo of Brown drinking beer (Photo-5)

(8) Photo of Brown drinking beer (Photo-6)

(9) Photo of Brown drinking beer (Photo-7)

(10) Photo of surveillance location of Randolf (Photo-8)

(11) Diagram of intersection (Diagram of Intersection)

(12) Brown depo transcript p. 23 (Brown depo-23)

(13) Brown depo transcript p. 29 (Brown depo-29)

(14) Brown depo transcript p. 37 (Brown depo-37)

(15) Video clip, Brown depo (Brown depo-23)

(16) Video clip, Brown depo (Brown depo-29)

(17) Video clip, Brown depo (Brown depo-37)

The CD also contains a PowerPoint slide show for this case containing the slides shown in this appendix so that you can see them in full color and with full motion.

The digital files on the CD-ROM can also be downloaded from the NITA web site, *www.nitastudent.org*. When you use exhibits from your file to create PowerPoint slides, you will take them from this CD or from the files you downloaded. When you open the CD, the Personal Injury Case folder looks like this:

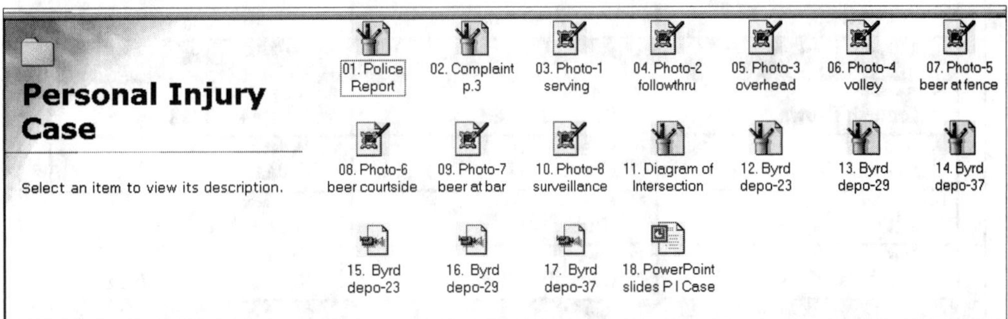

The illustrative aids used as examples in this Appendix assume you represent Robert Byrd, the defendant. Assume further that your approach to the case is that Brown stopped so suddenly that the accident was unavoidable. No personal injury was caused by the collision and Brown's injuries are faked. Brown told Byrd about no injuries when they talked right after the accident, and he reported no injuries to the police officer who investigated the accident. Surveillance photos of Brown playing tennis suggest that he did not suffer a permanent back injury, as claimed. Photos of Brown drinking beer suggest that he is not taking muscle relaxant prescription drugs that would require that he abstain from all alcoholic beverages.

NITA CITY POLICE DEPARTMENT
Accident Report

1. Investigating Officer: D. Pierce		2. Badge No: 2157
3. Date: April 20, YR-1	4. Time: 3:40 p.m.	5. Place: Nita City
VEHICLE # 1		
6. Operator: Kenneth Brown	7. Address: 5 Scott Pl. N. C.	8. Vehicle Title #: G18M4443798
9. Year: YR-3	10. Make: Honda	11. Model: Sedan
12. Lic. Plate: ALD-144	13. State: Nita	14. Insurance: State Farm
15. Pol. #: 00528-24-2234	16. Towed: Driveable	17. Damage: Rear bumper and trunk
VEHICLE # 2		
6. Operator: Robert Byrd	7. Address: 104 E. Main, N. C.	8. Vehicle Title #: IP644W5772
9. Year: YR-1	10. Make: Volvo	11. Model: Sedan
12. Lic. Plate: BYRD-10	13. State: Nita	14. Insurance: USAA
15. Pol. #: 3001-17750-1440	16. Towed: Driveable	17. Damage: Front fender
18. Principal Road: 12th Avenue	19. Speed Limit: 25	20. Intersecting Road: E. Main
21. Injuries: None - minor accident		
22. Narrative: Interviewed both drivers. Vehicle #1 was traveling south on 12th Avenue. When he neared intersection of E. Main light was green. Light changed to yellow and #1 stopped short and was rear-ended by Vehicle #2. #2 appeared to be traveling within posted speed limit of 25 mph and to have his vehicle under control. #2 may have been following too close, but accident was made unavoidable by the sudden and unnecessary stop by #1. Note also that timing of light was different than observed in the past in that yellow light was shorter than it had previously been. In light of all of above—No Citations—Both vehicles driveable—No injuries.		
23. Investigating Officer Signature: David Pierce		Date: 4/21/YR-1

9. As a direct and proximate result of the negligence of Defendant, Plaintiff has suffered severe and permanent injury, for which he must take pain medication, and pain and suffering, Plaintiff has become unable to engage in strenuous work or exercise, Plaintiff has incurred past and future medical and rehabilitative expenses, all in an amount which exceeds the tort threshold set forth in Chapter 431 of the Nita Revised Statutes, and Plaintiff has suffered mental and emotional distress, and has lost income and earning capacity.

WHEREFORE, Plaintiff prays that:

1. He be given judgment against Defendant for special and general damages that may be proven time of trial;

2. He be awarded his costs and such other relief as this Court deems just and proper.

DATED: Nita City, Nita, July 15, YR-1.

DARROW O. CLARENCE
Attorney for Plaintiff

- 3 -

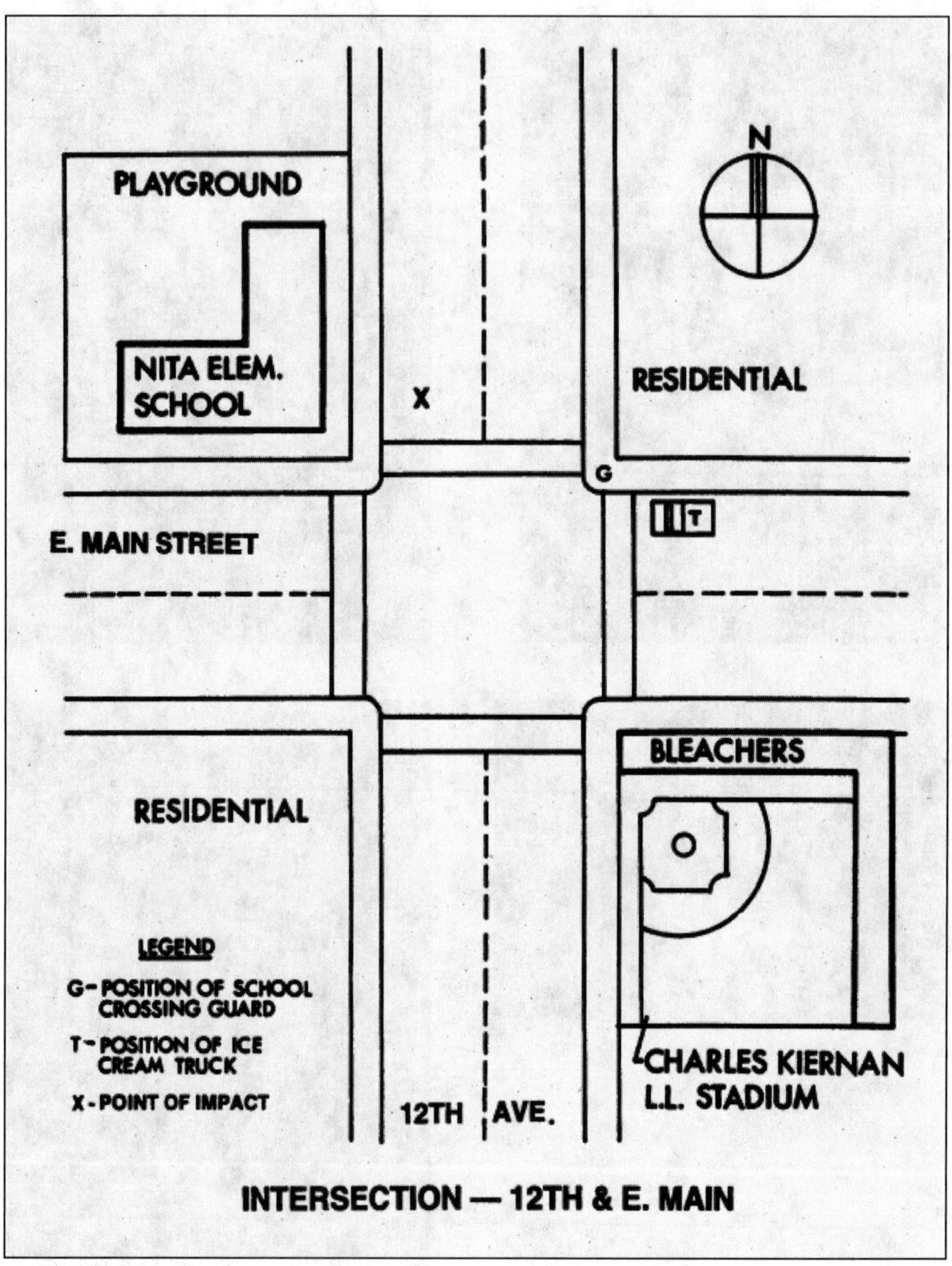

INTERSECTION — 12TH & E. MAIN

DEPOSITION OF ROBERT BYRD [10/10/YR-2]

Q: Where were you going at the time of the accident?
A: I had an appointment at Ferguson Auto Body.
Q: Where is that located?
A: In South Nita City.
Q: What time was the appointment?
A: At four.
Q: Why were you going there?
A: They are a client of mine.
Q: You sell them auto parts?
A: Yes.
Q: You had a ways to go, didn't you?
A: I know I was cutting it close, but if I wouldn't have been in this accident, I would have been able to just make it in time.

DEPOSITION OF ROBERT BYRD [10/10/YR-2]

Q: What time did the accident happen?
A: Just after 3:30.
Q: How do you know the time?
A: Given that I had an appointment at four, I was checking my watch, and besides you could tell that school had just gotten out, and that's at 3:30.
Q: How could you tell school had just let out?
A: There were lots of kids coming out from the school yard onto the sidewalk and the crossing guard was stationed right on the north corner across from the school.
Q: What was the guard doing?
A: Talking to little boy.
Q: Was the guard a man or a woman?
A: A woman.
Q: Did you see kids anywhere else?
A: Yes, there were a bunch crowded around an ice cream truck.
Q: Where was the truck parked?
A: On Main, just east of the intersection.
Q: Facing which way?
A: West, towards the school.
Q: You seemed to have seen a lot going on in and around that intersection?
A: Well, yes, I was being especially careful watching all the school kids wherever they were, that's what safe drivers are supposed to do, right?

DEPOSITION OF ROBERT BYRD [10/10/YR-2]

Q: Tell me how the accident happened?
A: I was driving behind Mr. Brown's car, about ten feet behind, going no more than twenty. When I got about twenty feet from the crosswalk on 12th the light turned yellow. I assumed Mr. Brown would continue through the intersection.
Q: Where was Mr. Brown's car at the time the light turned yellow?
A: At the crosswalk.
Q: Not into the intersection?
A: Well that's where he was headed.
Q: But not there yet?
A: Not yet, but I assumed he would continue through.
Q: Why did you make that assumption?
A: It was the only intelligent thing to do.
Q: Why's that?
A: Well, otherwise he would have had to jam on his brakes and stop suddenly.
Q: What's wrong with that?
A: Obviously, it can cause someone following behind to run into you.
Q: Which is what you did?
A: My point exactly.
Q: Had Mr. Brown continued as you assumed, what were you going to do?
A: I planned to follow him right through the intersection.
Q: On a red light?
A: I was hoping it would stay yellow until I got through.

Exercise 2.1: Construct a basic bullet point list

Although Byrd's counsel needs to address liability, the principal task is to ensure that no damages are assessed. For that reason, the construction of bullet point slides probably would start with that point. A key bullet point chart will draw together the reasons why Brown was not injured.

A first draft might look like this:

Why Brown Wasn't Injured

- Both cars drivable
- Minor damage
- Brown says nothing to officer of injury
- Two months later Brown plays tennis
- Shows no signs of injury playing tennis
- Drinks beer after tennis

Exercise 2.2: Edit the text

In editing the title for the first draft, take account of the possibility that (at least for opening statement) the title is argumentative and therefore objectionable. A key issue is "the injury" and the title can reflect that without being argumentative.

The first two points are short and readily understood. The third point, however, might be subject to the rebuttal that Brown simply said nothing although he really was injured. A better way to put the same fact is to focus on the conclusion that the officer drew from his own observations and investigation on the scene.

The plural "signs" in the fifth bullet point can be reduced to "sign" which is stronger.

The sixth bullet point can be deleted altogether. The point about drinking beer (and its relationship to the medication supposedly being taken) is ancillary to and not as important as the other points on the list.

Now the slide looks like this:

The Injury

- Both cars drivable
- Minor damage
- Officer concludes: "No injuries"
- Two months later Brown plays tennis
- No sign of injury playing tennis

The first two points might be consolidated in order to reduce the number of bullet points and to balance their importance.

The revised slide looks like this:

The Injury

- Both cars drivable, damage minor
- Officer concludes: "No injuries"
- Two months later Brown plays tennis
- No sign of injury playing tennis

Exercise 3.1: Set the typeface, size, and alignment

Change the typeface to Tahoma.

Change they type size for the title to 48-point.

Put the title in bold face.

Add shadowing to the title.

Change the type size for the text to 36-point.

Now your slide looks like this:

The Injury

- Both cars driveable, damage minor
- Officer concludes: "No injuries"
- 2 months later Brown plays tennis
- No sign of injury playing tennis

When the typeface is enlarged, the third bullet point becomes too long to fit on one line. One way to deal with this is to change "two" to "2."

Exercise 3.2: Put boxes around the title and text

The boxes around the title and text of this kind of slide will give it a more polished look. This example uses a 3/4-point line for each box. The slide that you have been working on will look like this:

The Injury

- Both cars drivable, damage minor
- Officer concludes: "No injuries"
- 2 months later Brown plays tennis
- No sign of injury playing tennis

If you try out a shadow around the title box, it should look like this:

The Injury

- Both cars driveable, damage minor
- Officer concludes: "No injuries"
- 2 months later Brown plays tennis
- No sign of injury playing tennis

Exercise 3.3: Add color to the components of the slide

When you add color to the background of the slide, it will look something like this:

The Injury

- Both cars driveable, damage minor
- Officer concludes: "No injuries"
- 2 months later Brown plays tennis
- No sign of injury playing tennis

When you add color to the title box, the slide looks like this:

The Injury

- Both cars drivable, damage minor
- Officer concludes: "No injuries"
- 2 months later Brown plays tennis
- No sign of injury playing tennis

You can also add colors for the fonts for the title and text; the border around title box; the border around text box; and the bullets. The PowerPoint slide show on your CD contains several examples of how this slide might be colored, styled, and animated.

Exercise 3.4: Change bullet shape, size, and spacing

In this slide, the bullets have been changed from the standard round shape to a check mark. The check mark is on the Bullets & Numbers screen in PowerPoint 2000 and is in the Monotype Sorts collection in PowerPoint 97.

Using check marks requires more space between the bullet point and the text. In this slide, an additional space has been added for each line.

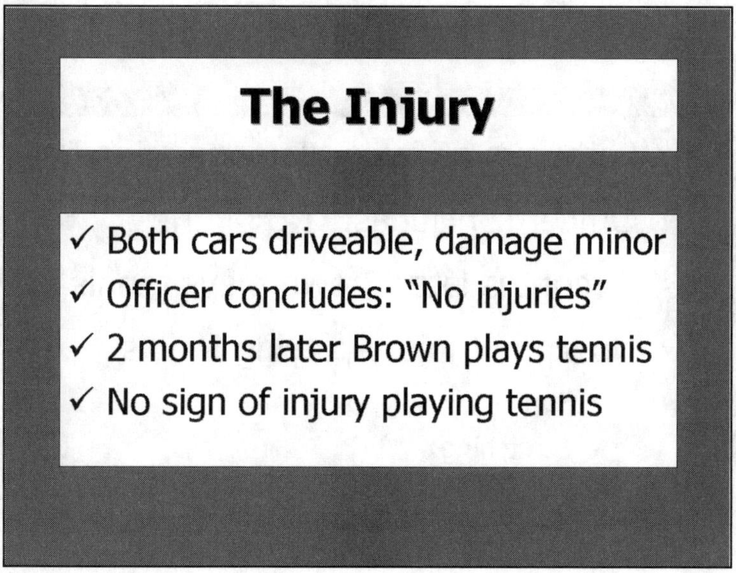

The CD shows slides with different bullet sizes and spacing.

Exercise 3.5: Create subordinate points

Another way to give emphasis to the point that Brown can exert himself playing tennis with no sign of injury would be to subordinate three bullet points about the kind of vigorous motion shown by the photos.

The slide now looks like this:

The Injury

- ✓ Both cars drivable, damage minor
- ✓ Officer concludes: "No injuries"
- ✓ 2 months later Brown plays tennis
- ✓ No sign of injury playing tennis
    - ✓ Running
    - ✓ Stretching
    - ✓ Bending

If you have changed the bullet shape on the main points, you may want to stick with the standard round shape for the subsidiary points to avoid having your slide look too cluttered.

Exercise 4.1: Make a companion slide

After dealing with the injury, which is the defense's primary target in this case, counsel might want to move to liability as the second principal issue. This slide might include the principal fact supporting a conclusion of no liability, including:

- the place where the accident occurred
- the low speed at which the cars were traveling
- the fact that Brown did not need to stop
- the unexpected nature of his stop such that Byrd could not anticipate it

Copy the initial slide to get all of the settings for typeface, type size, alignment, borders, and background. Put in the new material.

The companion slide looks like this:

The Accident

✓ 12th Avenue before Main Street
✓ Following Brown at 20 mph
✓ Car at crosswalk, light turns yellow
✓ Brown jams brakes, in intersection

Exercise 4.2: Construct a no-title slide

The police officer has contributed a theme on liability in his report – the conclusion that Brown's stop was sudden and unnecessary, thus something that Byrd would not expect under ordinary circumstances even if he was keeping a good lookout as required of all drivers.

This theme might be displayed as a no-title slide that could be used on several occasions as the testimony proceeded.

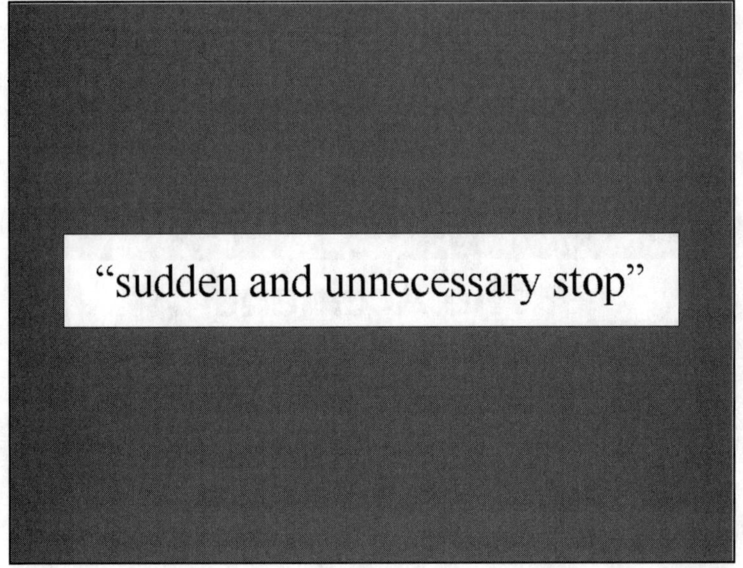

Exercise 5.1, 5.2, 5.3, and 5.4: Create a labeled photo

One of the points you want to make in your opening is that Brown is really not as injured as he claims. The best proof of this is the photographs taken by the insurance investigator of Brown playing tennis at the Nita Country Club.

Care must be taken with the titles for the photos so they are factual and not argumentative at this stage in the case. Thus, titles like "The Bogus Injury," or "Injury, What Injury?" should not be used. One option might be to time the showing of these photographs right after your discussion of the accident where no injuries were noted by the police officer, and your recap of plaintiff's alleged injuries, with the segue being "Let's look at how Mr. Brown was doing about two months later." Then bring up the photo with the title "Two Months Later." Another option would be to title the slide "Ken Brown, May 24, YR-1."

One such slide would look like this:

Exercise 6.1: Zap-Zap-I-Win relationship chart

In this case, the defense might want to highlight as part of closing argument three facts that suggest that Brown is not as injured as he claims. These facts might be that:

- Officer Pierce found no injuries and had none reported to him;
- Brown is healthy enough to play two vigorous sets of tennis without any obvious pain; and
- Brown can and does drink beer irrespective of what he claims his doctor has ordered him to do.

A relationship chart can highlight these facts and point to the conclusion that Brown simply was not injured as a result of this accident.

The chart would look like this:

The animation for this relationship chart is shown on the CD.

Exercise 6.2: All-Roads-Lead-to-Rome relationship chart

This model of relationship chart uses the familiar metaphor to suggest that a group of particular images in this case points to the same central theme that Brown was not really injured in this accident. The image at the center of the slide is taken directly from the police report and is surrounded by a series of linked photos to bolster that image.

The slide looks like this:

The animation for this relationship chart is shown on the CD.

Exercise 6.3: The basic time line

Here is a basic time line designed to suggest plaintiff has filed a bogus lawsuit in that he has not been injured by this accident.

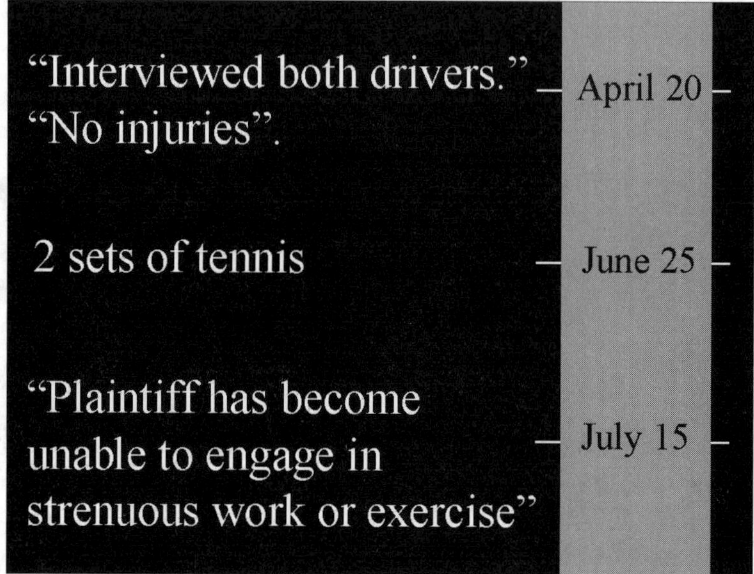

This emphasizes that the complaint was filed three months after the accident and only a few weeks after playing vigorous tennis.

Other versions of this slide showing the use of color are on the CD.

Exercise 7.1: Use a box for focus

In the opening statement for Byrd, it might be important to review the police report prepared by Officer Pierce. For purposes of these exercises, we assume that the comments in the narrative portion of the report are admissible. That would vary by jurisdiction.

You will start by importing, sizing, and centering the document on your screen.

To create a contrast between the document and the rest of the slide, put a border around the document and use a background color for the slide.

The slide looks like this:

NITA CITY POLICE DEPARTMENT
Accident Report

1. Investigating Officer: D. Pierce		2. Badge No: 2157
3. Date: April 20, YR-1	4. Time: 3:40 p.m.	5. Place: Nita City
VEHICLE #1		
6. Operator: Kenneth Brown	7. Address: 5 Scott Pl. N. C.	8. Vehicle Title #: G18M4443798
9. Year: YR-3	10. Make: Honda	11. Model: Sedan
12. Lic. Plate: ALD-144	13. State: Nita	14. Insurance: State Farm
15. Pol. #: 00528-24-2234	16. Towed: Driveable	17. Damage: Rear bumper and trunk
VEHICLE #2		
6. Operator: Robert Byrd	7. Address: 104 E. Main, N. C.	8. Vehicle Title #: IP644W5772
9. Year: YR-1	10. Make: Volvo	11. Model: Sedan
12. Lic. Plate: BYRD-10	13. State: Nita	14. Insurance: USAA
15. Pol. #: 3001-17750-1440	16. Towed: Driveable	17. Damage: Front fender
18. Principal Road: 12th Avenue	19. Speed Limit: 25	20. Intersecting Road: E. Main

21. Injuries:
None - minor accident

22. Narrative:
Interviewed both drivers. Vehicle #1 was traveling south on 12th Avenue. When he neared intersection of E. Main light was green. Light changed to yellow and #1 stopped short and was rear-ended by Vehicle #2. #2 appeared to be traveling within posted speed limit of 25 mph and to have his vehicle under control. #2 may have been following too close, but accident was made unavoidable by the sudden and unnecessary stop by #1. Note also that timing of light was different than observed in the past in that yellow light was shorter than it had previously been. In light of all of above—No Citations—Both vehicles driveable—No injuries.

23. Investigating Officer Signature: David Pierce	Date: 4/21/YR-1

Add a Rectangle to contain the exhibit number in order to identify the document on the slide.

You will want to orient the jury to significant aspects of the document by pointing out the date it was created and who created it. Use the Rectangle button to put boxes around them. Shape the rectangle so that it fits directly over each item but does not crowd the text.

Your slide will look like this:

Exhibit 12

NITA CITY POLICE DEPARTMENT
Accident Report

1. Investigating Officer: D. Pierce		2. Badge No: 2157
3. Date: April 20, YR-1	4. Time: 3:40 p.m.	5. Place: Nita City
VEHICLE #1		
6. Operator: Kenneth Brown	7. Address: 5 Scott Pl. N. C.	8. Vehicle Title #: G18M4443798
9. Year: YR-3	10. Make: Honda	11. Model: Sedan
12. Lic. Plate: ALD-144	13. State: Nita	14. Insurance: State Farm
15. Pol. #: 00528-24-2234	16. Towed: Driveable	17. Damage: Rear bumper and trunk
VEHICLE #2		
6. Operator: Robert Byrd	7. Address: 104 E. Main, N. C.	8. Vehicle Title #: IP644W5772
9. Year: YR-1	10. Make: Volvo	11. Model: Sedan
12. Lic. Plate: BYRD-10	13. State: Nita	14. Insurance: USAA
15. Pol. #: 3001-17750-1440	16. Towed: Driveable	17. Damage: Front fender
18. Principal Road: 12th Avenue	19. Speed Limit: 25	20. Intersecting Road: E. Main

21. Injuries:
None - minor accident

22. Narrative:
Interviewed both drivers. Vehicle #1 was traveling south on 12th Avenue. When he neared intersection of E. Main light was green. Light changed to yellow and #1 stopped short and was rear-ended by Vehicle #2. #2 appeared to be traveling within posted speed limit of 25 mph and to have his vehicle under control. #2 may have been following too close, but accident was made unavoidable by the sudden and unnecessary stop by #1. Note also that timing of light was different than observed in the past in that yellow light was shorter than it had previously been. In light of all of above—No Citations—Both vehicles driveable—No injuries.

23. Investigating Officer Signature: David Pierce	Date: 4/21/YR-1

Exercise 7.2: Circle words and phrases for emphasis

You may want to emphasize the words "No Citations" and "No injuries" at the end of the narrative section of the report.

When you add circles for this purpose, the slide will look like this:

Exhibit 12

NITA CITY POLICE DEPARTMENT
Accident Report

1. Investigating Officer: D. Pierce		2. Badge No: 2157
3. Date: April 20, YR-1	4. Time: 3:40 p.m.	5. Place: Nita City
VEHICLE # 1		
6. Operator: Kenneth Brown	7. Address: 5 Scott Pl. N. C.	8. Vehicle Title #: G18M4443798
9. Year: YR-3	10. Make: Honda	11. Model: Sedan
12. Lic. Plate: ALD-144	13. State: Nita	14. Insurance: State Farm
15. Pol. #: 00528-24-2234	16. Towed: Driveable	17. Damage: Rear bumper and trunk
VEHICLE # 2		
6. Operator: Robert Byrd	7. Address: 104 E. Main, N. C.	8. Vehicle Title #: IP644W5772
9. Year: YR-1	10. Make: Volvo	11. Model: Sedan
12. Lic. Plate: BYRD-10	13. State: Nita	14. Insurance: USAA
15. Pol. #: 3001-17750-1440	16. Towed: Driveable	17. Damage: Front fender
18. Principal Road: 12th Avenue	19. Speed Limit: 25	20. Intersecting Road: E. Main
21. Injuries: None - minor accident		
22. Narrative: Interviewed both drivers. Vehicle #1 was traveling south on 12th Avenue. When he neared intersection of E. Main light was green. Light changed to yellow and #1 stopped short and was rear-ended by Vehicle #2. #2 appeared to be traveling within posted speed limit of 25 mph and to have his vehicle under control. #2 may have been following too close, but accident was made unavoidable by the sudden and unnecessary stop by #1. Note also that timing of light was different than observed in the past in that yellow light was shorter than it had previously been. In light of all of above—No Citations—Both vehicles driveable—No injuries.		
23. Investigating Officer Signature: David Pierce		Date: 4/21/YR-1

Exercise 7.3: Link key terms with a line

Now you can link the date the accident happened and was investigated by Officer Pierce with his findings.

Your slide will look like this:

Exhibit 12

NITA CITY POLICE DEPARTMENT
Accident Report

1. Investigating Officer: D. Pierce		2. Badge No: 2157
3. Date: April 20, YR-1	4. Time: 3:40 p.m.	5. Place: Nita City
VEHICLE # 1		
6. Operator: Kenneth Brown	7. Address: 5 Scott Pl. N. C.	8. Vehicle Title #: G18M4443798
9. Year: YR-3	10. Make: Honda	11. Model: Sedan
12. Lic. Plate: ALD-144	13. State: Nita	14. Insurance: State Farm
15. Pol. #: 00528-24-2234	16. Towed: Driveable	17. Damage: Rear bumper and trunk
VEHICLE # 2		
6. Operator: Robert Byrd	7. Address: 104 E. Main, N. C.	8. Vehicle Title #: IP644W5772
9. Year: YR-1	10. Make: Volvo	11. Model: Sedan
12. Lic. Plate: BYRD-10	13. State: Nita	14. Insurance: USAA
15. Pol. #: 3001-17750-1440	16. Towed: Driveable	17. Damage: Front fender
18. Principal Road: 12th Avenue	19. Speed Limit: 25	20. Intersecting Road: E. Main
21. Injuries: None - minor accident		
22. Narrative: Interviewed both drivers. Vehicle #1 was traveling south on 12th Avenue. When he neared intersection of E. Main light was green. Light changed to yellow and #1 stopped short and was rear-ended by Vehicle #2. #2 appeared to be traveling within posted speed limit of 25 mph and to have his vehicle under control. #2 may have been following too close, but accident was made unavoidable by the sudden and unnecessary stop by #1. Note also that timing of light was different than observed in the past in that yellow light was shorter than it had previously been. In light of all of above—No Citations—Both vehicles driveable—No injuries.		
23. Investigating Officer Signature: David Pierce		Date: 4/21/YR-1

Exercise 7.4: Explain with a split screen and bullets

Another way to orient the jury to this police report and emphasize details found in the report would be to create a split screen with the document on the left and bullet points on the right.

The bullet points extract and summarize the key information from the document.

The slide would look like this:

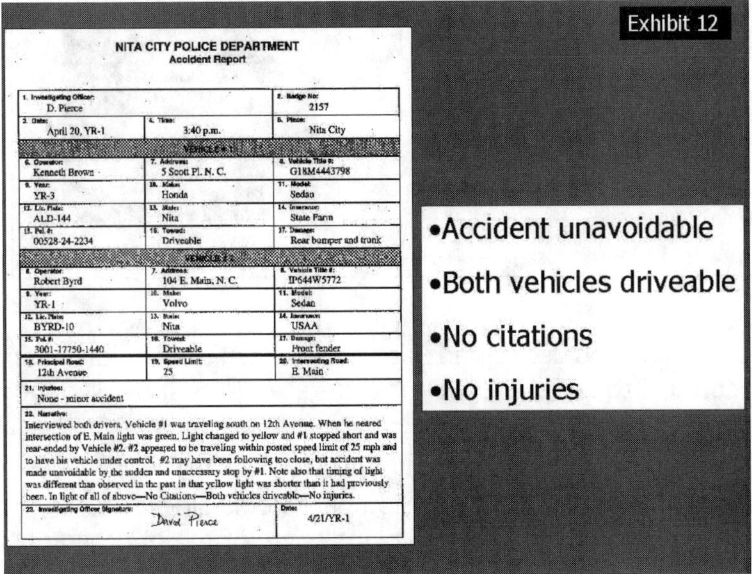

NITA CITY POLICE DEPARTMENT
Accident Report

1. Investigating Officer: D. Pierce		2. Badge No: 2157
3. Date: April 20, YR-1	4. Time: 3:40 p.m.	5. Place: Nita City
VEHICLE # 1		
6. Operator: Kenneth Brown	7. Address: 5 Scott Pl. N. C.	8. Vehicle Title #: G18M4443798
9. Year: YR-3	10. Make: Honda	11. Model: Sedan
12. Lic. Plate: ALD-144	13. State: Nita	14. Insurance: State Farm
15. Pol. #: 00528-24-2234	16. Towed: Driveable	17. Damage: Rear bumper and trunk
VEHICLE # 2		
6. Operator: Robert Byrd	7. Address: 104 E. Main, N. C.	8. Vehicle Title #: IP644W5772
9. Year: YR-1	10. Make: Volvo	11. Model: Sedan
12. Lic. Plate: BYRD-10	13. State: Nita	14. Insurance: USAA
15. Pol. #: 3001-17750-1440	16. Towed: Driveable	17. Damage: Front fender
18. Principal Road: 12th Avenue	19. Speed Limit: 25	20. Intersecting Road: E. Main
21. Injuries: None - minor accident		

22. Narrative:
Interviewed both drivers. Vehicle #1 was traveling south on 12th Avenue. When he neared intersection of E. Main light was green. Light changed to yellow and #1 stopped short and was rear-ended by Vehicle #2. #2 appeared to be traveling within posted speed limit of 25 mph and to have his vehicle under control. #2 may have been following too close, but accident was made unavoidable by the sudden and unnecessary stop by #1. Note also that timing of light was different than observed in the past in that yellow light was shorter than it had previously been. In light of all of above—No Citations—Both vehicles driveable—No injuries.

23. Investigating Officer Signature: David Pierce	Date: 4/21/YR-1

In closing argument, another way to show visually that Brown's claimed injuries are at best exaggerations, and at worst falsehoods, is to compare the complaint with the photos. You can underline the two portions of paragraph 9 of the complaint that state "he must take pain medication" and "unable to engage in strenuous work or exercise" and display the photos that contradict these claims. The photos show Brown drinking beer (which according to his doctor he should not be doing if, in fact, he is taking pain medication) and playing tennis with no obvious discomfort.

A slide in this format might look like this:

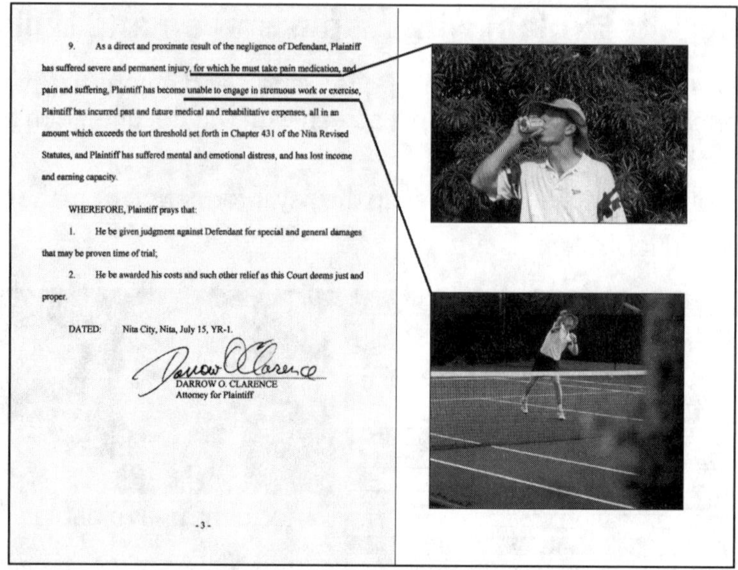

9. As a direct and proximate result of the negligence of Defendant, Plaintiff has suffered severe and permanent injury, for which he must take pain medication, and pain and suffering, Plaintiff has become unable to engage in strenuous work or exercise, Plaintiff has incurred past and future medical and rehabilitative expenses, all in an amount which exceeds the tort threshold set forth in Chapter 431 of the Nita Revised Statutes, and Plaintiff has suffered mental and emotional distress, and has lost income and earning capacity.

WHEREFORE, Plaintiff prays that:

1. He be given judgment against Defendant for special and general damages that may be proven time of trial;

2. He be awarded his costs and such other relief as this Court deems just and proper.

DATED: Nita City, Nita, July 15, YR-1.

DARROW O. CLARENCE
Attorney for Plaintiff

-3-

Be sure that the line you use to underline the claim in the complaint and the line you use to connect to the photo are the same size. They should connect cleanly. When you use two illustrations, connect them in the same way (in this illustration at the upper left corner).

Another use of the split screen is to compare items side-by-side. In this case, representing Byrd, you might want to place some of the photographs taken by the investigator side-by-side with Brown's principal claims.

A slide in this format would look like this:

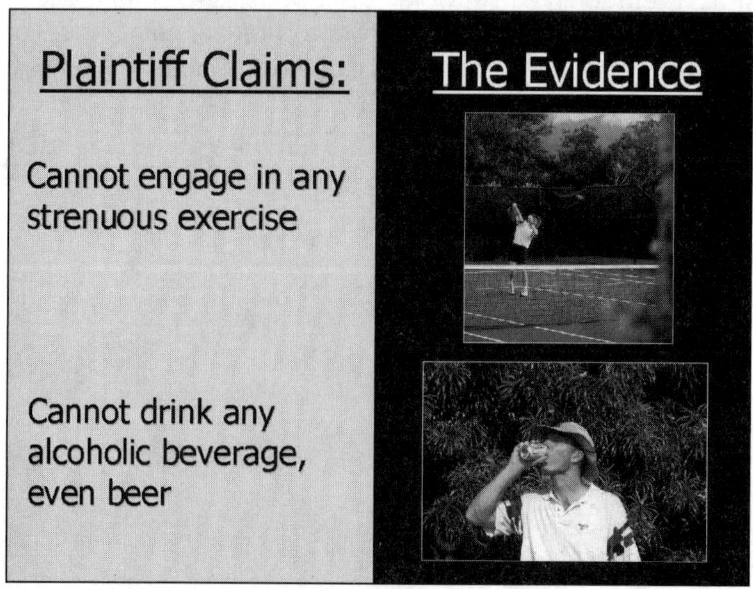

Exercise 7.5: Construct re-keyed callouts

The police report contains quotes that are useful to Byrd's case. One key phrase in the report is "accident was made unavoidable." Another is "by the sudden and unnecessary stop by #1." It would be difficult to create a direct callout of this material because it appears on two lines of text, making it difficult to crop and too wide for magnification. A re-keyed callout is more appropriate.

In this case, the quote refers to #1 and it is not self-evident who that is. To make this point clear, place a circle over "#1" and additional ovals over "Vehicle #1" and the operator "Kenneth Brown" so that the designation and the connection are now on the slide. These can be connected visually using the same color for the circle around #1 and the corresponding ovals in the document. This is shown on the CD.

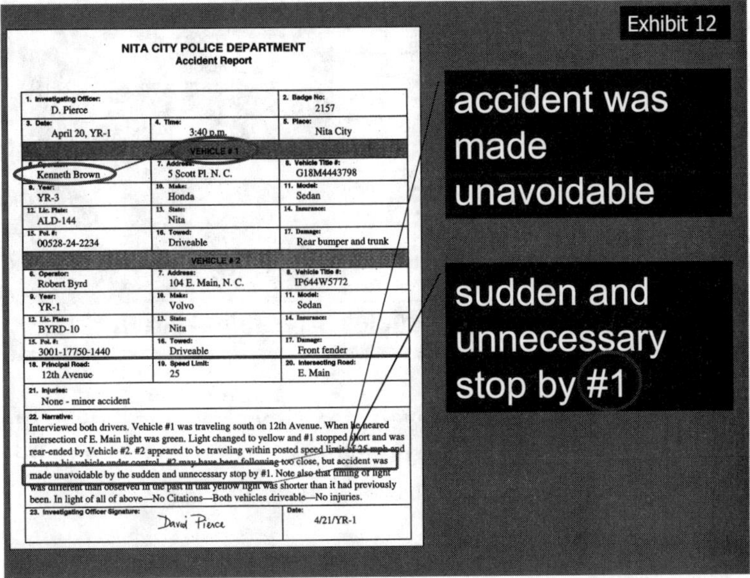

The indicator lines normally point to an anchor box in the text. In this case, the anchor box is unwieldy because of the location of the text excerpts relative to one another but it can be drawn using separate lines or the irregular shape on the Draw button menu.

If either counsel moved to eliminate any references to insurance in the trial, this part of the police report can be blocked out as shown above. Create a rectangle box over the entry that the police officer made just under item #14 for each vehicle and the word "insurance" just above. The fill color on this box is white to block out what is underneath, and the border is eliminated with the "no line" option.

Exercise 7.6: Extract direct callouts

One aspect of the police report that helps Byrd's case is the finding by the investigating officer that both vehicles were driveable and that neither driver was injured. These facts are stated in relatively compact form and can be extracted for direct callouts.

One layout for the slide would look like this:

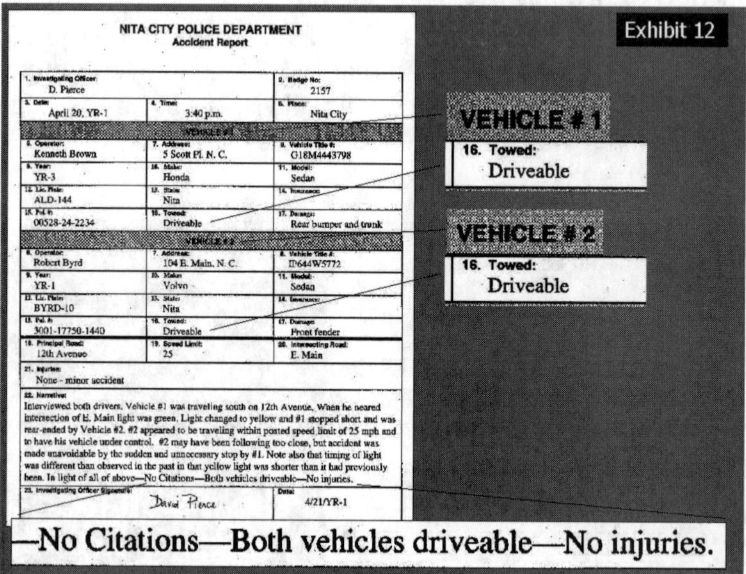

When portions of the text do not fit well into direct callouts as is the case for the last two boxes here on citations and injuries you can use rectangles with a white fill to cover portions of the text that you do not want.

Exercise 8.1: Add annotations to the diagram

In this case you have a diagram of the intersection where the accident took place. Both sides will want to use the diagram to orient the jurors to what happened at the time of the accident.

When you get the diagram and its exhibit number on the screen, and color the background, the slide will look like this:

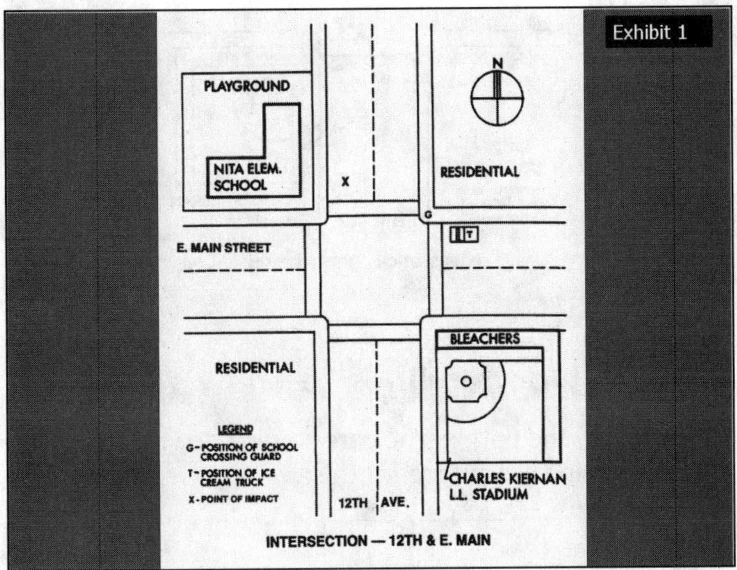

The diagram has marks on it to show where the school crossing guard was positioned, where the ice cream truck was located, and where the collision occurred. These marks are explained in a small legend in the lower left corner. Any important aspects of the diagram should be annotated to draw attention to the parts of the diagram most relevant to the case theory.

The labels might look like this:

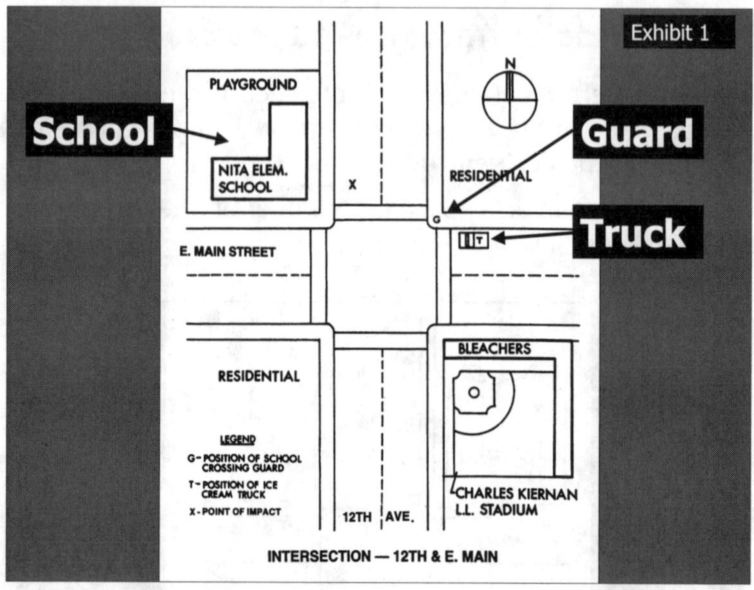

Exercise 8.2: Use dotted lines to show action

You might want to show the path of the cars coming down 12th Avenue into the intersection. A dotted line will suffice for this.

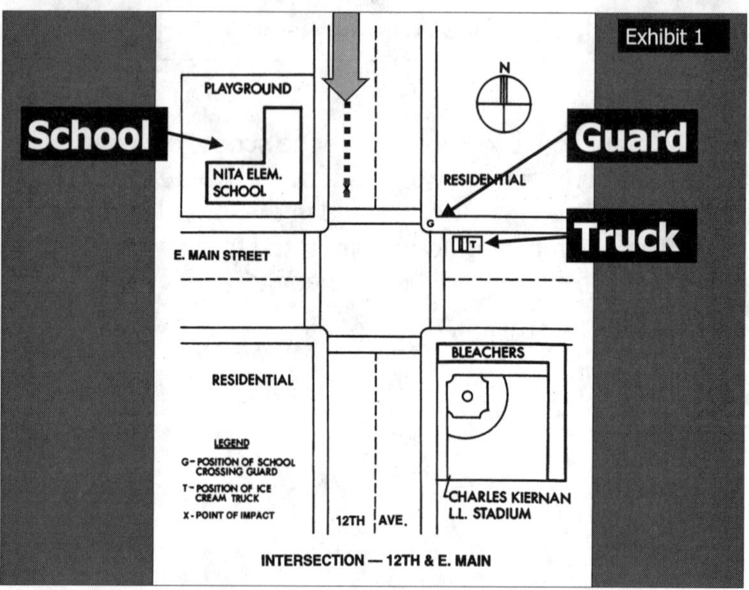

In this case, you need to be careful with the dotted line because there is a dashed line right next to it on the diagram indicating street markings. The line in this illustration uses 6-point square dots. Because the dotted line does not illustrate direction very well, a block arrow (Drawing Toolbar, AutoShapes button, block arrows option) has been added with a colored fill.

If you also want to show the relative distance these two cars were apart, a dotted line will not work because the two cars took the same path down the street. To do this, you have the option of creating boxes to signify each car or importing clip art cars of similar colors to represent each car. Your CD PowerPoint slide show has examples of each of these options.

If you use boxes, it is helpful to indicate who was driving by putting a letter designation in each. Because both parties have last names that begin with "B," that letter is not helpful. You can use the first letter of their first names to avoid confusion. You can also color the boxes to reflect the different colors of the cars or, if the cars are nearly the same color, just use red for Brown's car and black for Byrd's car.

Both cars were heading down 12th Avenue at about the same speed and about ten feet apart when Brown suddenly applied his brakes. To simulate this action, size and space the two boxes and place them where they would have been when Brown stopped.

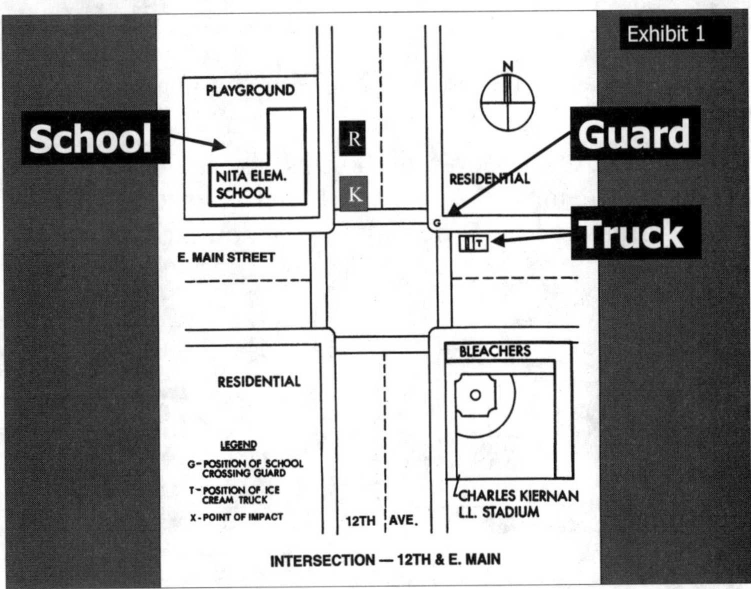

Then move the boxes together to show the impact.

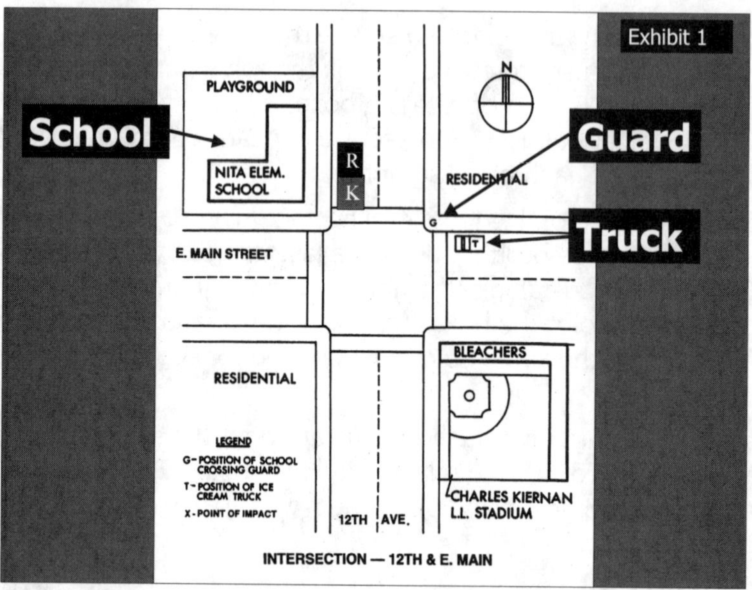

This effect can also be animated on one slide. See Chapter 9 on motion and special effects.

Instead of using text boxes to represent the cars, you can import two cars from a clip art CD-ROM, size them, and use them in the diagram. (See Chapter 12, Exercise 12.11 on importing clip art.) The diagram will now look like this:

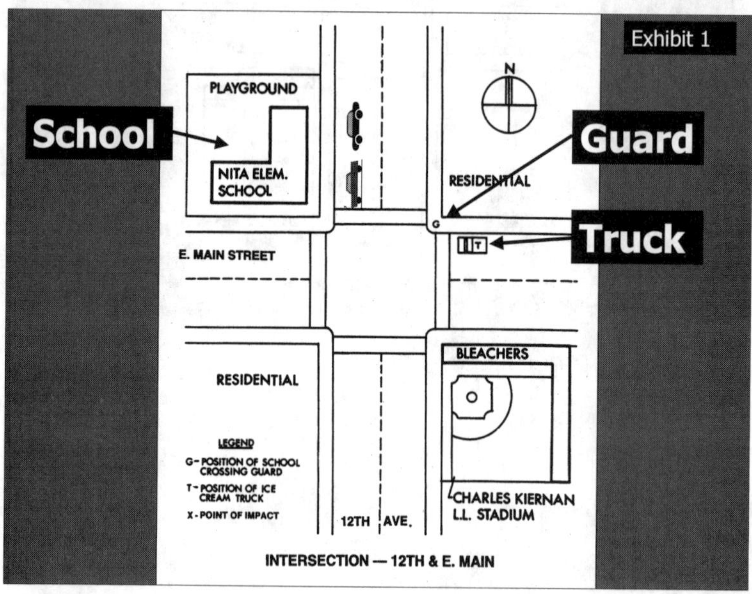

Exercises 9.1-9.8: Motion and special effects

Each type of slide for this case file has been animated as described Chapter 9 and is included in animated form on the CD that comes with this book. This slide show can also be downloaded from NITA's web site, *www.nitastudent.org*. To learn how these animations were done, deconstruct the slides as described in Chapter 12.13.

Exercises 10.1-10.5: Running your slide show

The slide show for this case on the CD includes slides with transitions. They can be viewed in slide sorter mode to see what transitions were added or in slide show mode to see the transitions in action.

Appendix D

PowerPoint 97 Supplement

PowerPoint 97 incorporates all of the features that lawyers need to make slides for courtroom use. In a few instances, the methods of accomplishing tasks were changed from PowerPoint 97 to PowerPoint 2000. In particular, these areas were substantially changed:

1. Motion and special effects

2. Speaker notes

Part I: Motion and Special Effects

If you are using PowerPoint 97 and have come to the point of animating your slides, use this appendix with Chapter 9. Consult the introductory sections of Chapter 9 for information of general applicability. Read each exercise in Chapter 9 for the explanatory material, illustrations, and notes. This appendix provides the detailed directions tailored to PowerPoint 97.

Exercise 9.1: Bulleted lists

Step 1: Display one bullet point at a time.

With the full slide on the screen—

A. Click on the text in the box containing the bullet points to activate it.

B. Click the right mouse button. A drop-down menu will appear.

C. Click on the Custom Animation option. The Custom Animation screen appears. It looks like this:

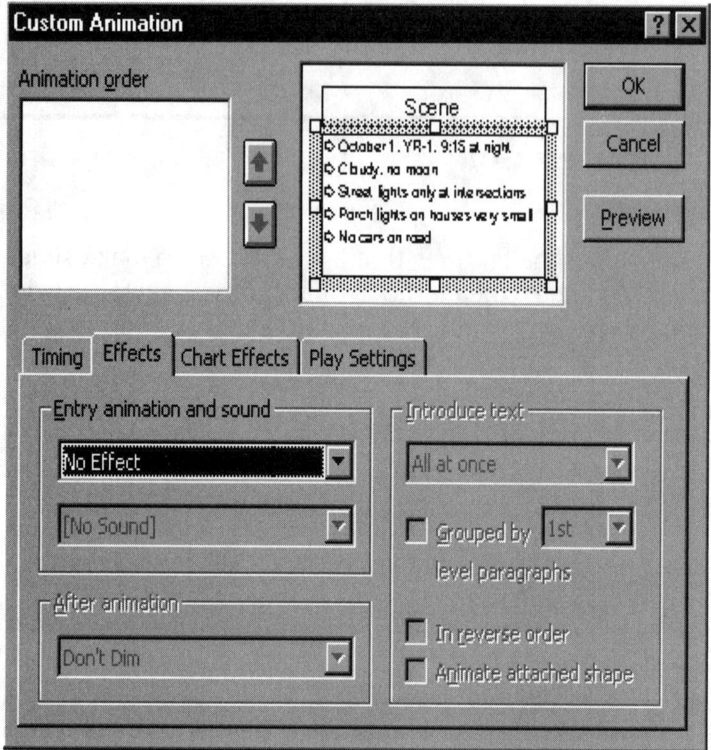

The Custom Animation screen should appear with the Effects Tab active. If the Effects Tab is not active (in the forefront), click on it.

D. Go to the Entry Animation and Sound area at the left side of the Effects box. The name in the top box indicates the animation effect that is currently active. The box may say "No Effect." The name in the second box indicates the sound effect that is currently active. That box may say "No Sound."

E. Click on the arrow next to the box to display the options.

F. Click on the Wipe Down option.

G. Click on the Preview button in the upper right area of the screen to see if you like the animation. It will run on the small thumbnail of your slide that appears in the adjacent box.

H. Click on the OK button in the upper right corner. This stores the work that you have done. (You still need to save your work when you finish.)

Step 2: Dim prior points so the current point is highlighted.

With the full slide on the screen—

A. Go back to the Custom Animation screen. (Step 1, A, B, C above.)

B. Go to the tabs in the middle of the screen. Make sure the Effects Tab is still active. If not, click on it.

C. Go to the After Animation box in the bottom left corner. It probably displays the option Don't Dim. (The After Animation box will only become active after some Effect has been chosen using the Effect box above.)

D. Click on the small arrow to the right of the box. A drop-down menu will appear. It shows eight colors, and the options More Colors, Hide After Animation, and Hide on Next Mouse Click.

E. Click on the gray color. The option box will now display the gray color you selected.

F. Click on the Preview button in the upper right area of the Custom Animation screen to see if the dimming works the way you want. The gray color will dim the text of a preceding bullet point (turning the letters from black to gray) when the next bullet point is selected.

G. Click on the OK button.

Step 3: Bring up letters or words one at a time.

With the Custom Animation screen in front of you, and the Effects tab active—

A. Go to the Introduce Text box in the middle of the screen at the right side. The white box should display the All At Once option.

B. Click on the small arrow to the right of the box. A drop down menu will appear displaying two more options, the By Word option, and the By Letter option.

C. Click on the By Letter option.

D. Preview this to see if it works by clicking on the Preview button at the top right of the Custom Animation screen.

E. Click on the OK button.

Step 4: Add a typing sound to the material introduced letter by letter.

With the Custom Animation screen in front of you and the Effects tab active—

A. Go to the Entry animation and sound area in the lower left of the screen. There are two white boxes in this area. The first is for effects and the second is for sound. The Sound box should display the message "No sound."

B. Click on the small arrow to the right of the Sound box. A drop-down menu will appear.

C. Click on the Typewriter option.

D. Click on the OK button.

Step 5: Preview all the animations for your slide using the full slide view.

With the full slide on the screen—

A. Go to the View Bar.

B. Click on the Slide Show button (1st button on right side). The slide title should appear with a blank space below where the bullet points will go.

C. Click once with the left mouse button. The first bullet point should appear.

D. Click again. Each time you click, another bullet point will appear displaying the entry effect and sound effect that you chose.

E. To end the slide show at any time, click the right mouse button. A drop-down menu will appear. Click on the End Show option.

Step 6: Save your work.

Exercise 9.2: Relationship charts

Step 1: Display the block arrow shapes and the conclusion box one at a time.

With the full slide on the screen—

A. Open the Custom Animation screen.

1. Go to the Menu Bar.

2. Click on the Slide Show button. A drop-down menu will appear.

3. Click on the Custom Animation option. The Custom Animation screen will appear. (Illustration, Exercise 9.2, Step 1.)

B. Open the Timing box.

1. Click on the Timing tab in the row of tabs in the middle of the screen.

2. This opens a box in the lower half of the Custom Animation screen.

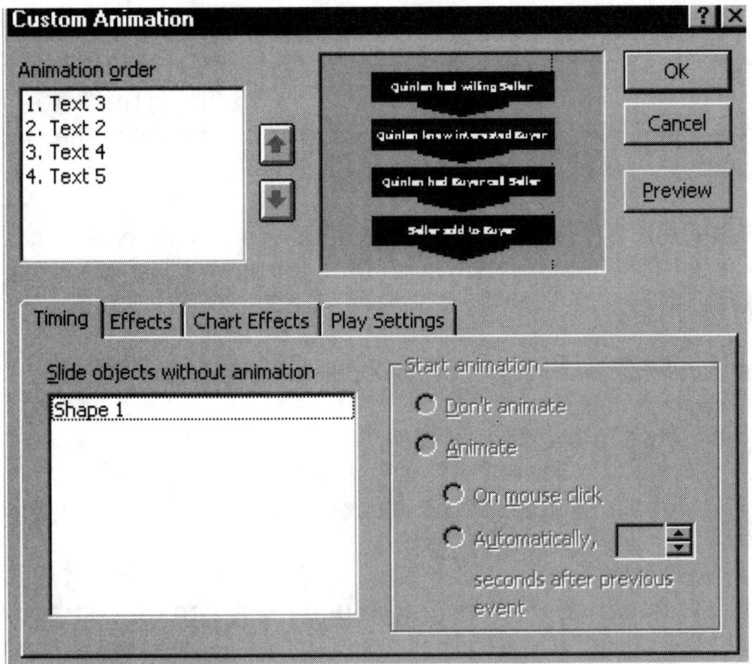

The upper half of the screen has a white box labeled "Animation order" on the left, which tells you if any animation has been selected for any of the objects on your slide. This should be blank at this point because you have not added any animations. The upper half of the screen also has a "Preview Box" on the left in which your current slide should be showing.

The lower left half of the screen has a white box labeled Slide objects without animation on the left, which should contain the names of the objects in the order you created them—"Text 1" (this is the first block arrow); Text 2, Text 3, and Rectangle 4. All of the block arrows get the name Text. There are two ways to create the last object showing the conclusion. If you used a Text Box for the conclusion, it will be called Text 4. If you used a Rectangle, it will be called Rectangle 4.

C. Animate the four objects.

1. Click on the name of the first of the four objects listed in the white box on the right side of the lower half of the screen. The name will then be highlighted.

2. The lower right half of the screen has a gray area labeled "Start animation," with two options—Don't Animate and Animate. The Don't Animate option should show a black button indicating that this choice is the one currently in force.

3. Click on the Animate button on the right side of the lower half of the screen. This animates the first object. The system indicate this status by deleting the name of this object from the list on the bottom part of the screen (objects not yet animated) and putting it in the box at the top part of the screen.

4. Make sure that the On Mouse Click option is active. The button is located under the Animate button on the right side of the lower half of the screen.

5. Repeat these steps for each of the other objects.

Step 2: Get the objects in the right order.

With the Custom Animation screen still in front of you, and the Timing tab still active—

A. Go to the Animation order box in the upper left corner. Your four objects should be listed there. They will be called Text 1, Text 2, Text 3, and Rectangle 4. The numbering reflects the order in which you created them.

B. If the objects are in the correct order in which you want them to appear, you do not need to do anything.

C. If any object is out of order, click on the name of the object that is out of order. The name will be highlighted. Then go to the Arrow buttons to the left of the Animation order box and click on the Up Arrow button or the Down Arrow button to get it into the right order. Each click will move the name up or down one place in the list.

D. Preview this part of the operation by clicking on the Preview button in the upper right part of the screen.

Step 3: Add the effects on entry.

A. Open the Effects box on the Custom Animation Screen.

1. Click on the Effects tab in the row of tabs in the middle of the Custom Animation Screen.

2. A new box opens on the bottom half of the screen. Under "Entry animation and sound," there are two white boxes. The first one is for the animation; the second one is for sound.

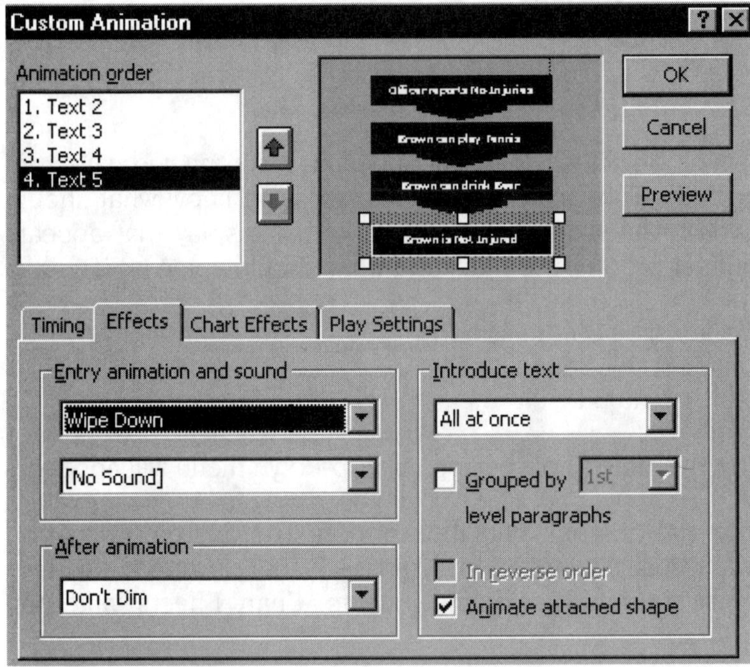

B. Select the effect to be used for each of the objects.

1. Click on the name of the object in the white box in the upper left part of the screen. This tells the software that you want to supply an effect for this particular object.

2. Go to the Effects box in the lower left area of the screen.

3. Click on the arrow next to the Entry animation and sound box. A drop-down menu appears.

4. Scroll to the option you want and click on it. Use Wipe Down for the block arrows and Box Out for the conclusion.

Step 4: Preview the animation by clicking the Preview button in Custom Animation screen.

Step 5: Click on the OK button to record your choices.

Step 6. Save your work.

Exercise 9.3: Photographs

Step 1: Display the photo with the slide and display the title later.

With the full slide on the screen—

A. Specify which object will make an appearance (entry) separate from the basic slide. This operation lets the software know what should come up with the slide (that is, a part of the display that appears when you first present the slide) and what should come up later.

1. Get the full slide on the screen.

2. Go to the Menu Bar.

3. Click on the Slide Show button. A drop-down menu will appear.

4. Click on the Custom Animation option. The Custom Animation screen will appear. (Illustration, Exercise 9.1.) This screen has four tabs across the middle—Timing, Effects, Chart Effects, and Play Settings.

5. Click on the Timing tab. A new box will appear. The screen now looks like this:

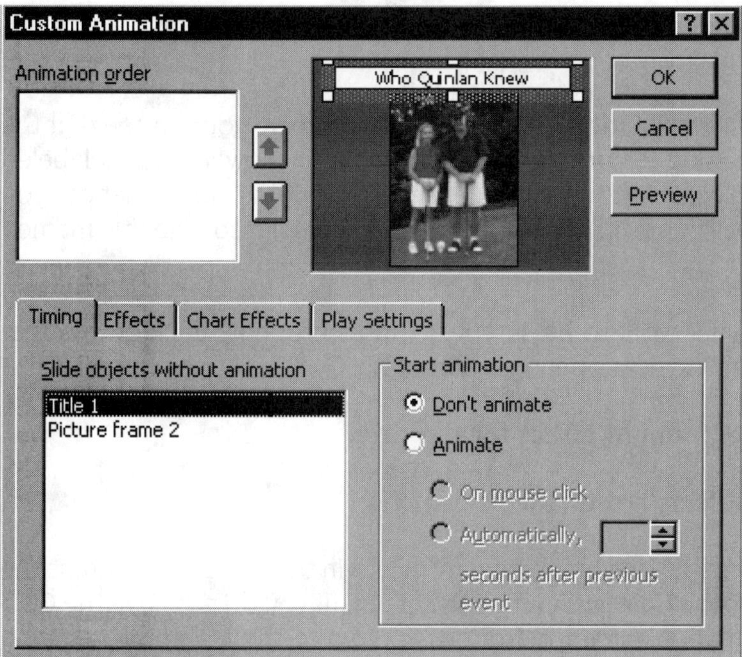

The upper half of the screen has a white box labeled "Animation order" on the left, which tells you if any of the objects on your slide have been animated. This should be blank at this point because you have not added any animations. The upper half of the screen also has a Preview Box on the left in which your current slide should be showing.

The lower half of the screen has a white box labeled "Slide objects without animation" on the left, which should contain the names "Title 1" and "Picture frame 2" representing the two objects you have on your slide.

6. Click on the Title 1 name within the "Slide objects without animation" box in the lower left. The Title 1 name will change color indicating that it is active.

7. The lower half of the screen also has a gray area labeled "Start animation" with two options—Don't Animate and Animate. The Don't Animate option should show a black button indicating that this choice is the one currently in force.

8. Click on the button in front of the Animate option on the right. The button will turn black indicating that it is on. The Title 1 name will disappear from the lower box (Slide objects without animation) and will

now appear in the upper box (Animation order) indicating that it has been animated.

When you look at the Custom Animation screen, you can see that the photo (named Picture frame 1) remains in the lower left box labeled "Slide objects without animation." Because it has no animation, you know it will come up when the slide is first displayed. The title (named Text 1).

B. Preview your work to be sure it operates properly. Click on the Preview button in the upper right part of the Custom Animation screen.

Step 2: Use the Zoom In effect for the title.

A. Get the Effects box on the screen.

1. Click on the Effects tab (2nd from left) in the row of tabs across the middle of the Custom Animation screen. (If you do not have the Custom Animation screen in front of you, go to the Menu Bar, click on the Slide Show button. A drop-down menu will appear. Click on the Custom Animation option. The Custom Animation screen will appear.)

2. The Effects tab will bring up a new display for the lower half of the screen. Under "Entry animation and sound," there are two white boxes. The first one is for the animation and the second one is for sound. Each box will display the name of the currently selected choice.

B. Click on the small arrow to the right of the Entry Animation box. A drop-down menu will appear listing special effects mostly alphabetically.

C. Click on the Zoom In Slightly option.

Step 3: Preview your work. Click on the Preview button in the upper right area of the screen.

Step 4: Click on the OK button if the Preview looks all right.

Step 5: Save your work.

Exercise 9.4: Text treatments—box, circle, and line

Step 1: Display the box, circle, and line objects one at a time.

With the box-circle-line slide on the screen in full slide view—

A. Animate all three objects.

1. Go to the Menu Bar.

2. Click on the Slide Show button. A drop-down menu will appear.

3. Click on the Custom Animation option. The Custom Animation screen will appear. (Illustration, Exercise 9.1.) This screen has four tabs across the middle—Timing, Effects, Chart Effects, and Play Settings.

4. Click on the Timing tab. A new box will appear. (Illustration, Exercise 9.3, Step 1).

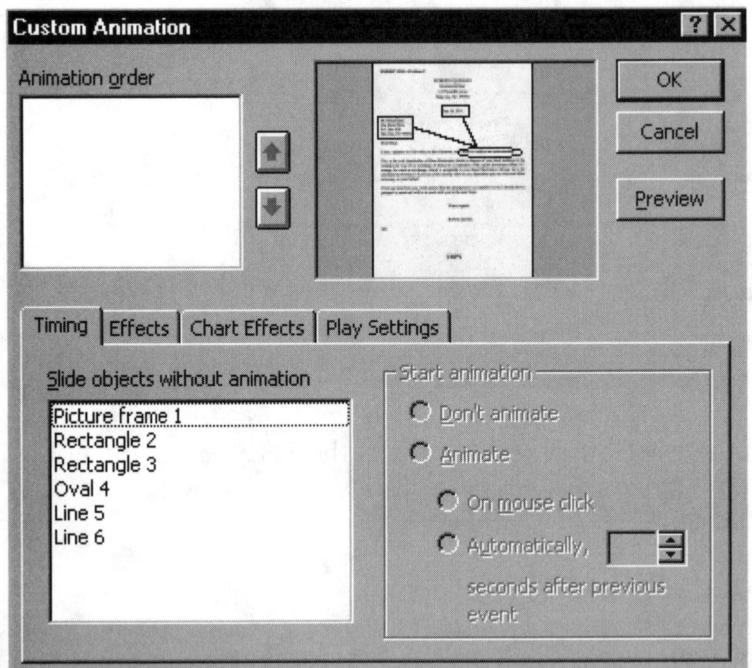

The upper half of the screen has a white box labeled "Animation order" on the left, which tells you if any animation has been selected for any of the objects on your slide. This should be blank at this point because you have not added any animations. The upper half of the screen also has a Preview Box on the left in which your current slide should be showing.

The lower half of the screen has a white box labeled "Slide objects without animation" on the left, which should contain the names of the objects in the order you created them—"Picture frame 1" (this is the document); Rectangle 2, Oval 3, and the lines that you used.

5. Click on the Rectangle 2 name within the "Slide objects without animation" box in the lower left. The name will change color indicating that it is active.

6. The lower half of the screen has a gray area labeled "Start animation," with two options—Don't Animate and Animate. The Don't

Animate options should show a black button indicating that this choice is the one currently in force.

7. Click on the button in front of the Animate option on the right. The button will turn black indicating that it is on. The name will disappear from the lower box (Slide objects without animation) and will now appear in the upper box (Animation order) indicating that it has been animated.

8. Repeat this operation for the objects named Oval 3 and the Line 4.

As you look at the Custom Animation screen, your Rectangle, Oval, and Line objects should be listed in the white box in the upper left called "Animation order." This means that these objects will not appear with the slide when it is first displayed. Your object named "Picture frame 1" is still in the white box in the lower left called "Slide objects without animation." This means that it has no animation and will come up when the slide is first displayed.

9. Preview this part of the work by clicking on the Preview button in the upper right part of the screen.

B. Specify the order in which the objects should appear.

With the Custom Animation screen still in front of you, and the Timing tab still active—

1. Go to the Animation order box in the upper left corner. Your three objects should be listed there. The Rectangle 2 object is probably listed first, the Oval 3 object is listed second, and the Line 4 object is listed third.

2. If the objects are in the order you want, you do not need to do anything.

3. If any object is out of order, click on the name of the object that is out of order. The name will be highlighted. Then go to the Arrow buttons to the right of the Animation order box and click on the Up Arrow button or the Down Arrow button to get it into the right order. Each click will move the name up or down one place in the list.

4. Preview this part of the operation by clicking on the Preview button in the upper right part of the screen.

Step 2: Add appropriate effects on entry.

With the Custom Animation screen still in front of you—

A. Get the Effects box on the screen.

1. Click on the Effects tab in the middle of the screen (2nd from left).

2. A new box will appear in the lower half of the screen. (Illustration, Exercise 9.1, Step 3.) Under "Entry animation and sound," there are two white boxes. The first one is for the animation; the second one is for sound. The name of the current choice should appear in the box.

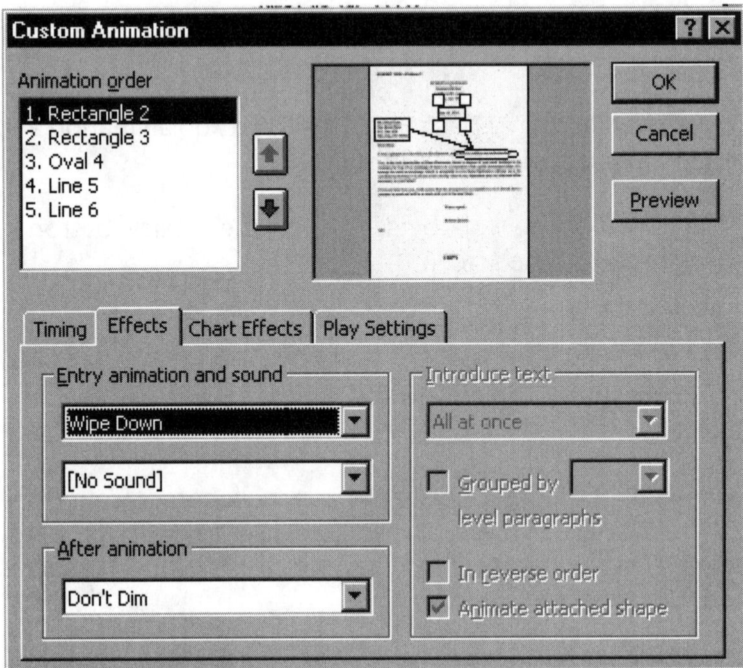

B. Select the effect that you want for each of your objects.

1. For the box: Go to the white box in the upper left corner that lists all your objects. Click on the Rectangle 2 name. This tells the software that you are now going to choose the entry effect for the box.

2. Go to the Entry animation and sound area. The animation box should say "No effect." Click on the small arrow to the right of the box. A drop-down menu will appear. Click on the Wipe Down option.

3. For the circle: Go back to the white box in the upper left corner that lists all your objects. Click on the Oval 3 name.

4. Go to the Entry animation and sound area. Click on the small arrow to the right of the animation box. A drop-down menu will appear. Click on the Wipe Right option.

5. For the line: Go back to the white box in the upper left corner that lists all your objects. Click on the Line 4 name.

6. Go to the Entry animation and sound area. Click on the small arrow to the right of the animation box. A drop-down menu will appear. Click on the Stretch from Bottom option. This will make the line start to appear at the circle and stretch toward the box (if the circle is below the box).

7. When you are finished, click on the OK button to preserve your work.

Step 3: Preview your work.

With your slide on the screen—

A. Go to the View Bar.

B. Click on the Slide Show button (5th from the left).

C. When your slide appears on the screen, it should show just the document. Click your left mouse button. The first object should appear. Click the mouse button again for successive actions.

D. When you are finished, click the right mouse button and a drop-down menu appears. Click on the End Show option.

You do not need to go through the entire slide show. You can stop at any point by right clicking and using the End Show option. That will take you back to the working Slide View mode.

Step 4: Save your work.

Exercise 9.5: Text documents—split screen with bullets

Step 1: Animate the identification box and the object containing the bullet points.

With the full slide on the screen—

A. Click on the object containing the bullet points to activate it.

B. Click with the right mouse button. The Custom Animation screen will appear.

C. Click on the Timing tab. A new box will appear. (Illustration, Exercise 9.3, Step 1.)

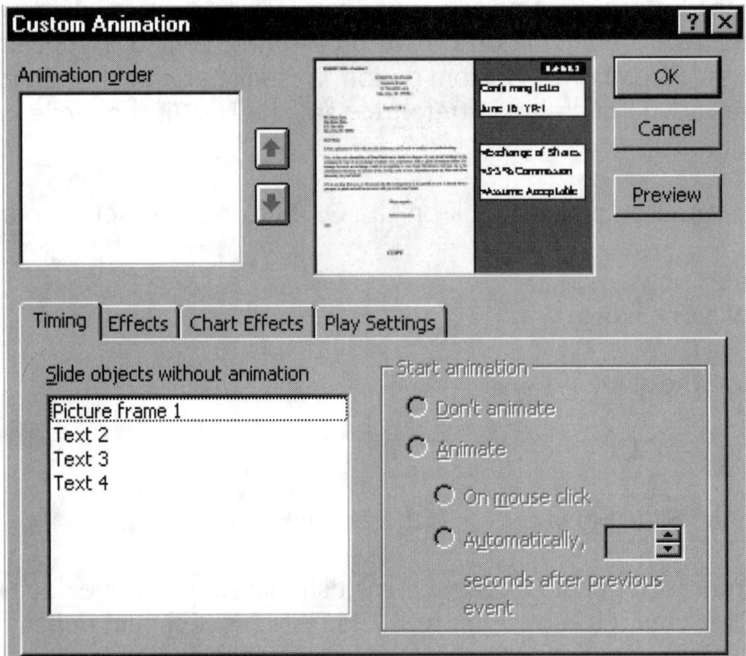

D. Animate the identification text box.

1. Click on the Text 2 name within the "Slide objects without animation" box in the lower left. The Text 2 name will change color indicating that it is active.

2. Click on the button in front of the Animate option on the right. The button will turn black indicating that it is on. The Text 2 name will disappear from the lower box (Slide objects without animation) and will now appear in the upper box (Animation order) indicating that it has been animated.

E. Animate the object containing the bullet points.

1. Click on the Text 3 name within the box in the lower left.

2. Click on the button in front of the Animate option on the right. The Text 3 name will disappear from the lower box and appear in the upper box.

Step 2: Put the objects in the proper order.

With the Custom Animation screen still in front of you, and the Timing tab still active—

A. Go to the Animation order box in the upper left corner. Your objects should be listed there.

B. If the objects are listed in the correct order in which they should be displayed on the screen, then you do not need to do anything further.

C. If the objects are not listed in the correct order, use the Arrow buttons to the right of the box to re-order them. Select (highlight) the name of the object that needs to be moved. Click on the Up Arrow or Down Arrow to move that object up or down in the order.

Step 3: Add appropriate effects on entry.

With the Custom Animation screen still in front of you—

A. Click on the Effects tab. A new box will appear in the lower half of the Custom Animation screen. (Illustration, Exercise 9.1, Step 3.)

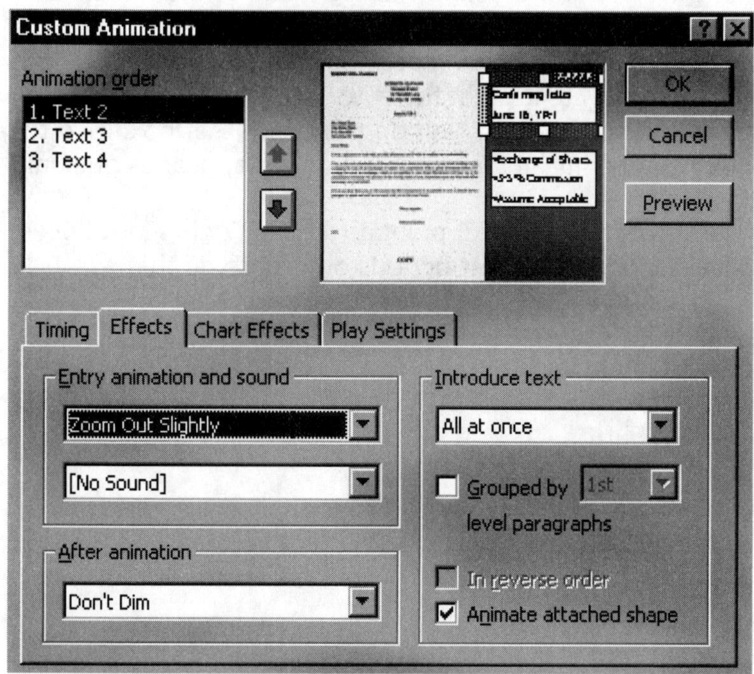

B. For the identification box:

1. Go to the white box in the upper left corner that lists all your objects. Click on the Text 2 name. This tells the software that you are now going to choose the entry effect for the box.

2. Go to the Entry animation and sound area. The animation box should say "No effect." If you choose this option, the identification box will simply appear in its correct place. This is usually the best way to deal with the small text boxes that contain exhibit numbers, dates, or other identifying features. Alternatively, click on the small arrow to the right of the box. A drop-down menu will appear. Scroll to the bottom where the Zoom out slightly option appears. Click on that option. This helps focus the eye on the identification box without the appearing too directive.

C. For the object containing the bullet points:

1. Go back to the white box in the upper left corner that lists all your objects. Click on the Text 3 name.

2. Go to the Entry animation and sound area. Click on the small arrow to the right of the animation box. A drop-down menu will appear. Click on the Wipe Down option.

3. Click on the small white box, on the left side of the Effects box, labeled Grouped by __ level paragraphs. Just to the right of the first line of text is a small white box that should display "1st." If it does not, use the arrow key to its right to get to 1st. This will make the bullet points appear separately. If you do not check that box, then the entire object containing all the bullet points will appear as one unit.

4. If you want to dim each bullet point as the next one is introduced, see Exercise 9.1, Step 3 for instructions on how to do that.

D. Preview your work. Click on the Preview button in the upper right of the Custom Animation screen.

E. Click on the OK button.

Step 4: Save your work.

Exercise 9.6: Text treatments—re-keyed callouts

Step 1: Animate the objects.

With the full slide on the screen—

You have four or more objects on this slide: the document, the identification box containing the Exhibit number, the first callout box, the second callout box, and the reference points within the document if you surrounded them with rectangles. PowerPoint names these objects in the order you created them. So they are probably called Picture frame 1 (for the document), Rectangle 2 (for the identification text box), Text 3 (for the first callout box), Text 4 (for the second callout box), Rectangle 5 (for the reference within the document for the first callout box), and Rectangle 6 (for the reference for the second callout box). You need to designate each of these objects for animation.

A. Go to the Menu Bar.

B. Click on the Slide Show button. A drop-down menu will appear.

C. Click on the Custom Animation option. The Custom Animation screen will appear. (Illustration, Exercise 9.1.) This screen has four tabs across the middle—Timing, Effects, Chart Effects, and Play Settings.

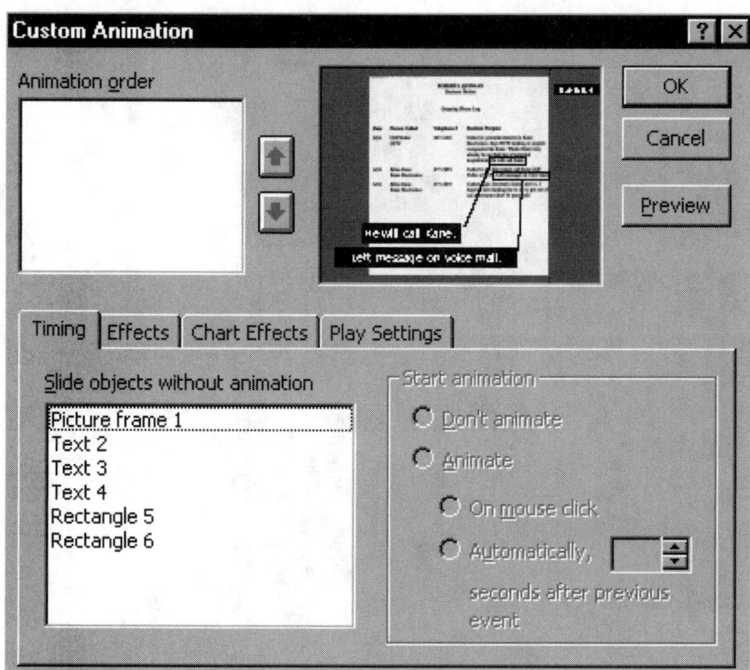

D. Click on the Timing tab if it is not already active. A new box will appear on the lower half of the screen. (Illustration, Exercise 9.3, Step 1.)

E. Click on the first name listed in the white box in the lower left corner labeled "Slide objects without animation." The name will change color indicating that it is active.

F. Click on the button in front of the Animate option on the right. The button will turn black indicating that it is on. The name will disappear from the lower box (Slide objects without animation) and will now appear in the upper box (Animation order) indicating that it has been animated.

G. Do the same operations for the second, third, and fourth objects.

Step 2: Put the objects in the correct order, if necessary. (Exercise 9.4, Step 1(B).)

Step 3: Add appropriate effects on entry.

With the Custom Animation screen still in front of you—

A. Click on the Effects tab. A new box will appear in the lower half of the Custom Animation screen.

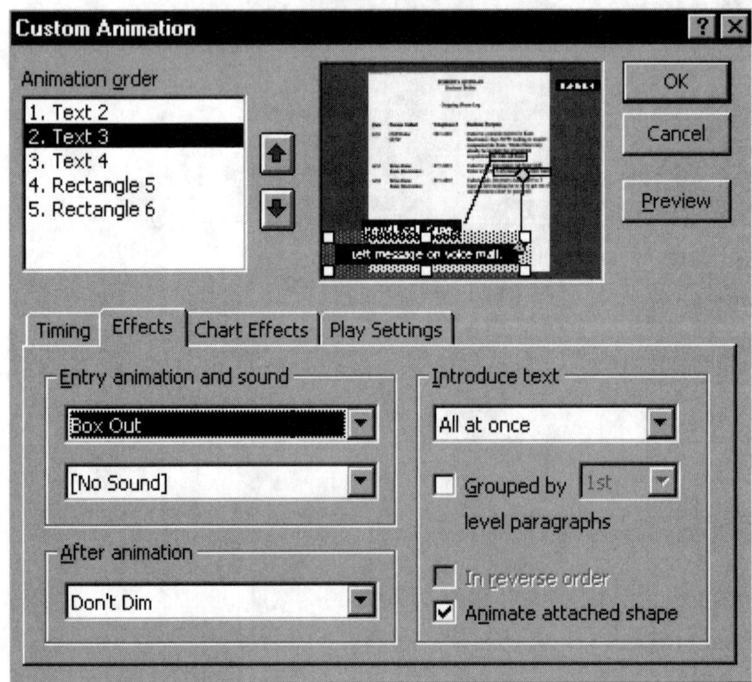

B. For the document, which is the first object, named Picture frame 1—

1. Click on the Picture frame 1 name in the white box in the upper left corner of the screen. This tells the software that you want to work on the object containing the document. Its name will be highlighted.

2. Go to the Animation Box in the lower left portion of the screen. If it says "No effect," this means that the document will appear directly with no special effects. This is usually the best choice for documents standing alone.

3. If the Animation Box says something else, then click on the small arrow to the right of the box and scroll up to the top where the "No effect" option is located. Click on that.

C. For the identification box, the second object, named Rectangle 2—

1. Click on the Rectangle 2 name in the white box in the upper left corner of the screen. The name will be highlighted.

2. Go to the Animation Box in the lower left portion of the screen.

3. Click on the small arrow to the right of the box. A drop-down menu will appear. 4. Click on the No effect option.

D. For the first callout, the third object, named Text 3—

1. Click on the Callout 3 name in the white box in the upper left corner of the screen. The name will be highlighted.

2. Go to the Animation box in the lower left portion of the screen.

3. Click on the small arrow to the right of the box. A drop-down menu will appear.

4. Scroll down to the Box Out option. Click on that.

E. For the second callout, the fourth object, named Text 4, do the same operations as described above for Text 3.

F. For the rectangles showing the reference points in the document for the callouts, do the same operations as described above for Rectangle 1.

G. Preview your work.

H. Click on the OK button.

Step 4: Save your work.

Exercise 9.7: Text treatments—direct callouts

Step 1: Animate the objects.

With the full slide on the screen—

A. Open the Timing box in the Custom Animation screen. (Illustration, Exercise 9.3, Step 1.)

1. Go to the Menu Bar.

2. Click on the Slide Show button. A drop-down menu will appear.

3. Click on the Custom Animation option. The Custom Animation screen will appear.

4. Click on the Timing tab in the row of tabs in the middle of the screen. This opens a box in the lower half of the Custom Animation screen.

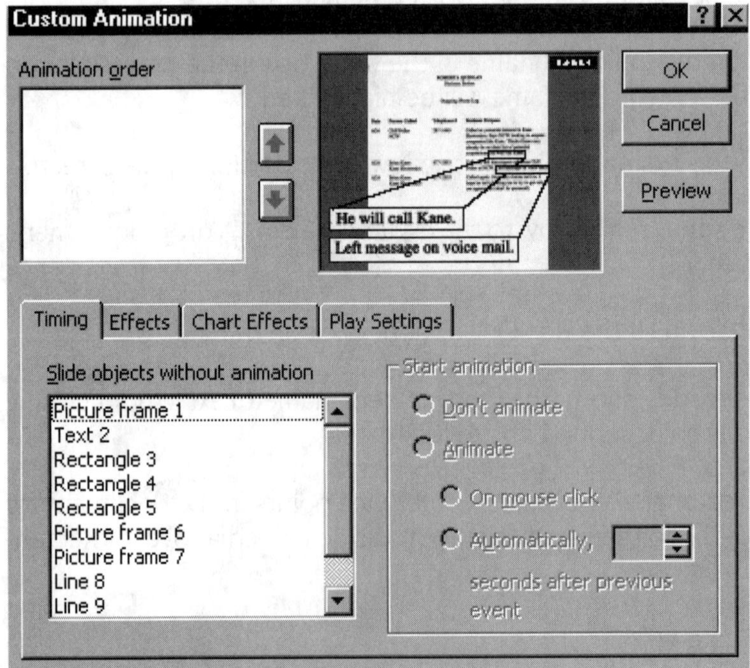

B. Click on the name of the first of the seven objects listed in the white box on the left side of the lower half of the screen. The name will then be highlighted.

C. Click on the Animate button on the right side of the lower half of the screen. This animates the first object. The system indicate this status by deleting the name of this object from the list on the bottom part of the screen (objects not yet animated) and putting it in the box at the top part of the screen.

D. Make sure that the On Mouse Click option is active. (The button is located under the Animate button on the right side of the lower half of the screen.)

E. Repeat these steps for each of the other objects.

Step 2: Get the objects in the right order. (Exercise 9.4, Step 1(B).)

A. Have the first rectangle showing the reference point in the document appear next.

B. If the callout box and its lines have been grouped (Ch. 6, Exercise 6.6, Step 8), then you can apply an effect to the whole group and that group, showing the callout for the first reference, would appear next. If you have not grouped these objects, then animate the lines first and then the callout box.

C. Then have the rectangle that is the reference point for the second callout appear.

D. The second callout box and its lines would appear at the end.

Step 3: Add the effects on entry.

A. Open the Effects box on the Custom Animation Screen.

1. Click on the Effects tab in the row of tabs in the middle of the Custom Animation Screen.

2. A new box opens on the bottom half of the screen.

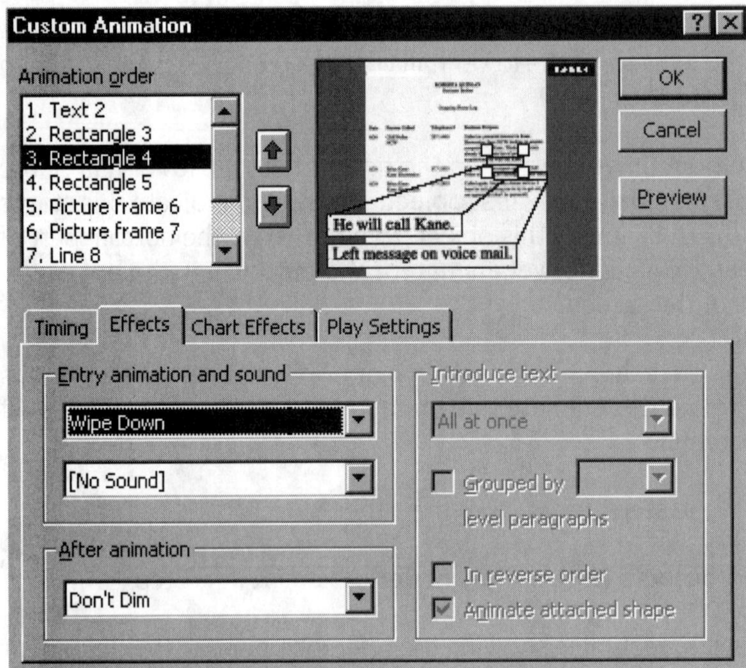

B. Select the effect to be used for each of the objects.

1. Click on the name of the object in the white box in the upper left part of the screen. This tells the software that you want to supply an effect for this particular object.

2. Go to the Effects box in the lower left area of the screen.

3. Click on the arrow next to the box. A drop-down menu appears.

4. Scroll down to the option that you want for the object. Click on it. Use No Effect for the document, Wipe Down for the callouts, and Wipe Left for the lines.

Step 4: Preview the animation.

Step 5: Click on the OK button to record your choices.

Step 6: Save your work.

Exercise 9.8: Annotated diagrams

Step 1: Specify that the diagram appears with the slide.

With the full slide on the screen—

A. Open the Timing box in the Custom Animation screen. (Illustration, Exercise 9.2, Step 1.)

1. Go to the Menu Bar.

2. Click on the Slide Show button. A drop-down menu will appear.

3. Click on the Custom Animation option. The Custom Animation screen will appear.

4. Click on the Timing tab in the row of tabs in the middle of the screen. This opens a box in the lower half of the Custom Animation screen. The names that the software has assigned to each of your objects should be listed there.

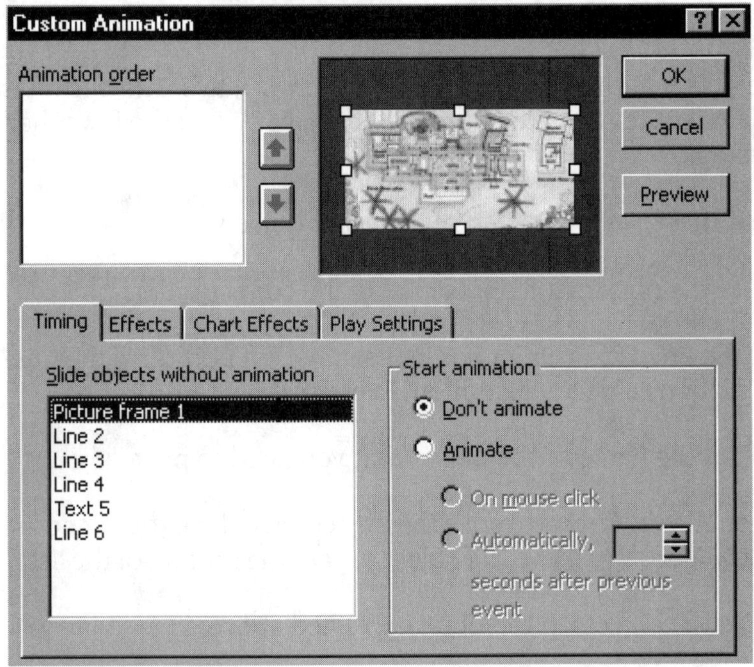

B. Click on the name assigned to the diagram (probably Picture frame 1).

C. Go to the right side of the Timing Box on the Custom Animations screen. Under the Start Animation caption, there are two choices—Don't Animate and Animate.

D. Click on the Don't Animate button. This will make the document appear when the slide first appears. It will have no animation of its own. The slide itself may have a transition when it appears. (Ch. 10, Exercise 10.2.)

Step 2: Display the annotations one at a time.

A. Animate the objects.

1. Click on the name of the first of the five objects to be animated. They listed in the white box on the left side of the lower half of the screen. The name will then be highlighted.

2. Click on the Animate button on the right side of the lower half of the screen. This animates the first object. The system indicate this status by deleting the name of this object from the list on the bottom part of the screen (objects not yet animated) and putting it in the box at the top part of the screen.

3. Make sure that the On Mouse Click option is active. The button is located under the Animate button on the right side of the lower half of the screen.

4. Repeat these steps for each of the other objects.

B. Make sure the objects will appear are in the correct order.

1. Go to the Animation Order box in the upper left portion of the Custom Animation screen. (Illustration, Exercise 9.3, Step 1.)

2. Highlight the name of the object that you need to move.

3. Click on the Up Arrow to move the object toward the top of the list or the Down Arrow to move the object toward the bottom of the list.

4. Arrange the objects in the order explained above.

C. Preview the order to check it by clicking on the Preview button in the upper right of the Custom Animation screen.

Step 3: Add the entry effect to each animated object to control how it first appears on the screen.

A. Open the Effects tab on the Custom Animation screen by clicking on that tab (2nd from left) in the row of tabs in the middle of the screen. A new box will appear in the lower half of the Custom Animation screen. The screen looks like this:

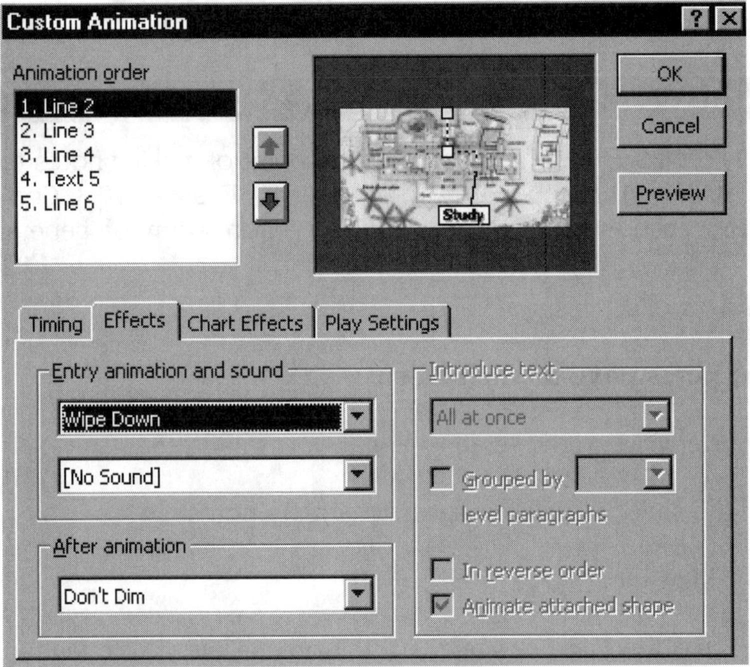

B. Select the effect to be used for each of the objects.

1. Click on the name of the object in the white box in the upper left part of the screen. This tells the software that you want to supply an effect for this particular object.

2. Go to the Effects box in the lower left area of the screen.

3. Click on the arrow next to the box. A drop-down menu appears.

4. Scroll down to the option that you want for the object. Click on it. Use No Effect for the document, Box Out for the annotations, and Wipe Right for the lines.

Step 4: Click on the OK button to record your choices.

Step 5: Preview the animation. (Exercise 9.4, Step 3.)

Step 6: Save your work.

Part II: Add Notes

If you are using PowerPoint 97 and have come to the point of making notes to accompany your slides, use this appendix with Chapter 10, Exercise 10.3. Consult the introductory sections of Exercise 10.3 for information of general applicability.

To create notes for a slide, do this:

Step 1: Get the notes page on the screen.

With the Slide Sorter view on the screen—

A. Click on the slide for which you want to create notes.

B. Go to the View Bar.

C. Click on the Notes Page View button (4th from the left). This brings up the Notes page. Your slide will be on the top. A text object on the bottom says "Click to add text."

Step 2: Adjust the type size so that you can see what you are doing.

The notes screen shows a very small type size when it first appears. This is because it is designed to be printed out on regular-size paper (which is larger than what is shown on the screen) and, when that is done, the type size will be in the normal size. There are two ways to deal with this.

A. If you will be working primarily on the screen, and not printing out your notes pages, you can adjust the type size permanently—

1. Put your mouse cursor at the beginning of the text in the notes box and click on it.

2. Go to the Formatting Toolbar.

3. Click on the arrow next to the type size box (2nd from the left).

4. Scroll down to 20, and click on that option.

5. This will increase the size of the type so that you can work with it easily on the screen. However, if you print out the page, the notes will be in 20-point size, which is quite large.

B. If you may want to print out your notes pages, you can adjust the type size temporarily—

1. Go to the Standard Toolbar.

2. Look at the Zoom box, a small white box on the far right. It will say 50% or some other percentage indicating how much smaller the current display is than full size.

3. Click on the arrow to the right of the box. A drop-down menu will appear.

4. Choose 100% by clicking on that option. Your screen will resize.

Step 3: Type in your notes.

Step 4: Resize the objects if you need more space for your notes.

Usually, you will want more space for notes than the software provides on the regular notes page. There are two objects on a notes page: the slide and the notes area. You can resize them just like any other objects. (Ch. 2, Exercise 2.3.) What you do on the notes page will not affect your slide.

A. Resize the notes object first. Click on the text in the object to activate it. A fuzzy border with handles will appear.

B. Position your mouse pointer over the handle in the middle of the top margin. Use the two-arrow mouse pointer to pull the top margin upward. This will partially obscure your slide. The top portion of your slide will still be showing.

C. Click on the slide.

D. Position your mouse pointer over the handle in the bottom left corner. Hold down the CTRL key on the keyboard and use the two-arrow mouse pointer to pull the bottom margin upward, thus reducing the size of your slide.

E. Now you should have a smaller version of your slide and a larger area in which to make notes.

Step 5: Print your notes pages if necessary.

A. Go to the Menu Bar.

B. Click on the File button. A drop-down menu will appear.

C. Click on the Print option. The Print screen will appear.

D. In the Print Range box in the middle of the screen, click on the Current Page option.

E. In the Print What box at the bottom of the screen, use the arrow button next to the box to scroll down to the Notes Pages option. Click on that.

F. Click on the OK button.

Glossary

Active	A box or shape surrounded by a special border indicating that the commands about to come will be applied here. See also *selection border* and *fuzzy border*.
Activate	The method of setting up a box or shape to take commands. To activate, move the mouse pointer to a text object, a picture object, or a shape and click the left mouse button. A fuzzy border with handles appears around the margin when something has been activated. (See illustration in Ch. 2, Exercise 2.3.) This means that the object or shape is ready to accept your work. See also *select*.
Alignment	The function that brings text or boxes and shapes into line. Text can be aligned to the left margin, right margin, both margins, or centered. These options are controlled by the alignment buttons on the Formatting Toolbar. (See illustration in Ch. 1.) Boxes and shapes can be aligned by their tops, bottoms, sides, or centers. These options are controlled by the Drawing Toolbar, Draw button, Align option.
Anchor box	A rectangle put around the words in the text of a document for which a re-keyed or direct callout is constructed. The anchor shows where the callout came from. The anchor is linked to the callout box by one or more indicator lines.
Animation	Directions to the software with respect to an object (such as bullet points, a photo, document image, or diagram) that is part of a slide, but will appear separately after the slide is on the screen. Animation uses various kinds of motion including Wipe, Fly, and Dissolve. (See Ch. 9.)
ANIX	A software product that enhances PowerPoint. (See Exercise 12.16.)
Aspect	PowerPoint slides are in a 4½ (length) by 3½ (tall) ratio, which is called the aspect.

Background	The area of the slide behind any of the objects on the slide. Usually relates to color.
Bar	The areas of the basic PowerPoint on-screen display that are always in view. These include the Title Bar, Menu Bar, Status Bar, Scroll Bar, and View Bar. (See illustration in Ch. 1, Section 1.5.)
Black slide	A kind of transition that uses a black (or blank) slide so that there is nothing on the screen for a period of time, until the next slide is brought up. (See Exercise 10.2, Steps 3-4.)
Border	Fuzzy edge around a box or shape indicating that it is active. (See illustration in Ch. 2, Exercise 2.3.)
Box	A text box is created using the Text Box button on the Drawing Toolbar. A title box appears on some layouts on the New Slide screen. (See illustration in Ch. 2, Exercise 2.1.) A rectangle box is created using the Rectangle button on the Drawing Toolbar. Other box shapes are accessed through the Autoshapes button on the Drawing Toolbar.
Button	The areas on bars and toolbars where you can click to use a PowerPoint function. (See illustrations in Ch. 1, Section 1.5.)
Callout	A text box used to enlarge words or phrases in documents for easy reference. (See illustrations in Ch. 6, Exercises 6.5 and 6.6.) The callout box is usually connected visually by a thin line to the spot in the document from which the words or phrases came.
Click on	To place the mouse pointer in the designated area and press the left mouse button once.
Clip art	Icons, stylized pictures, cartoons, symbols, and signs that come in pre-packaged files. (See Exercise 12.11.)
Crop	A method for cutting photos and other images down in size by eliminating unnecessary portions. (See Ch. 6, Exercise 6.2.) If you make an error and cut too far, the cropping tool also works backward to recapture lost material. Distinguished from *resize* in which the

entire photo is reduced in size without eliminating any parts.

Cursor (insertion pointer) The blinking vertical line that appears on the screen indicating where text will go when typing begins. The location of the cursor changes as you type, and also changes when you put the mouse pointer in a particular spot and click on it.

De-activate To click anywhere outside an active slide. The fuzzy border and handles disappear indicating that the item is no longer active.

Default The setting in PowerPoint as it comes out of the box. This is what PowerPoint will do if you don't tell it to do something else. For example, Fly From Left is the default special effect for animating an object. If you do not choose a different effect, PowerPoint will use this one.

Demonstrative exhibit An exhibit offered in evidence because it demonstrates something at issue (e.g. a photo, a document, a map). The standard for admitting it is whether it is fair and accurate. A principal objection is that it is not accurate (because something has been added or removed) or that it is unduly prejudicial. Distinguished from *illustrative aid* which is offered for use in trial (and not in evidence) because it helps illuminate the testimony.

Dialog box A display that appears when you click on certain buttons or select certain menu options. Dialog boxes allow you to mix-and-match the selection of related options. Also called a *screen*.

Direction box A box on the Custom Animation screen, displayed with the Effects tab, that tells the direction (up, down, right, left) in which a particular effect will be played.

Directory A storage area for files.

Display A visual aid created with presentation software that may be shown in a courtroom on a small monitor, a large monitor, or a large projection screen.

Distribute	A function that spaces objects evenly across a given distance (either horizontally or vertically).
Double click on	To press the left mouse button twice in rapid succession.
Drag	To move something on the screen from one place to another by placing the mouse pointer on the desired area, using the four-arrow mouse pointer while holding down the left mouse button and moving the mouse (thus "dragging" the object) to the new location, then releasing the left mouse button.
Drawing Toolbar	The second bar at the bottom of the screen under the View Bar. This contains buttons that control special functions for putting lines and shapes into PowerPoint slides. (See illustration in Ch. 1, Section 1.5.)
Drop-down menu	A subsidiary menu of related functions that appears when you click on some kinds of buttons. Options on the menu are selected with the mouse pointer. Some drop down menus have more options than are shown when the menu first appears. A small arrow at the bottom of the menu indicates that there is an extension. Click on the arrow.
Effect	The motion to go from one bullet point to the next or one object to the next within one slide. Distinguished from *transitions* which are motions when moving from one slide to the next.
Expansion arrow	An indicator at the end of a toolbar or a menu that provides access to additional buttons or options.
File	A collection of information you have created.
File name	The description of a file that is put into the system so you can find the file again.
Fill	The space within an object. Distinguished from *background* which is the space behind the objects on a slide. Usually relates to color.

Folder	A collection of files. Folders have names so that you can find them.
Font	A combination of typeface (e.g. Arial) and type size (e.g. 24 points) usually expressed as "24-point Arial."
Formatting Toolbar	The last toolbar on the top of the screen. The left half of this bar contains familiar word processing buttons for font, type size, bold, italic, underline, and alignment (left, center, and right) that you use on word processing software. These buttons have the same functions in PowerPoint when you are typing text. The right half of this bar has special PowerPoint functions. (See illustration in Ch. 1, Section 1.5.)
Full slide view	The screen display in PowerPoint when a single slide in full size is on the screen rather than the Slide Sorter view which shows thumbnails of all the slides in the group.
Fuzzy border	A highlighting around the edge of an object when it is active. (See illustration in Ch. 2, Exercise 2.3.)
Grouping	A method of linking objects so when you move one of the objects to a different place on the slide, all the attached or related objects move at the same time.
Handle	A small square box located in the middle of each border or edge and at each corner or end of an active object. (See illustration in Ch. 2, Exercise 2.3.) The handle is the control area that allows you to move each part of the border or edge independently to re-shape or resize the object. The handles in the middle of the top and bottom margins change height. The handles in the middle of the side margins change width. The handles in the corner change height and width at the same time. See also *move handle*.
Hard copy	Materials, such as slides, printed on paper.
Highlight	See *select a word or phrase*. The term "highlight" is also used for the function of emphasizing the text of a document by coloring it (usually yellow). PowerPoint has no colored highlighter function. See *semitransparent effect* (Ch. 12, Exercise 12.5.)

Icon	A small picture on a button, bar, or screen display indicating a function.
Illustrative aid	Something offered for use before a jury (but not to be admitted in evidence) because it is an aid to testimony (e.g. a bullet point list, a labeled photo, a text document treatment, a relationship chart, or an annotated diagram). The standard for using an illustrative aid before a jury is whether it is helpful. A principal objection is that it is misleading or argumentative and therefore not helpful. Distinguished from *demonstrative exhibit* which is used before a jury to demonstrate something at issue in the case.
Import	To bring a file or part of a file into the area you are working on. You can import a file from outside PowerPoint, and you can also import parts of one PowerPoint file into another PowerPoint file. Saves doing the work over again.
Indicator line	The line between an anchor box in the text and a callout box.
Insertion pointer	Cursor. See definition above.
Keyboard command	Commands to the software generated by the keys on the computer keyboard. Distinguished from *buttons* and *menus*.
Layout	A basic design for a slide. PowerPoint has 12 layouts. (See illustration in Ch. 2, Exercise 2.1.)
Margin	Border, edge. The side of a box or shape. When activated, the margin of the box or shape will have handles and a fuzzy appearance.
Menu	A list of options. Select an option by highlighting it with your mouse pointer and clicking on it.
Menu Bar	The second bar at the top of the screen, located just below the Title Bar. It contains familiar Windows buttons for the File, Edit, View, Insert, Format, Tools, Window, and Help functions. (See illustration in Ch. 1, Section 1.5.)

Mouse pointer — The indicator box that moves around the screen as you move the mouse. Changes shape (one arrow, I-beam, two-arrow, four-arrow, cross) as you set up to perform different functions. The shape of the mouse pointer tells you what function the system is prepared to perform. (See illustrations in Ch. 1, Section 1.3.) Distinguished from *cursor* which indicates where type will go.

Move handle — A vertical bar at the very front of each toolbar which is used to move the entire toolbar to a new location. (See Exercise 12.3.)

Object — A defined area on a slide. Types of objects include: text, photograph, line, shape, video, clip art, and drawing. If you want to put text on a slide, for example, you need to put a text object on the slide and put your text inside that object. You cannot put text directly on the slide. An object can be activated and de-activated. It has handles for resizing it and for moving it from one place to another on the slide. (See illustration in Ch. 1, Exercise 2.1, of a slide with two text objects, one for the title of the slide, and one for bullet points.)

Option — One of the choices listed on a drop-down menu or a dialog box.

Palette — A way of displaying color options.

Picture object — An object into which you can import a picture. (Also called a picture box.)

Picture Toolbar — The bar usually located to the right of the Drawing Toolbar on the bottom of the screen. It contains buttons related to working with pictures. The Crop button is the most important.

Point — A unit of measurement used for type size. 72 points equal one inch; 32 points equal one-half inch; 12 points equal one-sixth inch. This is the size in which a font will appear on your computer screen when working in 100% mode (see Zoom).

Presentation — A series of slides. (Also called a *slide show*.)

Presentation software	Specialized software for making visual displays usually described as slides. PowerPoint is one such software package.
Remote control	A handheld device for running a slide show.
Resize	To make a document, photo, or other image larger or smaller without changing it in any other respect. Distinguished from *cropping* in which unnecessary parts are cut out.
Resolution	The measure of how sharp and clear an image is. Photographs scanned at 200 dots per inch have a lower resolution than those scanned at 300 dots per inch.
Reveal	The action used to bring the object or the slide to the screen. (Used as a noun, as in "the reveal for that object or slide.") See animations and transitions.
Sans serif	A kind of typeface design without fine lines projecting from the main stroke of the letter. A sans serif type is preferred for litigation uses because it maintains clarity when enlarged.
Scanning	A process of turning paper copes into digital files. See Exercise 12.14.
Screen	The information shown on your computer monitor as you perform various operations. Sometimes also called a *dialog box*.
Scroll	The action of moving up or down on a page or in a box to bring additional material into view. The control for scrolling is an arrow on a scroll bar (see Ch. 1, Section 1.5) or an arrow at the right side of a box.
Select an object	To activate the object by clicking on it with the left mouse button.
Select a word or phrase	To highlight the text by dragging your mouse over it while holding down the left mouse button. The text changes from black letters on white to white letters on a black background.
Selection border	See *fuzzy border*.

Slide | A visual aid.

Slide show | A collection of slides related to one another and intended for presentation in a particular order one after another. (Also called a *presentation*.)

Split screen | A display that has a photo or document on one side and explanatory bullet points on the other, or a document on one side and an explanatory photo on the other, or visa versa.

Standard Toolbar | The toolbar located just below the Menu Bar. The left half contains the familiar Windows icons for open, save, print, cut, copy, paste, undo, and redo functions. The right half of this bar contains icons for special PowerPoint functions. (See illustration in Ch. 1, Section 1.5.)

Storage media | Alternatives for storing PowerPoint slides, including floppy disk drives, hard disk drives, CDs, file servers, or internet services.

Template | A pre-selected set of background and fill colors, text fonts, and other design features that come with PowerPoint for you to use in creating your slides. When you use a template, instead of selecting specific options among those available, PowerPoint makes the selection for you.

Text box | An object into which you can put text.

Text object | An object into which you can put text. Same as *text box*.

Thumbnail | A miniature picture of a slide. The Slide Sorter button on the View Bar displays thumbnails of each of the slides in a slide show. This allows the user to edit the slide show and to move from one slide to another while creating a slide show. (See illustration in Ch. 4, Exercise 4.1.)

Title Bar | The blue bar at the very top of the screen that lets you know you are in PowerPoint. At the far right corner, it provides the familiar Windows Minimize, Maximize,

	and Close buttons. These are the same on all Windows programs. (See illustration in Ch. 1, Section 1.5.)
Title box	A text object or text box into which you can put the title of your slide.
Title object	A text object or text box into which you can put the title of your slide. Same as *title box*.
Toolbar	A collection of buttons that control related functions. The toolbars used most often are the Standard Toolbar, Formatting Toolbar, Drawing Toolbar, Picture Toolbar. (See illustrations in Ch. 1, Section 1.5.)
Transition	The motion to go from one slide to the next. Distinguished from *animation* which is the motion going from one object to the next within one slide.
Treatment	A method for emphasis. Examples of treatments include: box, circle, line, callout, split screen.
Typeface	The name of a particular design for shape of letters.
Type size	The sizes available for a particular typeface. Type size is usually expressed in points.
View Bar	The first bar at the bottom left of the screen. Five buttons on this bar control various views of your slides: single slide, slide sorter, outline, speaker notes, and slide show.
Visual aid	Something used in a courtroom to help the jury understand the testimony. See also *illustrative aid, demonstrative exhibit*.
Wireless mouse	A mouse that operates by radio signals.
Wireless remote	A remote control that operates by infrared signals.
Wizard	A set of help instructions designed to guide you through constructing slides.

The NITA How-To Finder List

Index

A

T

U

V

W

X

Y

Z